Egermeier's BIBLE Story Book

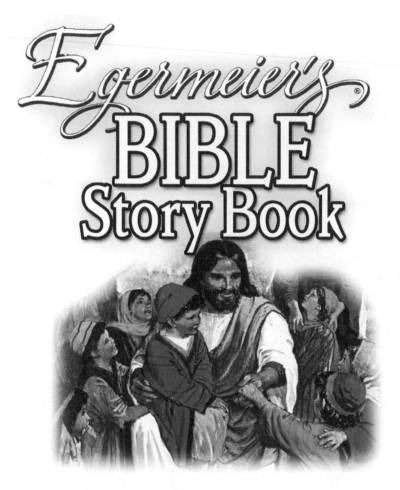

Presented to

Keith Moore   3rd Grade

By

Alex Poper   Michel Dohman

Date

December 2018

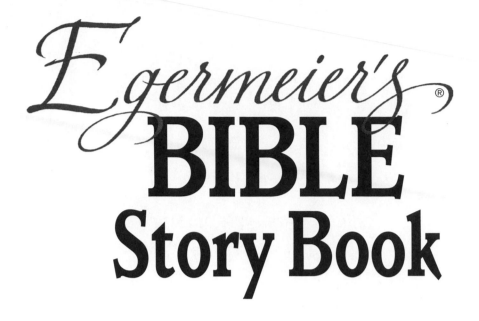

Egermeier's
BIBLE
Story Book

stories by
Elsie E. Egermeier

story revision by
Arlene S. Hall

W | **warner**
press

Warner Press, Anderson, Indiana, USA

**A Complete Narration from Genesis to Revelation
for Young and Old**

Preface

At its heart, the Bible is a story of how God has dealt with his people and revealed himself to them across the centuries. It tells the story of how God sent his only son to show us what he is like. Jesus Christ lived, died and rose again so we could live forever with him in heaven. The simple stories repeated in this book cover the full range of Bible history. Together, they provide an overall picture of the big story that the Bible as a whole tells.

When Elsie E. Egermeier first wrote these Bible stories she made this statement of purpose: "In the writing of the Bible Story Book the author has endeavored to familiarize herself with the viewpoint of children and to adapt her language accordingly. With vivid recollections of the capacity of the child mind to grasp and retain Scripture truths, she has labored prayerfully and conscientiously to present these stories in such a simple, direct manner that her youthful readers will have no difficulty in comprehending their teaching."

This new edition includes revised Questions and Answers, along with a new format for the Index that makes finding specific stories or scripture passages easier. A table of Helpful Bible Information is a useful resource for those who desire additional study. The addition of full-color story titles and headings on each page also make the book more appealing. This new edition of the Bible Story Book, however, does not depart from the book's original nature or purpose and the much-favored briefer stories of the previous edition have been retained.

Arlene S. Hall, who wrote the 1963 story revisions, is a graduate of Scarritt College for Christian Workers and the author of a number of books for children and children's workers.

The publishers join with Dr. Egermeier in her prayer "that He who said, 'Suffer the children to come to me,' may in this book find a way to draw them to Himself."

Contents

Contents

4

Contents

5

*Dedicated to the children
of the world. May God's
Word speak to them from
these pages.*

STORIES OF THE OLD TESTAMENT

in Six Parts

STORIES OF THE OLD TESTAMENT
in Six Parts

The Patriarchs

Genesis; Job

How the World Was Made

Genesis 1:1—2:24

Long, long ago there was no world at all. There was no sun to shine, no stars to twinkle, no moonbeams to play through the night shadows. But even then there was God, for he has always been the same unchanging God.

Then, at the beginning of time, God made the world. At first water covered everything, and darkness was everywhere. What a strange, unfriendly world this must have been! But God planned to make it beautiful, so he said, "Let there be light." He called the light Day and the darkness he called Night. This was the first day of time.

On the second day God made the beautiful blue sky and placed in it clouds to carry the moisture. He called the sky Heaven.

The third day God said, "Let the waters be gathered together unto one place, and let the dry land appear." He called the waters Seas and the dry land Earth. The whole earth was bare—no grasses, flowers or trees. So God caused a carpet of grass to grow and beautiful flowers to spring up from the earth. He made the trees and plants. God knew his work was good.

But God had more plans for his world. On the fourth day he made the sun, the moon and the stars. The sun was to rule the day and the moon, the night.

Next God began to create living creatures. He made all kinds of fish to swim about in the seas and birds of every description to fly in the sky. The fifth day passed, and the world had become a better place.

11

The Earth God created

It was on the sixth day that God said, "Let the earth bring forth living creatures." Living things appeared in the woods, on the plains, in the air and sea.

Still this was a strange world, for there were no people in it. There was not a home anywhere—not a man, woman or little child. What a very strange world indeed! But God had not yet finished creating his wonderful world. He planned to have the people live on the earth, enjoy its beauties and take care of it. They would know who had made all these things. More than that, they would be able to love and worship him.

So it was that God made the first man. Out of the dust of the earth he made the body, then he breathed into that body the breath of life. Man became a living soul.

God called the first man Adam. Adam was to name the birds and animals. It was his work to rule over all other living creatures.

Now Adam needed a helper. God said, "It is not good that man should be alone. I will make him a helpmeet." God made Adam a wife and Adam loved her deeply. He called his wife Eve.

When the sixth day ended God had made the world and placed everything in it just as he had planned. On the seventh day God rested.

The First Home

Genesis 2:8—3:24

Adam and Eve were very happy in their garden home. God had given them good things to enjoy, and they knew nothing about evil and wrongdoing. God walked and talked with them in the cool evenings.

In this garden God planted a wonderful tree called the tree of life. Whoever ate the fruit of this tree would live forever. Another tree was called the tree of knowledge of good and evil. God said, "You may eat the fruit of every tree in the garden except from the tree of the knowledge of good and evil. If you eat of this tree, you shall surely die."

One day the serpent asked Eve, "Will God let you eat the fruit of every tree in this garden?"

"We may eat of every tree except one," Eve answered. "God told us not to eat of the tree of knowledge of good and evil, lest we die."

"You will not die," the serpent replied. "God knows that if you eat fruit from this tree you will become as wise as God to know good and evil. That is why he has forbidden you to eat it."

Eve looked at the fruit. If it would really make her wise like God, she wanted to taste it. Reaching out her hand, she picked the fruit, ate it and gave some to Adam. He, too, ate the fruit.

At once Adam and Eve knew they had disobeyed God. Fear filled their hearts. How afraid they were to meet God! They had never been afraid before, but now they tried to find a hiding place among the beautiful trees in the garden. Their hearts had become wicked.

Soon a voice called, "Adam, where are you?"

Adam answered, "Lord, I heard your voice and I was afraid, so I hid."

"Why should you be afraid to meet me?" God asked. "Have you eaten the forbidden fruit?"

Adam said, "Eve gave me some of the fruit, and I ate it."

"What is this you have done?" God asked Eve.

She answered, "The serpent tempted me and I ate."

God's heart was full of sorrow and pain because Adam and Eve had given in to the tempter and had disobeyed him. Now they could no longer be with him because sin had spoiled their lives. They were no longer fit to live in the beautiful garden God had made for them.

God sent them out into the world to make a home for themselves. At the gate of the garden, he placed an angel so that Adam and Eve could not come back to eat of the tree of life.

To Eve God said, "Because you have disobeyed me, you shall have pain and trouble."

God punished Adam too. No longer would it be easy to grow fruits and vegetables. Weeds, thorns and thistles would grow in his fields.

When Adam and Eve died, their bodies would become dust again. All this came because of sin.

As the years passed, however, the children and grandchildren of Adam and Eve remembered a promise. Someday God would send a Savior to make men free from sin and death.

The First Children

Genesis 4

Because Adam and Eve had done wrong, they had to find another place to live, outside the Garden of Eden. They knew they were being punished for the wrong they had done.

Adam had to work hard and long to get food for Eve and himself. No doubt, his hands and feet were sometimes bruised and torn by thistles and thorns. Eve, too, had pain and sorrow. Her home was not so happy as it had been before she disobeyed God.

Adam and Eve could no longer walk and talk with God face to face. Yet they still worshiped him and confessed their sins to him. They offered him gifts upon their altars. On a pile of stone or earth, they placed wood for a fire. Then they laid their offering on the wood, set fire to it and the offering was burned.

Adam and Eve must have been lonely with no other people to talk to. But God planned there would be more people. A baby boy was born to Adam and Eve. They named him Cain. How they must have loved him! Later God gave them another little boy, and they named him Abel.

When Cain and his brother Abel grew old enough to understand, Adam and Eve told them about the great God. How much Adam and Eve wanted their sons to love and please God!

Cain and Abel grew to manhood. Like Adam, Cain worked in the fields. Abel took care of sheep. They built altars and offered their gifts to God. Cain brought food from the field for his offering. Abel brought a fat lamb. God must have looked on Abel and seen his sorrow for his sins and his desire to be forgiven. God must have seen his trust, and God was pleased with Abel's offering.

God was not pleased with Cain's offering, and Cain was very angry. God said to him, "Why are you angry? Why do you look so sad? If you do well, you will be accepted. If you do not, you will be taken by sin. Do not let sin get a hold on you. Master it instead."

Later when the brothers were in the field, Cain quarreled with Abel. Cain became so angry that he killed Abel.

Again God spoke to Cain. He asked, "Where is Abel, your brother?" Cain replied, "I do not know. Am I my brother's keeper?"

15

Adam and his family worship God

God knew what Cain had done. He told Cain, "Because you have done wrong, you will be punished. You will till the ground, but your crops will be poor. You will wander here and there without any one place to call your home."

Cain said, "O God, this punishment is greater than I can bear! What if people try to kill me when I wander from place to place?"

God answered, "I will put a mark on you. Then people will know they are to do you no harm."

Cain wandered far away into a land called Nod. There he lived for many years.

The Great Flood

Genesis 5:1–9:17

Adam and Eve's children lived to be very old. They had children, grandchildren, great-grandchildren and many great-great-grandchildren.

As the years passed there were more and more people in the world. Most of them were very wicked. Yet there was a man who tried to please God. This man was Enoch. He walked with God, talked to God and listened when God spoke to him. Because Enoch put his faith in God most of all, he did not die. Instead, when he became old, God took him to heaven.

Enoch's son Methuselah was the oldest man who ever lived. He lived to be nine hundred and sixty-nine years old. By this time there were many, many people in the world. Their hearts were full of sin. They did not try to please God, for they did not love him. They did not teach their children to love the good and do the right. Everywhere there was sin and wrongdoing. What a sad world!

How sorry God was that he had made man! The people were no longer fit to live. Finally God decided the only way to get rid of sin and wickedness in the world was to cover the earth with a great flood.

Then God remembered Noah. Even among these wicked people, Noah tried to do right. He taught his sons to do right also. This pleased God.

Sometimes God talked to Noah. Now he told Noah about his plan to destroy the world. He promised Noah and his family that they would not be destroyed with the wicked.

"Build an ark," God told Noah. "When it is finished you and your wife and your sons and their wives may go into the ark. You will live there until the flood is over."

God decided to save a pair of each kind of living thing. These would also stay in the ark during the flood.

Because Noah believed God, he began building the ark. God had told him how it should be built. While the people went their wicked way, Noah and his sons made the ark as God had said. It looked like a three-story houseboat perched up on dry land.

How the people must have laughed at Noah and his three sons. They must have thought Noah and his sons were crazy. Where was the water for their boat?

Again and again Noah warned the people to repent of their sins or they would be destroyed in the flood. None of them believed him.

When everything was ready, God told Noah to take into the ark his wife, his three sons and their wives. Then God caused two of every kind of animal, bird and creeping thing to go into the ark. Seven pairs of each kind of useful birds and animals came. When all were inside, God shut the door.

After a few days the rain began to fall. And such a rain! Great sheets of water poured down from the clouds. Soon the tiny streams were raging, and the rivers were overflowing their banks. People left their homes and rushed to the hills for safety. Animals ran pell-mell, trying to find refuge and shelter. Still it rained. Higher and higher the waters rose. Now the people knew Noah had told the truth.

For forty days and nights it rained. Only Noah and his family were safe. The waters lifted the ark off the ground, and the ark began to float. For more than six months it floated. Then one day it stood still on top of a mountain.

After waiting for some time, Noah opened a window and let out a raven. This bird had strong wings and could fly about until the waters had gone down. Several days later Noah sent out a dove. The dove returned because she could not find a place to build her nest. A week later Noah sent the dove out again. She stayed longer this time.

17

When evening came she flew back, bringing a green olive leaf in her mouth. Now Noah and his family knew the land was becoming green and beautiful. The next week when Noah sent out the dove, she flew away and never came back.

Now Noah believed it was time to uncover the ark and look out upon the earth. How glad he must have been to see dry land again! For more than a year they had been inside the ark.

God said to Noah, "Come out of the ark with your wife and your sons and their wives, and with every living thing that is in the ark." Noah opened the great door. He and his family stepped out on dry ground. All the animals, the birds and the creeping things came out.

Noah was thankful to be alive. As soon as he came out of the ark, he built an altar and made his offering to God. God accepted the offering and was pleased with Noah and his family.

God promised that he would never again send another flood to destroy every living creature. God said, "As long as the earth remains there will be summer and winter, springtime and autumn, and day and night." To remind men of his promise God made the rainbow in the sky.

The Tower of Babel

Genesis 9:18—11:9

A clean, new world lay before Noah and his three sons when they stepped out of the ark. There were no wicked people left.

Noah and his sons made new homes. The sons' names were Shem, Ham and Japheth. After a while God gave them children. These children grew up and made homes for themselves. Then there were other children. Again there were many people on the earth.

From a mountain in Ararat, where the ark lodged after the flood, the human family moved south into the valley of Mesopotamia and lived on a plain in the land of Shinar.

"Let us build a city," said the people, "and let us make a tower so great and high that its top will reach up to the sky. Then we shall not be scattered over the earth and separated from one another." And so the people set to work.

Noah sees God's rainbow

How busy they were! Some made brick, others mixed mortar
and still others carried brick and mortar to the workmen who were
building the city and the tower. They all dreamed of the time their
city and their wonderful tower would be finished.

Then a strange thing happened. God saw the city and the tower,
and he was not pleased. He knew that men would become more
sinful if they finished the great tower. Already they were thinking
more and more about their own work and less and less about the
God who gave them the strength to work. Soon they might forget
God entirely and worship the things they had made. God decided
to stop their building.

Until this time all the people spoke one language. Now God
caused them to speak different languages. The people of one family
could not understand what their neighbors were talking about. Nor
could these neighbors understand the people who talked
to them. They could not go on with their great building because the
workmen could not understand one another. The people of Babel
became restless and unhappy until finally those who spoke one
language moved off by themselves.

Abram Follows God

Genesis 11:27—12:20

The people who moved away from Babel forgot God and became
more sinful. They prayed, but not to God. Wherever they went they
worshiped something. Many worshiped things that God had made—
the sun, the moon and the stars. Later they even worshiped rivers,
mountains and hills. They made images or figures of wood and
stone. They called these images gods and worshiped them.

Near Babel another city was built. It was Ur of the Chaldees. The
people who lived there were known as Chaldeans. They worshiped
the moon-god, Ur. They named their city in honor of their god.

On the plains near Ur lived old Terah, a shepherd and farmer.
He had three grown sons—Abram, Nahor and Haran. They
worked with their father. Haran died while still young and left
a son named Lot. Abram did not worship the moon-god but
believed in the true God.

About this time the family left Ur. Terah took Abram and his wife, Nahor and his family and Lot. They took all they owned—their tents, their large flocks of sheep and their herds of cattle. Day after day they journeyed up the great river Euphrates until they came to a place they called Haran. Here they settled. Time passed, and old Terah died.

One day Abram heard God calling him. God said, "Leave this country, your relatives and your father's house. Go to a land that I will show you. I will bless you and make you a great blessing. Through you all the families of the earth will be blessed."

As many people came to realize later, this meant that a Savior would be born into the family of Abram. Jesus Christ would be a blessing to the whole world.

Leaving his brother Nahor and his family at Haran, Abram started out. He took his wife Sarai, his nephew Lot, and their servants. Driving their flocks and herds before them, they turned away from the great river and journeyed southwest, toward the land of Canaan. On one side the mountains rose wild and high. On the other side the barren desert stretched as far as they could see. On and on they traveled—across rivers, through valleys, over hills—each day farther from their homeland and nearer to the land God had promised.

When they reached the plain of Moreh, God spoke again to Abram, "This is the land that I will give to you and your children." Abram built an altar there and worshiped God.

Now this land was called Canaan and the people were known as Canaanites. Abram did not live in their cities but pitched his tents wherever he could pasture his cattle and sheep. His flocks and herds grew larger and larger. Abram became rich.

Later there was a famine in the land. The grass and water dried up. Nowhere could Abram find pasture, and so he moved to Egypt. When the famine was over, he returned to Canaan.

Abram and Lot Separate

Genesis 13

After Abram returned from Egypt, he and Lot moved to Bethel where they had first pitched their tents in Canaan. Here Abram had built an altar to worship God. Now he sacrificed another offering and again talked to God.

Abram had become a very rich man. Not only did he have many servants, flocks and herds but also much silver and gold. His nephew Lot owned many servants, sheep and cattle too. Wherever these men and their servants pitched their tents, the place looked like a tent town. The country all around them was dotted with cattle and sheep.

Later trouble arose between the servants of Abram and Lot. The servants who cared for the flocks quarreled. Abram's servants wanted the best pasture land for Abram's flocks. Lot's servants wanted the same land for their master's cattle. And so the trouble grew.

When Abram heard about the quarrel, he looked out over the countryside and saw how hard it must be for the servants. How could they always find places nearby where there were tender grasses and plenty of water? Abram saw, too, the nearby villages of the Canaanites. There was not room enough for all to live together peaceably.

Abram told Lot, "Let there be no quarrel between us or between our servants. There is not room enough for both of us to live together with our flocks and herds. But see, the whole land lies before us. Let us separate. If you choose the west country, I will go east; but if you want the east country, I will take the west."

Abram and Lot could see far to the east and the west. Because God had promised Abram all this land, Abram could have chosen the better part, or he could have sent Lot and his servants away. Instead he offered Lot the first choice.

Lot, forgetting the kindness of his uncle, chose the east country where the Jordan River flowed. "I can always find plenty of grass and water there," he reasoned. "My flocks and herds will increase until soon I shall be very rich."

23

Lot chooses the best land

Afterwards God told Abram, "Lift up your eyes and look northward and southward and eastward and westward. All the land that you can see I will give to you and your children and your children's children."

As yet Abram and Sarai had no children, but Abram believed God. God also told Abram to journey through all the land to see how large it was. So Abram came to a plain called Mamre. Here he pitched his tents under the oak trees near the city of Hebron and built another altar to worship God.

Lot Is Captured

Genesis 14

When Lot chose the fertile plains of Jordan, he thought he was making a wise choice. He saw in the distance the large cities Sodom and Gomorrah. He knew he could make much silver and gold by selling sheep and cattle in those cities. So Lot moved toward Sodom. Later he pitched his tents nearer the city walls. Finally he moved his family inside. What a mistake!

Now Sodom was not a place for good people to live. The people of that city cared nothing about God. Some were very rich, but they were also very wicked. Lot thought them rich and clever.

One day trouble came upon Sodom. There had been war, and the kings of Sodom, Gomorrah and three other cities had gone out to battle. They were defeated. The conquering soldiers entered Sodom and Gomorrah, crowded through the streets, pushed their way into rich men's houses and took everything they could carry away. They even captured people for slaves. Lot, his wife and his children were taken with the others.

One captive escaped and fled across the country to find Abram. He told about the battle and what had happened to Lot. When Abram heard this, he took a few friends and three hundred and eighteen menservants to go after the captives.

After a long, hard march they came upon the enemy's camp at a place called Dan. It was night. The enemies lay asleep. Abram and his men rushed upon them and frightened them. The enemy thought a great army had come to fight, and they were not prepared for battle. So they ran away, leaving their tents, all the goods and the captives.

24

Melchizedek, king of Salem, came out to meet Abram and gave him food. Melchizedek loved and worshiped the true God. He was a priest of God. He thanked God for giving Abram such a great victory and asked God to bless Abram. Because Melchizedek was a priest of the true God, Abram gave him a tenth of all the goods from the enemy's camp.

The people of Canaan honored Abram for his courage, and the king of Sodom went out to meet him. He offered Abram all the gold and silver and food and clothing that he had taken from the enemy's camp. He asked only that the people be returned to Sodom.

Abram would not accept any reward because he had promised God not to keep anything for himself. And so all the people and the things they owned were returned.

Lot, his wife and his children went back to live in wicked Sodom, but Abram returned to his quiet tent home under the oak trees near Hebron.

Abram's Tent Home

Genesis 15—17

Abram was growing old. Although he had great riches and many servants, he had no children. One night while he was asleep, God appeared to him and said, "Do not be afraid, for I will protect you and will give you a great reward because you are faithful."

"What will you give me for a reward?" Abram asked.

God promised that someday Abram would have a son. At God's bidding Abram got up, went outside and looked up at the starlit heavens. "Someday the children of your family," God said, "shall be as many as the stars—so many that no one can count them."

Abram understood that his family would one day own the land of Canaan. Even though Abram did not have any children, he believed God's promise.

God caused him to know that the children of his family would be slaves in a strange land for four hundred years. After that they would return to Canaan and possess the land. Later we shall see how this came to pass.

25

At one time Abram and his household went to Egypt during a famine in the land of Canaan. When they returned, they brought with them an Egyptian servant girl named Hagar. They taught Hagar about the true God.

One day Hagar displeased Sarai. Sarai punished Hagar severely and Hagar ran away. For some time Hagar followed the sandy desert road. When she got tired, she stopped to rest by a fountain. There an angel of the Lord found her.

"Hagar, Sarai's maid, where did you come from and where are you going?" the angel asked.

"I am running away from my mistress," Hagar replied, "because I am so unhappy."

"Go back," the angel said, "and try to please Sarai. God will give you a son. He will grow up to be a strong man."

Hagar knew a messenger from God had spoken to her. God had known about her all the time. She obeyed and returned to Sarai. Afterward the fountain in the wilderness where the angel had found her was called Beerlahairoi, which means, "A well of the Living One who sees me."

Hagar had a son as God had promised. Abram named him Ishmael, which means, "God hears." Abram loved Ishmael, but Ishmael was not the child that God had promised him.

When Abram was nearly one hundred years old, God spoke to him again. Abram fell on his face and listened.

God said, "I will make a covenant with you."

Abram knew a covenant was a promise between two people, each one agreeing to do something for the other. In this covenant God promised to give Abram a son, and Abram promised to serve God faithfully.

God said, "Your name shall no more be called Abram, but Abraham, which means, 'The father of many,' and your wife Sarai shall be called Sarah, which means 'Princess.'"

27

Abraham's tent home

Abraham's Strange Visitors

Genesis 18

As Abraham sat in the door of his tent, he saw three strangers. He knew they were from a far country, for they did not even look like the men he knew. He ran to meet them and bowed low.

"Do not go on, but stay here," Abraham said. "I will have water brought so you may wash your feet. Please rest under the tree. I will get you some food. Then you may go on." The three men agreed.

First Abraham sent for water to wash their feet. It was the custom for people to take off their sandals and wash their feet whenever they sat down to rest and visit.

Next Abraham told his wife to bake barley cakes upon the hearth while he prepared the meat for his guests. Abraham ran out to his herd, chose a young calf and had a servant dress and cook it. When all was ready, Abraham brought the food to his guests. They ate while he stood by.

As they ate one visitor asked, "Where is Sarah?"

Abraham answered, "She is in the tent."

The visitor then added, "Your wife Sarah will have a son."

When Sarah heard this, she laughed. Abraham and she were old. How could they have children?

The visitor turned to Abraham and asked, "Why did Sarah laugh and think she was too old to have a child? Doesn't she know that nothing is too hard for the Lord?"

When they had eaten, the men started on. Abraham walked with them a little way. By this time he knew they were not like other men. They were heavenly beings. Two of the visitors were angels. The other was the Lord. Abraham felt he was not good enough to entertain such wonderful visitors.

The Lord loved Abraham. He asked his companions, "Shall I tell Abraham what I am going to do? I know that he will teach his children to keep my ways and do right."

Turning to Abraham, the Lord said, "I am going to visit Sodom and Gomorrah to see whether these cities are as wicked as they seem."

The two men went on, but Abraham wanted to talk to the Lord. If the cities were destroyed, what would happen to Lot? Lot had gone back to live in Sodom after Abraham had rescued him from the enemy's camp.

Because Abraham loved Lot, he asked the Lord, "Will you destroy the righteous people with the wicked in Sodom?"

The Lord said, "If I can find fifty righteous people in Sodom, I will not destroy it."

Then Abraham feared there might be fewer than fifty, so he pleaded with the Lord. "Would you spare the city if there were only forty-five righteous?"

The Lord said, "If I find there are forty-five, I will not destroy it."

Still Abraham felt troubled. There might not be even forty-five. He asked, "What if you find only forty righteous?"

The Lord said, "I will not destroy the city for the sake of forty."

"What," thought poor Abraham, "if there are fewer than forty?" Again he said, "O Lord, be not angry with me, but if there are only thirty righteous people will you spare the city for their sakes?"

The Lord promised to spare the entire city if only thirty righteous people could be found. Abraham kept pleading until he had asked the Lord to spare the city for only ten righteous people. The Lord promised to do it. Then the Lord went on, and Abraham returned to his tent.

What Happened to Sodom

Genesis 19

As evening came the people of Sodom hurried to their homes. Soon the city gates would be closed, and the wise men who judged the people would leave the gate and go to their homes.

Lot was one of the wise men at Sodom's gate. This evening he saw two strangers approaching. He greeted them with a low bow. These were the angels who had dined with the Lord at Abraham's tent.

Lot said, "Come to my house and stay all night. You can get up early and be on your way."

At first the two refused. They would spend the night in the streets. Because Lot knew the wicked men of Sodom would harm these strangers, he insisted they come with him. Finally they did.

29

Lot brought water to wash their dusty feet and prepared good food for them to eat. Perhaps Lot did not know they were angels, but he knew they were not like the wicked men of Sodom.

Soon the news spread over the city that Lot had two strangers at his home. Men hurried to Lot's house. They planned to hurt the visitors. When Lot refused to let them see his guests, they pushed him aside and tried to break open the door. At this the angels pulled Lot inside, and the men of Sodom were blinded.

The two told Lot, "Sodom is so wicked that God is going to destroy it. You must get out of Sodom. Tell your daughters and sons-in-law to get out, too."

Lot went to the homes of his sons-in-law, two men of Sodom. He told them, "We must get out of Sodom, for the Lord is going to destroy it." But they did not believe him and would not leave.

Before the sun rose, the angels urged Lot, "Take your wife and two daughters and flee for your lives."

How hard it was for Lot to leave his home and his riches! But God was good to him, and the angels forced him and his family to leave the city.

The angels said, "Run to the mountains for your lives. Do not even stop long enough to look back."

But Lot's wife looked back, and she became a pillar of salt.

Poor, unhappy Lot! How afraid he was! He thought it would not be safe even in the mountains. So he prayed to God to spare a small city nearby and allow him and his daughters to go there. God granted his request, and they fled to that city. It was called "Zoar," which means "littleness."

Just as the sun rose, Lot and his daughters entered the gate of Zoar. Then a great rain of fire and brimstone fell upon Sodom, Gomorrah and all the neighboring cities. Everything was destroyed.

Later Lot and his daughters feared they were not safe in Zoar, so they went to the mountains. There they lived in a cave, far away from other people. This is the last we hear about Lot, the man whose home and riches were destroyed because he chose to live among the wicked people of Sodom.

Isaac is the child God promised

Hagar and Ishmael

Genesis 20:1–21:21

After Sodom and the other cities of the plain had been destroyed, Abraham left Hebron. He journeyed south and west, into the land of the Philistines. At Gerar near the Great Sea, he made his home. Here God gave him and Sarah a son. Abraham named the child Isaac which means "laughing." Both Abraham and Sarah had laughed when God told them they would have a son in their old age.

Isaac's parents thought he was a wonderful little baby. When Isaac grew old enough to toddle about the tent and to say a few words, Abraham gave a great feast for him.

Ishmael, the son of Sarah's maid Hagar, also lived in Abraham's tent. Although Ishmael was much older, he and Isaac sometimes played together. At the feast Ishmael made fun of Isaac. Perhaps he was jealous of the little boy.

When Sarah saw Ishmael do this, she became angry. She told Abraham, "You must send Ishmael and his mother away, for I do not want our little boy to grow up with Ishmael."

Now Abraham loved Ishmael too. He didn't know what to do. God told Abraham not to grieve but to send the boy and his mother away. God promised that Ishmael would begin a nation.

The next morning Abraham told Hagar that she must take Ishmael and go away. He gave her food and water for the journey. Abraham said good-bye and watched them as they started toward Egypt, where Hagar had lived as a girl.

As Hagar walked through the desert, she remembered the time the angel spoke to her when she had run away from Sarah. On this second journey Hagar got lost and wandered off into the wilderness. After a while there was no more food or water. The hot sun beat down upon the dry, burning sand all day.

Hagar and Ishmael grew so thirsty, faint and weak that they could go no farther. Lovingly Hagar laid her son beneath the shade of a little bush and went away. "I cannot bear to see him suffer and die," she sobbed.

But God had not forgotten about Hagar and her boy. Soon she heard a voice calling from heaven, "Why are you sad, Hagar?

Do not be afraid, for God has heard Ishmael's cry. I will save his life
and make of him a great nation. Go now and lift him up."

Then Hagar saw a spring of water bubbling out of the dry ground.
Quickly she filled her empty bottle and gave Ishmael a drink.

Hagar and Ishmael did not go on to Egypt, but made their home
in the wilderness, far from other people. God cared for them, and
Ishmael grew to be a strong man of the outdoors. He became a
hunter, skillful with bow and arrow. His children also grew up in the
wilderness and were like their father.

Abraham Offers Isaac

Genesis 22:1-19

God knew how much Abraham loved Isaac. As the boy grew,
Abraham loved him even more. Isaac was the child God had
promised, and Abraham loved the boy as a gift from God. Abraham
looked forward to the time when Isaac would become a man and
have children also. These children would grow up and become the
fathers of more people, even as God had promised.

As Isaac grew Abraham taught him to know and worship God.
Perhaps he took Isaac when he offered gifts upon the altar. Abraham
told Isaac that God would accept the gifts and hear prayer if one did
what was right and trusted in him.

The people in Abraham's day thought they must offer as a sacrifice
to their god the dearest things they had, even their own children.
God could never be pleased with such sacrifices. He wanted to teach
Abraham this lesson and also to test his love for God.

So God called to Abraham and Abraham answered, "Behold,
here am I."

God said, "Take your son, your only son, Isaac, whom you love so
much, and go into the land of Moriah. There give him back to me
as an offering upon an altar which you will build at the place I will
show you."

Abraham did not know why God asked him to do this. God had
promised to make of Isaac a great nation. How could God keep
his promise if Isaac were offered upon an altar? Abraham did not
understand, but he was sure God knew best. He would obey.

It would take several days to get to the land of Moriah. Abraham got ready to go. He called two menservants and Isaac. After saddling his donkey, they started away. They took wood and fire to burn the offering. For two days they traveled. At night they slept under the trees.

On the third day Abraham saw the mountain where God wanted the altar built. Abraham told the servants, "Stay here with the donkey while Isaac and I go to worship." Isaac carried the wood on his shoulder, and Abraham took the vessel of fire.

As they climbed the mountain together, Isaac began to wonder why his father had not brought a lamb for an offering. He said, "My father, see, here are wood and fire for the altar, but where is the lamb for an offering?"

Abraham replied, "God will provide a lamb."

When they reached the place God had chosen, Abraham built an altar, laid wood upon it, tied Isaac's hands and feet and placed him upon the altar. Then a loud voice called out, "Abraham! Abraham!" The old man stopped to listen.

The angel of God said, "Do no harm to Isaac. Now I know that you love God even better than you love your child. Untie his hands and his feet, and let him go."

At this Abraham saw a ram caught by his horns in the bushes. He offered the ram instead of his son Isaac.

Afterward the angel called to Abraham again and said, "Because you would have given me your dearly loved child, I will surely bless you and cause your family to be as many as the stars in the heavens and as the sands of the sea. And I will bless all the nations of the earth through your family because you have obeyed my voice."

It was a happy father and son who walked down the mountain. Now Abraham knew that he had pleased God, and Isaac knew that his life was precious in God's sight. Abraham called the place where he had built the altar, "The Lord will provide." The two returned to the servants who were waiting and went back to their home at Beersheba. Here Abraham lived for many years.

Rebekah gives Eliezer a drink

A Wife for Isaac

Genesis 23:1—25:18

When Sarah, Isaac's mother, was one hundred and twenty-seven years old, she died. Abraham bought a field that had a cave and buried Sarah in the cave. This burial place was called Machpelah.

After Sarah's death Abraham and Isaac felt lonely. Isaac was now a man. Abraham decided Isaac needed a wife. In those countries the parents usually chose husbands and wives for their children. Abraham wanted to choose a good wife for Isaac. He thought about his brother Nahor who lived in Haran. Nahor was the father of twelve sons. By this time these sons were married and had grown-up children.

Abraham called his trusted servant Eliezer and said, "Go back to my old home where my relatives are and get a wife for Isaac."

Eliezer knew the journey would be long and hard. Then what if Abraham's people were not willing to send a daughter into a strange country to become the wife of a man they had never seen?

Abraham said, "If the woman is not willing to come back with you, I will not blame you."

Faithful Eliezer said, "I will go."

Eliezer took with him ten camels, several servants and many rich presents. For days and days they traveled across valleys, hills and rivers, and by the great lonely desert. At last they came to the northern part of Mesopotamia and stopped near a well outside the city of Haran.

It was evening, and the women of the city were coming to fill their pitchers at the well. Eliezer had learned to trust in Abraham's God. Now he prayed that God would show him a good wife for Isaac. "Let it be, O Lord, that the young woman I shall ask to give me a drink will also water my camels. Then I shall know that she is the one you have chosen to be Isaac's wife."

While Eliezer prayed, a beautiful young woman came to get water. When she had filled the pitcher, Eliezer asked for a drink. Although he was a stranger, she spoke kindly to him and offered to draw water for his camels also. Again and again she filled her pitcher and poured the water into the trough for the thirsty camels.

When she finished Eliezer gave her two gold bracelets and an earring. He asked, "Whose daughter are you? Would your father have room to lodge us?"

The girl said, "I am Rebekah, the granddaughter of Nahor. There is plenty of room in my father's house for you." Then she hurried to tell her family about the man at the well and to show the beautiful presents he had given her.

Eliezer knew his prayer had been answered. He bowed his head and worshiped God.

When Rebekah's brother Laban heard her story and saw the rich ornaments Eliezer had given her, he ran to meet the strangers at the well. "We have room for you and your camels," he said.

They went with Laban. He brought water to wash their feet and food for them to eat. But Eliezer would not eat.

"First let me tell why I have come," he said. "I am Abraham's servant. God has blessed my master greatly, giving him flocks and herds, silver and gold, and many servants. God also gave him and Sarah a son in their old age. Now Abraham has given all his great riches to his son, Isaac. Because Isaac is not married, Abraham sent me to find a wife for Isaac." Eliezer told how Rebekah, in answer to his prayer, had offered water to him and his thirsty camels.

Rebekah's father and brother Laban were willing to let her go with Eliezer because they believed that God had sent him. Rebekah too was willing.

How thankful Eliezer was! He bowed his head once more to worship the great God who had helped him. Afterward he enjoyed the feast that had been prepared. That same night he gave other presents of silver, gold and beautiful clothing to Rebekah and her family.

The next morning Eliezer said, "Now let me return to my master."

Laban and his mother did not want Rebekah to leave them so soon. "Can you not stay for a few more days?" they asked. But Eliezer insisted that he must go at once.

They called Rebekah, and she said, "I will go." So they said good-bye and sent her away with her nurse and other maids.

On the homeward journey Rebekah and her maids rode the camels, and Eliezer led the way. Perhaps they traveled the same road

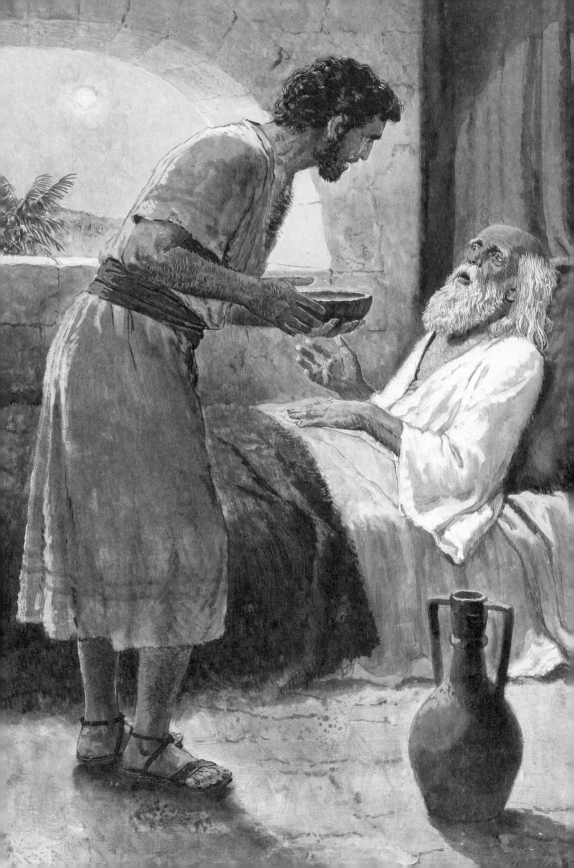

that Abraham had traveled many years before, when he went to the land that God had promised.

At last they were near the place where Abraham and Isaac lived. It was evening and Isaac was out in the fields alone, thinking about God. When he saw the camels coming, he hurried to meet them.

Rebekah asked, "Who is the man coming to meet us?"

"That is my master, Isaac," Eliezer replied. At that Rebekah got down from her camel and covered her face with a veil.

When Isaac met them, Eliezer told how God had answered prayer and sent Rebekah to him. Isaac took her to the tent that had been his mother's, and she became his wife. He loved her, and she comforted him in the loss of his mother.

Time passed and finally Abraham died, too. He was one hundred and seventy-five years old. Ishmael heard of his death and came to help Isaac bury his father. They placed Abraham's body in the cave where Sarah was buried.

Esau Sells His Birthright

Genesis 25:19-34

After some years twin sons were born to Rebekah and Isaac. One was Esau. He was redheaded and hairy. Isaac dearly loved Esau. The younger twin was Jacob. He was not at all like his brother. He liked to stay around the tents. Jacob was his mother's favorite.

As Esau and Jacob grew older, they were taught to work. They learned to take care of their father's cattle and sheep. Esau was fond of hunting. Often he took his bow and arrow to get a deer or other animal. When he got home, he dressed the meat and cooked it. This pleased Isaac very much. Maybe this was one reason Isaac loved Esau better than he did Jacob.

In those lands when the father died, the oldest son received twice as much of the property as did any of the other children. This double portion was called the "birthright." Because Esau was the oldest son, he was to receive the birthright.

One day when Esau came home from his work in the field, he was very hungry. Jacob had been cooking, and the air was full of good

Esau seeks his birthright

smells. Food had never smelled better to Esau. He felt weak from hunger. He said, "Jacob, give me some of that red pottage, for I am weak from hunger."

Jacob answered, "I will give it all to you if you will sell me your birthright for this food."

Esau grew hungrier. He cared more about getting something to eat than he did for his birthright. "What good will a birthright do me if I die of hunger?" Esau wondered. So he sold his birthright for something to eat. Later Esau was very sorry for what he had done.

Isaac and the Wells

Genesis 26

Isaac grew even richer and more powerful. His herds increased. He had many servants. His crops yielded a bountiful harvest. All this made his Philistine neighbors jealous. They didn't want anyone to be richer and more powerful than they.

Of course the Philistines knew that if Isaac didn't have water his cattle would die, his crops would fail and he wouldn't be able to keep so many servants. So they filled his wells with dirt.

Then came Abimelech, leader of the Philistines, to Isaac. He said, "Move away from us. You are much mightier than we Philistines are. We don't feel comfortable with you so near."

How easy it would have been for Isaac to stand on his rights and show the Philistines his power, but Isaac believed that peace was more important than getting one's way. Taking his cattle, his goods and his servants, he set up camp in the valley of Gerar.

Isaac called his servants to him and said, "In this valley are wells that my father Abraham dug, but the Philistines have stopped them up. We will find these wells, dig them out and have water for ourselves and the cattle."

Just as Isaac had said, the servants found an old well. How hard they worked to dig out the dirt! How glad they were to see the springing water! Now everything would be all right.

But all did not go well. The herdsmen of Gerar argued and fought with Isaac's herdsmen. "The water is ours!" they shouted.

"No!" came the angry answer. "We dug out this well, and the water belongs to us."

The fighting did not last long after Isaac heard about the trouble. Calling his servants to him, Isaac said, "Let us find another of my father's wells. He had other wells in this valley that we can use."

Maybe the servants didn't like the idea of looking for and digging out another well, but they obeyed. This second well Isaac called Sitnah. Surely there would be no more trouble this time. But again the herdsmen fought about who owned the water.

A third time Isaac and his company moved and dug another well. There was no trouble over the water. Isaac said, "This well shall be called Rehoboth, for now the Lord has made room for us, and we shall be fruitful in the land."

That night the Lord appeared to Isaac and said, "I am the God of Abraham thy father: fear not, for I am with thee, and will bless thee and multiply thy children for my servant Abraham's sake."

How Isaac must have rejoiced! His father's God had spoken to him and given him the promise. With great joy Isaac built an altar to give thanks to the one true God.

Soon thereafter Isaac had a new reason for joy and thanksgiving. Two visitors came from Gerar: Abimelech, the leader of the Philistines, and his chief captain. When Isaac saw them, he said, "You hate me and sent me away. Why have you come to see me now?"

Abimelech answered, "We know the Lord is with you. We want to make a treaty of peace."

Isaac agreed. He knew that hatred and fighting would never settle differences. Isaac became known throughout the land as one who lived peaceably and followed God's ways.

Isaac Blesses Jacob

Genesis 27:1–42

Isaac lived at Beersheba until he became old and blind. Because Isaac thought he would soon die, he wanted to give the birthright and his blessing to Esau. He called Esau and said, "My son, take your bow and arrow, go into the woods and hunt one more deer. Bring to me

41

the delicious venison that you can prepare. After I have eaten, I will give you my blessing, for I shall die soon."

Esau went to find a deer. How he wished he had not sold his birthright!

Rebekah wanted her younger son, Jacob, to receive the birthright. When she heard Isaac tell Esau to get the venison, she said to Jacob, "I will cook the tender meat of two young goats and season the food just as Esau does. You will wear Esau's clothes and take the food to your father. He will think you are Esau."

At first Jacob was afraid his father would discover the truth and give him a curse instead of a blessing. But Rebekah urged him to obey her orders. "Let the sin be mine," she said.

Isaac was surprised when Jacob brought the dish of food Rebekeh had prepared. He knew Esau had not been gone long enough to kill a deer and prepare the meat. "How have you come so soon?" he asked.

Jacob replied, "Your God helped me to find the deer at once."

Still Isaac wondered how it could be Esau. The voice sounded like Jacob's. Isaac said, "Come near that I may feel you and know you are Esau."

Now Rebekeh had covered Jacob's hands and neck with goat's skin. When blind old Isaac touched the hairy hands he said, "These are Esau's hands." Finally he ate the delicious meat and gave Jacob the blessing of his grandfather Abraham.

After Jacob had gone away, Esau came. "Rise up, my father, and eat of my venison," he said. "Then give me your blessing."

"Who are you?" exclaimed Isaac.

Esau replied, "I am your son Esau."

The old man trembled. "Someone has come in your stead," he told Esau, "and to him I have given the blessing."

Esau knew at once that Jacob had received the blessing. He wept bitterly. "Have you not one blessing for me also?" he pleaded.

Isaac was deeply troubled. "How can I bless you after I have given the best of everything to your brother?"

Still Esau pleaded for a blessing. Finally Isaac blessed him too, with a lesser promise of greatness.

Now Esau hated his brother. "Soon our father will die," he thought. "Then I shall kill Jacob and take everything that has been given him."

Jacob's Dream

Genesis 27:42—29:12

Rebekeh heard that Esau planned to kill Jacob as soon as their father died. She sent for Jacob at once. "You must go far away," she told him. "It is not safe here. Let me send you to my brother Laban who lives in Haran. Perhaps Esau will forget his anger. Then you can come back to me, for why should I lose both you and your father?"

Rebekeh did not tell Isaac that she was afraid Esau would kill Jacob. Instead she told her blind husband, "I am very unhappy because our son Esau has married Canaanite wives. If Jacob did that I would not want to go on living."

Isaac called Jacob and said, "Do not marry a woman of Canaan, but go back to Padanaram and find a wife among your mother's people. God's blessing shall be upon you, and he will give you the blessings of your grandfather Abraham."

Jacob said good-bye to his mother and his blind old father before starting on his long journey. He traveled alone. How afraid he was of Esau! Jacob wondered if he would ever return to his home and feel safe. What good was the birthright now? He could not wait until Isaac died to get the double share of his father's wealth, for then Esau would kill him.

Poor, discouraged Jacob! How unhappy he must have felt as he climbed the rocky slopes of Canaan. Perhaps Jacob was afraid that Esau was already looking for him. Perhaps he was sorry he had tricked his old father. Now he might never see his father again. Perhaps he was even sorry he had bought Esau's birthright. Whatever his thoughts were as he traveled, God knew all about Jacob.

When the sun went down, Jacob felt even lonelier. He was very tired, and so he chose a stone for his pillow, wrapped his cloak about him and lay down on the ground to sleep. He dreamed of a wonderful ladder that reached to heaven. Beautiful angels were going up and down the ladder. God was standing at the top.

Jacob dreamed that God spoke to him and said, "I am the God of your grandfather Abraham and the God of your father Isaac. The land upon which you are lying I will give to you and to your descendants. And your descendants shall be as many as the dust of the earth. Through your family I will bless all people. I will be

43

with you and protect you wherever you go. I will bring you back to this land. I will never leave you until I have fulfilled this promise."

Jacob awoke from his dream and looked about. Although he saw no one, he felt sure that God was there. In the morning he set up the stone that he had used for a pillow, poured oil upon it and consecrated it to God. He called this place Bethel, which means, "The house of God." Then he promised to give back to God a tenth of everything if God would go with him and bless him.

After this wonderful dream Jacob's heart must have felt lighter. He hurried on his way. Every day he drew nearer the end of his long tiresome journey through the desert.

One evening he saw men in a field near a well. Around them were three flocks of sheep waiting to be watered. He came nearer and asked the men, "Where are you from?"

They replied, "We are from Haran."

At last Jacob was near his uncle Laban's home. "Do you know a man named Laban?" he asked eagerly.

"Yes, we know him," they said. "Here comes his daughter Rachel with his sheep."

Jacob saw a beautiful young shepherdess coming to the well, and he hurried to meet her. He rolled the stone away from the well and watered her sheep. Then he said, "I am one of your relatives, the son of your father's sister, Rebekeh." Jacob was so glad to see a relative after such a long journey that he kissed Rachel and the tears rolled down his cheeks.

Rachel hurried home to tell her father that Rebekah's son had come from Canaan and was at the well with the sheep.

Laban Tricks Jacob

Genesis 29:13—31:55

When Laban heard that Jacob had arrived, he hurried to welcome him. Laban was glad to hear from his sister Rebekah and to meet her favorite son. At first he was very kind to Jacob.

Jacob helped his uncle. By the end of the month Laban said, "Let me pay you for your work. How much do you want?"

Jacob sleeps at Bethel

Jacob replied, "I will serve you faithfully for seven years if then you will give me your beautiful daughter Rachel to be my wife." Jacob loved Rachel and wanted to marry her. He loved her so much that the seven years seemed like only a few days.

When the seven years were up, Jacob reminded his uncle of their agreement. Laban arranged a marriage feast and invited many friends to the wedding. In the evening he brought the bride to Jacob. A veil covered her face and no one could see her. This was the custom.

After the ceremony Jacob wanted to see his bride. He lifted the veil, but it was not the beautiful Rachel whom he loved. Instead it was her older sister, Leah. How unhappy he was! His uncle had tricked him. Perhaps Jacob remembered how he had tricked his blind father and cheated his brother out of the blessing.

Jacob demanded of Laban, "What have you done to me? Didn't I work seven years for Rachel? Then why did you cheat me?"

Laban said, "It is not the custom in our country to let the younger daughter marry first. If you will serve me for seven more years, you may have Rachel also for your wife."

In those days most men had several wives. Because Jacob loved Rachel, he decided to work for her, too. And Rachel, too, became his wife.

After fourteen years Jacob wanted to return to Canaan. Laban did not want to let him go. "While you have been with me," he told Jacob, "the Lord has blessed me for your sake."

Jacob said, "But how am I to provide for my family?"

Laban agreed to let Jacob have part of the cattle and sheep and goats. Jacob separated these from Laban's. Jacob had his sons take care of them while he looked after Laban's flocks.

And God blessed Jacob and increased his possessions. Jacob became rich. By this time Jacob was the father of eleven sons and a daughter.

Because Jacob became rich, Laban's sons were jealous. They said Jacob got his riches dishonestly. Laban, too, began to feel envious.

The angel of God spoke to Jacob in a dream and said, "I am the God of Bethel where you anointed the stone and made a promise to me.

Jacob speaks to Laban

The time has come for you to return to your people in Canaan. I will be with you."

Jacob was afraid Laban would not let him take Leah and Rachel to far-off Canaan. Jacob decided to go away secretly. He waited until Laban went to shear the sheep. Then he called Leah and Rachel out into the field and said, "Your father no longer feels kindly toward me. God has told me to return to Canaan."

"We are ready to go," they replied. "God is with you."

Busy days followed. Jacob got ready to start out on the long road that he had traveled twenty years before. The sheep, the goats, the cattle and the camels were all brought from the fields. The servants drove the animals while Jacob's wives and children rode on camels.

Across the fields they went and onto the road which wound along the lonely wilderness. Wild mountains were on one side and on the other side the dreary desert sand stretched into space. Finally they came to a camping place at Mount Gilead. Here they stopped to rest.

Things were happening back at Haran. Someone told Laban that Jacob had gone away and had taken everything he owned. How angry Laban was! "I shall overtake him," Laban decided.

Perhaps he planned to make Jacob return to Haran. He took several men and hurried after Jacob's company. For seven days they followed fast. At last they saw the tents Jacob had pitched at Mount Gilead. Before they reached Gilead God warned Laban not to harm Jacob. God caused Laban's anger to cool. He did not even quarrel with Jacob.

Afterward Jacob set up a stone for a pillar and the other men gathered stones together in a heap. Laban called this heap of stones Mizpah, which means, "A watchtower." And he said to Jacob, "May God watch over us while we are absent from each other." Then, bidding his daughters and their children a loving good-bye, he started back to his home at Haran. Jacob and his family traveled on toward Canaan.

Jacob and Esau Meet Again

Genesis 32—35

Although twenty years had passed since Jacob's flight from Canaan, he never forgot his fear of Esau. What if Esau never forgave him? What if Esau still wanted to kill him?

God knew about Jacob's fear and sent a company of angels to meet him. That gave Jacob courage. He sent messengers to tell Esau of his coming. If Esau didn't welcome him home, Jacob could not be happy in Canaan.

But Esau no longer lived in Canaan. With his family he had moved to the country of Edom, south and east of the Dead Sea. There the messengers told him of Jacob's coming. He said he would come to meet Jacob and bring four hundred men with him.

Jacob was terribly afraid. He thought Esau planned to kill him and his wives and children. He quickly divided his company into two groups. If Esau attacked one group, the other would be safe. Jacob asked God to protect him. In the morning he sent sheep and oxen, camels and other animals to his brother. How much Jacob wanted to please Esau!

That night a strange man wrestled with Jacob. At dawn Jacob saw he had been wrestling with an angel of God. The angel said, "Let me go, for the day is breaking."

Jacob answered, "I will not let you go until you bless me." The angel asked, "What is your name?"

"My name is Jacob," he answered.

The angel said, "You will be called Israel because you have power with God and man." Israel means, "A prince of God."

Jacob called this place Peniel, which means, "The face of God."

Jacob walked on with his company. When he looked up, he saw Esau coming to meet him. His heart pounded as he stepped forward to meet his brother. Jacob bowed himself to the ground. Seven times he bowed. Esau ran to Jacob, threw his arms about him and kissed him. All was forgiven.

Jacob presented his wives and their children to his brother and told him how God had blessed him.

Esau asked, "What about the animals that were brought to us?"

"They are a present for you," Jacob said.

At first Esau refused them because he, too, was rich in cattle. Finally he accepted them as a gift from Jacob.

After a short visit Esau returned to his home in Edom, and Jacob went on to Canaan. At Shechem he bought a field, built an altar and worshiped God. He thanked God for the safe journey from Haran.

Later Jacob moved to Bethel, then toward his old home at Hebron where his father, Isaac, still lived. Many years had passed since Jacob had traveled that same road, alone and afraid. Now he was returning to his father's house bringing his family and many servants.

Surely God had blessed him, and his heart was glad.

Before they arrived at Hebron, Rachel died. She left a tiny baby boy whose name was Benjamin. Jacob buried her at Bethlehem and marked her grave with a stone.

When Jacob reached Hebron, he found his father expecting to die. How happy Isaac must have been to have Jacob home again! Isaac was now one hundred and eighty years old. When he died, Esau came and helped Jacob bury him.

Joseph Becomes a Slave

Genesis 37

Of his twelve sons Jacob loved Joseph most. Joseph was the eleventh boy. He was Rachel's oldest son.

Because Jacob loved Joseph most, his brothers were jealous. When Jacob made a wonderful coat of many colors for Joseph, the older sons hated their brother.

One day Joseph saw four of his brothers do wrong. As soon as he could he told his father what his brothers had done. They hated Joseph even more for telling on them.

One night seventeen-year-old Joseph had a strange dream. He told his brothers about it. "We were together in the field binding sheaves. My sheaf stood upright while yours bowed down around it."

How angry the brothers were! "Do you think you will someday rule over us?" they asked.

51

Jacob gives Joseph a beautiful coat

Soon Joseph dreamed again. This dream was stranger than the other. He told his father and brothers, "In my dream I saw the sun, the moon and eleven stars bowing down before me."

Jacob said, "Indeed, shall your father and your mother and your brothers bow down to you?" That dream seemed to make Joseph greater, better and wiser than his family. Still Jacob wondered what such a dream could mean.

Jacob and his family lived at Hebron, where Abraham had lived long before. Jacob's flocks were so large the brothers could not find enough pasture nearby. Sometimes they had to take the flocks far from home to find grass and water. This time Jacob sent his ten older sons to Shechem with the cattle and sheep. After they had been away for several weeks, Jacob sent Joseph to find out how they were getting along.

Joseph started out alone. It was fifty miles to Shechem. When he got there, he could not find his brothers and their flocks. What should he do now?

A man from a nearby town told Joseph, "Your brothers have gone to Dothan to find better pasture."

Joseph journeyed on, over the hills and across the valleys to Dothan, fifteen miles away. Long before he was within calling distance, he could see the flocks.

When the brothers saw a young man in a beautiful coat coming across the fields, they said to each other, "Here comes the dreamer. Let us kill him and see what will become of his dreams."

Reuben, the oldest, did not want to harm Joseph. Because he thought the others would not listen if he told them not to harm Joseph, he said, "Let us not kill him; only throw him down into this pit and leave him alone to die."

The others quickly agreed. When Joseph approached, they seized him, tore off his beautiful coat and threw him into the pit. Paying no attention to Joseph's shouts, they sat down on the ground and ate their lunch.

Reuben did not intend to let Joseph die in the pit. He planned to rescue Joseph as soon as the others went away.

While Reuben went to care for the flocks, a company of merchants came by on camels. Some of these travelers were called Ishmaelites because they were descendants of Ishmael. They were on their way to Egypt to sell rich spices and perfumed gum.

"Now," thought Judah, "we can get rid of our brother and make some money!" He said, "It would be better to sell Joseph to these merchants than to let him die in the pit. For even though we hate him, he is our brother."

The others were quite willing to sell Joseph, so they pulled him out of the pit and sold him to the Ishmaelites for twenty pieces of silver.

Poor Joseph! Now he knew that he was being taken far away by rough strangers. All his pleading and all his tears did not make any difference to his brothers. They divided the money and thought they were rid of Joseph forever.

After the Ishmaelites passed on, the brothers returned to their work. At once Reuben hurried back to the pit. Stooping down, he called to Joseph. There was no answer. Again and again he called, but Joseph did not reply. He ran to his brothers. "The child is gone. What shall I do?" As the oldest Reuben felt responsible for his brother.

The brothers told Reuben what they had done. "But what shall we tell our father about Joseph?" they wondered. Finally they decided to dip Joseph's coat in the blood of an animal, take the bloodstained coat to their father and tell him that they had found it.

Jacob was alarmed when his sons returned without Joseph. When he saw the blood-covered coat he knew it was Joseph's. At once he believed that wild animals had killed Joseph. Jacob tore his clothes and dressed in sackcloth. He mourned bitterly and would not be comforted.

Joseph, a Prisoner in Egypt

Genesis 37:36—40:23

After a long, dusty journey the Ishmaelites arrived with Joseph in Egypt. Here Joseph saw dark-skinned people who spoke a different language. He saw large cities, beautiful temples for the worship of idols, mighty pyramids and the great river Nile. How strange all this was to a youth who had always lived in tents!

The Ishmaelites took Joseph to the chief city and sold him to an officer in the king's army. Joseph could never forget how terrified he was when his own brothers sold him as a slave. Nothing could be done about it now. He would just have to learn to be a good slave.

God did not forget Joseph or the wonderful dreams He had given him. God was preparing Joseph for the time when those dreams would come true. Joseph did not understand God's plan, but he trusted God.

Joseph's master, Potiphar, was a very rich man with many servants. Joseph learned quickly. He learned to speak the language and to be cheerful and obedient. Potiphar noticed that Joseph was honest and had a good understanding of business. After a while he put Joseph in charge of his household and his wealth. Joseph did so well that he became a slave in name only.

Then a strange thing happened. One day Potiphar's wife tried to make love to Joseph, but Joseph would not let her. She became so angry that she lied about Joseph to her husband. "He tried to make love to me while you were away," she said. Potiphar believed his wife and had Joseph thrown into the king's prison.

How unfair this was! To be a slave had seemed bad enough, but to be put in prison for doing right was even worse. But Joseph did not pout and feel sorry for himself. Instead he was cheerful. The prison keeper was attracted to Joseph. Day after day the keeper watched him. Finally he decided that Joseph was the very person he needed to help care for the prisoners. Later he gave Joseph full charge of all the prisoners. Now Joseph was as busy as he had been in Potiphar's house.

About this time Pharaoh, the king of Egypt, was much displeased with two special servants—the chief butler and the chief baker. Pharaoh put both servants in prison, and Joseph cared for them.

One morning Joseph noticed that these men were troubled. "Why are you troubled?" he asked.

"We have had strange dreams," they told Joseph, "and there is no one here to tell us what they mean. In the king's court there are wise men who often tell the meaning of dreams, but they will not come to us in prison."

"Surely God knows the meaning of your dreams," Joseph said, "and I am his servant. Tell me what you have dreamed. God may show me the true meaning."

The chief butler said, "I saw a grapevine with three branches. While I looked at it the buds shot forth and became blossoms, and the blossoms became clusters of grapes. Then I squeezed the juice of the grapes into Pharaoh's cup. This I gave to the king as I did when I waited on him."

God helped Joseph know the meaning of the dream. Joseph said, "The three branches are three days. In three days you will be back at your job in the king's palace. I beg you to tell Pharaoh about me. I was stolen from my father's house and sold a slave. For no fault of mine, I was put into prison." And the chief butler promised to tell Pharaoh about Joseph.

Then the chief baker told Joseph his dream. "There were three baskets upon my head. In the top one there were bake meats for the king's table. The birds flew down and ate the food in the top basket."

Through the wisdom of God, Joseph knew the meaning of this dream too. He hated to tell its meaning, but the chief baker insisted. "In your dream the three baskets mean three days. In three days the king will hang you."

Three days later Pharaoh had a great birthday feast. During the feast he had the chief butler returned to the palace and the chief baker hanged. But the chief butler soon forgot about Joseph. Two years passed before he remembered to tell the king about Joseph.

Joseph, a Ruler in Egypt

Genesis 41

One morning Pharaoh called the wise men of Egypt to tell him the meaning of two strange dreams. But they could not explain the dreams. Pharaoh was greatly troubled.

When the chief butler heard about this, he remembered his dream in prison and Joseph's kindness. How could he have forgotten Joseph? Now he told Pharaoh about Joseph. Immediately the king sent for him.

Joseph was busy caring for the prisoners when the messenger came from the king's palace. "Pharaoh wants to see you at once," the messenger said.

"Why did Pharaoh send for me?" Joseph wondered. "If only he would set me free!" Joseph shaved and put on clean clothes. Then he hurried to the royal palace.

At the palace Pharaoh was anxiously waiting. Everyone was deeply troubled. "If this strange young man cannot help, what shall we do?" they wondered. They heard footsteps outside the door, and Joseph was brought in. Fair-skinned and handsome, he was the center of attention at once.

Pharaoh said, "I have heard that you can tell the meaning of dreams. I have had two dreams which trouble me greatly, and none of the wise men of Egypt can tell me what these dreams mean."

Joseph replied, "This wisdom does not belong to me, but to the God I serve. He will help me know the meaning of your dreams."

Then Pharaoh explained, "In my dream I was standing by the river Nile when seven fat cattle came up out of the river and fed in the green meadow. Later seven very lean cattle came up out of the river and stood on the bank. The lean cattle ate the fat ones. Still they were as thin as they had been at first. Then I awoke.

"Afterwards I fell asleep and dreamed again. This time I saw seven ears of corn grow up out of one stalk. Full, good ears they were. Then seven other ears sprang up—withered, thin and blasted with the east wind. These thin ears ate the good ones, and once more I awoke."

Joseph told the king, "Both dreams have the same meaning. God wants you to know what is going to happen. The seven fat cattle and the seven full ears are seven years. The seven lean cattle and the seven thin ears are the next seven years. God is telling you there will be seven years of plenty throughout all Egypt. Afterwards there will be seven years of famine. These years of famine will be so hard that the good years will be forgotten. All the food will be gone.

"God has given you these two dreams to show you that these things will happen soon. He has warned you to prepare for the famine, or it could destroy you and your kingdom. You should appoint a wise man to look after the food supply. During the seven plentiful years, let him save enough grain each year so there will be food for all during the famine."

Pharaoh and his attendants listened carefully to Joseph's words. The king said, "Surely the Spirit of God is in this man. His words are good. Can we find another who could manage the affairs of this kingdom more wisely than he?"

Pharaoh made Joseph ruler over all the land of Egypt. He dressed Joseph in royal robes and put a gold chain about his neck. He took off his signet ring and put it on Joseph's finger. Pharaoh said, "You shall be overseer of my house, and your word shall govern my people in all Egypt. I am the only one who will be greater than you."

And Pharaoh gave Joseph a chariot. In this Joseph rode through the streets of the city, and the people bowed before him. Pharaoh called Joseph "Zaphenath-paneah," which means, "The man to whom secrets are revealed." He also gave Joseph an Egyptian girl, the daughter of a priest, for his wife.

All this honor did not change Joseph's heart. He was still kind and fair to all. Day after day he rode through the land and gathered up the food which grew everywhere in abundance. He stored this food for the years of famine.

During this time God blessed Joseph with two sons. Joseph named them Manasseh and Ephraim. And Joseph was grateful to God for all his blessings. He realized that all his troubles had brought about this great honor he now enjoyed.

When the seven years of plenty had passed, the years of trouble began. Nowhere in all Egypt would grain grow. When the people needed food, they came to Joseph. Opening the storehouses that had been filled during the years of plenty, he sold food to the Egyptians.

Not only in Egypt was there a terrible famine, but also in the countries round about. From far and near people came to Joseph, begging him to sell them corn lest they die of hunger.

Joseph's Dreams Come True

Genesis 42

The great famine reached the land of Canaan also. Food became scarce, and the people were worried. "What are we going to eat?" they wondered.

Jacob said to his sons, "I have heard there is corn in Egypt. Go there and buy food." The brothers left, but Benjamin did not go with them. Since he had lost Joseph, Jacob loved Benjamin best. Jacob was so afraid of losing Benjamin too that he would not let his youngest son go so far from home.

More than twenty years had passed since the ten older brothers had sold Joseph as a slave. The brothers had grown more thoughtful of each other. They were not even jealous because their father loved Benjamin best. How often they must have remembered the time they sold Joseph!

As the brothers traveled to Egypt, they saw new stretches of country. Eagerly they watched for the first glimpse of Egypt. But Egypt did not look as they had expected. The fields were just as bare as those of Canaan. Soon they learned there was plenty of food here in spite of the famine. Great storehouses were filled with corn.

Like everyone who wanted to buy food, they went to Joseph. Little did they dream that this man who sat on a throne and dressed like an Egyptian prince was their brother. In these twenty years he had become a man. Everyone bowed before him just as if he were king. His ten brothers bowed also.

Joseph knew his brothers at once. When they bowed he remembered his dreams. Now he knew those dreams had come true, and he understood why God had let him be sold into Egypt. But Joseph wanted to know whether his brothers had changed. So he pretended not to know them. He spoke like an Egyptian and pretended to be harsh and stern.

Joseph becomes a ruler in Egypt

"Who are you?" he demanded roughly.

They replied, "We are men of Canaan, and we are brothers."

"You are spies," he told them, "and I know you have come to see the stricken condition of our country. You plan to bring an army against us."

"Indeed we are not spies," they answered. "We have come to buy food for ourselves and our families."

Still Joseph insisted they were spies. Again they told him they were brothers, the sons of one man.

"Is your father yet alive?" he asked. "And have you another brother?" The brothers told about their old father and his great love for Benjamin.

Now Joseph wondered whether they were kind to Benjamin. Did they care more for their father's happiness now than they did when they sold Joseph to the Ishmaelites? Joseph decided he must find out before he told them who he was. So he said, "You must prove you are not spies. I will put nine of you in prison and send the other one back to Canaan. If he returns with your youngest brother, then I will believe that you are true men."

Joseph had his brothers put in the prison where he had spent several long years. He would see if they were better men than they used to be. After three days he sent for them and said, "I fear God, and I want to do the right thing. If you are true men, you can prove it this way: I will send nine of you back to your old father with food and keep one of you in prison. You must bring back your younger brother or I will know you are spies."

To each other they said, "We are suffering now because of our sin. Now we know how terrified Joseph felt when we sold him. He pleaded with us, but we would not listen."

Reuben, the oldest brother and the one who had planned to save Joseph's life, reminded them, "I told you then that you should not sin against the boy. You would not listen to me. By your sin you have brought this trouble on us all."

Joseph pretended not to know what they were saying, but he heard every word. His heart was touched. They were sorry for their sin.

He turned his face away and cried for joy. Then he dried his tears and spoke to them again like an Egyptian. He took Simeon, the second oldest, tied him up and put him back in prison. Then he ordered his servants, "Fill their sacks with corn and put each man's money back into his sack."

The heavyhearted brothers started home. What would their father say? Joseph was lost to him. Simeon was a prisoner. Now Benjamin must go to Egypt or Simeon would be killed. No wonder they were worried!

At the end of the first day they stopped to feed their animals. One brother opened his sack and found his bag of money with the corn. They were even more afraid when they saw the money. The stern ruler would think they had stolen the money.

At last they reached home, tired and afraid. They told their father what had happened. "We cannot return unless we take Benjamin," they said.

"I can never let you take my youngest son," Jacob replied. "I no longer have Joseph or Simeon. I would die if something happened to Benjamin too."

Then the brothers emptied their sacks of food. When they found that each one's money had been replaced in his sack, they were more frightened than ever.

Joseph's Brothers Return to Egypt

Genesis 43

Still the famine continued. The brooks dried up, and the wells became more shallow every day. After a time the food Jacob's sons had brought from Egypt was almost gone. "You must go again," said Jacob, "and buy more corn."

But Judah answered, "We cannot go unless we take Benjamin. That is the only way the ruler will sell us more corn."

"Why did you tell him you had a younger brother?" Jacob asked.

Judah explained, "The man asked us if we had another brother. We only answered his questions. We didn't know what he would say."

Reuben brought his two sons to Jacob and said, "You may kill my sons if I do not bring Benjamin back safely."

Still Jacob shook his head and refused to let Benjamin go. The days dragged on and the food supply grew less and less. What should they do? Even though the brothers were grown men, they would not return to Egypt without their father's consent. In that land the father ruled his household as long as he lived.

Finally Judah said, "Father, if you do not send us soon, we shall all die of hunger. I will certainly take care of Benjamin. Should any harm come to him, I will bear the blame forever."

At last poor old Jacob let Benjamin go with his brothers. "If my children must all be taken away from me, then I must bear the loss," he said.

At once they prepared for the journey. Jacob told his sons to take the ruler presents. They took rich spices and perfumes, wild honey and nuts. Jacob said, "Take twice as much money as before. Maybe the money was put back into your sacks by mistake."

When the brothers returned to Egypt, Joseph saw Benjamin with his brothers. At once he sent them to his own house and ordered his servants to prepare a feast. "The men of Canaan are to dine with me," he told his steward.

The brothers did not know what Joseph told his servants. Why had they been brought to the ruler's house? The brothers were afraid. "He thinks we stole the money," they said, "and now he will accuse us and put us in prison with Simeon." What should they do? They decided to tell the steward their troubles.

"Do not be afraid," the steward said. "I had your money." The steward gave them food for their animals. Then he gave the brothers water to wash their feet. Afterwards he brought Simeon to them. "You are all invited to eat dinner with my master," he said.

At noon Joseph came home. He spoke to the brothers kindly and asked if their father was still alive. Next he turned to Benjamin and asked, "Is this your youngest brother?" The brothers nodded.

Joseph said to Benjamin, "The Lord be gracious to you, my son." He longed to throw his arms around Benjamin, but there was still more he wanted to find out about his ten older brothers. So he hurried out of the room to hide his tears.

63

Joseph and his brothers

The brothers were beginning to feel better. They were glad to find Simeon well. Soon they hoped to be on their way to Canaan with food and good news for their anxious father.

After the tables had been arranged, Joseph and his brothers entered the dining hall. Other guests were present—possibly Egyptian officers. The brothers saw three tables—one for Joseph the ruler, another for the Egyptians and the third for them. The brothers were seated at the table according to their ages, from the oldest to the youngest. "How strange!" they thought. "How can this man know our ages?"

Joseph sent each brother food from his table, but to Benjamin he sent five times as much as to the others.

Joseph Makes Himself Known

Genesis 44:1—45:24

When the meal was over, the brothers wanted to go home. "Fill their sacks with corn," Joseph told the steward, "and put their money back into the sacks. But in Benjamin's sack put my silver cup also." And the steward did it.

The next morning the brothers started home. But they had not gone far when the steward came hurrying after them. "My master's silver cup is gone," he said. "Why have you taken it?"

"God forbid that we should steal the cup," they answered. "We are honest men. Didn't we return the money that we found in our sacks? Why then should your master think we took his cup?"

So sure were they that none of them had taken the cup that they said, "Search us and see for yourself. If the cup is found, let that one die in whose sack it is discovered, and the rest of us will become your servants."

"If I find the cup," said the steward, "I will take him for my servant in whose sack it is found. The others may go free."

Then the search began. Every man lowered his sack to the ground and opened it. And one by one the men rejoiced when the missing cup was not found. At last the steward opened Benjamin's sack. Here he found the missing cup.

How astonished the brothers were! They could not believe it. What should they do now? They could not part with Benjamin. How afraid they were as they turned back to the city with the steward!

Joseph was waiting for them. "What is this you have done?" he demanded sternly, as they fell to the ground before him.

"Surely God is punishing us for our sins. We are all your servants," exclaimed Judah.

"God forbid that I should keep all of you," answered Joseph. "I will punish only the one who took the cup. The rest of you may return home." Joseph wondered if his brothers would let Benjamin suffer so they could escape.

Judah remembered his promise to bring Benjamin safely home or bear the blame forever. He fell on his face at Joseph's feet. "Please do not be angry with me, but listen to my words," he said. "The last time we came you asked if we had a father or a younger brother. We told you that we had. We told you about our father's love for Benjamin to prove that we were not spies. We told you our father would not be willing to let him come, because he feared something might happen to Benjamin. Still you insisted that we bring him if we wanted to buy more food.

"When we got home, we told our father what you said. How sad he was! He said he could never let Benjamin leave him. But when the food was almost gone, he wanted to send us again. We reminded him that we could not see you unless Benjamin was with us. Several days later our father said, 'If anything happened to Benjamin, I would die.' Now if we go back without Benjamin our father will die, for he is old and feeble. He lives for Benjamin. Let Benjamin return, I beg you, and let me take his place. I promised our father that if anything happened to Benjamin I would bear the blame forever."

Judah's words touched Joseph deeply. How different they sounded from the words Judah had spoken so long ago when he suggested they sell Joseph to the Ishmaelites! Now Judah was offering himself as a lifetime slave in the place of Benjamin. A changed Judah indeed!

Now Joseph was sure his brothers were better men. Quickly he ordered the Egyptian servants to leave the room. Turning to his brothers, he said in their language, "I am your brother Joseph. Does my father yet live?"

65

Surprise and fear came over the brothers. They could not say a word. Joseph saw they were afraid. The tears were streaming down his face as he called them to come nearer.

"I am the same Joseph you sold into Egypt, but do not be afraid. Do not be angry with yourselves, for God sent me here to save your lives. This terrible famine will last five more years. You must bring your families and all your things to Egypt or else you may die. I will take care of you. Here God has made me a father even to Pharaoh. Here I am the ruler of all his people."

Then Joseph kissed Benjamin and embraced him. Joseph greeted each brother with the same forgiving tenderness.

The Egyptian servants heard Joseph weeping, and they hurried to tell Pharaoh that Joseph's brothers had come. Everyone was glad, for everyone loved Joseph.

Pharaoh said, "Have your brothers go home and bring their households and your father back to Egypt. Send wagons to bring the women and children."

The brothers started home, taking Egyptian wagons loaded with presents. Joseph sent special gifts to his father. To each brother he gave five outfits of Egyptian clothing. To Benjamin he gave five times as much as to the others.

Joseph's Family Moves to Egypt

Genesis 45:25–50:26

Jacob waited and waited for his sons. How anxious he was to see them. At last they came, followed by a train of Egyptian wagons.

Jacob's joy was greatest when he saw Benjamin and Simeon. At once the brothers told the good news. "We found Joseph!" they exclaimed, "and he is alive and well. More than that, he is the ruler of all Egypt, and he sent us to bring you and our wives and our children to live in Egypt."

At first Jacob could not believe their words. How could this be? But when he saw the wagons filled with presents, he said, "It is enough; Joseph my son is yet alive. I will go and see him before I die."

The third journey to Egypt was a happy one. Jacob and his sons' wives and their little children rode in the wagons. The men drove

Joseph welcomes his father

the herds of cattle. Jacob's sons and grandchildren—sixty-seven persons besides the mothers who, of course, went too—made up the company.

One night they made camp at Beer-sheba where Abraham and Isaac had lived long before. Here Jacob offered sacrifices to God. And God spoke to him in a night vision. "Do not be afraid to go to Egypt, for I will go with you. I will make your family a great nation. Then I will bring that nation back to the land that I promised to Abraham and Isaac." From this time on Jacob was called Israel, and his children were known as Israelites.

At the Egyptian border, the Israelites camped again. They waited for Judah to go tell Joseph of their coming. Joseph took his royal chariot and rode into Goshen to meet his father and his relatives.

What a happy meeting! Both father and son cried for joy and said many tender words. Then Joseph took five of his brothers and his father to see Pharaoh, the king.

Pharaoh was glad to see them. When he learned they were shepherds, he told them they could live in the land of Goshen. Watered by the Nile River, Goshen was a fertile country between the river and the desert. Until the famine was over, Joseph provided food for his relatives and their cattle.

After the famine Joseph's people continued to live in Goshen. Israel was one hundred and thirty years old when he left Canaan, and he lived seventeen years in Goshen. Before he died he asked his sons to take his body back to Canaan and bury it in the cave where Abraham and Isaac were buried. Then he gave each son a blessing.

Joseph brought his two boys, Manasseh and Ephraim, to see their grandfather and to receive his blessing. Israel said, "Surely God has been good to me, for I thought I should never see your face again. Now I see both you and your children." He placed his trembling, wrinkled hands upon the boys' heads to bless them. His right hand was on Ephraim, the younger and his left hand on Manasseh.

"Not so, my father," Joseph said gently, trying to place his father's right hand on Manasseh's head.

But Israel would not allow the change. "I know what I am doing," he answered. "Your younger son will become greater than the older. To the younger belongs the greater blessing."

After Israel died Joseph commanded the Egyptian physicians to prepare his father's body for burial. This took forty days. For seventy days the people mourned the death of Joseph's father. Then Joseph asked Pharaoh, "May I go with my brothers to bury my father in Canaan?"

And Pharaoh said, "Go."

When they returned the brothers thought, "Perhaps Joseph has been kind to us only for our father's sake. Now he may treat us cruelly because we wronged him so long ago."

So they sent a messenger to Joseph, saying, "Before our father died, he asked you to forgive us. Please forgive us, for we are servants of the God of our father."

Joseph wept when he heard this. His brothers were afraid. He sent for them and said, "Do not be afraid. Am I in God's place that I should punish you? No! I will care for you and your children as long as I live." How relieved the brothers were! Now they were sure Joseph had forgiven them.

As the years passed, Joseph's relatives grew in number until they became a great nation. Joseph was one hundred and ten years old when he knew he was about to die. He called the old men of Israel to his bedside and said, "I am going to die, but God will watch over you. By and by he will lead you back to the land of your fathers. Do not bury me here in Egypt, but put my body in a coffin and take it with you when you return to Canaan."

And the men of Israel wept as they promised. Afterwards whenever they looked at Joseph's coffin they remembered his words. They knew they would not always live in Egypt. They would yet be a great nation, and God would still send a Savior.

Job, a Man Who Loved God

Job 1:1—42:17

In a country called Uz lived a very rich man named Job. His cattle were numbered by thousands. He had seven sons, three daughters and many servants.

Not only was Job rich, but he was godly. With all his heart he wanted to please God. He built altars of earth or of stone and made

offerings to God. He prayed and asked God to forgive his sins and to bless him.

When Job's sons grew to manhood and had homes of their own, they loved to have great feasts. The brothers took turns giving the feasts, and their three sisters were always invited.

On the morning after the feasts, Job always got up early and placed offerings on the altar for each of his children. Perhaps they had sinned in their hearts during the feast.

God loved Job. He blessed him with health and happiness. He gave him many friends and great honors.

But one day Satan complained to God about Job. He said, "Job serves you just because you bless him. If he had lots of trouble, he would turn away from you."

God knew Satan was wrong, but God told him to find out for himself. And Satan did. He sent Job lots of trouble.

One day while Job's children were feasting, a messenger came running to Job with bad news. "The oxen were plowing and the asses were feeding beside them, but the Sabeans came and stole all the animals and killed all the servants. I am the only one that escaped."

Before the servant was through telling Job about it, another servant brought more bad news. He said, "Lightning has killed all the sheep and the servants. I alone escaped to tell you."

Then came another servant to Job, saying, "The Chaldeans have taken the camels and killed the servants. I am the only one that got away."

Before Job knew what was happening, a fourth messenger announced, "Your children were feasting and a great wind blew down the house. They are all dead. Only I escaped to tell you."

When Job heard all this bad news, he tore his clothes and fell down on his face. But he did not turn away from God.

Then Satan planned another trouble for Job. Satan thought, "I will make life so miserable for Job that he will blame God for his suffering. Then he will want to die."

In those days many people believed troubles were always sent from God as a punishment for sins. Satan thought Job, too, believed this, so Satan caused great, ugly sores to break out all over Job's

God sends Job new blessings

body. These sores were very painful. Everybody looked upon Job with horror, and even his wife wished he would die. Poor Job!

Three friends came to see Job. They had heard about his troubles and wanted to comfort him. For several days they sat with Job but did not say a single word to him. When they saw how much he was suffering, they believed God was punishing Job for awful sins. They said God had sent this suffering because Job was trying to hide his wrongdoing from God. Poor Job! Even his friends did not believe in him.

Then God spoke to Job out of a whirlwind, and Job bowed low on the ground and worshiped. God said, "I am angry with your three friends, for they have not spoken rightly of me."

When Job heard this, he prayed for his friends. God knew Job was a servant of his. He sent Job many blessings. The sores went away. Every year Job grew richer until he had twice as much as before the troubles came, and God again gave him seven sons and three daughters. His daughters were the most beautiful women in all that country. And so health, happiness, riches and honor came again to Job.

Even to this day Job is remembered as a man who would not let any kind of trouble or sorrow turn him away from God.

MOSES, LAWGIVER AND LEADER

Exodus; Leviticus; Numbers; Deuteronomy

~~~~~~

A Baby and a Basket

Exodus 1:1—2:10

After Jacob's name was changed to Israel, his children were called Israelites. They lived in the land of Goshen more than four hundred years. And their numbers grew until they became a strong nation.

Joseph and the kind Pharaoh had been dead a long time. Another Pharaoh had come to the Egyptian throne. This new Pharaoh was afraid of the Israelites. He thought, "Soon there will be more Israelites than Egyptians. If they should turn against us, we would be in serious trouble. What if they joined our enemies? I must not let them leave Goshen. I will keep them for slaves."

Pharaoh called his people together and told them his fear. "We must do something," he said, "to stop the Israelites from becoming stronger and more powerful than we are."

Finally he and his officers decided to make the Israelites work even harder. Pharaoh wanted new cities, and he commanded the Israelites to build them. Then the officers put taskmasters over the workmen. The taskmasters were to make them work hard and fast.

But the harder they worked the stronger the Israelites became. Pharaoh was even more afraid. "This will never do," he reasoned. "I must make life more miserable for them." And he did.

One morning Pharaoh sent the Israelites this message: "Every baby boy that is born among your people must be thrown into the Nile River."

Into such a world Moses was born. How much his mother loved him! For three months she hid him from the soldiers. Then the baby was too old to hide. So she gathered bulrushes that grew along the river. These she wove into a basket. To keep the water out, she plastered it with pitch. Then she made a soft bed in the bottom.

Next came the very hardest part. She put the baby in the basket and carried the basket to the river. There among the tall reeds at the

73

water's edge, she placed her precious basket and went back home. Sister Miriam played along the riverbank and watched the basket.

Soon a company of richly dressed women appeared. One of them was the Egyptian princess, Pharaoh's daughter. They had come to bathe in the river. When the princess saw the strange-looking basket floating among the reeds, she sent her maid to get it.

"What can be inside this basket?" the women wondered as they gathered round to see it opened. How surprised they were to see a little baby! The baby was crying, and the princess lifted him lovingly.

"This is one of the Israelite's children," the princess said. She knew about the cruel command her father had given, but how could she let this sweet little baby be killed? "I'll take him for my own," she decided.

When Miriam heard this, she ran to the princess and asked, "Shall I get an Israelite woman to nurse this baby for you?" Of course the baby would need a nurse, and the princess was glad to hire an Israelite woman.

Miriam ran home and quickly brought her mother. How happy and thankful they were to carry the baby back home! No longer were they afraid of the soldiers, for everyone knew this baby had been adopted by Pharaoh's daughter.

When the baby grew old enough to leave his mother, he was taken to live with the princess at Pharaoh's palace. The princess called him Moses, which means "drawn out," because she had drawn him out of the water.

Moses was given a royal education. As a prince he would one day be a leader in the government—perhaps even the king of all Egypt.

Moses Becomes a Shepherd

Exodus 2:11-25

When the boy Moses grew to manhood, he did not forget his own people—the Israelites. Whenever he left the beautiful palace, he saw his people being mistreated by their taskmasters. What could Moses do?

In his heart he believed God had saved his life as a baby so he could help his people. How he longed for that time to come!

75

He despised the riches of Egypt when he saw the hardships and poverty of the Israelites. He despised the Egyptian worship of the sun and the Nile River.

One day when Moses was with the Israelites, he did wrong. As he came to one place, he saw an Egyptian beating an Israelite. How angry Moses was! He had seen Egyptians beating poor Israelites too often. Moses could stand it no longer. He killed the Egyptian and buried him in the sand. Surely the Israelite understood that Moses was trying to help him.

The next day Moses saw two Israelites quarrel and begin to fight. Stepping between them, he asked, "Why are you so unkind to each other?"

One answered crossly, "Who made you a ruler and a judge over us? Do you intend to kill me as you killed that Egyptian yesterday?"

When Moses heard this, he was afraid. Didn't his people know how much he loved them and how he longed to help? Now Pharaoh would want to kill him. He must find a place to hide. Perhaps he would be safe in the wilderness.

After a long, tiresome journey across the desert, Moses came to a well. Here he sat down to rest. Soon seven young sisters came to draw water for their father's flocks. As they watered the sheep, other shepherds came and tried to drive the sheep away. This had happened many times before, but this time Moses was there to help the sisters.

When the sisters returned home with the flocks, their father asked, "Why are you home so early today?"

They replied, "We met a stranger at the well. He helped us when the men tried to drive our sheep away."

"But where is the stranger?" their father asked. "Why didn't you bring him with you? Go and invite him to eat with us."

When Moses came the father said, "I am Jethro, the priest of Midian. These are my daughters." As they talked, Jethro invited Moses to live among his people and to care for his flocks.

Later one of Jethro's daughters became Moses' wife. For many years Moses worked as a shepherd in the land of Midian. Because he was a stranger among the people of Midian, Moses named his first son Gershom, which means "a stranger here."

Changes were taking place in Egypt. The old Pharaoh had died, and a new Pharaoh ruled. Daily he oppressed the Israelites and made life even harder and more miserable for them. Their hearts grew heavy. They groaned beneath their heavy burdens. In anguish they cried to God, and he heard their prayers.

Moses and the Burning Bush

Exodus 3—4

Moses looked much different now from the young man who had lived at Pharaoh's palace. No longer did he wear the princely Egyptian robes. Now he wore the coarse mantle of a shepherd. In his hand was a long shepherd's staff. Day after day and year after year he had cared for his father-in-law's sheep. During this time the sun and the wind had tanned his face and hands while the years had whitened his hair.

One day Moses led his flock to a green pasture near the foot of Mount Horeb. There he saw a flame of fire spring out of a bush. He watched, expecting to see the bush become ashes, but the flame did not burn the bush.

"What a strange sight!" thought Moses. "I must take a closer look at this."

As he started toward the bush, a voice called from the flame, "Moses! Moses!"

And Moses replied, "Here am I."

"Do not come near the bush," the voice said. "Take off your shoes, for you are standing on holy ground."

Moses knew at once that God was speaking to him, for it was the custom for a person to remove his shoes when approaching a sacred place. Quickly he stooped down and unfastened his sandals. Then he hid his face, for he was afraid to look at the flame again.

"I am the God of Abraham, of Isaac and of Jacob," the voice said. "I have seen the suffering of my people, the Israelites. I have heard their cries. Now I am come to deliver them from the Egyptians and to bring them into the land that I promised their fathers."

How glad Moses must have been to hear this good news! But the voice continued, "Come now, and I will send you to Pharaoh, that you may lead my people out of Egypt."

Moses asked the Lord, "Who am I that I should lead my people out of Egypt? This is too big a job for me to do."

"I will surely go with you and help you do it," answered the voice. "And when you bring the Israelites to this mountain to worship me, you will know that I have been with you."

Moses said, "What if the Israelites have forgotten you? If they ask, 'Who is this God?' What shall I say?"

And God said, "Tell them that my name is I AM, the One who is always living. Tell them that I AM has sent you to help them. Do not be afraid, Moses, for they will believe you. With the elders of your families, go to Pharaoh and tell him, 'Our God, the God of the Hebrews, has met with us. Now let us go three days' journey into the wilderness to worship him.'"

Moses listened carefully. He heard God say, "At first the king will refuse to let you go, but after I have shown my power in Egypt, he will send you out of the land."

Still Moses was afraid his people would not believe God had sent him unless he could show them some sign for proof. So he asked God to give him a sign.

God said, "What is that in your hand?"

"It is a rod," answered Moses.

"Throw it on the ground," God said.

Moses obeyed, and the rod became a snake. When Moses saw the snake, he tried to get away from it.

God said, "Do not be afraid. Take hold of its tail."

Again Moses obeyed, and the snake became a rod once more.

Then God told Moses, "Put your hand on your chest under your cloak and bring it out again."

When Moses did this, his hand was white with leprosy. How afraid he was!

But God said, "Put your hand on your chest again."

When Moses obeyed his hand became normal. This sign was to prove to the Israelites and the Egyptians that God had sent Moses.

78

Moses helps Jethro's daughters

If the people did not believe these signs, Moses was to take water from the river and pour it on the ground. The water would become blood. This would be the third sign.

Still Moses felt unwilling to go. He told God, "You know I cannot speak well. You know I am slow to speak."

Then the Lord reminded Moses, "Am I not the Lord who made man's mouth? Go, and I will teach you what to say."

Then Moses pleaded, "Oh, my Lord, please send someone else."

God said, "I will send your brother Aaron with you. He will speak the words you tell him. Aaron is already on his way to meet you."

At last Moses was ready to obey God. He led his flock back to Jethro, his father-in-law, and said, "Let me return to my people in Egypt and see if they are still alive."

And Jethro said, "Go in peace."

God spoke again to Moses, "Return to Egypt, for those who wanted to kill you are dead."

Moses took his wife and sons and started for Egypt. On the way he met Aaron. How glad the brothers were to see each other! Moses told all that God had said, and together the two brothers returned to Egypt.

When they arrived they gathered the elders of Israel. Aaron told them that God had sent Moses to be their deliverer. When the people heard the words of the Lord and saw his signs, they believed and were glad. They bowed their heads and thanked God for hearing their prayers.

Moses and Aaron Before Pharaoh

Exodus 5:1—7:24

One day a messenger told Pharaoh, "Two Israelites want to see you."

And the king said, "Bring them in."

The messenger returned with Moses and Aaron. They told Pharaoh, "The Lord God of the Israelites has said, 'Let my people go, that they may worship me in the wilderness.'"

But Pharaoh answered, "Who is the Lord, that I should obey him? I do not know the Lord, and I will not let the Israelites leave the country to worship him."

Moses and Aaron answered, "The God of the Hebrews has met with us. Let his people go on a three days' journey into the wilderness to worship him. If you refuse there will be sickness and death."

Pharaoh only frowned and replied crossly, "Why are you trying to take the people away from their work? Get back to work, both of you, and let the Israelites alone." With these words he sent Moses and Aaron out of his court.

At this time the Israelites were making bricks and building houses for the Egyptian rulers. To hold the clay together for the bricks, they used chopped straw.

Now Pharaoh commanded the taskmasters, "Do not give the people straw to make brick any more. Let them find the straw. But be sure they make as many bricks as before. That will keep them so busy they will not have time to think about going away to worship their God."

Now the Israelites had more trouble than ever! Of course they could not gather straw from the fields and still make as many bricks as before. Then the taskmasters beat them.

The people told Moses and Aaron, "You promised to lead us out of Egypt, and you are only making more trouble for us."

How sorry Moses was! He loved his people and wanted to help them. Moses asked the Lord, "Why did you send me to Pharaoh? He will not let the people go, and he is making life more miserable for them."

And the Lord said, "I am the God of Abraham, Isaac and Jacob. I have heard the cries of the Israelites, and I will free them from the Egyptians."

Moses went to encourage his people, but they felt so downhearted they would not listen to him.

Then God said, "Speak to Pharaoh again and show him the signs I have given you."

But Moses answered, "If my people won't listen to me, surely Pharaoh won't listen either." Moses was ready to give up because

81

Pharaoh would not let the people go at once. He did not understand God's plan.

The Lord told Moses, "You will seem like a god to Pharaoh, and Aaron will be your prophet. Pharaoh will hear your words even though he refuses to obey me."

Moses took Aaron and went again to talk with Pharaoh. Now Aaron had in his hand the rod Moses had brought from the wilderness. When Aaron threw the rod to the ground, it became a snake.

Pharaoh sent for his magicians. When they came they, too, threw their rods before Pharaoh. Their rods also became snakes, but Aaron's rod swallowed their rods and became a harmless cane in Aaron's hand again. Even after Pharaoh saw this, he would not listen to Moses and Aaron or believe their sign.

On the next morning God sent Moses and Aaron to Pharaoh again. This time they met him on the bank of the river Nile. Because God had sent them, Moses and Aaron were not afraid. They told the king, "The Lord our God has sent us to you again."

Moses told Aaron to wave the rod over the river. The water became blood. Soon all the fish died, and a terrible odor filled the air. Aaron stretched his rod toward all the waters and streams of Egypt, and the water became blood.

Pharaoh's magicians brought to him water in a stone jar and turned the water to blood. Then the king returned to his palace. The Egyptians were alarmed. Nowhere in all the land could they find a drop of water.

"Let My People Go"

Exodus 7:25–10:29

A week later God told Moses and Aaron to say to Pharaoh, "Let my people go to worship me."

When Pharaoh refused, Aaron did as God commanded. He stretched his rod over the rivers, lakes and ponds. Thousands of frogs came hopping up out of the water. Frogs were everywhere—in the people's houses and in the palace. They hopped onto beds and into

Moses and Aaron face Pharaoh

the cooking. When the magicians tried, they too brought frogs out of the water.

Pharaoh was greatly troubled. He had been too stubborn to let anyone know how much he hated the bloody water. Now there were frogs to make him miserable. Finally he begged Moses and Aaron to ask God to take the frogs away. "I will let your people go to sacrifice to the Lord," he promised.

And Moses asked, "When do you want God to destroy the frogs?"

Pharaoh answered, "Tomorrow."

Moses prayed, and on the next day all the frogs died except those in the river. But Pharaoh got stubborn again and would not let the Israelites go. So there was another plague. This time Aaron struck the dust with his rod, and the dust became lice and fleas.

When the magicians tried, they could not do this. They told Pharaoh, "This is the work of God." Still Pharaoh would not listen.

One morning when Pharaoh walked along the river, God sent Moses and Aaron to him. "Because you will not let Israel go," they said, "tomorrow God will send another plague. Great swarms of flies will fill your palace and the houses of the Egyptians. Everywhere you go the flies will bother you. But there will be no flies in the houses of the Israelites."

When the swarms of flies came, Pharaoh called for Moses and Aaron again. "Tell your people to sacrifice to their God in Goshen," he said.

But Moses replied, "That will not do. If the Egyptians see us offering sacrifices to God, they will kill us." Because the Egyptians believed oxen were sacred, they would be very angry if they saw the Israelites kill oxen to sacrifice to God.

When Moses refused Pharaoh's offer, the king said, "I will let them go to the wilderness, only do not take them very far away."

Moses answered, "We must go three days' journey, and you must not break your promise."

But when the flies were gone, Pharaoh grew stubborn again and refused to let the Israelites go.

The next great plague was a cattle disease. Many cattle died of it, and Pharaoh became alarmed. When he sent a messenger to Goshen, he learned that the Israelites' cattle were all alive and well. Even after this Pharaoh did not let the Israelites go.

God kept telling Moses what to do next. This time Moses sprinkled a handful of dust in the air before Pharaoh. Painful boils broke out on all the Egyptians. The magicians had so many boils they could not come to Pharaoh. Still the king would not obey God.

Then Moses said, "Tomorrow there will be a great hailstorm. Get all your cattle out of the field and have the people stay in their houses. If they don't they will be killed."

Some of the Egyptians believed Moses and hurried to their homes. Others did not listen to the warning and stayed in the fields. When the sky grew black and the thunder roared, the Egyptians were afraid. They had never heard thunder or seen lightning before. Hailstones began to fall as fast as raindrops, and the lightning ran like fire along the ground. In the fields every living thing was killed. But no storm came to Goshen.

Pharaoh was frightened. He called loudly to Moses and Aaron, "I have sinned. I and my people are wicked." He promised that the Israelites could go at once if God would stop the great storm.

Moses answered, "I will spread out my hands toward heaven as soon as I am outside the city, and the storm will stop. Then you will know the earth belongs to God. But I know that you and your people do not yet fear the Lord God."

When the storm passed, Pharaoh looked out upon the bright sunshine, and his heart grew stubborn again. He was not willing to obey God.

The hailstorm had destroyed all the growing crops, but the wheat and spelt were unharmed because they had not sprouted. The next plague, God told Moses, would be locusts. They would eat every green thing above the ground.

When the Egyptians heard this, they hurried to Pharaoh and said, "How long are you going to let these men bother us? Let the Israelites go to worship their God."

So Pharaoh called Moses and Aaron and asked, "Whom do you intend to take with you to worship God?"

Moses replied, "We will take all our people, our flocks and herds."

"Take only your men and let them sacrifice," Pharaoh said and sent Moses and Aaron away.

When Moses left the palace, the Lord said, "Stretch out your hand for the locusts to come."

Moses obeyed. An east wind began to blow. All day and all night it blew. In the morning a great cloud of locusts appeared in the sky. They covered all Egypt except the land of Goshen.

Again Pharaoh was afraid. Hurriedly he sent for Moses and Aaron. "I have sinned against the Lord your God and against you," he said. "Now forgive me. Pray that God will take these locusts away, or I and my people will die."

When Moses prayed the Lord sent a strong west wind and the locusts were blown into the Red Sea and drowned. But again Pharaoh hardened his heart.

God told Moses to stretch his hand toward heaven, and a great darkness would come upon the land. And so it was. For three days there was no light—no daylight and no starlight.

Pharaoh sent the last time for Moses and Aaron. He said, "I will let all the people go, but they must not take their flocks and herds."

Moses answered boldly, "We will take everything we have when we go to serve our God."

How angry Pharaoh was! He shouted, "Get out of my sight! And if I ever see your face again I will kill you."

Bravely Moses answered, "It will be just as you say, for you will never see my face again. But know this: God will send one more terrible plague upon you and your people. Then the Israelites will leave your land."

The Death Angel

Exodus 11:1–13:19

It was evening in the land of Goshen and across the barren fields of Egypt. Everything had grown quiet around the walls and buildings where the Israelites had worked. Never again would the men return to their jobs. The time had come for them to leave Egypt.

God told Moses that Pharaoh would send the Israelites out of the land after the last plague. "Tell the people to get ready to leave quickly," the Lord said, "for they must start as soon as Pharaoh's messenger comes."

The Israelites believed now that God had sent Moses to help them. They obeyed him as a man of God. For many years they had been slaves and owned no money. Now, at God's command, Moses told the people, "Ask your Egyptian neighbors for jewels of silver and gold." And the Egyptians opened their treasure boxes to the Israelites.

"Tonight at midnight," Moses said, "God will send an angel through the land. The angel will enter every house that does not have blood on the door. The oldest child in that home will die."

Moses told the Israelites to kill a lamb for each family and sprinkle their door frames with blood. "Then roast the lamb and cook vegetables with it for a midnight supper. When the death angel passes over the land, you must be dressed and ready to start on your journey. Eat your supper standing around the table."

No wonder every household in Goshen was very busy. Instead of getting ready for bed, every man, woman and child was wide-awake and excited. All the boys and girls helped gather the cattle from the pasture lands or ran errands for their parents. Every father killed a lamb and sprinkled blood on the door frame of his house. Every mother prepared vegetables to cook for the midnight supper.

The midnight supper was called the "Passover" because the angel passed over the houses of those who obeyed the command God gave Moses. To remind them of this night when God saved them from death, God commanded the Israelites to eat such a supper each year at this time.

Now the Egyptians had not sprinkled blood on their door frames or prepared a midnight meal. Every one of them had gone to bed as usual, expecting to sleep all night. But at midnight all were awakened, even Pharaoh. He hurried to the bedside of his oldest son and found him dead. Pharaoh cried aloud. In every Egyptian home there was the same sad cry.

At once Pharaoh sent a swift messenger to Moses and Aaron at Goshen. There all were awake and ready to start on their journey. "Pharaoh wants all of you to leave Goshen at once," the messenger said. "He demands that you take everything with you just as you have said. Do not leave anything behind."

The Egyptians, too, sent messengers to Goshen. They wanted the Israelites to get out of the land quickly. "We shall all die if you stay here any longer," they said.

And the Israelites started out of Goshen. Like a great army, six hundred thousand men with their wives and children marched out of Egypt. With them were their flocks and herds.

The women had mixed dough in pans for bread but had not put leaven or yeast in it. When they stopped to eat, they baked the dough over coals of fire. Such bread was called unleavened bread. One week every year thereafter the Israelites ate bread without leaven in it. This week was celebrated as the Feast of Unleavened Bread.

Among the things the Israelites carried out of Egypt was Joseph's coffin. Before he died Joseph had requested, "When you leave Egypt, take my body with you and bury it in Canaan."

Crossing the Red Sea

Exodus 13:20–15:21

Moses and Aaron led the people out of Egypt, but they did not choose the way to go. God went with them, and he chose the way. In the daytime he was in a great cloud that moved slowly before the people. At night the cloud became a pillar of fire, and God watched over them while they rested. By day or by night the Israelites could look at the cloud or pillar and say, "Our God is going with us, and he is leading the way."

After the great company left Goshen, God led them by the cloud to the Red Sea. Here they camped. They planned to rest from their march. But suddenly someone ran through the camp shouting, "Pharaoh's army is coming! We shall be taken prisoners or killed!"

The people looked, and sure enough, Pharaoh's army was coming behind them. The Israelites could not swim across the Red Sea. Neither could they fight against Pharaoh's skillful soldiers. How frightened they were!

At first the people blamed Moses, "Why did you bring us out here in the wilderness to die? Why have you done this to us? We would rather have been slaves to the Egyptians than to die here."

But Moses was not to blame. He had only followed the cloud, and the cloud had led them there.

When Moses cried to God for help, the Lord told Moses to speak to the people and quiet them. They were all crying in fear.

Moses told the people, "Fear not. Stand still and see the salvation of the Lord, which he will show you today. For the Egyptians you have seen today you will see no more forever."

The cloud moved backward and stopped between their camp and Pharaoh's army. To the Israelites the cloud became a pillar of fire and lighted their camp all night, but to the Egyptians the cloud was all darkness.

God told Moses, "Tell the Israelites to go forward. Lift your rod over the Red Sea and divide it."

Moses obeyed, and God sent a strong wind. The wind swept a wide path through the waters and dried the ground. On each side of this path the waters rose like a high wall until every one of the Israelites and all their cattle had crossed to the other side.

Pharaoh's heart had hardened again after he sent the Israelites out of Goshen. He said, "I have made a great mistake by letting all my slaves go free. I must send my army after them and bring them back." So he followed the Israelites. With him were all the chariots of Egypt and their captains.

When the cloud lifted, Pharaoh and his army saw the Israelites walking through the sea on a dry path between two walls of water. The Egyptians rushed after them. When Pharaoh's army was far out from shore, trouble began. The horses got tangled in the harness and their feet began to sink in the sand. The chariot wheels came off.

"Let us go back!" the soldiers cried. "Israel's God is against us!" But it was too late. They could not go back, for the walls of water fell down and the whole army was drowned.

At last the Israelites were free. They knew God had saved them from their enemies. Moses wrote a beautiful song about the crossing of the Red Sea, and the people sang and rejoiced. Playing musical instruments called timbrels, the women went through the camp singing to God.

Water for Thirsty Travelers

Exodus 15:22-27

After the Israelites had celebrated their great deliverance from the Egyptian army, they began their march across the wilderness of Shur. This country was not like the land of Goshen. There were no waving fields of grain, no grassy pasture lands for their flocks and herds.

By and by they came to a camping place called Marah. How thirsty they were! The cattle needed water too. Everyone was hot and tired from the long march across the wilderness.

At Marah the Israelites were happy to find a spring of water, but when they tasted the water, it was so bitter they could not swallow it. Again they were ready to blame Moses for their troubles. "What shall we drink?" they asked.

Moses, too, was thirsty. He felt sorry for the people. He cried to God for help, and God told him what to do.

Near the spring grew a tree. God told Moses to cut this tree down and throw it into the spring. When Moses did this, the water became sweet. The people drank deeply and were satisfied. There was plenty of water for the cattle and sheep too.

God wanted to teach the people to trust him for help when troubles came. He said, "If you will do what is right in my sight, I will be with you. I will be your healer."

From the camp at Marah the Israelites moved on until they found a beautiful grove of palm trees and twelve wells of water. The name of this place was Elim. Here the people pitched their tents beneath the trees and drank from the wells. How glad they were to find such a pleasant camping place in the wilderness!

Food for Hungry Travelers

Exodus 16

The Israelites enjoyed their rest at Elim, but the cloud of God's presence lifted and began to move slowly ahead. By this sign the people knew God wanted to lead them farther on their journey. Taking down their tents, they moved on.

Now they entered a great desert country between Elim and the mountain where God had spoken to Moses from the burning bush. This country was called the wilderness of Sin.

Like fretful children, the Israelites began to find fault with Moses and Aaron. First it was one thing, then another. There was little food to eat in the great wilderness, and they grew hungry. Then they forgot how much they had suffered in Egypt. They forgot how many times God had helped them out of trouble. They thought only of how hungry and unhappy they were.

"We wish we had never left Egypt," they said. "There we had plenty of meat and bread. But you have brought us out into this wilderness to die of hunger."

How it hurt Moses to hear the people complain! God heard them too. He told Moses, "The people are sinning against me when they find fault with you for leading them out of Egypt. I will not let them die of hunger. I want them to know that I am the giver of all their blessings. In the evening I will send meat to them, and in the morning I will give them bread from heaven."

In the evening quail flew into the camp, and the people had them for meat. The next morning what looked like a white frost covered the ground. "What is this?" the people asked when they looked out of their tents.

In their language the words *man hu* meant, "What is this?" So the people were really saying to each other, *"Man hu, man hu?"* And the food became known as manna. When the sun grew hot, the manna melted on the ground.

Moses told the people that God had sent this food to be their bread. "Go and gather it," said he, "and get as much as you will need for today. Do not keep any for tomorrow because God will send a fresh supply. Each morning he will cause this bread to fall, except on the seventh day. On the sixth day you must gather twice as much as usual, and what is left over, you may keep for the seventh day. It will not spoil because God wants you to keep that day holy and do no work."

At Moses' word the people rushed out and gathered manna from the ground. They made it into cakes. How good they tasted—like wafers made with honey.

Now some of the people did not obey Moses. They tried to keep manna from one day to the next, but the bread spoiled. Some people did not gather twice as much on the sixth morning. When they went out on the Sabbath, they could find no manna.

Except on the Sabbath, God sent manna to the Israelites every morning until they reached the land of Canaan.

Water from a Rock

Exodus 17:1-7

Leaving the wilderness of Sin, the Israelites came to a place called Rephidim. Here again the cloud stopped as a sign that they should make camp and rest from their journey.

But the people began to complain at once. Although God was sending them bread every day, now he had led them to a place where there was no water. How thirsty they were! Instead of asking God to help them, the people complained to Moses, "Did you bring us out of Egypt to die here of thirst?"

Moses asked God, "What shall I do for my people? They are so angry they are almost ready to kill me."

The Lord answered, "Take the elders of Israel and go to Mount Horeb. When you strike the rock with the rod, water will come out. Then all the people can drink."

Moses did as the Lord commanded. With the elders he went to Mount Horeb. There were no springs or rivers in sight. But when Moses struck the rock, a stream of clear water flowed out. Down the mountainside and into the valley, the water ran. All the people hurried to drink.

Because the people did not trust God for help, Moses was ashamed of them. He scolded them for doubting the Lord.

Moses Holds Up His Hands

Exodus 17:8-16

In this country lived a wild people called Amalekites. When the Israelites camped at Rephidim, the Amalekites attacked them and tried to steal their goods.

Moses chose a brave young man named Joshua to lead the Israelites against their enemies. Moses told Joshua, "Choose men to fight the Amalekites tomorrow. I will stand on top of the hill with God's rod in my hand."

The next morning Moses, Aaron and Hur watched the battle from the hilltop. Moses stretched his arms toward heaven and asked God to help his people. In Moses' hand was the rod. At first the men of Israel drove their enemies back into the wilderness. Then Moses' arms became very tired from holding up the rod. When his arms fell to his sides, the Amalekites turned around and drove the men of Israel back.

Moses lifted the rod toward heaven again, and the Israelites began to win. Aaron and Hur found a large stone for Moses to sit on.

Then they stood beside him and held up his arms all day. At evening when the battle was over, Joshua returned to camp with his men. The people knew God had helped them drive their enemies away. In thanks to God, Moses built an altar at this place.

Jethro Advises Moses

Exodus 18

News reached Midian about all the things God had done for Moses and his people. Jethro, Moses' father-in-law, heard about it. He went to find Moses and hear more.

Jethro asked, "What is this the Lord has done for you?"

How much Moses had to tell! Tears ran down Jethro's cheeks as he heard how the Lord had helped the Israelites in their trouble with Pharaoh and the Egyptians. God had helped them many times since they had left Egypt too. Jethro and Moses praised God. How good the Lord had been!

Israelites gather manna

The next day Moses was very busy. From morning till evening, the people came to him with their problems. When Jethro saw all that Moses did for his people, he said, "My son, why do the people stand around you from morning till evening?"

Moses explained, "When the people have a dispute or quarrel, they come to me and I decide what is right. I tell the people God's way."

Jethro shook his head seriously, "Moses, Moses, what you are doing is not good. You will wear yourself out. It is too much for you to do alone."

Moses knew how tired he was, but more than anything else, he wanted to be a good leader to his people.

When the two sat down together Jethro said, "Moses, let me tell you what to do. You should represent the people before God and tell him about them. And be sure to teach the people God's laws and ways. Then they will know how God wants them to live.

"You should choose able men to work with you—men who love God, who are trustworthy, who will not be bribed. Make these men rulers of thousands, of hundreds, of fifties and of tens. Let them judge the people at all times. Whenever a big matter comes up, they can bring it to you, but they can settle little things themselves."

Moses nodded. Jethro's plan sounded good.

Jethro went on, "This will make it easier for you, Moses. You will last longer, and there will be more peace among your people."

And Moses did as Jethro suggested.

God Gives the Ten Commandments

Exodus 19—24

At Mount Horeb, or Sinai, God had talked to Moses from a burning bush. In front of the mountain was the wilderness of Sinai. When Moses tended sheep for Jethro, he led the flocks through this wilderness. He knew where to find grassy plains and plenty of water. And now the Israelites camped under the shadow of the great, rock-walled mountain.

While the people were busy pitching their tents and preparing food, Moses climbed the mountain to talk with God. And the Lord said, "Tell the people that I shall speak to them from this mountain.

On the third day, they shall hear my voice. Go, now, and tell them to wash their clothes and get ready to meet me."

When the Israelites heard Moses' words, they began to get ready. Everyone found something to do. Some carried water from the springs, and others washed clothes. In three days they would stand with Moses before God.

On the third morning a thick, dark cloud rested on top of Mount Sinai. Thunder rolled down the mountainsides into the valley, and lightning broke through the thick cloud. The whole mountain shook. The Israelites had never seen or heard anything like this.

Moses gathered the people near the foot of the mountain. But they said, "Don't let God speak to us in this voice of thunder, for we are afraid. We will listen when you tell us his words, and we will obey."

Moses answered, "Do not be afraid when God speaks. He wants to teach you that he is a great and holy God. He wants you to serve him only and never bow down to other gods."

Still the people stood far off, for they were afraid. But Moses was not afraid. He went into the thick darkness where God was. God told Moses the many laws he wanted the Israelites to obey. Moses wrote God's words in a book.

When Moses came down the mountain, he told the people all that God had said. And the people answered, "All that God has said we will do."

Early the next morning Moses built an altar near the great mountain, and the young men brought offerings of oxen to give to the Lord. The people gathered again, and Moses read to them from the book of the covenant.

After the service the people went back to their tents in the valley. Moses took Aaron and his two sons, Nadab and Abihu, and seventy elders up the mountain. They saw the glory of God, and they were not afraid. But they did not come near to the wonderful brightness of God's glory.

And the Lord said to Moses, "Come up to me and I will give you tables of stone on which the law and the commandments are written. Teach these to the people."

Before Moses went up to the cloud-covered mountaintop, he told Aaron and Hur to care for the people while he was with the Lord.

As Moses climbed the mountain Joshua was with him. For forty days Moses listened to God's words.

The Ten Commandments

Exodus 20:3-17

Thou shalt have no other gods before me.

Thou shalt not make unto thee any graven image, or any likeness of anything that is in heaven above, or that is in the earth beneath, or that is in the water under the earth: thou shalt not bow down thyself to them, nor serve them: for I the Lord thy God am a jealous God, visiting the iniquity of the fathers upon the children unto the third and fourth generation of them that hate me; and showing mercy unto thousands of them that love me and keep my commandments.

Thou shalt not take the name of the Lord thy God in vain; for the Lord will not hold him guiltless that taketh his name in vain.

Remember the Sabbath day to keep it holy. Six days shalt thou labor, and do all thy work; but the seventh day is the Sabbath of the Lord thy God: in it thou shalt not do any work, thou, nor thy son, nor thy daughter, thy manservant, nor thy maidservant, nor thy cattle, nor thy stranger that is within thy gates: for in six days the Lord made heaven and earth, the sea, and all that in them is, and rested the seventh day: wherefore the Lord blessed the Sabbath day, and hallowed it.

Honor thy father and thy mother: that thy days may be long upon the land which the Lord thy God giveth thee.

Thou shalt not kill.

Thou shalt not commit adultery.

Thou shalt not steal.

Thou shalt not bear false witness against thy neighbor.

Thou shalt not covet thy neighbor's house.

Thou shalt not covet thy neighbor's wife, nor his manservant, nor his maidservant, nor his ox, nor his ass, nor anything that is thy neighbor's.

Moses climbs the mountain to talk with God

The Golden Calf

Exodus 24:17-18; 32:1-35

While Moses was on top of Mount Sinai talking with God, Joshua waited for him on the mountainside. From their tents in the valley, the Israelites looked at the mountain. The top looked like fire and flames shot up into the sky day and night. The people knew Moses was in the thick cloud with God.

When the days became weeks and still Moses did not return, the Israelites wondered if he would ever come back. They grew restless. They soon forgot how afraid they had been when God's voice thundered from the smoking mountain. They seemed to forget even the words that God had spoken. They forgot they had promised Moses to obey the words of the Lord.

One day they said to Aaron, "We know something dreadful has happened to Moses, because he does not come back." Of course, they complained because Moses had led them into the lonely wilderness and left them without a brave leader to take his place. Every day they grew more restless. Finally they told Aaron, "Make us gods to go before us and show us the way."

Aaron was not brave. He feared the people. He remembered the time when they wanted to kill Moses because they could find no water. Perhaps he thought they would kill him if he refused to do as they asked. He did not remind them of their promise to serve no gods but God. Instead he told them, "Bring your gold earrings to me." And the people did.

Aaron melted the gold carefully in the fire. Then he shaped the gold into the form of a calf like the ones the Egyptians worshiped.

And the people said to one another, "These are the gods, O Israel, that brought you up out of the land of Egypt."

When Aaron saw how much the people liked the calf, he put it in the middle of the camp and built an altar before it. "Tomorrow we shall have a feast to our god," he announced.

The next day the Israelites had a great feast and worshiped the gold calf just as they had seen their Egyptian neighbors do. As they bowed themselves before the idol and sang and danced around it, they broke two of the Ten Commandments that God had told them

Moses discovers the Israelites worshiping the golden calf

to obey. God had said, "Thou shalt serve no other gods. Thou shalt not worship any graven image."

God saw the gold calf. He saw the Israelites bow down and worship it. He heard them singing and dancing around it, and he was greatly displeased. God said to Moses, "The Israelites have sinned against me. They have broken their promise and made a god of gold. Now they are worshiping it and crying, 'This is the god that led us out of Egypt!' Let me alone, Moses, and I will quickly destroy them all, for they are not fit to be called my people. But I will make of you, Moses, a great nation."

Moses loved his people even though they were often childish and unkind. He did not want God to destroy them. So he said, "Please, Lord, do not be so angry with your people. Did you not bring them out of Egypt by your power? What would the Egyptians say if your people died in the wilderness? And remember your promises to Abraham, Isaac and Jacob." And because Moses prayed for them, the Lord did not destroy the Israelites.

Moses hurried down the mountainside with Joshua. In his arms were the two wonderful tablets of stone upon which God had written the Ten Commandments. It was hard for Moses to believe the Israelites had sinned so greatly.

As they came nearer the camp Joshua said, "I hear the sound of war in camp." Then he added, "That's strange. It is not the noise of victory or of defeat. It is singing that I hear."

When they came into camp, they saw the people dancing and shouting before the gold calf. Moses was so angry that he threw the Commandments to the ground and they broke into many pieces. No wonder God had wanted to destroy the Israelites!

Moses ran into the camp and tore down the idol while the people watched. He broke it into pieces and threw it into the fire. Then he ground it into fine dust and put it in the drinking water. This made the water taste very bitter, but Moses insisted that the people drink it.

Moses' sudden appearance broke up the merry feast. His anger quieted the people, but many were sorry he had come back. They wanted to worship the god Aaron had made.

Sternly Moses asked Aaron, "What have these people done that made you bring this terrible sin upon them?"

Aaron answered, "Do not be angry with me! You know how evil these people are in their hearts. They said to me, 'Make us gods to go before us, for we don't know what has become of Moses.' So I told them to bring their gold earrings. When I threw the earrings into the fire, this calf came out!"

How angry Moses was! He stood at the gate of the camp and called out in a loud voice, "You who are on the Lord's side, come and stand by me!" Then every man who belonged to the tribe of Levi came and stood by Moses. He told these brave men to kill every person who still wanted to worship the gold calf. "Do not spare one of them," he commanded.

Everyone was sad, but no one was quite so sad as Moses. He knew how his people had sinned, and he was afraid God might not forgive them.

The next day Moses told the people, "You have been very wicked and in God's sight your sin is great. I will go up to him now, and I will make an offering for your sin. Perhaps he will forgive you."

And Moses went before the Lord and offered himself to die if God would not forgive the people. But God said, "Those who have sinned against me must suffer for their own sins."

God Writes the Commandments Again

Exodus 34

And the Lord told Moses, "Cut two stone tablets and bring them to me on Mount Sinai tomorrow. I will write on them the words that were on the tablets you broke."

Moses did what God commanded. In the morning he climbed Mount Sinai with the tablets under his arm.

God talked with Moses and told him how to lead the children of Israel. For forty days and nights, God taught Moses. On the tablets God again wrote the Ten Commandments.

How glad the Israelites were when they heard that Moses was coming down the mountain! This time while he was gone, they did not complain or worship another god. They went out to meet him, but when they saw him, they were afraid and started back to camp.

"Why are the people so frightened?" Moses wondered. He called to them. Aaron and the rulers of the people came back to talk to Moses.

They said, "Your face shines with a strange light, like the sun. It is so bright we cannot look at you."

Moses did not know God's glory was shining on his face. He put a veil over it. Then all the people came back and listened to his words.

God had given Moses rules for the people to follow, and Moses wrote them in a book. But God himself wrote the Ten Commandments on the two stone tablets. Ever after, Moses wore a veil when he told the people God's words. Whenever he talked with God, he took the veil off.

Gifts for the Tabernacle

Exodus 25—29

God wanted the people to know he was living among them, right in their camp. He wanted them to have a special place where they could always worship him. He wanted them to build a place of worship. Here God would be in the cloud by day and the pillar of fire by night.

God wanted the Israelites to be his own people and to act like his people. He wanted them to worship him only because he is the only true God.

He told Moses, "Have all the people who are willing give an offering." God explained that each person could give something for the tabernacle. The things needed for the tabernacle were gold, silver, brass, bright-colored cloth, animal skins, oil and precious stones. God even showed Moses how to build the tabernacle.

When the people heard about God's plan to live among them, they were glad. They offered cheerfully to give the best of everything to help build a place where they could worship the Lord. Men and women brought their gold bracelets, earrings, rings and ornaments. Those who had beautiful cloth and fine animal skins brought those. Others gave silver, brass and wood. Women who knew how to spin made more bright-colored cloth. Some even spun strong cloth from goat's hair. The rulers of the people brought jewels, spices and oils. With joy the people gave for the house of the Lord.

And God chose two wise men, Bezaleel and Aholiah, to teach others how to carve, engrave, weave and embroider. Together they made everything for the place of worship.

Now the people lived in tents. These could be moved easily from one camp to another as they journeyed toward Canaan. God told Moses to build the place of worship something like a tent. It was to have board walls and a top of cloth and animal skins. Then it could be taken apart and moved when the people broke camp.

God told Moses the kind of furniture to put inside the tabernacle. He told how the furniture should be made and where it should be placed.

The people obeyed. They worked faithfully and brought even more gifts as they were needed for the building.

When everything was finished, God told Moses to set up the tabernacle in the middle of camp. Then he commanded, "Bring the tribe of Levi to Aaron the priest. They will work with him and do as he says. They will care for the tabernacle."

God told Moses to divide the whole tribe of Levi into three groups, one group for each of Levi's sons. These were to camp one on the north side, one on the south side, and one on the west side of the tabernacle. Moses and Aaron pitched their tents on the east side, in front of the tabernacle door.

The Tabernacle

Exodus 40

After two years of work, the tabernacle was finished. All around it was an uncovered space called a court. Fine linen curtains, about seven or eight feet long, made the outside wall of the court,

Near the door of the court was a great altar called the altar of burnt offering. To worship God the people built altars of earth or stone. On them they laid their gifts and sacrifices to be burned.

The altar of the tabernacle was different. It was a brass-covered box without bottom or top. Inside, a metal grate was fastened. Here the fire was kindled. The altar was about five feet high and seven feet square. On the sides were two long poles. Whenever the Israelites moved camp, the priests put the poles upon their shoulders and carried the altar along.

Near the altar was a large basin called a laver. It was filled with water for the priests to wash their hands and feet.

Farther inside the court stood the tabernacle itself. The walls were made of boards covered with gold and placed on silver bases. The roof was made of four curtains, one laid above the other. The inner curtain was beautiful cloth, but the outer curtains were made of skins to keep the rain out. The front of the tabernacle opened into the court. There was no door, but sometimes a curtain hung across the opening.

From the roof hung a beautiful linen curtain that divided the tabernacle into two rooms. The first room opened into the courts. It was called the "holy place." The second room was called the "holy of holies."

In the holy place were three pieces of furniture: a table, a golden candlestick and a small altar. The table was covered with gold. On it were twelve loaves of bread, as if each tribe were giving an offering to God. The golden candlestick held seven burning lights. The small altar was called the altar of incense because sweet perfumes were burned there. The fire was lighted from the altar of burnt offering. Everything in this room was made of gold or was covered with gold— even the board walls on each side. And the curtain hangings and the curtain ceiling were decorated with beautiful colors.

The second room contained only the ark of the covenant. This ark was a box or chest covered inside and outside with gold. The lid was called the "mercy seat." At each end of the mercy seat was a gold cherubim. The stone tables upon which God had written the Ten Commandments were inside the ark of the covenant.

When the tabernacle was set up in the middle of the camp, God moved the cloud above it and filled it with his glory. Every day the cloud rested upon the tabernacle, and every night a cloud of fire was there. When the people saw these things, they knew that God was living among them.

People bring gifts for the tabernacle

Worship at the Tabernacle

Leviticus 1–9

After the tabernacle was set up, Moses did not need to climb Mount Sinai to talk with God. Now he entered the tabernacle where God lived among the people. There he heard the words of the Lord.

Before this anyone who wanted to worship God built an altar, burned his offering upon it and called on the Lord to forgive his sins. And the Lord would hear him.

Now Moses told the people, "Whenever you want to worship God and have him forgive your sins, bring your sacrifice to the priests at the door of the court. They will tend the altar of the burnt offering. The priests will offer the sacrifices before the Lord, and God will accept them."

God chose Aaron to be the high priest. To him God gave the most important work in the tabernacle of worship. God chose Aaron's sons to be priests also. They were to help their father.

On the morning when the tabernacle worship first began, God told Moses to call the people together before the door of the tabernacle. Before everyone Moses was to anoint Aaron and his sons with oil and put on them the beautiful priestly robes. God wanted the people to see that he had chosen these men to do his work in the court and in the tabernacle.

After Aaron was made high priest he offered a lamb on the altar of burnt offering as a sacrifice for the sins of the people. He did not put any fire on the altar, but God sent fire to burn up the lamb.

When the people saw this, they shouted for joy and fell on their faces. They knew God was pleased with their offering and with their priests.

Morning and evening every day thereafter the priests offered sacrifices for sin upon the altar of burnt offering. By these sacrifices God reminded the people that sin is an awful thing.

And the fire that God had kindled on the great altar was never allowed to go out. Every morning at sunrise, the priests raked the coals and placed fresh wood on them. Even when the tabernacle was moved from one place to another, the priests carried burning coals from the altar in a covered pan. God had lighted this fire, and he wanted it kept burning always.

Inside the holy place was a second altar, the altar of incense. Here sweet perfumes were burned before the Lord. Every morning and evening, the priests carried a shovelful of burning coals from the great altar to light the fire on the altar of incense. They carried these coals in a censer, a bowl that hung on chains. God commanded that the altar of incense should be lighted only from the fire that he had kindled on the great altar.

The priests also kept twelve loaves of bread on the golden table in the holy place. Each Sabbath morning they brought fresh loaves and removed the stale ones. These loaves were called showbread. Only the priests were allowed to eat this bread.

The priests also tended the seven lamps that burned on the golden candlestick. Every day they filled the lamp bowls with fresh oil and kept the light burning.

The Second Passover

Numbers 9–10

One day while the Israelites were still near Mount Sinai God reminded Moses that a whole year had passed since they left Egypt. And God said, "The time has come for you to eat another Passover Supper, for I want you to remember how the death angel passed over your homes in Goshen."

Moses told the people the words of the Lord. Every family prepared a supper like the one they had eaten before Pharaoh sent them out of Egypt.

The Lord commanded, "At evening eat the Passover with unleavened bread and bitter herbs. Do not leave any of it." And the people obeyed.

Not many days after the Passover Supper, the Israelites saw the cloud lift from above the tabernacle and float slowly toward the north. They knew the Lord wanted them to journey on. They had lived nearly a year in the wilderness of Sinai, under the shadow of the great mountain. How glad they must have been to be on their way to Canaan!

For three days they followed the floating cloud on and on across the barren country. Then the cloud stopped, and they rested in their tents.

Quail for a Complaining People

Numbers 11—12

While they rested in their tents, some complained. When the Lord heard their complaining, he was displeased. Fire fell on part of the camp, and some were killed.

How afraid the people were when they saw the fire! What if their tents were burned too? What if they were caught in the flames? They cried to Moses for help.

Moses prayed and God put out the fire. Moses called this camping place Taberah, which means a burning.

From Taberah the cloud led the Israelites farther north and brought them to the second stopping place. Here the people rested again. They forgot what had happened when they complained at Taberah. They forgot the many blessings God had given them. They said, "We are hungry for meat—oh, so hungry."

The people began to think about all the things they would like to eat. One said, "Remember the good fish we had in Egypt?"

Another added, "What about the cucumbers and the melons?"

"I miss the leeks, onions and garlic," a third said. The more they thought about the food of Egypt, the hungrier and unhappier they became.

When they saw the manna on the ground around their camp, they said, "We're tired of this manna. We want meat!" They complained as they gathered the food and grumbled while they ate it. Finally, like pouting children, they stood in front of their tents and cried because they had no meat.

Moses heard them crying. He was unhappy and ashamed of them. Time after time, they had complained, and just as often, he had prayed for them. This time he did not feel like praying for them.

Moses asked the Lord, "Why do I have to lead these people? They act like children—crying because they wish they had meat to eat!

The Hebrews obtain quail to eat

Leading these people is too hard. I cannot do it alone." Moses was so discouraged that he wished he were dead.

The Israelites were complaining again! The Lord knew they were unthankful and childish. He knew they needed to be punished. He felt sorry for Moses because the work was so heavy.

"Choose seventy men to be leaders of the people," God told Moses. "Take them to the tabernacle with you. I will come down and talk with you there. I will give my Spirit to the seventy men so they can help you lead the people. Then you will not have to carry all the responsibility by yourself." And so it was.

Of the people the Lord said, "Tell them they will have meat—not one day or two days, or five days, or ten days, or twenty days, but a whole month. They will have so much meat they will be sick of it."

In a wind from the sea came quail. About a day's journey from camp, great flocks of quail flew near the ground. All day, all night and all the next day, the people gathered quail. Those who gathered the least had more than one hundred bushels. It was enough meat for a month.

When they got back to camp, they cooked the quail. Then they ate and ate and ate. Many became sick—so sick that they died.

When the cloud moved on it stopped next at Hazeroth. Here Moses married an Ethiopian woman. Miriam and Aaron found fault with their brother because he did not marry an Israelite woman. They wondered, "Why should he be the chief ruler when God has sometimes spoken to us too?" They were jealous because Moses was great in the eyes of the people. They, too, wanted to be rulers, to be called great and wise.

But God was displeased because they spoke against Moses. Miriam got leprosy. Her skin became white as snow.

When Aaron saw what had happened, he was sorry they had sinned against Moses and against God. Aaron begged Moses, "Oh, Moses, we have been foolish. Do not lay this sin upon us. Do not let Miriam be a leper."

And Moses cried to the Lord, "Heal her now, O God, I beg you." God heard his prayer. After seven days Miriam was well again.

When the cloud lifted from Hazeroth, it led them to the wilderness of Paran, just outside the land of Canaan.

The Twelve Spies

Numbers 13—14

When the Israelites came to the wilderness of Paran, they were very close to the land God had promised them. One more march would take them across the border and into the beautiful country.

And the Lord told Moses, "Send twelve men into the land of Canaan to spy out the land."

Moses chose twelve good men and told them, "Cross over the plain and go up into the hills. See what the land is like. See what kind of people live there, whether they are weak or strong, few or many. Find out whether the land is good or bad, whether there is wood on it. Notice what kind of cities they have, whether they live in tents or strongholds. Bring back fruit from the land. The first grapes should be ripe now. Finally go with good courage."

For forty days the spies went here and there through the Promised Land. They saw strong cities and small towns. They saw fields of grain and large vineyards of grapes. The land was beautiful and full of all kinds of food. In this land they would not become hungry for meat, fruit or vegetables.

When the spies returned to Israel's camp, they brought samples of the fruit that grew in Canaan. Two men carried one large cluster of grapes on a pole between them. Never before had the people seen such wonderful fruit.

Then ten of the spies told about Canaan. "It is a rich land. We brought you some of the fruit that grows there. But the people live in great walled cities." And the Israelites talked to one another about the report.

Finally Caleb, another spy, quieted the people and told them, "Let us go at once and take the land, for we are well able to overcome it."

But the ten spies did not agree. They said, "We cannot go into the land, for the people are stronger than we." The people were frightened when the spies said, "The men of that land are so big they make us look like grasshoppers."

The people were so disappointed that they cried all night. When morning came they complained against Moses and Aaron. "We wish we had stayed in Egypt! We wish we had died back in the wilderness rather than be killed by the giants of Canaan. Why has God brought us out here to die? Our wives and our children will be taken prisoners." The people even planned to choose a captain and go back to Egypt.

When Moses and Aaron heard about the plan, they fell on their faces and begged the people to obey God. How could these people doubt God's great power after he had brought them out of Egypt, led them through the Red Sea on dry land, given them water from a solid rock, rained food from heaven, and protected them from their enemies?

Caleb and Joshua, the two spies who had faith in God, tore their clothes because the people did not trust God to give them Canaan. They pleaded with the people, "The land we searched is a wonderful land. The Lord promised it to us. Do not turn back or be afraid. The Lord is with us. Let us go forward!"

The people would not listen to Caleb and Joshua. Instead they wanted to kill the two faithful spies. But as the people looked for stones to throw at Caleb and Joshua, they saw the glory of the Lord come down upon the tabernacle.

The Lord said to Moses, "How long will these people provoke me? How long will it be before they have faith in me?" The Lord was so angry with the children of Israel that he thought he could not put up with them any longer.

Moses prayed earnestly for his people. He reminded the Lord, "If our people die here in the wilderness, the Egyptians will say you were not able to take the Israelites to Canaan." And Moses pleaded, "Pardon, I beg you, the sin of this people according to your great mercy, even as you have forgiven them from the day they left Egypt until now."

For Moses' sake God forgave the Israelites, but he refused to let them change their minds and enter Canaan now. God said, "All of you who are twenty years old and older will never live in Canaan because you have complained against me." To punish them God commanded them to turn back into the wilderness and camp until every person who had complained was dead.

How sorry the people were when Moses told them this! The next morning they got up very early, for they had big plans. They said, "We will go forward as the Lord first commanded us." And their men who had been trained for battle hurried out of camp to fight the men of Canaan.

Moses called after them, "Don't go! God is not with you. You will be defeated because you have turned away from the Lord."

The men rushed on, paying no attention to Moses' warning. The battle did not last long, for the men of Canaan drove the invaders out of the land.

Korah Rebels

Numbers 16

Korah thought he was as great as Moses and Aaron. As time passed he grew more and more jealous, and wrong thoughts filled his mind. "I am a Levite just like Aaron," Korah thought, "and I'm just as good as he."

Like Moses and Aaron, Korah belonged to the tribe of Levi. When the tabernacle was first built, God chose this tribe to care for it. God appointed Aaron the high priest and Aaron's sons to be priests. Only Moses, the high priest and the priests were allowed to enter the tabernacle.

When two others, Dathan and Abiram, heard that Korah envied Aaron, they told him, "You know, we could be just as good rulers as Moses."

These three talked against Moses and Aaron among the children of Israel, and they found two hundred and fifty others who felt the same way. Korah and these followers went to Moses and Aaron. They said, "You think you are great men. Every person in the congregation is holy, and the Lord is with all the people. Then why do you make yourselves leaders of the congregation of the Lord?"

When Moses heard this, he fell on his face. He had not tried to be great, but he knew God had chosen him to be the leader. He knew, too, that God had chosen Aaron to be the high priest. These men were not speaking against Moses and Aaron but against God.

Moses told Korah, "Tomorrow the Lord will show you whom he has chosen and who is holy. Bring censers with fire and incense before the Lord." Then he added, "Listen, you sons of Levi. Does it seem a small thing to you that the Lord chose you to care for his

tabernacle and to minister to the congregation? He has let you be
near to him; do you want to be priests too? Why are you gathered
against the Lord?"

Then Moses sent for Dathan and Abiram, but they sent word,
"We will not come. Is it a small thing that you made us leave the
good land of Egypt and brought us into this wilderness so you
could rule over us? You even promised us a rich land with fields and
vineyards. No, we will not come to see you."

Moses talked to the Lord about it. Then Moses reminded Korah
again, "You, your company and Aaron bring your censers before the
Lord tomorrow."

The next day Korah and his company brought all the congregation
with them to the door of the tabernacle. There the people saw the
glory of the Lord. And the Lord told Moses and Aaron, "Get away
from this congregation so I can destroy them."

Moses and Aaron fell on their faces and prayed, "O God, do not
punish all the congregation for the sin of one man."

The Lord told Moses what to do. Moses went to the tents of Dathan
and Abiram. The elders and the people followed. He told the people,
"Get away from these men and their tents lest something happen
to you. Now we shall prove whether I have ruled by God's command
or whether I have chosen myself as the ruler. If the ground opens
up and swallows these men, we shall know God has chosen me
for this work."

As soon as Moses said these words, there was an earthquake, and
the ground opened up. The men, their tents and their goods fell
into the earth. The people watching ran in fear.

The two hundred and fifty men who had followed Korah, Dathan
and Abiram were killed by fire. And the Lord told Moses to have
the two hundred and fifty brass censers flattened to cover the altar.
When the people saw the brass covering on the altar they would
remember that only Aaron and his children were chosen to offer
incense to the Lord.

Aaron's Rod

Numbers 17

Still the children of Israel complained about Moses and Aaron. And the Lord told Moses, "Take a rod for each of the twelve tribes of Israel, and write the name of the leader of the tribe on each rod. On the rod for the tribe of Levi, write Aaron's name. Then put all the rods in the tabernacle before the ark. The rod of the man I want to be my priest will blossom. Then the children of Israel will know for sure whom I have chosen."

Moses did as the Lord had said. The next day when he went into the tabernacle, eleven rods looked the same as they had the day before. But one rod was blossoming like a growing branch on a tree. Moses looked for the name on the rod. It was Aaron's.

All the children of Israel looked at the rods Moses brought out of the tabernacle. They could see that Aaron's was different from all the rest. The leaders of the tribes took back their rods.

God commanded Moses to keep Aaron's rod in the tabernacle so the people would never forget that God had chosen Aaron and his sons to be his priests.

Water at Meribah

Numbers 20:1-13

The children of Israel wandered through the wilderness of Sin and made camp at Kadesh. Here, Miriam, the sister of Moses and Aaron died and was buried.

About this time the wells at Kadesh dried up. The people and their cattle could not find water to drink. Again they began to complain. Again they said, "Moses, did you bring us into the wilderness so all of us would die here? Why did you take us out of Egypt and bring us to this terrible place? Nothing can grow here without water—no seeds, or figs, or vines or pomegranates. There is not even water for us to drink."

As always Moses and Aaron left the people and went into the tabernacle to pray. There the glory of the Lord appeared to them.

The Lord told Moses, "Take Aaron and the rod and have all the people gather around the rock. Then speak to the rock and water will flow out. There will be water for all the people and their cattle."

Moses and Aaron gathered all the people and stood before the great rock. Then, instead of speaking to the rock as God had commanded, Moses spoke to the people in an angry voice and asked, "Must we bring you water out of this rock?" He did not speak to the rock at all but hit it with his rod.

A clear stream of water gushed out and flowed across the sand. The people ran quickly to drink. Then they filled their pitchers. They brought the cattle to drink from the stream.

God was displeased because Moses and Aaron had not obeyed him. He told them, "Because you disobeyed, and the people thought you gave them the water instead of me, I will not allow either of you to lead these people into the land of Canaan."

The place where the Israelites had water from the rock was called Meribah.

Troubles on the Way

Numbers 20:14-29

For thirty-eight years the people wandered in the great wilderness. Then Moses planned to lead them to the border of Canaan. He wanted to go through the country of Edom to reach Canaan. The Edomites and the Israelites were somewhat related. They were descended from the brothers Jacob and Esau—the Edomites from Esau and the Israelites from Jacob. Moses wanted to be friendly with these people.

From Kadesh he sent a messenger to the king of Edom, saying, "You know all the trouble that has come to us in Egypt and on our journey through the wilderness. We are now at Kadesh, on the edge of your territory. I pray you, let us pass through your country. We will promise to stay on your roads and not go through your fields or vineyards. We will not drink your water."

But the king of Edom did not feel friendly toward the Israelites. He was afraid to let so many people go through his country. He sent this

Moses explains the Law

message to Moses, "You must not lead your people through Edom. If you try to go through our land, I will bring out my army against you."

Moses even promised to pay the king of Edom if he would let the children of Israel go through, but the king refused. So Moses led the people around the country of Edom—south and east and north toward Canaan.

On this long tiresome journey across the bare wilderness and rocky plains, the Israelites came to Mount Hor. Here they camped. God reminded Moses and Aaron that they would never enter Canaan because they had disobeyed him. Then he told Moses, "Take Aaron and his son Eleazer up on the mountain."

Aaron was now an old, old man about to die. God told Moses to take the priestly robes off Aaron and put them on Eleazer. In this way God chose Eleazer to take his father's place. How proud Aaron must have been of his son! Now he could rest in peace, for Eleazer would do well. And here Aaron died.

When Moses and Eleazer returned to camp, the people saw that Aaron was not with them. They saw Eleazer wearing his father's priestly robes, and they understood that God had chosen Eleazer to take Aaron's place. They knew Aaron had died on the mountain, and they mourned for him thirty days.

The Brass Serpent

Numbers 21:4-9

After the Israelites left Mount Hor, they came into a desert country. The hot sands burned their feet. Everything looked dreary, and Canaan seemed very far away.

The people were tired and unhappy. As usual they complained against God and against Moses. "Did you bring us out of Egypt to die in this wilderness?" they asked. "We have no water, and we are so tired of this manna that we hate it."

While they were complaining, snakes crawled into the camp and bit many people. These snakes or serpents looked like fire, and the poison from their bite felt like fire. Those who were bitten died.

At once the people knew they were being punished for complaining against God and Moses. They knew they had done wrong, and they were sorry. Quickly they came to Moses and said, "We have sinned, for we have spoken against the Lord and against you. Pray to the Lord and ask him to take away these snakes."

Moses prayed for the people. The Lord told him, "Make a fiery serpent and put it on a pole. Then whenever anyone is bitten, he can look at the pole and be made well."

And Moses made a serpent of brass and put it on a tall pole in the middle of the camp. From then on whenever anyone was bitten by a snake, the person looked up at the great pole and the snakebite was made well.

Victory for the Israelites

Numbers 21:12—22:2

The Israelites broke up camp and moved ahead. The wilderness of Arnon was their next stopping place. Here they found no water, but this time they did not complain. Instead they trusted God.

The Lord told Moses, "Gather the people together, and I will give them water."

Moses told the chief men of the tribes to dig a well in the sand. While they dug all the people sang praises. They believed God would fill the well with good water even before they saw it bubble up from the deep springs. Their faith pleased God. How the people enjoyed drinking from this well!

Again the Israelites moved on until they came to the country of the Amorites. The Amorites worshiped idols.

Moses wanted to lead his people through their country, so he sent a messenger to Sihon, the king of the Amorites. "Let us pass through your land," Moses asked. "We will keep on the highway and not bother your fields or your vineyards. We will not even drink water from your wells if you will let us pass through."

Sihon not only refused, but he took his army and marched against the Israelites. God helped the Israelites when they were attacked and gave them a great victory. They marched through the land of the Amorites and took their cities and villages. Even the king's own city of Heshbon became theirs. And the Israelites lived in the land of the Amorites for a time.

Later they moved on toward the land of Bashan. Og, the king of Bashan, brought out his army against them.

The Lord told Moses, "Do not be afraid of him, for I will give you victory over Bashan." When the army of Bashan fought the Israelites, the Israelites won.

Now the long forty years' journey through the wilderness had ended. All the old men except Moses and the two faithful spies, Caleb and Joshua, had died in the wilderness. Again the Israelites stood on the border of Canaan. Only the Jordan River separated them from the green hills and beautiful valleys of the Promised Land. They could look across the river and see the rich country God had promised them.

King Balak Sends for Balaam

Numbers 22:1-35

The Israelites pitched their tents on the plains of Moab near the Jordan River. When Balak, king of Moab, heard they were there, he was afraid. He had heard what the Israelites did to the Amorites. He knew they had taken both the land of the Amorites and the land of Bashan. Because he knew the Israelite army was larger than his, he thought: they will take my country away from me. Maybe they will even kill me.

Finally King Balak decided to send for Balaam, a wise man of Midian. Surely Balaam could help. King Balak called some of his princes and sent them to Balaam with this message: "The Israelites have come from Egypt to the border of my country. There are so many of them that they seem to cover the earth. I am afraid they will take our country, for they are mighty. I want you to come and help me. You are very wise. It is said that if you speak against a people they become weak. If you bless them they become strong."

The princes went to Balaam with the king's message. In their hands was the money King Balak had sent to Balaam for his help.

Balaam told the princes, "I do not know whether the Lord wants me to go with you. Stay here tonight. In the morning I will know."

During the night God asked Balaam, "Who are the men in your house?"

Balaam answered, "They are the princes of Moab. King Balak sent them to ask me to help him. From Egypt the Israelites have come into his land. There are so many of these people that he is afraid. He wants me to speak against them in your name so they will become weak."

God told Balaam, "Do not go with the princes of Moab. You must not speak against the Israelites, for I have blessed them."

In the morning Balaam told the princes God did not want him to go with them. And the princes took Balaam's message to their king.

When King Balak heard this, he sent even greater princes to Balaam. They said, "King Balak said to let nothing stand in your way, but come to him. He will give you great honor, and he will do whatever you ask him."

Balaam told these princes, "If King Balak would give me his house full of gold and silver, I could not change the word of the Lord. But if you want to wait until morning, I will talk to the Lord again."

While the princes slept, God told Balaam, "If the men come to call you, get up and go with them. Be sure to do whatever I tell you."

In the morning Balaam did not wait for the princes to call him. Instead he got up and saddled his ass. When they awakened he took two servants and went with them.

God sent an angel to trouble Balaam. The angel stood in the road with a sword in his hand.

Now Balaam did not see the angel, but the ass did. The animal ran off the road into the field. Balaam hit the animal to get her back on the road.

Soon they came to a path that went through a vineyard. On either side was a stone wall. Again the angel stood before them. The ass was so frightened that she ran into the wall. Balaam's foot was crushed against the wall. He was so angry at the ass that he hit her again.

Finally the angel stood in a narrow place in the path, and the ass could not get around the angel. This time the animal sank to the ground. Balaam grew even angrier. He hit the animal with his staff.

And God gave the ass a voice. She asked Balaam, "What have I done that you should hit me three times?"

123

Because Balaam was so angry, he did not think it strange for the ass to speak. Balaam said, "If I had a sword, I would kill you."

The ass reminded Balaam that she had always carried him safely since the day he bought her. Balaam knew this was right. Then the Lord let Balaam see the angel. Balaam bowed his head and fell on his face.

The angel asked, "Why did you hit the ass three times? Three times she saw me in your path and turned away. Three times she saved your life."

Balaam said to the angel, "I have sinned. I did not know you were standing in front of me. I will go back home if you do not want me to go on."

The angel told Balaam to go on with the princes of Moab and to be careful to speak only the words of the Lord.

Balaam Before the King

Numbers 22:36—31:9

When King Balak heard Balaam was coming, he rushed to meet him. "Why didn't you come sooner?" The king asked. "Don't you know that I am able to honor you?"

Balaam answered, "I cannot promise to help you even though I have come. I can speak only the words that God gives me."

Perhaps King Balak thought the wise man was trying to get more money from him. He did not understand that Balaam could not speak against people in the name of the Lord if God did not approve. As an idol worshiper, King Balak did not understand about the one true God.

The next day King Balak took Balaam to the top of a mountain. They looked down on the plain where the Israelites camped. Balaam told the king to build seven altars and offer to the Lord an ox and a sheep on each altar.

Then Balaam went farther up the mountain to talk to the Lord. And the Lord told Balaam what to say to the king.

Balaam returned to the king and the princes and said, "How can I say anything against this people when God does not?" And Balaam blessed the Israelites and told how great they would become.

King Balak demanded, "What have you done to me? I did not want you to bless these people. I wanted you to speak evil of them."

Balaam reminded the king, "I must say what the Lord puts in my mouth."

The king thought he would try again. So he took Balaam to another place where he could see a part of the Israelite camp. Here again he built seven altars and offered sheep and oxen to the Lord.

After Balaam spoke to the Lord again, he told the king, "What the Lord has promised he will do. He commanded me to bless the Israelites, and I cannot change it. God brought them out of Egypt and made them strong."

Now the king said, "Balaam, if you can't say evil of them, don't say anything at all."

Still the king thought he could change Balaam's mind. He took him to a third place where he built altars and offered sacrifices. Now Balaam knew it pleased the Lord to bless Israel, and he said, "How good are thy tents, O Israel! Your land will be rich and beautiful. Your king will be great, and your kingdom will be exalted."

How angry King Balak was! He said, "I had planned to give you riches and honor, but your God has kept them from you. Now get away from here as fast as you can."

Although Balaam had spoken only the words of the Lord, yet in his heart, he wished he could please the king. Because he was a clever man, he thought of another way to help Balak. If they could get the Israelites to worship idols, then God would not be with them.

And that's what they did. The Moabites and the Midianites made friends with the Israelites. Soon the young men of Israel married young women from Moab and Midian. Since the Moabites and the Midianites worshiped idols, these young women took their husbands to the feast of their gods. In this way many Israelites bowed down to idols.

God could not have his people worshiping idols. At Moses' command all those who had sinned in this way were killed.

The Israelites were victorious over the Moabites and the Midianites. In the battle Balaam was killed because he had caused the children of Israel to sin.

The Tribes of Reuben and Gad

Numbers 32

At this time the Israelites lived in the land they had taken from their enemies. This land was good for pasture, and the Israelites, especially the tribes of Reuben and Gad, had many cattle and sheep. These tribes liked the rich pasture lands of the country east of the Jordan so well that they said to Moses, "If it is all right with you, let us have this land for our own instead of going over into Canaan."

Moses asked them, "Would you want your relatives to go to war and take Canaan while you stayed here? The people would be very discouraged if they knew you were not going to help them take the land of Canaan."

Then the two tribes promised Moses, "We will build sheepfolds here for our cattle and cities for our families. Then we will go with you and help you take the land of Canaan. We will not return to our homes until Canaan is yours."

When Moses heard this, he agreed. To the children of Gad and Reuben and to half the tribe of Manasseh, he gave the land that had belonged to Sihon, king of the Amorites and to Og, king of Bashan.

And these tribes settled in the cities east of Jordan, built folds for their sheep and planned to make that country their home.

Moses' Last Journey

Numbers 27:12-23; Deuteronomy 34

Moses was now an old, old man. He knew he was about to die, and he wanted to be sure the people would have another leader. Moses asked the Lord, "Choose a man to lead the people so they will not be like sheep without a shepherd."

The Lord answered, "Take Joshua, a man who is filled with the Spirit, and lay your hands on him. Before all the people, bring him to Eleazer. Tell Joshua and the people what to do. And give Joshua some of your honor so all the children of Israel will obey him."

Moses did as the Lord commanded, and the people understood that Joshua would soon take Moses' place as their leader.

Again Moses called all the people together. He told them many things they needed to know before they went into Canaan to live. He wrote all these words into a book called Deuteronomy.

Finally Moses said, "I am one hundred and twenty years old. I am not able to lead you any longer. Remember that Joshua will lead you into Canaan and the Lord will be with you. Canaan will be yours.

"Be strong and go with good courage. Fear not, nor be afraid. The Lord your God goes with you. He will not fail you or forsake you."

As the people listened, they knew Moses was about to leave them forever. How faithful he had been! He had loved them as a father loves his children. He had been their leader a long, long time.

When Moses finished his long farewell message to the people, he walked out of the camp. As he went the people watched him with tears in their eyes. When he got to Mount Nebo, he began to climb up and up. At last the people could see him no more.

On the top of the mountain, Moses looked over into the land of Canaan. What a beautiful country it was! As Moses looked across its wooded hills and green valleys, he knew his people would soon be in the land God had promised them.

Here Moses died, and God buried him somewhere in the plain. Moses was one of the greatest men who ever lived. He was the only person who ever talked with God face to face.

For thirty days the Israelites mourned the death of Moses.

JOSHUA AND THE JUDGES

Joshua; Judges; Ruth; 1 Samuel 1—8

Rahab Helps the Spies

Joshua 1—2

Across the Jordan River, several miles from the Israelites' camp, was Jericho. A high wall had been built around this city to keep enemies out. There was a gate in the wall through which the people came and went.

The people of Jericho were afraid because the Israelites camped near the Jordan River. They had been hearing about the Israelites for a long time. They knew how God had led Israel out of Egypt and through the Red Sea. They heard how God helped the Israelites fight their enemies. What if Israel should cross the Jordan and take Jericho? The people of Jericho trembled at the thought.

After Moses died God told Joshua, "Take the people across the Jordan to the land I have given them. Everywhere they go, the land will be theirs. Be strong and of a good courage, for I will be with you. I will not fail you or forsake you."

Then Joshua told his officers, "Go through the camp and tell the people to get ready, for in three days we will cross the Jordan. In three days we will possess the land."

The people gathered their belongings and prepared food for the march. The men of the tribes of Reuben, Gad and Manasseh got ready to go with their kinsmen.

While the Israelites broke camp, Joshua sent two men across the river to learn all they could about the city of Jericho. Because Jericho was so large, Joshua believed they needed to capture it before going farther into Canaan.

When the two spies came to Jericho, they found the gate open. In they walked. They came to a house on the wall that belonged to a woman named Rahab. While they talked to her, someone hurried to tell the king, "Two men from the Israelite camp have come to spy on our land tonight."

The king knew he dared not let the spies get back to their camp. At once he sent officers to Rahab's house to capture the spies.

The officers told Rahab, "Bring us the spies that are in your house." When she did not obey, they searched the house, but they could not find the spies. Rahab had hidden the Israelites in the stalks of flax on her roof.

She said to the officers, "I told you the men went out the gate just before dark. If you hurry, you will overtake them."

Out the gate the officers ran. They must capture the two spies. The gates were locked as soon as the officers were gone. Now the spies could not get out of Jericho and return to their camp.

Rahab told them, "I know the Lord has given you the land. I know we cannot win against you. We have heard all the wonders God has done for you, and we are afraid. The Lord God is with you."

As the spies listened, they decided it would be easy to take Jericho because the people were so afraid. But how could they get back to camp to tell Joshua? Rahab said, "Promise me that when you come back to take the city you will save me and my family."

The men promised. She was to hang a red cord in her window, and her family would be saved.

Rahab took them to a window that opened above the wall. "Hide in the mountains for three days before you return to your camp. Then the officers will not find you."

With a strong rope, she let the men down the wall, outside the city. As soon as they were gone, she tied a red cord in her window.

After three days the spies returned safely to Joshua. They told him all that had happened. How glad Joshua was when he heard the spies say, "Surely God has given us that beautiful country, for the people are afraid of us. They think they are too weak to fight against us."

The spies meet with Joshua

Crossing the Jordan

Joshua 3:1—5:12

It was early morning in the Israelites' camp. The people were
ready and waiting to start on their last march to the Promised Land.
Joshua, their new leader, was brave. God had given him courage. He
knew the time had come to move forward, so he gave the command.

Leading the way were the priests carrying the ark. Behind them
came the Levites carrying the pieces of the tabernacle. Then all the
people followed.

When they came to the Jordan, it was flooded over its banks.
On the other side, they saw the green hills and beautiful fields
of Canaan, but the river was too deep and swift for them to cross.
They camped by the river and waited for the flood to pass.

Perhaps the people of Jericho looked at the flooded river and
thought, "We are safe from the Israelites for a while. They will never
be able to cross the river while it is flooded."

After three days of waiting the officers went through the camp and
told the people, "When you see the priests carrying the ark of the
Lord, be ready to follow it."

And Joshua said, "Tomorrow the Lord will do wonders among
you." How excited the people were! At last they were going
to enter Canaan.

The next day Joshua told the priests, "Take up the ark and pass
before the people." Soon everyone was ready to go.

God told Joshua, "As I was with Moses so I will be with you. Tell
the priests to carry the ark to the Jordan. When they come to the
brink of the water, have them stand still."

They did as the Lord commanded. When the priests stepped
into the water, the flooded waters stopped flowing and stood up
on one side. All the water ran off the river's bed, and the people
crossed on dry land.

God wanted the Israelites always to remember how he had helped
them cross the Jordan. He told Joshua, "Command one man from each
tribe to take a stone from the middle of the river where the priests
stand with the ark. When your children see these twelve large
stones, they will ask their fathers, 'Where did these stones come

from?' Then the fathers will tell their children how I brought them across the Jordan. These stones will be a memorial to the children of Israel for ever and ever."

After the men had picked up their stones, the priests carried the ark to the Canaan side of the river. As soon as the priests' feet touched the shore, the waters flooded the river as before.

Soon news reached Jericho and all their neighbors that the Israelites had crossed the river. They heard that God had dried up the flooded Jordan River to let the Israelites cross over. And all the people of Canaan were afraid because the Israelites served such a mighty God.

On the plains near Jericho, the Israelites made camp. They called the place Gilgal. Here they gathered grain from the fields around Jericho. Those who had been born in the wilderness had never eaten grain before. They found fruit too. How much they enjoyed the good food of Canaan.

For forty years God had sent the Israelites fresh manna from heaven each day except the Sabbath. Now they did not need manna any more, for they had come to a good land of grain, fruit and vegetables. Never again did manna fall.

The Walls of Jericho

Joshua 5:13—6:27

While the Israelites camped at Gilgal, Joshua went out to see the city of Jericho. As he looked at the great stone wall that surrounded the city, he must have wondered how his army could ever force its way inside. Since the people of Jericho were expecting the Israelites to attack, they had locked the gate and made it secure. No one even wanted to leave the city while the Israelites were outside.

As Joshua walked about and wondered what to do, he saw a strange man who was dressed like a soldier and who carried a bright sword. Joshua asked, "Are you for us or for the people of Jericho?"

The stranger answered, "I am the captain of the army of the Lord."

Joshua fell on his face and worshiped. Then he asked, "What does the Lord want me to do?"

"Take off your shoes," the captain said, "for the place where you stand is holy ground."

And the Lord let Joshua know how the Israelites were to attack Jericho. The great city would be theirs if they obeyed the Lord's commands.

When Joshua returned to camp, he told the people what the Lord wanted them to do. All the people were ready to obey. They marched around the great city of Jericho the first day. On the next day they did the same, for God had commanded them to march around the great stone walls for a week.

When the people of Jericho looked out their windows, they saw a great army marching around their city. Behind the soldiers were seven priests blowing trumpets made of rams' horns. Following were other priests carrying a strange-looking box on poles. Then came all the people of Israel. What a long parade they made!

None of the Israelites shouted or talked loudly. The only sound was the tread of their feet and the noise of the trumpets. The people of Jericho watched until the great company had marched all around the wall and returned to camp.

"What can this mean?" The people of Jericho wondered. "We cannot understand these Israelites. They don't even fight like other men."

When Rahab saw the Israelites marching around the wall, she knew they were going to capture Jericho. She brought her father, mother, sisters and brothers into her house. Together they looked out the window where the red cord hung. Together they watched the people who worshiped the one true God.

The next day the people of Jericho saw again the strange company march around their city. They saw the same thing on the third, fourth, fifth and sixth day. Finally they decided the Israelites were only trying to scare them.

On the seventh day, the Israelites got up early and prepared for a long march. They knew the day of victory had come. This time they walked around the walls of Jericho not once, but seven times. Then the priests blew loudly on their trumpets. At that signal all the people shouted, for they knew the Lord had given them the city. At that moment the stone wall began to tremble, then it shook and then it fell down flat.

Joshua told the two men who had spied on Jericho, "Go to Rahab's house. Bring her and her family to safety as you promised."

To the soldiers he said, "Take all the gold, silver and brass from the city for the tabernacle of the Lord. Do not take anything for yourselves, or you and all the camp of Israel will be in great trouble."

Finally they burned the city of Jericho. Only Rahab and her family were saved. So the Lord was with Joshua, and his fame was spread through all the country.

Because Achan Stole

Joshua 7:1—8:29

After the victory at Jericho, the Israelites wanted to move farther into the land of Canaan. Joshua sent spies to Ai, the next town. "Go up and view the country," he told them.

When they returned they told Joshua, "We will need only three thousand men to take this city because it is small."

So Joshua sent three thousand soldiers to Ai. This time the soldiers did not return with shouts of victory. Instead they came running with the men of Ai right behind them. A few brave Israelites even lost their lives in the battle.

How discouraged the Israelites were at their defeat! Joshua was so troubled that he tore his clothes and fell on his face before the ark. It was a long time before he could find words to say. Finally he prayed, "O Lord God, why did this happen? Why did our men turn their backs on their enemies? What will people say about our God when they know we have been defeated?"

And God said, "I cannot help the Israelites when there is sin in the camp. I commanded that no one should take anything for himself from Jericho, but one has disobeyed."

The next day Joshua searched for the man who had done this. Joshua discovered that Achan was the guilty man. Joshua told him, "My son, confess your wrong to the Lord, and tell me what you have done. Do not hide it from me."

Achan said, "Yes, I have sinned against the Lord. In one of the houses of Jericho, I saw a beautiful robe and much silver and gold. I wanted them so much that I took them. They are buried beneath my tent. You will find the robe on top with the silver and gold under it."

Joshua sent messengers to Achan's tent. They dug and found the things Achan had taken. At Joshua's command Achan and everything that belonged to him were brought to a valley outside the camp. The Israelites stoned and burned them. On top of the ashes, they piled stones. Whenever the Israelites saw the pile of stones, they remembered that God had punished the man who disobeyed him.

Then the Lord told Joshua, "Do not be afraid or dismayed. Go to Ai. The city and the land will be yours. The cattle and the things you find there will belong to you."

Joshua chose thirty thousand brave men and sent them to Ai at night. "Go a little beyond the city," he told them, "and wait there."

In the morning Joshua and his people started toward Ai and pitched their camp on the north side of the city. Then he sent five thousand soldiers to the west side of the city.

Joshua and some of his men came out to fight the soldiers of Ai. The Israelites pretended they were beaten and ran. After them came the soldiers of Ai in hot pursuit. When they were far enough away from the city, Joshua gave the signal. The soldiers who were waiting behind the city entered it.

As the soldiers of Ai ran after Joshua's men, they must have thought, "What cowardly men these Israelites are!" But when they started back to their city, they saw that Joshua had trapped them. More soldiers were coming behind them, and their city was on fire. This was another victory for the people who obeyed God.

Joshua Builds the Altar of God's Law

Deuteronomy 27—28; Joshua 8:30-35

After the victory at Ai, Joshua led the Israelites farther north to Mount Ebal. They stopped at a place where Abraham had once built an altar to worship God.

Before Moses died he had commanded Joshua, "When you get to Mount Ebal, you shall set up stones and plaster them together to make an altar to the Lord. On the stones of the altar, you are to write very clearly all the words of the Law. When you are finished, all the people will worship and rejoice together."

Now that Joshua had come to Mount Ebal, he did just as he had promised.

All the men of Israel, all the women and all the boys and girls went with Joshua to the place of worship. It was a beautiful valley, shaped like a bowl, lying between two mountains. Mount Ebal was on the north and Mount Gerizim on the south.

As Moses had commanded, six of the tribes stood on the slope of one mountain, and the other six stood on the slope of the opposite mountain. In the valley between was the altar. Here Joshua and the Levites offered sacrifices to God.

The priests and the Levites read to the people all of God's laws that Moses had written in a book. The people remembered the words of the Lord that Moses had told them. They remembered that they had promised to obey these words.

As the priests and the Levites read each blessing God had promised if the Israelites would obey him, the tribes on the slope of Mount Gerizim shouted, "Amen!" And their voices rang out across the valley to the people who stood on the other slope.

Then the priests and the Levites read each trouble that would come to the people if they disobeyed God. And the people on Mount Ebal shouted, "Amen!" Their voices echoed through the whole valley. By saying "Amen" to the words of God's law, the Israelites meant, "Let it be so."

What a wonderful meeting it was! After the words of the Law were read aloud, they were written on the stones of the altar for everyone to read. At evening the Israelites returned to their camp at Gilgal.

Joshua Is Tricked by Strangers

Joshua 9:3-27

One day strange men came to the camp at Gilgal. Their clothes were in tatters, and their shoes were full of holes. The donkeys carried old, ragged sacks. The leather bottles from which the men drank were old and worn. The little bit of bread that was left in their sacks was dry and moldy.

The strangers asked to see Joshua and his officers. To them the strangers explained, "We have come from a far country to make peace with you."

The officers asked, "How do we know you are not our neighbors? How could we make a treaty with you?"

Joshua questioned the strangers further, "Who are you and where do you come from?"

They said, "We have come from a far country. We have heard about your great God, and we were afraid you would defeat us as you did the other kingdoms. Then our elders told us to take food, come to you and make a treaty.

"We took bread hot out of the ovens. See how dry and moldy it is. These leather bottles were new, but see how torn they are. We came so far that our clothes and shoes are worn out."

As Joshua and his officers listened, they thought, "Surely these men have come a long way." They felt sorry for these poor people. What harm could they do to Israel? Joshua and his officers felt so sure that the strangers spoke the truth that no one asked God what to do. Instead Joshua promised to let these men and their people live when the Israelites came to their country.

Three days later the Israelites moved on and came to the land of Gibeon. There they learned that the strange visitors had come from this nearby land. They had taken dry, moldy bread and worn-out clothes just to make Joshua and his officers believe they had come from a far country.

The people blamed the officers for making such a foolish promise without asking God's advice. And the officers were angry and ashamed. They said, "We have promised them by the Lord God of Israel that we would let them live. We cannot break our promise."

139

After some time the officers thought of a plan. "We have to let these people live, but we will make them our servants."

Joshua sent for the strangers who had come to Gilgal. "Why did you lie to us?" He asked.

The men answered, "We knew what had happened to Jericho and Ai and we were afraid. We knew you would not promise to save our lives if you knew we lived close by, so we acted as though our land were far away. Now we are in your hands. It is up to you to do what seems right."

Joshua said, "Because you did not tell the truth, you and your people will never again own houses and lands. You will be our slaves. You will cut our wood and carry our water."

Although the Gibeonites had to work hard, they were glad to be alive. They thought it was better to be slaves than to be killed.

The Sun and the Moon Stand Still

Joshua 10–12

News came to the king of Jerusalem that Joshua had taken Ai and destroyed Jericho. Even the great royal city of Gibeon with her many warriors had made peace with the Israelites.

Because the king of Jerusalem was afraid, he sent word to neighboring kings, "Come and help me war against the people of Gibeon because they have made peace with the Israelites."

So five kings gathered their armies and marched across the hills and valleys to Gibeon. They camped around the great city and made war against it.

The people of Gibeon were terrified. They sent word to Joshua, "Remember we are your servants. Come quickly and save us. All the kings of the Amorites are attacking us."

Joshua took his army and his mighty warriors and went up to Gibeon.

The Lord told Joshua, "Do not be afraid, for I will be with you. Your enemies will not win."

After marching all night, the Israelites came upon the soldiers at Gibeon in a surprise attack. The enemy turned and ran. As they ran hail began to fall. More men were killed in the hailstorm than in the battle.

As the five kings ran from the Israelites, they found a mountain cave and hid there. When Joshua heard of this, he told his men, "Roll great stones in front of the cave and guard it."

The men did as Joshua told them. The cave became a prison, for the kings could not escape.

Afterward the five kings were taken out of the cave and killed. Then they were buried in the cave and stones were piled against the opening.

When Joshua saw the enemy running everywhere, he thought they might hide in the woods and return to fight the next day. He knew the day would not be long enough to find and take the enemy, so he said, "Sun, stand still above Gibeon; and moon, stay above the valley of Ajalon."

And the sun and the moon did stand still. Never had there been a day so long. The Israelite soldiers chased their enemies over the hills and through the valleys. No one escaped. Because the sun and the moon stood still, the Israelites won a great victory.

News of this battle soon reached other cities of Canaan, and everywhere the people were afraid of the Israelites. Joshua obeyed all the commands God had given Moses. So Joshua took all that land, the hills, the south country, the valley and the plain. He defeated thirty-one kings and took the cities and country where they had ruled. Then the Israelites rested from war in their camp at Gilgal.

The Israelites Settle in Canaan

Joshua 13–19

The Israelites had conquered much of the land of Canaan, but Joshua was getting too old to lead them in more battles. Nearby there were no enemies to harm them, and the people had much of the beautiful land to call their own.

But God wanted the Israelites to have all the land of Canaan, not just a part of it. That had been his promise. He did not want Canaan to be a home for people who worshiped idols. The Israelites were the only people in all the land who worshiped the one true God.

141

The Lord told Joshua, "You are growing too old to fight, and there is still land that has not been taken from your enemies. Divide this country among the twelve tribes of Israel and give each tribe a part for their own. Then let each tribe drive out all the wicked people who live in the section given to it."

Joshua, the high priest Eleazar, and the elders from each tribe divided the land as God told them to do. Since two and a half tribes had already chosen the cattle country east of the Jordan River, the other nine and one-half tribes shared the land of Canaan. From this time on Canaan was called the land of Israel even though some Canaanite people still lived in the far corners.

One day the rulers of the tribe of Judah came to see Joshua. With them was Caleb. Of the twelve spies Moses had sent into Canaan forty years before, only Caleb and Joshua had reported that they could take the land with God's help.

Caleb reminded Joshua, "I was forty years old when Moses sent me to spy out this land, and I reported to him what I believed was true. The people were afraid when they heard the stories the ten spies told, but I followed the Lord with all my heart. Moses promised that the land I had spied out would belong to me and my children forever."

Joshua nodded his head. He remembered how Caleb and he had tried to quiet the people when they cried in fear because giants lived in Canaan.

Then Caleb continued, "Now the Lord has kept me alive these forty-five years since Moses made his promise. I am eighty-five years old, but I am as strong as I was the day Moses sent me into Canaan. I can still fight."

What Caleb said was true. Joshua knew it well.

Finally Caleb asked, "Remember the mountains where the giants, the Anakims, lived in great fenced cities? If the Lord goes with me, I can drive them out and possess the land."

There were beautiful valleys near Gilgal where the enemies had been driven away. Here the fields were green and fruit trees grew. But Caleb did not want an easy place.

How happy Joshua was when he knew Caleb still had great courage and faith. He blessed Caleb and gave him the mountain country and the city of Hebron where the giants lived.

With the Lord's help, Caleb drove out the giants. Then he took his sons and daughters and other relatives to live at Hebron.

From the time the Israelites crossed the Jordan River, the tabernacle had been at Gilgal. Now the time came for it to be moved again. And the Levites carried it to Shiloh. Here it stayed for many years.

Shiloh was nearer the center of the land of Israel, and all the people were commanded to worship God at the tabernacle three times a year. They came for the Passover feast where they killed and roasted a lamb as their fathers had done on the night they left Egypt. Fifty days later they brought their first-ripe grain and laid it on the altar for the Feast of Pentecost. Last was the Feast of Tabernacles when they built booths of branches and lived out of doors. This reminded them of the long years they had lived in the wilderness.

Although the Levites were settled in different parts of the land, some of the priests and Levites always stayed at Shiloh to care for the tabernacle just as God had commanded.

Cities of Refuge

Joshua 20—21

When the Israelites left Gilgal to make their homes in various parts of the Promised Land, they had no Bible to take with them. They had no tabernacle nearby, and no longer were they reminded of God's nearness in the cloud by day and the pillar of fire by night.

God knew how much these people would need to be reminded of him. So he sent some of the Levites with the people to every part of the land.

Ever since the tabernacle was built, the Levites had assisted in the worship. Also they had taught the people God's law. Only a part of the Levites were needed at one time to serve in the tabernacle at Shiloh. Since there were many Levites, they took turns helping in the tabernacle. When they were not serving at Shiloh, they went home to their families who lived in various cities throughout the land.

The Levites made their homes in forty-eight different cities. Fields outside the city walls were given to them for pastures. It was their duty to help all the people round about to remember God's laws.

God told Joshua, "Choose six cities of refuge. Then if anyone kills a person accidentally, he can run into one of these cities and be safe." Even if the killing was an accident, the Israelites had always believed that the relatives of the dead person had a right to kill the offender. But God planned there should be punishment only when people did wrong on purpose.

The cities of refuge stood on high hills and could be seen from a distance. A man who had killed a person accidentally would be safe as soon as he entered the gate of a city of refuge. The gatekeeper would let him enter but not those who followed him.

Inside the city of refuge, he was given a fair trial. If he had killed someone by accident or in self-defense, he was allowed to live in the city in peace. When the one who was then high priest died, the slayer could go to his own home in safety.

The Altar Beside the Jordan

Joshua 22

When the tribes went to the various parts of the land to make their homes, Joshua sent for the men of the tribes of Reuben, Gad and the half tribe of Manasseh. He told them, "You have kept your promise to Moses and you have obeyed all that I commanded you. Now that your brethren are settling their own land, you may get your tents and go back to your land across the Jordan."

How glad the men must have been to be able to return to their wives and children! They had fought many battles in helping their relatives drive the enemy out of Canaan.

As they departed Joshua said, "Keep the Lord's commandment and the law that Moses gave you. Love the Lord your God and walk in all his ways. Serve him with all your heart and soul." Joshua blessed them and sent with them Levites to live in their cities and remind them of God's law.

As they returned to Gilead, they took with them riches. Joshua had given them a part of the cattle, gold, silver, iron, brass and clothing they had taken from the cities they had conquered.

When they came to the Jordan River and looked across to their own country, they thought, "This river divides us from the rest of the land of Israel. But we cannot let this river cut us off from the worship of the true God at Shiloh."

There on the high banks of the river they built an altar like the one on which the priests offered sacrifices to God at Shiloh. Then they traveled on to their homes.

God had commanded the Israelites to offer sacrifices only on the altar at the tabernacle. When the men of the other tribes of Israel heard about the new altar by the Jordan River, they were angry. They thought their kinsmen were trying to worship God in their own way instead of coming to the tabernacle at Shiloh. They remembered how God had punished all the people when a part of them sinned. What if God allowed a new trouble to come to the Israelites because those men had built a new altar?

In fear they gathered together and planned to cross the river to fight those who had disobeyed God's word. Before attacking they sent Phinehas, the son of Eleazar the priest, with a prince from each tribe to talk to the men who had built the altar.

How surprised the men were to see Phinehas and the ten princes of Israel coming to see them! Why, they had seen them at Shiloh just a short time before. But they were even more surprised when the visitors said, "Why have you rebelled against the Lord and built this altar? Don't you know that he will honor only the sacrifices offered at Shiloh? He will punish all of us for your sin."

The men who had built the altar said, "The Lord God knows why we built the altar. We do not intend to use it to worship God. No sacrifices will be offered on it. We built it because we were afraid that someday your children would not allow our children to come to Shiloh to worship the true God. Then our children could show them this altar built like the one at the tabernacle. Seeing it your children would understand that the tribes east of the river also worship the Lord."

Phinehas and the ten princes felt glad when they heard these words. "Now we understand," they said. "You have not committed

any sin against the Lord." With light hearts they hurried back to Shiloh to tell the people why the altar had been built by the river.

And all the people were glad. Now they knew the tribes on the other side of the Jordan wanted always to serve the true God. The men returned to their homes throughout Canaan.

The children of Reuben and Gad called their altar Ed which means "a witness." For they said, "This altar shall be a witness between the tribes of Israel that the Lord is God."

Joshua's Farewell

Joshua 23—24

For many years the Israelites lived in Canaan. They built homes and cities. They cultivated the land and lived in peace. How much they enjoyed the land God had given them!

Joshua was now one hundred and ten years old. No longer could he lead the Israelites against the heathen people who still lived in the land, but Joshua knew God would help the Israelites.

Now that Joshua was about to die, he wanted to talk to his people one more time. He sent messengers throughout the land calling all the people and their elders to meet at Shechem.

And all the people came, for they loved and honored Joshua. They had never refused to obey him. Together they remembered all the wonderful things God had done for them.

Now Joshua their leader spoke to them for the last time. "Be very courageous," he told them, "and keep all God's laws that Moses wrote in the book. There are still heathen in the land, but you must drive them out. Have nothing to do with them. Do not bow down and serve their gods. Do not marry with them. If you do all this, God will give you success and good things. If you disobey great trouble will come to you."

Joshua reminded the people how God had been with them since the days of Abraham. He told them the words of the Lord. " 'When Abraham worshiped me instead of idols, I led him into this land and promised that it would belong to his descendants. Here Isaac lived. This was Jacob's home until he went with his children to live in Egypt. When your fathers suffered as slaves in Egypt, I sent Moses and

147

Joshua says good-bye to his people

Aaron to lead them out. When the Egyptians overtook your fathers at the Red Sea, I led them across the sea, but the Egyptians were drowned.'"

As Joshua spoke the people must have nodded their heads. They had heard about Abraham, Isaac and Jacob. From earliest childhood they had known how God led the Israelites out of Egypt.

As Joshua spoke the words of the Lord, the people's hearts beat faster, for now Joshua was telling about the wonderful things God had done during their own lifetime. "And the Lord said, 'I brought you across the Jordan and gave you victory over all your enemies. Now you have a good land for your own.'"

The people knew that the words of the Lord were true! God had done great things for them.

At last Joshua said, "Today you must choose whether you will serve the Lord God or worship other gods. But as for me and my house, we will serve the Lord."

And all the people answered, "We will serve the Lord and obey his commands."

Joshua knew that he could not live much longer. Because he wanted the people to be reminded of their promise after he was gone, he wrote their promise in a book. Then he set up a great stone under an oak tree at Shechem. Afterward, whenever the people saw that stone, they remembered their promise to God and to Joshua.

Soon after this meeting, Joshua died, and the Israelites buried him on a hillside near his home. At Shechem they buried Joseph's body, which they had carried from Egypt in a coffin. Nearby were the fields Joseph had known as a boy. Later Eleazar died and Phinehas became high priest in his father's place.

And the people served the Lord as long as there were elders in their tribes who knew the great works God had done for the children of Israel.

The Israelites Forget God

Judges 1:1–3:11

After Joshua was dead, the Israelites remembered their promise to obey God. God had commanded them to drive the heathen out of Canaan. When the Israelites fought against their heathen neighbors, God helped them. Their enemies were afraid because God was with the Israelites.

After a time the Israelites got tired of fighting. Perhaps they wanted to rest and enjoy their new land. Maybe they planned to take just a short rest before going back to battle. But while they rested, they made friends with their idol-worshiping neighbors.

Time passed and the Israelite children grew up with the heathen children. When they were older, many Israelites married heathen men and women. Because they wanted to please their husbands and wives, the Israelites bowed down to idols and worshiped them. Little by little the Israelites forgot their promise to serve the one true God.

Although the Israelites forgot, God did not. He sent a messenger to tell them, "I brought you out of slavery in Egypt and you promised to serve me always. You promised to drive the heathen out of the land and tear down their altars. But you have not obeyed my voice. Why have you done wrong? You knew that great trouble would come if you disobeyed."

When the people heard these words, they wept. At once they offered sacrifices to the Lord. They wanted to repent of the wrong they had done.

Even though the people were sorry, it was not long until they had forgotten again. They bowed down to the idols that were set up under the trees instead of going to Shiloh to worship the true God. It was too easy for them to act like their heathen neighbors.

Perhaps at first the Israelites thought, "Three trips to Shiloh every year are too many. We will go just twice this year." Then maybe the next year they went only once. Finally they did not go at all.

When the Israelites began to worship idols, God allowed troubles to come upon them. No longer did he help them win their battles. The king of Mesopotamia defeated the Israelites and ruled over them. For eight unhappy years, the people served that king.

When the people found themselves in trouble, they remembered how God used to help them. Again they called on the Lord for help. Although they had done wrong, God heard their prayers. He spoke to Othniel, a brave man among them.

Like his uncle Caleb, Othniel followed the Lord. He called together the soldiers of Israel and led them to battle against the king of Mesopotamia. And God gave them the victory.

For forty years Othniel ruled Israel as a judge. As long as he lived, the Israelites were not troubled by their heathen neighbors. When he died the people began to forget God again. They did not go to the tabernacle at Shiloh to worship. They would not listen to the words of the Levites who lived among them. They wanted to worship gods they could see. Soon they were worshiping idols again.

Ehud Judges Israel

Judges 3:12-31

The Israelites broke their promise to God and began to worship idols again. Trouble came to them because they had done wrong. Eglon, king of nearby Moab, looked with greedy eyes on the rich land of Israel. He thought, "I must rule that country too."

He called other enemies of the Israelites. Together they attacked the Israelites. Because God did not help the Israelites, they were defeated. King Eglon became their ruler. For eighteen years they served him.

The people hated serving King Eglon. Every year they had to bring fruit, grain and cattle to the king. They were not paid for these things. The king had demanded they bring him these gifts each year.

As time passed the Moabites grew richer and the Israelites became poorer. The Moabites had an ambitious king, but the Israelites did not even have a leader. They had forsaken God.

After suffering for a long time, the Israelites remembered again the victories God had given their fathers. They talked about the days when God had blessed their people. "If only we had not turned away from the Lord to serve idols," they groaned.

Again they felt sorry for their sin and took offerings for sacrifices to Shiloh. The high priest put their sacrifices on the great altar of the tabernacle. Earnestly they asked God to forgive their sins and help them once more.

God answered their prayer and sent them a second deliverer, or judge. His name was Ehud. He was a left-handed man who belonged to the smallest of the twelve tribes, the tribe of Benjamin.

How glad the Israelites were to have a leader again! Ehud's job was to take the required fruit, grain and cattle to King Eglon. Ehud took several men with him to help.

Now Ehud despised King Eglon because he made life so miserable for the Israelites. Ehud thought he could never deliver his people as long as the Moabites had such a powerful king. "If the king were out of the way," reasoned Ehud, "our enemies would be so upset that we could easily defeat them." With this idea in mind, Ehud planned to deliver Israel.

When Ehud and his men brought the required gifts, King Eglon was at his summer house. The king received the gifts and sent the Israelites away.

Ehud and his men left the king and started for home. They had not gone far when Ehud sent his men on home, but he returned to the king. "I have a secret message for you, O king," Ehud said.

The king commanded, "Keep silence," and sent everyone except Ehud out of the room. When they were gone, the fat king arose from his chair and waited to hear the secret message.

At that moment Ehud drew a sword from under his coat and killed the king. Then he quietly locked the doors of the room and returned to his people.

When Ehud left the servants wondered why the king did not recall them. They waited. Finally they tried the door, but it was locked. Perhaps the king was resting. Again they waited. At last they became alarmed and forced their way into the room. There they found the king dead.

At once the servants sent out the word, "Ehud has killed the king." The army gathered and marched toward the land of Israel.

As soon as Ehud reached his home, he sounded the trumpet throughout the mountain. And the children of Israel gathered to see what he wanted.

Ehud said, "The Lord has delivered your enemies the Moabites into your hand."

The people believed him, and the soldiers followed Ehud. In the battle Israel won a great victory, and again the Israelites were free.

For the next eighty years, their enemies did not trouble them. Then the Philistines rose up against Israel. God sent Shamgar to be their judge, and he helped them defeat the Philistines. Shamgar was the third judge of Israel.

Deborah Leads Israel

Judges 4—5

Again the Israelites worshiped idols. When Jabin, king of Canaan, attacked them, the Lord did not help the Israelites. The Canaanites won the battle and ruled Israel harshly for twenty years.

Near Shiloh lived a brave woman named Deborah. Because she loved and worshiped the true God, she was made the judge of Israel. Her job was to remind the people of God's commands. Sometimes God told her things that were going to happen. Deborah was known as a prophetess.

The people honored Deborah. They came from every part of the land to get her advice. Usually they found her sitting under the shade of a palm tree near her home.

These were hard days for all Israelites. Jabin, king of Canaan, made life unbearable for them. They did not know how to free themselves from him. Sisera, the captain of Jabin's large army, was very cruel. Many of his soldiers rode in iron chariots pulled by horses. From these chariots they shot arrows or threw spears at their enemies. The Israelites were more afraid of the iron chariots than they were of the foot soldiers.

After suffering under Jabin's rule for twenty years, the people cried to God for help. God heard their cries and told Deborah what to do.

Deborah leads her people

At once she sent for Barak, a brave soldier. When he came she said, "The Lord wants you to take ten thousand men and go toward Mount Tabor. Sisera will come after you with his army and chariots, but the Lord will give you the victory."

Barak said, "If you will go with me, I will do it."

"I will go with you," Deborah said, "but you will not get the honor for this victory. Sisera will be taken by a woman."

Barak may have thought Deborah meant she would take Sisera, but he was wrong. When they reached the North Country, Barak called ten thousand soldiers from the tribes of Naphtali and Zebulun. With these men Barak and Deborah marched toward Mount Tabor and made camp.

When Sisera heard that the Israelites were getting ready to fight near Mount Tabor, he took his army out after them. Perhaps he thought, "How do these Israelites dare fight against me and my great army?"

From the camp at Mount Tabor, Deborah and Barak could see the little river Kishon. It wound like a silver ribbon through the valley far below. As they watched they saw people gathering along the river's bend. Soon they knew this was Sisera's army. They saw the hundreds of iron chariots. The soldiers must have felt a little afraid when they saw Sisera's battle array.

Deborah told Barak, "Up! This is the day the Lord will help you take Sisera. The Lord is with you. Go at once!"

Barak and his soldiers obeyed quickly. They rushed down the mountainside toward Sisera's army. Suddenly Sisera and all his army were afraid. As the Israelites came toward them, they began to run.

When Sisera saw his men being defeated and killed, he jumped out of his chariot and ran as fast as he could. As he ran to find safety, he saw a tent near the valley.

In the door of the tent stood a woman named Jael. When she saw Sisera desperately looking for a hiding place, she said, "Come in, come in. Do not be afraid."

How glad Sisera was to get out of sight of his enemies! Surely no one would look for him here. He asked Jael, "Give me, I pray you, water to drink. I am thirsty."

Jael took a leather bottle filled with milk and poured Sisera a drink.

Then he said, "Stand in the door of the tent. If anyone comes looking for me, do not let him know I am here."

At last Sisera felt safe. He lay down and went to sleep while Jael stood guard at the door. When he was sound asleep, Jael killed him because she knew how cruelly he had treated the Israelites.

How happy all the people were to be delivered from their enemies! They thanked God for the victory. Deborah and Barak sang praises to the Lord.

For forty years the children of Israel prospered and had peace.

Gideon Tears Down an Altar of Baal

Judges 6:1-32

After forty years of peace and prosperity under Deborah, the Israelites became careless again. Soon they forgot how good God had been to them. They made images of the gods the Canaanites worshiped. They even built altars, offered sacrifices and bowed down to these gods. Again the Israelites lived like their heathen neighbors.

When God saw the Israelites bowing down to other gods, he was displeased. He could not help a people who did not love and serve him.

About this time the Midianites began to make trouble. For many years they had occupied the land to the east of Israel. They lived in tents and moved often in search of good pasture and water for their cattle.

Finally the Midianites camped along the borders of Israel. Because the Israelites were too weak to drive them away, they grew bolder. At first they allowed their flocks and herds to graze on the pasture lands of Israel. Then they began to steal the food that grew in Israel's fields and vineyards. They even crowded the Israelites out of their homes. Like grasshoppers, they filled the valleys with their tents and ate up everything the Israelites grew.

With their homes gone, the Israelites had no place to live. The mountain dens and the caves were the only places they could find. They were uncomfortable, hungry and unhappy.

In their trouble the Israelites remembered God and cried again for his help. God knew the people had brought all this trouble on themselves, but he sent a prophet to remind them of all the wonderful things God had done for their fathers.

The prophet told the people, "The Lord God of Israel brought you out of slavery in Egypt and gave you this land. You have disobeyed him. Do not be afraid of the gods your neighbors worship. The Lord, he is God."

After the prophet had spoken to the people, they returned to their caves. Gideon decided to thresh some of his wheat and hide it before the Midianites came and took it. As he worked, an angel came and sat down under an oak tree nearby. Gideon was surprised when he looked up from his work and saw the strange visitor.

The visitor said, "Gideon, the Lord is with you. You are a mighty man of valor."

"But, sir," Gideon answered, "if the Lord is with us, why has all this trouble come? Why doesn't he do great things for us as he did for our fathers when he brought them out of Egypt? Why has he forsaken us and let the Midianites oppress us?"

"Go," the angel said, "in all your might, and the Lord will save Israel from the Midianites."

How could a man like Gideon save his people from their enemies? He asked the visitor, "I come from a poor family. Of all of my father's sons, I am the least. How could I do such a great work?"

"The Lord will be with you," the angel answered, "and you will smite the Midianites."

After all the troubles that had come upon the Israelites, Gideon was so discouraged that it was hard for him to believe the words he heard. How could he be sure God would help him? He told the visitor, "Show me a sign that what you say is true. Stay here, I ask you, until I bring you a present and set it before you." And the angel promised to wait.

When Gideon had prepared meat, broth and bread and brought it, the angel said, "Place the meat and the bread on this rock. Then pour out the broth." And Gideon did it.

156

Gideon threshes wheat

When the angel touched the food with his staff, fire flamed out of the rock and burned up all the food. When Gideon looked around, the visitor was gone.

At once Gideon knew his visitor had been an angel of the Lord. How afraid he was! God told him, "Peace be with you, do not be afraid."

And Gideon built an altar here. He called it, "The Lord is peace."

Now the Israelites worshiped an idol called Baal. Even Gideon's father had a grove of trees for his images of Baal. Here the people worshiped.

That night the Lord told Gideon, "Take one of your father's oxen and tear down the altar of Baal. Then cut down all the trees that are around it. In its place, build an altar to the Lord God. Place the wood of the grove on the altar and offer sacrifice to the Lord."

While it was still night, Gideon called ten servants to help. They tore down the altar of Baal, cut down the trees and built an altar to the true God. On it they sacrificed an ox to the Lord.

The next morning when the people came to worship Baal, they found his altar torn down and the grove gone. They saw the ox on the altar of the Lord. "Who did this?" they asked angrily.

Someone answered, "Gideon, the son of Joash."

At once the men went to Joash and said, "Bring Gideon out at once. He has torn down the altar to Baal and cut down all the trees in the grove. We will kill him for this."

Joash told the men, "If Baal is a god, let him take care of Gideon."

When the people saw that Baal could not harm the man who had destroyed his altar, they ceased to be angry with Gideon. Instead they felt foolish for having worshiped such a god.

Gideon and the Fleece

Judges 6:33-40

Gideon sent messengers throughout the land to call the soldiers of Israel together. As they gathered Gideon wanted to be sure the Lord would help them drive the Midianites away. At evening he put a piece of wool on an outdoor floor. Gideon said to God, "If you will help me save Israel, let there be dew on this piece of wool and let the ground all around it be dry."

When morning came the ground was dry all around, but the fleece was covered with dew. It was so wet that Gideon wrung water out of it.

Still Gideon wondered. Again he prayed. "Do not be angry, O God, but give me another sign that you will be with me. This time let the fleece be dry and the ground around it be wet."

The next morning when Gideon found the fleece dry and the ground wet, he believed that God would help him. Now Gideon was ready to lead the Israelite soldiers against the Midianites.

Gideon Attacks the Midianites

Judges 7:1—8:28

Thirty-two thousand soldiers gathered at Gideon's command. They pitched their camp beside the well of Harod on Mount Gilboa. The Midianites camped in the broad valley below.

And God told Gideon, "You have too many soldiers. When the Midianites are defeated, the Israelites will think they won the victory in their own strength. I want them to know my power. Tell all the men who are afraid to go home."

Gideon did as the Lord commanded and twenty-two thousand men left camp. Still the Lord thought Gideon's army was too large. He said, "Take the men down to the water. Put in one group those who lay down their weapons and kneel to drink the water. In the other group put those who hold their weapons in one hand and drink from the other hand."

Gideon did this. Except for three hundred soldiers, all the men threw their weapons on the grass and knelt down to drink.

"With these three hundred you will defeat the Midianites," the Lord said. "Send the other men home."

Now Gideon had so few men that they didn't even look like an army. Because Gideon knew the Lord had promised to help, he was not afraid. He would do everything the Lord commanded.

That night the Lord said to Gideon, "Get up and go down to the Midianites. You will defeat them. If you feel the least bit afraid to attack them, take your servant Phurah and go down to their tents. Listen to what they say. Then you will feel confident that your men can win this battle."

Gideon took Phurah and went down to the tents on the outskirts of the enemy camp. Gideon was a little afraid when he saw all their tents and their camels. At one tent he heard a man telling about his dream. The man said, "In my dream I saw a cake of barley bread come tumbling into our camp. It rolled against one of the tents and upset it."

Gideon listened and heard another man inside the tent explain the dream: "Your dream means that Gideon will come against us and defeat us, for God is with him." When Gideon heard these words, he thanked God and hurried back to his waiting men.

First Gideon divided the men into three companies, one hundred men in each. Next he gave each man a trumpet to blow when the company made their attack. And to every man he gave a pitcher with a burning torch hidden inside.

With trumpets in one hand and pitchers in the other, Gideon and his three hundred men crept down the mountain toward the enemy camp. Here they parted and quietly took their places around the camp until Gideon gave the signal.

Except for the watchmen, all the Midianites were asleep. At midnight Gideon gave the signal, a long loud blast on the trumpet. When Gideon's men heard that, they too made long loud blasts on their trumpets. All around the camp they shouted, "The sword of the Lord and of Gideon!" At that instant every soldier broke his pitcher, and all around the camp a glare of light flamed from the smoking torches.

The sleeping Midianites awakened with a start. What could be happening? They decided Gideon had attacked them with a great army. Every man ran for fear of being killed by Gideon's army. As they plunged through the darkness, they stumbled over one another. Many died from being trampled by their own men. Many fell on their swords as they stumbled. Others hurried toward the Jordan River where they hoped to be safe.

Gideon and his brave men followed the fleeing Midianites. Many other Israelites gathered to help drive their enemies away. The Midianites lost many men, their princes and two of their kings in this battle. After this the Midianites did not trouble the Israelites any more.

After Gideon had led his people to victory, they begged him, "Be our ruler. Then when you die, your son can be the ruler. He can be followed by his son."

Gideon answered, "I will not rule over you, nor will my son. The Lord shall be your ruler." Although Gideon would not become their king, he judged Israel by God's word for forty years.

Abimelech Makes Himself King

Judges 8:31–10:5

After Gideon died Abimelech, one of his sons, remembered that the Israelites had tried to make his father king. He remembered, too, that his father had refused. "Now," thought Abimelech, "I will be their king."

To become king Abimelech needed the help of many people. He went to Shechem to get his mother's relatives to help. He asked his grandfather, "Wouldn't you like to have your grandson be the king of Israel?"

Abimelech's relatives thought of all he could do for them if he were king. They decided to help him all they could. They took money from the temple of their idol and gave it to Abimelech. With this money Abimelech hired scoundrels to do his dirty work.

Abimelech was afraid his brothers might want to rule Israel. If they were out of the way, none of them could stop him from becoming king. So he killed his brothers. Only Jotham, the youngest brother, got away. Jotham hid in the mountains where Abimelech could not find him.

After this Abimelech returned to Shechem to become king. The men of the city took him out into the country and crowned him under an oak tree. Even though they knew what he had done to his brothers, still they wanted him to be their king.

When Jotham heard that Abimelech was king, he knew God was not pleased. He knew Abimelech and the people of Shechem had sinned. Jotham climbed a mountain near Shechem and called out loudly, "Listen to me, ye men of Shechem."

The people in the valley below listened while Jotham told them a story about the trees.

"One day the trees decided they wanted a king. They said to the olive tree, 'You be our king and rule over us.'

"The olive tree replied, 'Should I quit making olive oil for God and man just to become a ruler of trees?' And the olive tree refused to be their king.

"Next they said to the fig tree, 'Come, rule over us.'

"But the fig tree replied, 'Shall I quit making sweet fruit for mankind to become only a ruler over the trees?' And the fig tree would not be their king.

"Then they asked the grapevine to rule over them, but even the vine refused. At last they spoke to the sharp, prickly bramble bush. 'You be our king,' they said.

"And the bramble replied, 'If you will trust yourselves under my shadow, I will become your king. If you do not trust me, then I will send out fire to destroy all of you, even the great cedars!'"

When Jotham finished his story, he told what it meant. He said, "The men of Shechem are like the trees that wanted a king to rule over them. Abimelech is like the bramble bush, sharp and prickly. He will cause much sorrow and ruin. He will destroy you just as fire destroys trees. Abimelech will stir up trouble that will kill himself and all you people of Shechem."

At that Jotham ran away to find safety in another part of Israel. His life would always be in danger where Abimelech ruled.

For three years Abimelech ruled as king. Then trouble arose between him and the men of Shechem. They planned to kill their king, but he learned of their plan. Abimelech led an army against Shechem and destroyed it. He caused much trouble and bloodshed in many places until he lost his own life.

After Abimelech died the Israelites were judged by Tola for twenty-three years. Then Jair became judge and helped the people settle their quarrels. For twenty-two years he served his people.

Jephthah Leads Israel to Victory

Judges 10:6–12:7

Jephthah had lived in the land of Tob ever since his brothers drove him away from home. He became a strong man, and many people told about his mighty deeds. Even his brothers heard about them.

The Israelites were in great trouble again. They had quit going to the tabernacle at Shiloh to worship God. Everywhere they bowed down to the gods of their heathen neighbors. The people round about made war on the Israelites and took their riches. The Ammonites came from the east and the Philistines from the west to rule over the Israelites. The Ammonites even threatened to take the homes of the Israelites and drive them out of the country.

After eighteen years of suffering under the rule of their enemies, the Israelites remembered how God had given them this land long ago and made them stronger than all the nations round about. In their trouble, they cried to God. They expected God to send a deliverer, just as he had done many times before.

Instead God told them, "You have forsaken me and served other gods. For that reason I will not deliver you any more. Go and cry unto your new gods. Let them help you out of your trouble."

And the people prayed to the Lord, "We have sinned. Do to us what you think is best, but deliver us." They knew their idols could never help them. Only God could save them. They tore down their idols and began to serve the Lord.

God saw the people worshiping him, and he felt sorry for them. He saw them gather their soldiers at Mizpeh to fight the Ammonites, but they did not have a leader.

Then they remembered Jephthah who was famous for his brave deeds. And the elders went to Jephthah in the land of Tob. They begged, "Come, be our captain in a battle against the Ammonites."

Jephthah said, "You sent me away from my father's house. Now why are you coming to me with your troubles?"

Finally the elders promised Jephthah that he could be the leader of Israel if he would command their forces against their enemies. And Jephthah agreed.

Jephthah knew he could not defeat the Ammonites without God's help. Not only did he ask God's help but he promised to give God the first thing that came out of his house when he returned from battle. How foolish Jephthah was! He did not know what he would see when he came back. God did not want Jephthah to make such a promise.

Before the battle the Ammonites ordered the Israelites to give up the land east of the Jordan River. The Israelites said, "When we came out of Egypt to this land, the Lord gave us the land east of the Jordan. Why should you have it now? It was not yours in the first place, but belonged to the Amorites whom we defeated."

The Ammonites still demanded the land and Jephthah sent back the answer, "You do wrong to fight against us, but today the Lord will judge between the children of Israel and the children of Ammon."

The battle raged, and the Israelites won. News of the victory reached Jephthah's home before he returned. How glad his family was! When Jephthah's daughter saw her father coming, she ran out to meet him.

As soon as Jephthah saw his daughter, he remembered his promise. He thought he had to give her as an offering to God. How brokenhearted he was!

Their heathen neighbors sometimes offered children to their gods, but the Law of Moses forbade the Israelites to do this. Perhaps Jephthah did not know that law. He knew his promise had been foolish, but both he and his daughter thought he should keep it. And he did.

Jephthah judged Israel for six years. When he died the people buried him in his hometown.

Samson's Birth Is Announced

Judges 13

For twenty-five years the Israelites served the Lord. When the Israelite children grew up, they wanted to worship gods as their heathen neighbors did. They made images and placed them in their cities and under the trees in their dooryards. They bowed down and worshiped these idols.

Not all the Israelites turned to idol worship. Here and there throughout the land, a few people feared the Lord and served him.

Because there was idol worship among the Israelites, trouble came to them. On the seacoast lived the strong, cruel Philistines. For forty years they ruled the tribes of Israel that lived near their country. The Philistines worshiped a god called Dagon. This ugly idol had the face and hands of a man but the body of a fish. In their capital city the Philistines built a temple to Dagon.

Among the Israelites who served the Lord were Manoah and his wife. They had no children. An angel of the Lord told Manoah's wife she would have a son. The angel said, "Your son will deliver Israel from the Philistines. You must never cut his hair, for his long hair will be a sign that he belongs to God."

When the woman told her husband about the angel's visit, Manoah prayed, "O my Lord, let the man of God return and teach us what to do for the boy when he is born."

When the woman was out in the field, the angel returned. She ran to tell her husband the angel had come.

Manoah asked the angel, "What kind of boy shall we have and what will his work be?"

The angel answered, "It is just as I told your wife before."

And Manoah and his wife made a burnt offering unto the Lord. How thankful they were for the Lord's goodness!

When the son was born, they called him Samson. He grew strong and the Lord blessed him. His parents never cut his hair or let him drink wine, for the angel had said that Samson belonged to God. Such a one was called a Nazarite.

Samson Chooses a Wife

Judges 14

When Samson grew up, his body became very strong. His will, too, was very strong. Often Samson got into trouble because he used his great strength unwisely.

Even though Samson was a man, his hair remained uncut and he drank no wine. If he should break either of these rules, he knew that God would not bless him with unusual strength.

Samson wanted to marry a Philistine girl who lived in Timnah. His parents objected. They asked, "Isn't there a girl among your own people? Why do you have to marry one of our enemies?"

Samson said, "But this girl is the one I want." And arrangements were made for the wedding.

On the way to Timnah, Samson saw a lion that was about ready to attack him. With his bare hands, Samson killed the lion and went on his way.

Then came time for the wedding. Samson started to Timnah. He walked the familiar path. Along the way he saw that bees had made a nest in the lion he had killed. He took the honey from the hive and went on.

After the wedding Samson told thirty young men, "I have a riddle for you. If you can tell me the answer before my wedding feast is over, I will give each of you a shirt and a cloak."

The young men thought they could surely guess the riddle before the seven days of feasting were over.

Samson said, "This is the riddle:

Out of the eater came something to eat.

Out of the strong came something sweet."

The young men tried and tried, but they could not find the answer. Finally they told Samson's wife, "Get your husband to tell you the answer to the riddle or we will make trouble for you."

Samson's wife cried, begged and coaxed, but Samson would not tell her. Finally on the last day of the feast, he could stand her crying no longer. He told her the answer. Soon the young men had the answer too, and Samson knew he had been tricked.

Young Samson with his father and mother

In a rage Samson took the shirts and cloaks from thirty other Philistines and gave them to his guests. Then he left his wife at her father's house and went home.

The girl's father was much displeased that Samson had left her right after the wedding. Many days they waited for Samson's return. When he did not come, the father gave his daughter in marriage to another man.

Samson Angers the Philistines

Judges 15:1—16:3

By harvest time Samson was sorry he had let his temper get the best of him at his wedding. He took a present and went to see his wife, but her father would not let him in the house.

The man told Samson, "You left the wedding, and I thought you did not want her. Now I have given her in marriage to someone else. But I have another beautiful young daughter. You may marry her."

Samson was angry, and he started home. On the way he caught three hundred foxes, tied their tails together two by two and tied torches between the tails of each pair. After lighting the torches, he turned the foxes loose in the Philistines' fields. The fire destroyed their corn, their olive trees and their vineyards.

Now it was the Philistines' turn to be angry. They asked, "Who did this?" It did not take them long to find out that it was Samson. They blamed Samson's wife and her father for what Samson had done. This only made Samson angrier.

After much trouble and bloodshed, the Philistines took an army to capture Samson. When they got to the tribe of Judah, the Israelites asked, "Why are you coming to our land?"

The Philistines said they wanted Samson. The men of Judah did not want trouble with the Philistines so they promised to tie Samson up and bring him to them.

Samson let himself be tied and given to the Philistines. They took him back to their country. When they thought their troubles with Samson were over, he broke the ropes off his arms and hands. He picked up a bone from the ground and killed all his enemies.

Now the Philistines determined to get even with Samson. When he came to Gaza, their capital city, they had the men lock the gates and keep him prisoner. During the night Samson went out to the gates, tore them out of the wall and carried them twenty miles across the fields and hills. He placed the gates on top of a hill in his own land.

The Philistines were greatly surprised when they got up the next morning and found Samson had gone. How amazed they were to discover he had taken the gates of the city with him!

Samson and Delilah

Judges 16:4-20

Even though Samson knew the Philistines hated him, he still dared to go in and out of their country. He knew they were afraid to try to hurt him.

Samson was in love with a Philistine woman named Delilah. He went to see her often.

When the Philistine rulers heard about this, they, too, went to see Delilah. They promised her, "If you can get him to tell you the secret of his great strength, we will each give you eleven hundred pieces of silver."

Delilah must have thought of the many things she could buy with all that money. Also she knew she loved her own people more than she loved Samson. She agreed to find out Samson's secret.

The next time Samson came to visit her, Delilah acted just as she had at other times. Finally she asked, "Samson, tell me the secret of your great strength."

Samson said, "If I were tied with seven moist cords, my strength would be the same as any other man's."

Delilah sent word to the rulers that she knew Samson's secret. While Samson was asleep, they brought her seven moist cords and hid in her house. She tied him securely and called, "Samson, wake up! The Philistines are after you."

With no effort at all Samson broke the cords as if they were threads. Delilah scolded him, "You were just making fun of me, Samson. Now tell me the truth. What is the secret of your strength?"

Samson pretended to be very serious when he said, "If you tied me with new ropes, I would be the same as any man."

Again Delilah believed him. She sent for the rulers and they brought new ropes. While he slept they hid in Delilah's house and she tied him up. Again she called, "Samson, the Philistines are upon you." And Samson easily broke the new ropes.

The next time Samson visited Delilah she again coaxed to know the secret of his strength. This time he told her he could not free himself if his hair was woven together and fastened. When he was asleep, she wove and fastened his hair. Again Samson freed himself easily.

Delilah wondered if she would ever get the money the rulers had offered. The more she thought about it the unhappier she became. Day after day she pleaded with Samson to tell her the secret of his strength. She said, "How can you say you love me when you won't even tell me your secret?"

Samson finally became so tired of Delilah's coaxing and pleading that he said, "Because I am a Nazarite my hair has never been cut. If it were, the strength of the Lord would leave me, and I would be like other men."

This time Delilah knew Samson had told her the truth. She sent word to the rulers. They came with the money and hid as before. While Samson was asleep, a man cut his hair. Then Delilah called, "Samson, the Philistines are here."

Samson opened his eyes and saw the Philistine rulers in the room. He tried to get away, but he could not. The strength of the Lord had left him.

Samson Dies

Judges 16:21-31

How glad the Philistines were to have Samson in their power and know he could not hurt them. They tied him up and took him to Gaza. Before placing him in prison, they put out his eyes.

In prison it was Samson's job to grind the grain. They chained him and made him turn a heavy millstone to make the flour. Day after day he worked in prison. And with each passing day, his hair grew longer.

Poor Samson! He had made a bad mistake. Delilah had not been his friend. He should never have told her the secret of his great strength. Now he was blind and would have to suffer for the rest of his life.

About this time the Philistine rulers gave a great feast in honor of their god Dagon. They wanted to thank their god for giving them power over Samson. All the Philistines rejoiced and made merry.

During the feast the people said, "Bring Samson so he can amuse us."

A boy led in the once-great Samson. When the people saw him blinded and in chains, they made fun of him. They thought he could no longer harm them.

Samson knew the temple was crowded with people. On the flat roof there were three thousand people. Samson told the boy who led him, "Take me where I can lean against the pillars of the building."

As the people made fun, Samson prayed, "O Lord God, remember me and strengthen me this once, for the Philistines have put out my eyes."

Standing between the two main pillars of the house, Samson put an arm around each pillar and pulled with all his might. The house fell down and everyone was killed.

Ruth Goes with Naomi

Ruth 1:1–1:19

A famine spread throughout all the land of Judah. Because there was so little rain, the people could not raise enough food to eat. When the word came that there was food in the country of Moab, Elimelech moved there with his wife and two sons. They decided to stay in Moab until the famine was over.

The family was glad to have enough food to eat, but life was very different in a heathen land. Here many people had never heard about the true God. They worshiped an idol called Chemosh. Because they worshiped Chemosh with fire, he was sometimes called a fire god. His image was made of brass, and sacrifices were burned in his outstretched brass arms.

Even though heathen surrounded Elimelech and Naomi, they worshiped the one true God. They taught their sons to worship him too.

Then Elimelech died. How much Naomi and her two sons missed him! Now Mahlon and Chilion cared for their mother.

Later Mahlon and Chilion married and had homes of their own. Their wives, Ruth and Orpah, were Moabite girls. Instead of teaching her young husband to serve Chemosh, the fire god, Ruth learned to serve the true God.

Things went well with Naomi, her sons and their wives for about ten years. Then both Mahlon and Chilion died. How sad and lonely Naomi felt! She was not able to care for herself. When she learned that Bethlehem was no longer suffering from famine, she decided to return to her own people.

Both Ruth and Orpah loved Naomi. They wanted to go with her. Naomi agreed that they could go part of the way.

After the three had walked some distance, Naomi told her daughters-in-law, "Go back, each of you, to your mother's house. And may the Lord be as good to you as you have been to me and my two sons . May the Lord help each of you to find a good husband." Then she kissed them.

Through their tears they said, "We want to go with you."

Naomi answered, "Go back, my daughters. I do not have more sons for you to marry, and I am too old to get a husband to care for us. Go back."

Once Naomi had been a stranger in Moab. She knew how it felt to live in a strange land. She thought the girls would be happier among their own people.

Then Orpah kissed her mother-in-law good-bye and started back to Moab. But Ruth did not want to return.

Naomi told Ruth, "See, your sister-in-law has gone back to her people and her gods. You do the same."

"Do not make me leave you," Ruth begged. "I want to go wherever you go. I want to live wherever you live. Your people shall be my people, and your God, my God."

Now Naomi realized how much Ruth wanted to go with her. Naomi did not say any more about returning to Moab. Instead the two walked on and on, over the hills and through the valleys. At last they came to Bethlehem where Naomi had lived with her husband and two little boys.

Ruth Gleans in Boaz' Fields

Ruth 1:19—2:23

How glad Naomi's friends were to see her again! They noticed how much older she looked. They knew by the lines on her face that she had suffered trouble and sorrow. They could hardly believe this was the same Naomi who had left Bethlehem during the famine. They even asked one another, "Is this really Naomi?"

She told her friends, "Do not call me Naomi now, but call me Mara instead. Because I have lost my husband and sons, life has become bitter for me." "Naomi" meant "pleasant" and "Mara" meant "bitter." She wanted to change her name because her happiness had been changed to sorrow.

The friends wanted to know what Naomi planned to do. Naomi told them about Ruth, her daughter-in-law who had returned from Moab with her. The two would live together.

It was harvest time in Bethlehem. The grain was ripe in the fields. The reapers were busy cutting the grain and binding it into bundles. As was the custom among the Israelites, the reapers left some stalks of grain for the poor to gather.

When Ruth heard of this custom, she asked Naomi, "Let me go to the fields and glean from the grain that is left."

"Go, my daughter," Naomi answered.

It happened that Ruth began to glean in the field of a very rich man named Boaz. When he came to see how his servants were getting along with the reaping, he saw a strange young woman picking up the grain that had been dropped. "Who is she?" he asked.

The overseer explained. "She is the Moabite maiden who came back with Naomi. She asked permission to glean after the reapers. Ever since, she has worked steadily without resting."

Boaz watched as Ruth worked patiently among the people who were strange to her. He knew she was trying to find food for Naomi and herself. No wonder Boaz admired this beautiful young woman.

Boaz told Ruth, "Young woman, do not go to another field to glean but work with my maidens here. When you are thirsty, you may get a drink from the water jars."

Ruth was very thankful for this kindness. She bowed her head and asked, "Why are you so kind to me a foreigner?"

"I have heard about your kindness to your mother-in-law since your husband died," Boaz said. "I have heard how you left your own people and came to a people who are strange to you. May the Lord reward you with many blessings because you trust in him."

Ruth's heart was warmed by these kind words.

When mealtime came Boaz invited Ruth to eat lunch with his servants. "Treat her kindly and be sure to leave some grain for her to gather," he told his workers.

By evening Ruth had a bushel of grain. She carried it to Naomi. Ruth had even saved part of her lunch for Naomi.

Naomi was surprised to see so much grain. "Where did you glean today?" she asked.

Ruth told about Boaz and his kindness. And Naomi said, "Boaz is one of my husband's relatives. It is good that you are working in his fields."

And all during the harvest Ruth gleaned grain from Boaz' fields.

Boaz Marries Ruth

Ruth 3—4

When the harvest was over, there was a feast. Rich and poor rejoiced together because God had given them food for another year.

Naomi sent Ruth to Boaz' feast. When Boaz recognized Ruth, he said, "May the Lord bless you, young woman. Even though you do not have a husband, you have not followed after the young men. Everyone in the city knows you are a good woman. Now I was

Ruth gleans in the fields

closely related to your husband who died. Yet there is one person who is more closely related than I."

Ruth listened. According to the custom, she knew her husband's closest relative was expected to marry her and care for Naomi.

"Tomorrow," Boaz said, "I will talk to the other relative about this. If he will give up his rights, I would like very much to have you for my wife." Boaz told Ruth how much he loved her.

When Ruth got home, she gave Naomi the grain Boaz had sent and told her what had happened. How excited Ruth was!

Naomi said, "Tomorrow you will know for sure whether Boaz can marry you. He will not rest until he has taken care of the matter."

When Boaz got up in the morning, he went to the city gate to see his relative. Before the ten elders of the city, the relative said he could not marry Ruth and care for Naomi.

Boaz told the elders, "You are witnesses that I want to marry Ruth and care for Naomi."

"We are witnesses," the elders said. And they asked the Lord to bless Ruth and Boaz.

When Ruth and Boaz were married, he took her to live in his own house. How happy they were! Naomi was happy too, for Ruth and Boaz were good to her.

Later a little boy was born to Ruth and Boaz. Naomi loved being grandmother to little Obed. She helped Ruth care for him. How good God was to them!

Hannah Gives Samuel to the Lord

1 Samuel 1:1—2:21

Near Shiloh lived a man named Elkanah. Because he loved the Lord, he took his offerings to the tabernacle at Shiloh every year. With him went his family. Together they worshiped the Lord.

But Hannah, Elkanah's wife, was unhappy because she did not have any children. Even though Elkanah loved and honored her, still Hannah was sad. More than anything else, she wanted a baby.

This year when Hannah went with her husband to take their offering, she opened her heart to the Lord. "O Lord," she prayed, "if you will give me a baby boy, I will give him back to you to serve you the rest of his life."

Eli, the priest, saw Hannah. He noticed that her lips moved, but he did not hear a sound. He wondered what was wrong. Hannah explained, "I am very distressed, and I have told the Lord the trouble."

"Go in peace," Eli told her, "and may the Lord give you what you have asked."

No longer was Hannah sad. She knew the Lord had answered her prayer. Her heart was light as she and Elkanah returned home.

Before another year passed, God gave Hannah and Elkanah a baby boy. Hannah named him Samuel, which means, "asked of God."

When Samuel was old enough to help in the tabernacle, Hannah packed his clothes in a neat bundle and took him to Shiloh. She brought him to Eli, the high priest. Hannah said, "One year when I came up to the tabernacle with Elkanah, I prayed for this child. Because the Lord answered my prayer, I have brought Samuel to serve in the tabernacle. As long as he lives he shall belong to the Lord."

Eli knew God was pleased with Hannah. He promised to take care of Samuel and teach him to serve God. Then Hannah and her husband returned to their home.

Every year thereafter when Elkanah came to present his offerings at Shiloh, Hannah came too. Each time she brought a new coat for Samuel. Each year she was glad to see how much taller he had grown, and she was thankful when Eli told her how Samuel helped in the tabernacle.

Hannah was always glad that God had answered her prayer. And God gave Hannah other children besides Samuel.

God Speaks to Samuel

1 Samuel 2:22—3:18

Now Eli had two sons who were priests. They did many things that displeased God. Because Eli's sons did so much wrong, the good people of Israel dreaded to go to Shiloh with their offerings.

Even though Eli knew his sons did wrong, he still allowed them to serve as priests at the tabernacle. He tried to get them to change their ways, but they would not listen to him.

Then God sent a prophet to warn Eli about his sons' wrongdoing. The prophet said the sons would be punished. Because Eli let them serve as priests, he would be punished too. No longer would the high priest be a member of Eli's family.

After the prophet went away, God spoke to Samuel one night. Samuel did not know it was God speaking. When he heard a voice calling him, he thought it was Eli. Quickly Samuel got up out of bed and ran to Eli. "Here I am," he said, and he waited for Eli to say what he wanted.

But Eli had not called Samuel. He said, "I did not call you, my boy. Go back and lie down again." And Samuel obeyed.

Soon the voice spoke again, "Samuel!" The boy rubbed his sleepy eyes and hurried to Eli's bedside.

"Here I am," he said, "for I heard you call."

Again Eli told him, "I did not call. You may go back to bed."

The voice called Samuel a third time. When Samuel ran to Eli, the old man knew that God wanted to speak to the boy. Eli said, "Go and lie down. If the voice calls you again, say, 'Speak, Lord, for your servant listens.'"

Samuel went back and lay down again. Soon he heard the voice of God calling, "Samuel! Samuel!"

And the boy answered, "Speak, Lord, for your servant listens."

God talked with Samuel that night and told him that Eli and his sons would soon be punished, just as the prophet had said.

When morning came Samuel hated to tell Eli what the Lord had said. Perhaps he had lain awake for a long time, wondering what he should say to kind old Eli.

When Samuel did not come to tell Eli God's message, Eli called the boy to him.

Samuel came as he had during the night. "Here I am," he said.

"What did the Lord tell you?" Eli asked. "Do not hide it from me." And Samuel told him the words of the Lord.

Eli bowed his head and said, "Let the Lord do what he sees is best."

Hannah brings Samuel to Eli

The Ark of God Is Captured

1 Samuel 3:19—4:22

As Samuel grew older, God spoke to him again and again. And Samuel always told the people what God said. Finally throughout all Israel people began to say to each other, "Surely Samuel is God's prophet."

At this time people in many parts of Israel worshiped idols. They had turned completely away from God to serve images made of wood, silver or gold. They had disobeyed God.

Trouble came to the Israelites. The Philistines, their old-time enemies, fought against them and killed many Israelites. After the battle the chief men of Israel met to talk things over. They asked themselves, "Why did the Philistines win against us? How can we defeat them?"

Finally the leaders agreed, "Let us get the ark of God at the tabernacle in Shiloh and take it with us into battle. Then the Philistines will not be able to beat us."

Instead of praying and asking God to help them, they went to Shiloh and told Eli's wicked sons about their plan. And these priests said, "We will take the ark and go with you to battle." They too thought God would help if his ark were there.

When the priests carried the ark into camp, all the soldiers shouted for joy. They made so much noise that their shouts were heard in the Philistines' camp.

The Philistines wondered, "Why are the Israelites shouting after they were defeated in battle?" Then word came that the Israelites had brought the ark of God into camp.

The Philistines were afraid when they heard this. They worshiped idols, and they thought the ark was like an idol and that its presence would strengthen the Israelites when they carried it into battle. The Philistines remembered the stories they had heard about the wonderful things God had done for the Israelites. Surely the Israelites would win now. Then they would rule over the Philistines.

Before the next battle the captains of the Philistine army told their men, "Be strong and fight bravely unless you want to be servants to the

Israelites. Don't turn back, but fight with all your might." And the soldiers did their very best.

The Israelites started out bravely enough. Eli's sons carried the ark into the battle. Soon the Israelites knew they were being driven back and defeated. Israelites began to fall on every side. Even the priests were killed, and the Philistines carried away the ark of the Lord.

All the Israelite soldiers left alive ran away in great fear. They knew that God had forsaken them because they had sinned. To have the ark of God taken away from them—what could be worse?

One soldier ran to Shiloh. He tore his clothes so the people would know he brought bad news.

By the roadside near the tabernacle sat blind old Eli. He was anxiously awaiting news about the ark. How troubled he was because his sons had taken it out of the tabernacle! His sons were always making trouble.

When the messenger came into the city, he reported that the Philistines had beaten the Israelites, killed Eli's sons and taken the ark of God. The people were so alarmed that they cried aloud. Eli heard their cries. He asked, "What has happened?" And the messenger told Eli the news.

Eli was saddened by the defeat and the death of his sons. This was bad enough, but when he heard that the ark of God had been taken, he fell dead.

For forty years Eli had been judge and high priest of Israel. He was ninety-eight years old when he died.

With the ark of the Lord gone, the Israelites felt that God was no longer with them. They became a discouraged, fearful people.

The Ark of God Troubles the Philistines

1 Samuel 5:1–7:2

The Philistines rejoiced greatly in their victory over the Israelites. Now they thought their god was greater than the God of the Israelites. They carried the ark from the battlefield to their capital city. Here they placed it in the temple of Dagon, the fish god.

At once trouble began for Dagon and his worshipers. When the people came to worship their god early the next morning, they found Dagon lying face down before the ark. They put him back in his place and returned to their homes.

The next morning they found Dagon on the floor. This time his head and his hands had broken off in the fall. And the people began to be afraid.

Before long all the people in that city and the country round about broke out in painful sores. The people suffered a great deal. Finally the men of the city said, "Let's not keep the ark of the Lord any longer."

And the rulers asked, "But what shall we do with the ark?"

"Send it to Gath," the men decided.

When the ark reached Gath, the people there began to suffer with painful sores. Many men became so sick that they died. The people became so afraid of the ark that they sent it to another city called Ekron.

The people of Ekron saw the ark coming. How afraid they were! They asked, "Have you brought this ark here to kill us? Send it back to Israel where it belongs."

For seven months the Philistines were troubled. They called their wise men and asked, "What shall we do with the ark of the Lord? Where can we send it?"

After much thought the wise men advised, "Build a new cart and yoke two cows to pull it. Put the ark on the cart. With it put a box of golden jewels as a present. Then send the cows down the road toward Israel."

When the cart was finished and everything was ready, they started the cows down the road. No one led them, but the cows moved on toward Israel. They did not stop by the way to eat grass but kept on going until they crossed the border into Israel.

The Israelites of Bethshemesh were reaping their wheat in the valley. When they looked up and saw the cows and cart returning the ark, they rejoiced. Perhaps they had thought they would never see the ark again. They watched as the cows turned off the road into a field. The animals stopped by a great stone.

Quickly the Levites of Bethshemesh gathered and lifted the ark off the cart. They brought axes and chopped the cart into pieces.

Samuel serves as judge

Placing the wood on the stones, they sacrificed the two cows in thanks to God. All the people rejoiced.

Now the men of Bethshemesh were very curious to see what was inside the ark. They knew God had commanded that only the priests should touch it. Perhaps they wondered if the Philistines had stolen the Ten Commandments. Lifting the lid, they looked inside. Each man died who disobeyed God's command and opened the ark.

Now the men of Bethshemesh did not even want the ark in their town. They sent messengers to the people at Kirjath-jearim, saying, "The Philistines have returned the ark of the Lord. Come down and get it."

The ark was taken to the home of Abinadab, a Levite. He charged his son Eleazar to care for it.

After this time the Israelites never went to Shiloh again to worship God.

Freedom from the Philistines

1 Samuel 7:2-14

The Israelites hated having the Philistines rule over them. Everywhere the people mourned because they thought the Lord had forsaken them entirely. Then they remembered Samuel and how God had talked to him in the past. Perhaps Samuel could help them out of their troubles.

Samuel told the people of Israel. "If you return to the Lord with all your hearts, you must destroy all the idols that are among you. Then prepare your hearts for the Lord and serve him only. It is he who will deliver you from the Philistines."

What a time of cleaning up followed! Everywhere the people tore down the idols of Baal and Ashtaroth, the heathen gods they had worshiped. And throughout the land, the people began to call on God.

Samuel knew the people really wanted to follow God. He sent word to them, "All of you come to Mizpeh, and I will pray for you."

All the people came. They confessed their sins and prayed to the Lord. Samuel advised them in their problems.

When the Philistines learned that the Israelites were meeting at Mizpeh, they decided the Israelites were getting ready for battle. At once, the Philistines called their bravest soldiers. Then they marched toward Mizpeh to fight against Israel.

The Israelites trembled as they looked over the hills and saw the Philistines coming to battle. The Israelites had not brought weapons to fight with. They had come to Mizpeh to pray. What could they do? They told Samuel, "Pray to the Lord and ask him to deliver us from the Philistines."

Samuel took a lamb and sacrificed it to God. He prayed for God's help, and God heard his prayer.

Strangely enough, the Philistines did not get near enough to the Israelites to use their swords and spears. A terrible thunderstorm came up. The Philistines became so frightened and confused that they dropped their weapons and ran. The Israelites picked up these weapons and drove the Philistines back into their own land.

This was a great victory for the Israelites. Everyone rejoiced and praised the Lord. Samuel set up a stone pillar on the battlefield and called it Ebenezer, which means, "Here the Lord helped us."

As long as Samuel lived and judged the people, the Philistines did not return to Israel. They even gave back some of the cities that belonged to the Israelites.

The Israelites Want a King

1 Samuel 7:15—8:22

Samuel made his home at Ramah and built an altar to the Lord. During the year he went from city to city throughout Israel and judged the people. He was the last of fifteen judges who ruled the people of Israel.

When Samuel grew old, he had his sons help him in judging the Israelites. But the two young men were not fair in their judgments. They decided matters in favor of the person who gave them the most money.

The elders of Israel were so concerned about these two young men that they came to Ramah to talk to Samuel. They said, "Samuel, you are getting old, and your sons are not fair in their judgments like you. Give us a king to rule over us."

Samuel did not answer the elders then. Instead he talked to God about it. The Lord told him, "Do what the people want. They are not rejecting you, but they are rejecting me. They do not want me to be their king. Do as they say, but let them know how you feel about this matter. Help them know what it will be like to have a king rule over them."

And Samuel told the elders what the Lord had said. "If you have a king," Samuel said, "he will take your sons to drive his chariots, be his horsemen, serve in his army, run his farm. He will take your daughters to work in the palace. He will take the best food you grow for himself and his servants. Of all you own, he will take a tenth. Then you will complain about the king you have chosen, and the Lord will not listen to you."

Even after the elders heard this, they said, "We want a king. Then we will be like other nations. Our king can judge us and lead us in battle."

Again Samuel told the Lord what the people had said. Again the Lord told him, "Listen to them, and give them a king."

Finally Samuel told the elders, "Return to your homes, for God will give you what you have asked."

THE THREE KINGS OF UNITED ISRAEL

1 and 2 Samuel; 1 Kings 1—12; 1 Chronicles; 2 Chronicles 1—11

Samuel Anoints Saul

1 Samuel 9:1—10:16

Kish was a rich man who owned wide fields and green pastures in the land of Benjamin. He had many cattle to care for. Sometimes his son Saul helped.

One day several donkeys wandered away from the pasture and got lost in the woods. Kish told his son, "Take one of the servants and go to find the lost donkeys."

For two days Saul and the servant hunted for the animals but could find them nowhere. Finally Saul said, "Let's go back. My father will soon forget about his animals and think we are lost."

But Saul's servant did not want to return home without the lost animals. He said, "Let us stop in this city and ask the man of God to tell us where the animals are."

Saul did not want to stop because he had no present for the man of God. The servant said, "See, I have a small piece of money. I will give that to him."

When Saul saw the piece of money, the two went to look for the man of God. As they climbed the hill to the city gate, they met young girls coming to get water. They asked the girls, "Is the man of God here?"

"If you go in through the gate right now, you will find him," the girls said. "We are getting ready for a great feast."

Saul and his servant hurried on. At the gate they met Samuel, the man of God. At once Samuel knew that Saul was the man God had told him about the day before. "Tomorrow about this time," God had said, "I will send you a man from the tribe of Benjamin. Him you must anoint to be king of my people. He will be the captain of the army, and he will save Israel from the Philistines."

Even before Saul could ask about the lost animals, Samuel told him, "Come to the feast with me. Then you may go home tomorrow, for the animals you lost three days ago have been found. And now you are the man to whom all Israel is looking."

How surprised Saul was! He said, "I am a Benjamite, of the smallest tribe of Israel. My family is least in the whole tribe. Why should you say that to me?"

Samuel took Saul to the feast and gave him a place among the most important guests. The best food was placed before Saul. Samuel told him, "I had the best saved for you."

After the feast Samuel took Saul to a quiet place where they could talk. The next morning early Saul and his servant started home. Samuel walked out of the city with them. Finally he told Saul, "Tell your servant to go ahead, for I want to tell you the word of the Lord."

When the servant was gone, Samuel anointed Saul's head with oil. He kissed the tall young man and said, "I am doing this because God has chosen you to be king of the Israelites."

So Saul would believe God had chosen him, Samuel told him three things that would happen on the way home. At Zelzah he would meet two men with word that his father's donkeys had been found and now he was worried about Saul. At Bethel three men would give him two loaves of bread. Finally he would meet a group of prophets near a Philistine stronghold.

As Saul walked toward his home, he became a changed man. He knew God was with him, for he met men who brought news from his father and others who gave him bread. Even the prophets talked to him.

When Saul got near home, he stopped to offer a sacrifice. There his uncle met him.

"Where have you been?" his uncle asked.

Saul answered, "When we couldn't find the donkeys, we went to see Samuel." Saul told his uncle about the visit with Samuel but not about being anointed as Israel's first king.

Saul Is Proclaimed King

1 Samuel 10:17-27

Samuel sent messengers throughout the land to call all the Israelites to Mizpeh, the place where God had helped them defeat the Philistines. When the people came, Samuel reminded them of the many times God had blessed them and helped them out of their troubles. He spoke of the time God had led their grandfathers out of slavery in Egypt.

"Now," Samuel said, "you want a king to rule over you instead of letting God be your ruler and king. You dishonor God in asking for a king. Today God will give you what you want. Today he will choose a king for you."

Then the twelve tribes came before the Lord. First the strong tribes passed by, but God did not choose one of them. From the very smallest tribe, God chose a family, the family of Kish. And God let it be known that he had chosen Kish's son Saul to be king.

Everyone wanted to see the man God had chosen, but Saul could not be found. He had hidden from the crowd. And the Lord told Samuel, "Look, he has hidden himself in the baggage."

The people were so eager to see their king that they ran and found him. When Saul stood before the people, he was head and shoulders above every man in the crowd. How handsome he was!

Samuel said, "See the man God has chosen. None is like him."

And all the people shouted, "God save the king!"

Then Samuel told the people the kind of kingdom they should have. Samuel knew the people would forget his words, and so he wrote in a book all the words he had told the people.

Finally Samuel dismissed the people and every man returned home. Saul, too, went back to his home at Gibeah. With him went a company of men who loved God and their new king.

Not all the people approved of the man God had chosen. They wanted to choose their own ruler. They insulted Saul by saying, "How can this man save us?" Because they hated him, they did not bring him presents.

Saul pretended not to notice their angry looks and rude actions. He went quietly about his work and paid no attention to them.

Saul Rescues His People

1 Samuel 11—13

Soon after God had chosen Saul to be king, great trouble came to the Israelites who lived at Jabesh. The Ammonites, a fierce desert people, besieged their city.

The men of Jabesh knew they could not drive the Ammonites away. "It would be better to have the Ammonites rule over us than to fight them and be killed," the men thought. They sent messengers to tell Nahash, king of the Ammonites, "Make peace with us and we will serve you."

King Nahash replied, "We will make peace with you on one condition. If you will let us come among you and put out each person's right eye, we will make peace. Then all Israel will know you have disgraced them."

What a terrible condition for peace! Finally the elders of the city told Nahash, "Give us seven days to send messengers throughout Israel asking for help. If none come to help us, we will do as you say."

Swift messengers were sent across the Jordan River to Gibeah, the city where Saul lived. When the people heard the bad news, they cried aloud.

Saul heard the wails of his neighbors as he returned from the field. He went to see what was wrong, and they told him the bad news from Jabesh.

Up to this time, Saul had quietly gone about his own work even though he had been anointed king. Now the Spirit of the Lord stirred within him. He must help his people. He sent stern messages to all the Israelites that they would be punished severely if they did not come to help the men of Jabesh.

Everywhere the soldiers of Israel left their homes and hurried to Saul at Bezek. Soon he had a large army. Together they marched across the hills of Benjamin to the Jordan River. Here they waded through the water and climbed the bank on the other side.

They sent messengers to the men of Jabesh, saying, "By the time the sun is hot tomorrow, we will be there to help you."

191

Saul becomes king

How glad and thankful the men of Jabesh were! No longer were they afraid of their enemies. They told the Ammonites, "Tomorrow you can do to us what you think best."

The next day the soldiers of Israel arrived. Saul had divided his men into three companies to fight against the cruel Ammonites. The enemy was so scattered that there were not even two soldiers together in any place. The men of Jabesh were saved from much suffering, and Nahash did not return to fight again.

The Israelites were proud of their king when they saw how brave he was. They praised him. Now they remembered the men who had insulted Saul. "Where are those good-for-nothing men who did not want Saul to be our king? Let us get rid of them right now."

Saul would not permit it. He said, "No man shall be killed today, for the Lord has saved us from our enemies."

Samuel Resigns as Judge of Israel

1 Samuel 11:14—12:25

After the victory against the Ammonites, the men of Israel crossed the Jordan River again. They stopped at Gilgal, the place where their fathers had camped when they first came to Canaan. Here the Israelites sacrificed to the Lord. Saul and all the people rejoiced.

At this time Samuel announced he would no longer be their judge, but he would continue to live among them and tell them God's words. While the people rejoiced with their new king, Samuel looked on sadly. He was disappointed that the people had refused to let God rule over them any longer. Samuel felt he had to warn them once more.

"Now," Samuel said, "your king walks before you, and I am old and gray. I have lived among you since I was a child. You know all about me. Tell me, have I ever judged you wrongly?"

"No," the people answered.

"Have I ever taken anything that did not belong to me or accepted a bribe?"

Again they answered, "No."

Then Samuel said, "The Lord is witness to this truth."

And all the people answered, "He is witness."

Samuel reminded the people of the many ways God had cared for them. God had delivered them from cruel enemies many times, but often the people turned away from God and served idols. Then when trouble came, again the people would cry unto the Lord, "We have sinned when we turned away from you and served idols. Now deliver us from our enemies and we will serve you."

Samuel told the people, "When your enemies were all around you, God protected you. Now you want a man to be your king instead of God. Because you insisted, the Lord has given you a king. If you and your king serve the Lord and obey all his commands, it will be well with you. If you do not, the Lord cannot help you."

Because the people forgot God so easily, Samuel wanted to remind them of God's great power. He told them, "The Lord will send a great thunder and rain. Then you will remember the wrong you have done."

The sky grew dark with heavy clouds. The thunder roared so loudly that the men were afraid. The rain was heavy. In fear the people cried to Samuel, "Pray for us. We have sinned against God. We only added to our wrongdoing when we asked for a king."

Samuel comforted the people, "Do not be afraid. You have done wrong in the past. Now follow the Lord and serve him with all your heart. The Lord will not forsake you. I will pray for you. I will teach you the good and the right. But you must serve the Lord always and remember the great things he has done for you."

As the people returned to their homes, they thought about Samuel's words.

King Saul Offers a Sacrifice

1 Samuel 13

After two years King Saul built a standing army of three thousand soldiers. He stationed two thousand at Michmash and put one thousand under his son Jonathan at Gibeah.

Again the Philistines were causing much trouble in Israel. They were not afraid of King Saul. Throughout the land, they had forts and garrisons.

On a hill not far from Gibeah was an important Philistine garrison. Jonathan and his soldiers attacked that garrison and drove the Philistines away. This only angered the Philistines. Gathering a large army of chariots and horsemen, they came to fight against King Saul.

By now the Israelites must have realized that a king did not help them keep their enemies away. The Philistines had even taken the Israelites' swords and spears and would not allow them to make new weapons. This meant that very few men of Israel were prepared to fight.

King Saul sent swift messengers through the land. They blew trumpets and announced, "Listen, all you people. Saul has taken a Philistine garrison. Now the Philistines are marching against us. Let every man come to Saul at Gilgal."

Because Saul was king, the people answered his call, but they were afraid! The Philistines were a fighting people, and the Israelites did not even have weapons.

When Samuel heard about the trouble, he sent word to Saul that he would come to Gilgal in seven days. Then he would offer sacrifices to God and pray for the king and the people. God would show Samuel what they should do.

At Gilgal King Saul and his men waited for Samuel, but Samuel did not come. While they waited, the Philistines grew stronger. More men came into the Philistine camp. With each new Philistine soldier, the Israelites became more afraid. They were so frightened that they hid in caves, thickets, deep holes and between rocks. Some even deserted and crossed the Jordan.

When Saul saw his men becoming even more afraid, he thought he had to do something to give them courage. Samuel had not come as he had promised. If Saul did not do something quickly, he would have no army left.

Finally he said, "Bring the sacrifices to me and I will offer them." And Saul offered the sacrifices even though he knew God had commanded that only the priests and Levites should do this.

The sacrifice was still burning when Samuel arrived. When he saw what Saul had done he said, "Why have you done this?"

Saul answered, "Because my men were afraid and were running away. We waited for you, but you did not come when you promised. All the time the Philistines were gathering more forces. I was afraid they would attack before we had asked the blessing of the Lord, so I forced myself to offer the sacrifice."

"You have been very foolish," Samuel said sadly. "If you had not disobeyed the Lord, your family would have ruled Israel down through the years. Now your kingdom cannot endure. The Lord is looking for a man who will follow in his ways. He will become king over the people because you have disobeyed the Lord."

Instead of telling Saul what to do about the Philistines, Samuel walked away. When Saul counted his soldiers, there were only six hundred still with him. He marched them back to Gibeah, and the Philistines held their garrison at Michmash.

Jonathan Attacks the Philistines

1 Samuel 14:1-46

While King Saul and his six hundred men stayed at Gibeah, Jonathan took his servant and slipped away. Jonathan, Saul's son, told his armor-bearer, "Come, let us go over to the Philistine camp. Perhaps the Lord will help us. He can save his people by a few as easily as he can by many soldiers."

And the armor-bearer answered, "Do as you wish, and I will be with you."

Then Jonathan explained his plan. "When the Philistines see us, they will call out. If they say, 'Stay there and we will come to you,' we will stand still and not go up to the garrison. But if they say, 'Come up here,' that will be the sign the Lord is with us, and we will take the garrison."

The armor-bearer nodded, and the two started on their way. When they got close to the garrison, the Philistines called out, "Come up and we will show you something."

Jonathan told his servant, "Let us go up, for the Lord is with us."

And the two Israelites took one Philistine after another. Then there was an earthquake, and the ground began to tremble. The Philistines thought a strong army had come to fight them. When they heard the cries of the men Jonathan and his servant had attacked, the Philistines grabbed their weapons and got ready to fight. But instead of attacking Jonathan and his servant, they fought one another. The cry of battle rang out across the valley, and the people at Gibeah heard it.

The men King Saul had appointed to watch the Philistines night and day saw much excitement in the enemy camp. They sent messengers to tell the king, "Men are moving about in every direction. Some are falling and others are running away."

Saul called his soldiers quickly and counted them to see if anyone was missing. They discovered that Jonathan and his armor-bearer were gone. Saul and his men prepared for battle and ran out to join the fight. Even the Israelites who had been hiding in caves and thickets among the rocks crept out to see what all the excitement was about. Then they hurried to join the fight against the Philistines.

The mighty Philistines ran like cowards into the woods. The men of Israel chased after them. In time the Israelites grew tired and weak because they had not eaten all day. Saul had commanded that anyone who stopped long enough to eat would be put to death. Because the soldiers were afraid, they obeyed. Of course they became so tired from the chase and the fighting that many of their enemies got away.

Jonathan did not know about his father's command. As he passed through the woods with a band of men, he found wild honey and ate it.

The men with him said, "Your father commanded that no one should touch food until evening." But their warning was too late.

When Saul heard that Jonathan had eaten, he said, "You have disobeyed my order. Now I must keep my word even though you are my son."

The people asked Saul, "Why should Jonathan die when he has helped us win a great victory over the Philistines?" Because the people interceded, Jonathan was saved.

Saul Disobeys God

1 Samuel 14:47–15:35

The Philistines stayed in their own country after they were defeated at Michmash, but King Saul made war against other nations that troubled his people. He was victorious, and his soldiers honored him as a brave leader.

Saul added to his army every strong and brave young man he could find. No wonder his army grew larger and stronger. Finally Saul chose his cousin Abner to be captain of the forces.

King Saul got along so well that he seemed to forget his success came from God. He felt proud of his many victories. Wrong thoughts crept into his mind. He began to decide what was right to do instead of obeying God's commands.

Before the battle against the Amalekites, Samuel told Saul, "You must destroy everything. You must not take anything you find there."

Saul gathered an army of two hundred and ten thousand men and started for Amalek. On the way he sent messengers to the Kenites who lived among the Amalekites. Saul told them, "I am coming to destroy the Amalekites. Because you have shown kindness to the Israelites, I want you to leave the country at once. If you do not, you will be in the battle against us."

The battle against the Amalekites was a great victory for Saul. Even though Samuel had told him not to keep anything from the battle or take anything that belonged to their enemies, Saul took King Agag prisoner. Then when they discovered the Amalekites' valuable cattle, the Israelites decided, "We will save the best for ourselves." With King Agag and the best cattle, they returned to Israel.

While Saul and his men marched back to their homes, the Lord spoke to Samuel, "I am sorry that I ever made Saul king. He does not follow my ways any more. He does not obey my commandments."

And Samuel, too, was greatly disappointed in Saul. All night he shed bitter tears and prayed for the king.

The next morning Samuel went to meet Saul. When Saul saw the Lord's prophet, he said, "You are blessed of the Lord. I have done just as God commanded."

Samuel looked straight into the king's eyes and asked, "What about the bleating of sheep and the lowing of oxen that I hear?"

Saul explained, "From the battle we brought back the best of the sheep and oxen to sacrifice to the Lord."

Samuel told Saul how God had spoken to him during the night. Still Saul tried to excuse himself and blame the soldiers for wanting to keep the cattle. Samuel reminded the king, "It is better to obey God than to offer him sacrifices. Because you have rejected the word of the Lord, he has rejected you as king of Israel."

At last Saul cried out, "I have sinned because I was afraid of the people and did what they wanted. Go with me, I beg you, that I may worship the Lord."

As Samuel turned away from the king, Saul grabbed his cloak and it was torn. Samuel said, "Just as you have torn my cloak, the Lord has torn your kingdom away from you and given it to your neighbor who is a better man."

Again Saul begged the prophet to pray with him and to go with him to worship the Lord. And Samuel went to Gilgal and offered a sacrifice upon the altar for the sins of the people.

After this Samuel never saw King Saul again. Samuel returned to his home at Ramah. He mourned and wept as if Saul had died, for he knew God could not lead Israel while Saul ruled. How much the Lord wanted a king who would follow his ways!

Samuel Anoints David

1 Samuel 16:1-13

As the days passed, Samuel still mourned that Saul had turned away from the Lord. God asked him, "How long will you mourn for Saul after I have rejected him as the ruler of my people? Now I have chosen another to take his place."

Samuel raised his head and listened to God's words. "Fill your horn with oil, for I want you to go to Bethlehem and anoint the man I have chosen to be the new king."

At first Samuel was afraid to go. He told the Lord, "If Saul learns that I have anointed another king, he will kill me."

God told Samuel to take an offering and go to Bethlehem. Then Samuel was to offer a sacrifice and make a feast for the people. Among the guests he was to invite Jesse and his sons.

The Lord said, "I have chosen one of Jesse's sons. I will tell you which one is to be Israel's next king."

Now Samuel was not afraid to obey God. He quit weeping and filled his horn with oil. Taking a meat offering, he started toward Bethlehem.

When the rulers of the city saw Samuel coming, they were afraid. They asked, "Why have you come?"

Samuel explained, "I have come in peace to sacrifice to the Lord." And Samuel invited the rulers to the feast. Jesse and his sons were to come to the feast too.

Now Jesse had eight sons, but only seven came to the feast. The youngest kept his father's sheep in the fields outside the city.

When Samuel looked at Eliab, Jesse's oldest son, the prophet thought, "Surely this must be the man God has chosen." Samuel liked the looks of this tall, handsome young man.

God told Samuel, "This is not the man. You judge by outward appearance, but I look at the heart."

Then Jesse introduced his son Abinadab to the prophet, but Samuel said, "This is not the man the Lord has chosen."

One after another, Jesse brought his seven sons to Samuel. The prophet only shook his head and said, "God has not chosen any of these. Haven't you another son?"

Jesse replied, "I have one more, but I did not bring him to the feast. He is my youngest. Right now he is in the field caring for the sheep."

"Send for him at once," Samuel said. "We will not eat the feast until he comes." And they waited while a messenger hurried to bring the boy to Samuel.

How surprised David was to see a messenger running toward him! He knew his father and brothers were attending a religious feast. They had been getting ready when he left home that morning. Now as he watched the messenger he wondered if something had happened to his family.

Quickly David rose and pulled his shepherd coat about him. Picking up his rod, he hurried to meet the breathless runner.

"You are wanted in Bethlehem at once," said the messenger. "Samuel, the old prophet, wants to see you. Your father wants you to leave the sheep and come at once."

Samuel waited. Finally a rosy-cheeked, bright-eyed shepherd boy entered the room. What a fine-looking young fellow he was!

And the Lord told Samuel, "Arise and anoint him, for this is the one."

Samuel poured oil on David's head as God had commanded. David knew this was the sign that he would one day be leader of Israel.

After the feast Samuel went home. No longer did he grieve about King Saul, for God had chosen a better person to become king.

David Plays for King Saul

1 Samuel 16:14-23

David did not become king for a long time after Samuel anointed him. The shepherd boy returned to his father's fields near Bethlehem and cared for the sheep. But God sent his Spirit into David's heart at the anointing. Afterwards David thought much about God. As he cared for his sheep, he played sweet music on his harp and made up songs. He praised God as he played and sang. Many of his songs or psalms are recorded in the Bible.

As a shepherd boy David loved the out-of-doors. He liked to see the change of seasons. The hills and valleys, the trees and flowers, the animals, all reminded him of God the Creator. David made songs about these things. He sang so well that he was called the "Sweet Singer of Israel."

When Samuel told Saul that God had rejected him, Saul did not take off his kingly robes and lay aside his crown. He acted as though nothing had happened and went on ruling the people as long as he lived.

After Saul refused to obey God's commands, God took away the good spirit he had given him. Then Saul's heart and mind were troubled. He spent long days feeling downcast and in despair. He acted strangely, almost as if he did not have the right use of his mind.

The servants noticed the change that had come over King Saul. They said to him, "An evil spirit is troubling you. Let us send for a young man who can play sweet, soothing music on his harp. When you hear the music, the evil spirit will leave you."

201

Saul felt so miserable he was willing to try anything. He said, "Find a man who can play the harp well and bring him to me."

One of the servants answered, "Jesse of Bethlehem has a son who plays very well. He is a courageous young man. Also he is tactful, handsome and godly. I have seen this young man myself."

When Saul heard this, he sent a messenger to Jesse at once. "Send me your son David," he said.

Jesse called David from the field and told him about the king's message. After giving David a present for the king, Jesse sent him on his way.

David played his harp for the king, and Saul began to feel better. Soon he felt well again. As Saul listened to David's music and talked with him, Saul loved him greatly. He appointed David as his armor-bearer. Saul felt he needed David so much that he sent word to Jesse, "Let David stay with me, for he pleases me greatly."

From that time David spent much time at the palace. Whenever Saul's mind and heart were tormented, David played his sweet music and Saul was relieved and refreshed. Later David returned to his sheep at Bethlehem.

Little did Saul know that David had been anointed to become king. But David learned much about the duties of a king as he served Saul. Already he was filling his heart and mind with the things he would need to know.

David Kills Goliath

1 Samuel 17:1-54

The Philistines gathered their armies and marched into Israel to fight King Saul and his soldiers. On one mountain the Philistines pitched their tents. On the opposite mountain, the Israelites made camp.

But the battle between the two armies did not begin at once. Instead the Philistines sent one of their soldiers, a giant, to challenge Saul's men. He thundered to the men of Israel, "Why should your whole army battle with us. I am a Philistine. Choose one of your men

203

David plays for King Saul

to fight with me. If I kill him, you will be our servants. If he kills me, we will be your servants."

When the men of Israel saw the great tall giant covered with armor and heard his bellowing voice, they were afraid. No one wanted to fight him. Goliath was nearly twice as large as the ordinary man. Even King Saul, who was head and shoulders taller than any of his men, looked small beside this mighty giant.

Every morning and every evening Goliath called to the Israelite soldiers. Every morning and every evening the men of Israel trembled when they saw the giant and heard his mighty voice. Forty days passed and still no one would fight with him.

Meanwhile David was at home caring for his father's sheep. Three of Jesse's sons were in Saul's army, and Jesse wanted to know how they were getting along. He called David from the field and told him, "Take this corn and these ten loaves of bread to your brothers and give these cheeses to their captain. Find out how your brothers are getting along. Then come back and tell me."

Early the next morning David started to the camp of Israel. When he arrived the soldiers were standing in line for battle. At once David ran to find his brothers. As he talked to them, he noticed how anxiously the soldiers watched the Philistine camp. Their faces even grew pale in fear.

David wondered, "What can this mean?" Then he saw the great giant Goliath and heard his thunderous shouts. He saw Saul's soldiers turn and run like frightened sheep.

When David talked with the men, they told him about Goliath. "Have you noticed what a giant he is? If a man kills Goliath, the king will give him riches and let him marry his daughter. King Saul has even promised to pay the debts the man's father owes." Even with such a reward, no one would fight with the giant.

David said, "Why should this wicked Philistine bother us? I will go out and kill him."

How surprised the soldiers were when they heard that! Again they told him how terrible Goliath was. Still David did not back down. The soldiers ran to tell the king.

Eliab was angry and embarrassed that his young brother would say such a thing in front of the soldiers. "Why did you come here?" Eliab asked angrily. "And who is taking care of the sheep while you are gone? Did you just come here to watch?"

"What have I done to make you angry?" David wanted to know. Just then a messenger came to take David to the king.

When David was brought to the king, he said, "Don't let anyone be afraid of Goliath. I will fight with him."

Saul looked at the young shepherd who stood before him. "You cannot fight against this Philistine," Saul said. "You are just a youth, and he has had long years of experience in battle."

David told the king, "I take care of my father's sheep. At different times a lion and a bear grabbed a lamb out of the flock. Both times, I rescued the lamb and killed the wild animal. This Philistine giant will be just like one of those wild animals. The Lord who helps me protect my sheep will help me defeat this Philistine."

When Saul heard this, he said to David, "Go, and the Lord be with you."

Since David was wearing the clothes of a shepherd, Saul ordered that his own armor be given to the youth. The brass helmet was put on David's head. The heavy metal coat was fastened around him. A sword was placed in his hand. But David could not move in this heavy armor.

He told Saul, "I cannot wear these. I am not used to them." He took off the armor and put on his own clothes. Then he went to meet Goliath.

At the brook he bent down and picked up five smooth stones. These he put in his shepherd's bag. Taking out his sling, he walked toward the giant.

How surprised Goliath was when he saw David coming toward him without a weapon! Were the Israelites making fun of him by sending this youth? Goliath roared out, "Am I a dog that you come to fight me with a stick?" He threatened to tear David to pieces.

David did not turn back. Instead he called out, "You come against me with a sword and a spear and a shield, but I come against you in the name of the Lord God of hosts. You have defied the Lord, and today the Lord will deliver you into my hand. Then all the earth will know there is a Lord God in Israel. And all those who watch will know that the Lord does not give victory with the sword and spear. The Lord will help us win this battle."

The giant in his heavy armor moved slowly toward David. David took a stone out of his bag and ran toward Goliath. David put the stone in his sling and threw it. The stone hit the giant on the forehead, and he fell to the earth with a great thud.

The Philistines did not wait to see more. They knew God was against them, and they ran. They left their tents and belongings behind and raced as fast as they could go. Saul's army chased after them.

There was great rejoicing among the men of Israel. They knew God had delivered them from their strong enemies.

Saul Becomes David's Enemy

1 Samuel 17:55—18:30

Before David fought against Goliath, few people had heard of him. When the king saw David's bravery, he must have wondered whether David came from a family of warriors. Perhaps the king wanted to find out about David's family because he had promised one of his daughters to the person who killed Goliath.

When David returned from the fight, Saul asked, "What family do you come from?"

David reminded him, "I am the son of Jesse. My father lives at Bethlehem."

As Saul's son Jonathan watched the young hero return to the palace, he admired David greatly. The two became acquainted. After Saul commanded David to stay at the palace, Jonathan and David were together often.

To show David how much he loved him, Jonathan took off his princely robe and gave it to David. Also he gave David his sword and his bow. With these gifts went Jonathan's promise always to be David's friend.

Because David had defeated Goliath, Saul made him captain of the army. David did whatever the king commanded.

And David became the favorite—of his men, of the people, of the servants. At first Saul did not pay any attention to David's popularity. Then Saul heard the women going through the streets singing, playing their instruments and making merry. They sang that Saul had defeated thousands of their enemies. And Saul felt proud as he listened. But then the women sang that David had defeated tens of thousands.

How angry Saul became! The women thought David was greater than he. In his heart Saul was jealous of David. He thought, "The next thing I know David will have my kingdom. I must watch him closely." From that day on Saul hated David.

Saul was so angry and jealous that the evil spirit swept over him. Again his mind and heart were tormented. As before David played on the harp for the king. This time David's sweet music only made the king feel worse. Two different times as David played Saul threw a spear at him. Both times David saw the spear coming and dodged.

Now Saul was sure that God was with David, and the king was afraid. No longer could he have David as head of the army, so he let David be captain of just one thousand men.

In spite of this treatment, David acted wisely. The Lord was helping him.

When Saul noticed how well David took his demotion, he was even more afraid. Even though he had promised his daughter to the man who defeated Goliath, Saul had her marry another man.

Everyone loved David, even Saul's younger daughter Michal. When Saul heard about this, he planned another way to get rid of David. If David could kill one hundred Philistines, he could marry Michal. Saul believed that David would be killed in the fight.

How surprised Saul was when David returned from battle after killing twice as many enemies as the king had ordered! Now Saul had to let David marry Michal.

As the days passed, the king noticed how much his daughter loved David. That made Saul all the more jealous and afraid. Again he sent David into battle, and David did so well that he was honored throughout the land.

Jonathan and Michal Save David's Life

1 Samuel 19

At first King Saul tried to keep secret his hatred and jealousy of David. He pretended to be friendly while he planned David's death. When his plans failed, Saul became bolder. Finally he ordered Jonathan and his servants to kill David.

How terrible Jonathan felt when he heard this! David was his friend. It hurt Jonathan to see his father act like this. Jonathan ran to David and said, "My father wants to kill you. Find a safe place to hide until morning. I will talk to him and try to change his mind. Then I will tell you what happens."

As soon as David had run outside the city to hide, Jonathan went to his father. He said, "Do not let yourself sin against David. He has never done any wrong to you, but he has done many good things for you. He risked his own life to kill the giant and deliver Israel. You were glad when you saw it. Why then do you want to kill an innocent man?"

Saul listened and felt ashamed of how jealous he had been. He promised, "David shall not be killed."

Jonathan hurried to David's hiding place to tell him the good news. Together they returned to Gibeah. David came and went in Saul's presence as before. Saul did not try to harm him.

Then war broke out with the old-time enemies, the Philistines. Saul sent David to fight against them. Once more David defeated the Philistines and drove them back into their own land.

When David returned victorious from battle, Saul was more jealous than ever before. Again his heart and mind were sorely troubled. David came to play sweet music, but having David around only made the king more troubled. How he wished to be rid of David! Picking up his spear, he threw it at the young man. Because David was on his guard, the spear missed its mark, and he ran out of the room.

Saul was so angry he sent messengers to guard David's house during the night and capture him in the morning.

When Michal found out about the plan, she told her husband, "If you don't get away tonight, you will be killed tomorrow."

She let David down through a window, and he escaped. Then she put pillows in the bed to make it look as if David was sleeping there.

In the morning Saul sent messengers to get David. Michal told them, "He is ill."

When Saul heard this he commanded, "Bring him to me, bed and all."

The messengers obeyed. When the covers were pulled back, they saw only pillows in the bed. Saul knew his daughter had saved David's life.

When David left his home, he went to Ramah where Samuel lived. He told the old prophet everything that had happened. Samuel took David to Naioth. Here Samuel taught the young prophets.

Saul heard that David was with Samuel at Naioth. He sent messengers to capture David. When the messengers came to Naioth, they found Samuel teaching the prophets. As Saul's men listened, the Spirit of God filled their hearts and they worshiped the Lord.

How angry Saul was that his messengers had disobeyed him! He sent more men and the same thing happened. A third time he sent messengers, but this time, too, the men worshiped God instead of doing as Saul commanded.

Finally Saul said, "I myself will go, and I will capture David." But when he came to Naioth and heard the prophets praying and worshiping God, Saul bowed down and worshiped too. For a night and a day, he stayed with the prophets.

Jonathan Warns David

1 Samuel 20

While Saul was at Naioth, David returned and found Jonathan. "What have I done?" David wanted to know. "Why does your father want to kill me?"

Jonathan said, "Don't worry. You won't be killed. My father doesn't do anything, large or small, without talking it over with me first. He would not hide any plans from me."

Still David did not feel safe. "Your father knows we are friends, and he will not tell you about his plans for me. I tell you I am only one step away from death."

When Jonathan promised to do anything he could to help, David explained, "Tomorrow is the beginning of the feast. Saul will expect me to eat at his table. I will hide during the feast. If Saul becomes angry because I do not come, you will know he intends to take my life. But if he speaks well of me, then you will know it is safe for me to return."

Jonathan promised to let David know. On the third day David was to hide behind a great rock in the field. Jonathan would come in the morning with a little boy to pick up the arrows. If he told the boy the arrows were on one side of the rock, David would know it was safe to return to his home. If he told the boy the arrows were beyond him, David would know he should run for his life.

Saul's family and guests sat around his table at the feast, but David's place was empty. The first day Saul did not mention it. The second day Saul lashed out against David. When Jonathan defended his friend, his father said in anger, "You foolish son. Don't you know you will never be king as long as David lives?"

Jonathan asked, "What has he done to deserve death?"

Saul was so angry that he threw his spear at Jonathan. Now Jonathan knew that David's life was in great danger. He left the table and would not eat anything all day.

In the morning Jonathan told the boy, "Come with me to the field near the city. I am going to shoot with my bow and arrows. You can watch where the arrows fall and get them for me."

The two started off together. Outside the city they came to a wide field. The little boy felt proud to be walking with a prince. Perhaps he even tried to make his steps as long as Jonathan's. Perhaps his eyes sparkled when he saw Jonathan's shining bow.

Finally they stopped and Jonathan fitted an arrow into his bow. He aimed carefully and shot. The boy watched the arrow fall and ran to pick it up. As he ran Jonathan shot another arrow farther away. He called to the boy, "The arrow is beyond you. Run, hurry, don't wait!"

The boy did not know this was a signal. After he got the arrows, Jonathan sent him back to the city.

David came out of hiding, and Jonathan ran to meet him. The two friends were so sad that their eyes were filled with tears. Jonathan told David, "Go in peace and may the Lord be with you."

David hurried away and Jonathan walked slowly back to the city.

David Flees for His Life

1 Samuel 21:1–22:5

Because Saul was about to take David's life, David ran to find safety. He came to a city called Nob. The tabernacle had been moved here after the Philistines stole the ark of God. The priests cared for the tabernacle every day. Ahimelech was the high priest.

How surprised Ahimelech was to see David come running into the tabernacle! He knew David was a brave captain, and it seemed very strange to see David by himself. Ahimelech asked, "Why are you alone?"

David did not want anyone to know he was running from King Saul lest someone report him to the king. He said, "The king has sent me on a secret mission."

As David looked at the bread in Ahimelech's hand, he remembered how hungry he was. "Give me the five loaves of bread you have, for I am very hungry," he said.

While David ate the bread, one of Saul's servants saw him. It was Doeg, Saul's head herdsman. Now David knew he must find another place to hide.

"Give me a sword," David told Ahimelech. "I left in such a hurry that I forgot mine." The priest handed David Goliath's sword.

Just having this sword in his hand made David feel better. He remembered how God had helped him when he faced Goliath. "There is no sword like this one," he said.

Poor David! He did not know where to hide, but he had to go somewhere. Surely Saul would not look for him among the Philistines, so David crossed the border into enemy territory. He went to Achish, king of the Philistines.

When the Philistines saw David, they asked Achish, "Isn't this David of Israel? Do not the people sing of him, 'Saul has slain his

Jonathan aims carefully

thousands, but David his ten thousands?'" And the Philistines wanted to keep David as their prisoner.

David soon discovered he was not safe here either. He wished he had never come to this city. Achish might even try to kill him. Finally David decided to pretend he was crazy. Maybe the Philistines would be afraid of him and let him go.

Achish brought David before the people and said, "Look, this man is crazy. Why bring him to me? Do you think I need a crazy man in my court?"

When the Philistines saw how David acted, they decided they did not want him. David escaped and returned to Israel. As he went through the wilderness, he found a cave among the rocks. Here in the cave of Adullam he hid for many days.

David's family found out about his hiding place and came to live with him there. Their lives, too, were in danger.

How sorry David felt to see his old father and mother driven away from their home with no place to live! He left his hiding place and took them to Moab where his great-grandmother Ruth had lived.

He asked the king of Moab, "Let my father and mother live here until I know what the Lord will do for me." The king of Moab agreed, and David's parents were safe.

David returned to the cave of Adullam. Somehow word got around that David was hiding there. Many people joined him. All who were in trouble or in debt or in any distress came. They thought life would be better for them if David were their leader. Soon David had an army of four hundred men.

Saul Orders the Priests' Death

1 Samuel 22:6-23

After David fled from Gibeah, Saul tried to find him. Strangely enough no one seemed to know where David had gone. No one wanted to get David into trouble with bad-tempered Saul.

Saul made his headquarters under a tree and sat with spear in hand waiting to hear of David's whereabouts. One day someone told Saul that David had a small army near the cave of Adullam.

"Why haven't my servants told me about David's hiding place?" Saul wondered. Saul snarled at them, "Listen to me! What can David do for you? Will he give you fields and vineyards and make you captains of his army? Is that why none of you will tell me about David? Even my own son Jonathan is against me and stirs up the people to take sides with David."

Among the servants that day was Doeg, the head of all Saul's herdsmen. He stepped up boldly and told the king, "I saw David in the city of Nob. He was talking to the high priest, Ahimelech. Ahimelech prayed for David, gave him food and handed him Goliath's sword."

Saul believed that Ahimelech, the high priest, had helped David find a safe hiding place. Quickly he sent for all the priests who lived at Nob.

When they came Saul spoke harshly, "Listen to me, Ahimelech!"

The priest did not know why Saul was so disturbed. He answered, "Here am I, my lord."

Saul ignored Ahimelech's politeness and lashed out, "Why have you and David plotted against me? Why did you give him bread and Goliath's sword? Did you pray that the Lord would help him get the better of me?"

How surprised Ahimelech was to hear these words! He said, "Why, David is one of your most faithful servants. Isn't he your son-in-law? Doesn't he go wherever you send him? That is why I talked to the Lord about him. My king, do not hold this against me or against my family. I knew nothing about the trouble between you and David."

Saul hated to be reminded of David's good qualities. He hated to think David was his son-in-law. Even the high priest honored David. This made Saul furious. He cried, "You and all your priests who helped David get away from me will be punished. You must die."

It didn't matter to Saul that the priests were God's men. He commanded the soldiers, "Kill these priests because they have helped David get away from me."

But the soldiers feared God more than they feared Saul. They said, "We cannot kill the Lord's priests."

So Saul commanded dishonorable Doeg to do this terrible deed. And Doeg obeyed. He even hurried to Nob and killed others there.

One of Ahimelech's sons, Abiathar, escaped and ran to David with the terrible news.

David was greatly troubled. He said, "The day I saw Doeg in the tabernacle, I knew he would tell Saul. I feel to blame for your father's death."

Then David thought about Abiathar. Saul would want to kill this young man too. David said, "Stay with me. The man who wants to kill me is after you too. With me you will be safe."

Later Abiathar became the high priest. He was with David through all his years of trouble and served David faithfully.

Saul Hunts David

1 Samuel 23

Not far from David's hiding place was the city of Keilah. The Philistines fought against the men of Keilah and stole their grain.

When David heard this, he prayed, "Shall I go and save the people of Keilah from the Philistines?" God told him to go.

David told his men the words of the Lord. They said, "We are afraid here, but we would be even more afraid to fight against the Philistine armies."

A second time David prayed, and God gave the men courage. David and his men defeated the Philistines and saved the people of Keilah.

When Saul heard that David had driven the Philistines out of Keilah and marched into the city, he thought of a plan. "Now is my chance," he decided. "I will capture my enemy, for he is in a trap." Saul thought it would be easy to capture David inside the walls of Keilah. Saul gathered his army together and started after David.

Abiathar, the priest, had gone with David to Keilah. When they heard that Saul was coming, David told Abiathar to find out from God what they should do.

David also prayed, and God told David he was not safe inside the city. Taking his soldiers, David hurried out of the city and hid in the thick woodland.

There Jonathan came to see David. How glad they were to see each other again! Jonathan said, "Don't be afraid, for my father will not find you. You will be the next king of Israel, and I will be next in power to you. My father knows that."

David and Jonathan renewed their promise of friendship, and the two parted. This was the last time they saw each other.

David went from one place to another to hide in the mountains, woods and caves. Everywhere he went Saul followed after with his army of three thousand men.

At one time Saul and his men were on one side of the mountain and David and his men were on the other. David thought Saul was about to overtake him, but a messenger brought news that the Philistines had invaded Israel again.

Saul did not pursue David any farther but went to fight the enemy. Again David was safe for a time.

David Spares Saul's Life

1 Samuel 24—25

After Saul had taken care of the troublesome Philistines, he went looking for David again. With his army he came to the wilderness of Engedi where David and his men were hiding in a great cave.

Saul became so tired from the march that he went into the cave to rest awhile. He did not see David and his soldiers standing in the shadows at the sides of the cave.

They watched Saul lie down. When he fell asleep, David crept up to him and cut off part of his robe. David's soldiers wanted to kill Saul. They knew he was not a good ruler and God was displeased with him. David reminded his men, "Do not touch him, for he has been anointed of God."

Saul awoke and walked out of the cave to join his men. David followed and said, "My lord and king."

The king turned and saw David bowing before him.

David said, "Why do you listen to people who say I want to take your life? Today I could have killed you while you slept in the cave.

Some of my men wanted me to do that, but I would not do anything to harm the Lord's anointed."

Saul was so surprised to see David that he didn't know what to say.

David went on, "See, I have a piece of your robe that I cut off. Now you know I would not harm you, yet you would take my life. The Lord judge between us."

The king was so moved that the tears rolled down his cheeks. He remembered how much he had once loved David. Saul said, "You are a better man than I, for you have done good to me while I was trying to kill you. Today the Lord let me fall into your hands, and you spared my life. I know that you will one day be king of Israel."

After this talk Saul took his army and returned to his home at Gibeah. Perhaps he thought he would never trouble David again.

David believed Saul would soon change his mind and come looking for him again. He took his men and found another place to hide.

About this time Samuel died. All the Israelites gathered to mourn his death and to bury him at Ramah.

David Finds Saul Asleep

1 Samuel 26—27

David hid in the wilderness of Ziph, but he was not safe. The people of Ziph told Saul where David was. As soon as Saul heard the news, he took his army of three thousand men and went after David. After weary marching Saul and his army camped in the wilderness.

Saul's coming was no surprise to David, for he had spies on the watch. They told him about Saul's doings.

"Now," thought David, "I will go and visit Saul's camp tonight. Perhaps I can show him again that I would not harm him." David turned to his men and asked, "Who will go with me to see Saul at his camp?"

Abishai said, "I will go with you."

When the two entered Saul's camp, all the soldiers were sound asleep—even Abner, Saul's brave captain. David and Abishai made their way to the center of the camp. There they found Saul asleep.

His spear was stuck in the ground near his head. His bottle of water was within reach.

Abishai wanted to kill Saul, but David insisted, "We cannot do that, for Saul is God's anointed. The Lord will take care of Saul for the wrong he has done. Let as take his spear and the bottle of water."

Quietly one reached for the bottle while the other pulled Saul's spear out of the ground. Then without making a sound, they crept out of camp. No one heard them come and no one heard them go away.

The two climbed the hill outside of camp. Then David called loudly to Abner, the captain of Saul's army. "Abner, Abner!" he called. "Why don't you answer, Abner?"

Abner awoke with a start. He knew it was David's voice, and he was afraid.

David said, "Are you one of the bravest men in all Israel? Why then did you leave the king without your protection? While you were asleep, someone stole into your camp to kill Saul. Instead he took Saul's spear and bottle of water. I have them here."

Saul, too, was awakened by David's voice. He called out, "Is that you, my son David?" Again he felt ashamed when he found out how easily David could have harmed him. Saul said, "I have sinned. Return, my son David, for I will not harm you. I have been a fool and made many mistakes."

From the other hill David answered, "Send one of your soldiers to get your spear. I could not harm God's anointed."

Even though Saul wanted David to return to Gibeah, David remembered other times Saul had broken his promise. He was afraid to believe the king. Instead of going back to live in Gibeah, he took his soldiers and went to live in a city the Philistines gave them. Here David lived until he learned about Saul's death.

Saul Dies

1 Samuel 28:3-25; 31

Saul's troubles began when he disobeyed God and did just as he pleased. His troubles grew bigger and bigger as he allowed wrong thoughts to creep into his mind. His mind became so filled with wrong thoughts that it was easier for him to do wrong than to do right.

After many years of trouble, Saul became an old man. And what a miserable old man he was! He thought everyone was against him. Nowhere could he find happiness and contentment.

Again the Philistines invaded Israel. Not only did they steal from Saul's people, but they even took his cities. All the while they became bolder and bolder. Saul knew he was no longer able to drive them out of the land. He must have remembered the times he had sent David to fight against the Philistines. He must have thought about how God had helped David to be victorious.

Since Saul did not have a great leader to send against the Philistines, he had to go himself. He gathered all the soldiers of Israel and led them out to the battlefield where Gideon had led three hundred brave men to a great victory many years before.

But Saul did not feel as courageous as Gideon had. How afraid he was when he saw the Philistines mustering their forces in the valley! What should he do?

Since Saul had commanded so many of the priests to be killed, he could not find a single priest in all the land who would tell him God's will. Nor was there any prophet who would help Saul. Even old faithful Samuel was dead, and God would not speak to Saul.

Saul was so desperate that he went to see a witch who lived at Endor. Perhaps she could tell him what to do to win the battle. Instead Saul heard words that frightened him more than ever. He learned that he and his three sons would be killed the next day and that the Philistines would win a great victory.

On the next day the battle began. The Philistines overpowered the men of Israel and killed many of them. Saul's three sons, Jonathan and his two brothers, fell dead on the battlefield. Saul was badly wounded by an arrow. He knew he would die, and he was afraid the Philistines would torture him if they found him alive.

Saul commanded his armor-bearer to kill him, but the armor-bearer said, "I cannot kill the Lord's anointed."

In despair Saul fell on his own sword and died. At night brave men of Israel took the bodies of Saul and his sons to bury them.

David Mourns for Saul and Jonathan

1 Samuel 29–30; 2 Samuel 1:1–2:3

David, his men and their families had been living in Ziklag, the city the Philistines had given them. While David and his men were away, the Amalekites set fire to Ziklag and captured all the women and children. When David discovered what had happened, he took his men and went after the Amalekites. They recovered their wives and children, but when they returned to Ziklag, they had no homes to live in.

As they wondered what to do, a messenger came running to David. When David saw that the messenger's clothes were torn, he knew the messenger had bad news. David asked, "Where have you come from?"

The man answered, "I escaped from the camp of Israel."

David urged the man, "How did the battle go? Hurry up, tell me the news!"

"The men of Israel ran from the battle," the man said, "and many were killed. Saul and Jonathan were killed too."

It was hard for David to believe that Saul and Jonathan were dead. He asked, "How do you know this is so?"

The messenger explained that he had seen Saul fall on his sword. "I took the crown off his head and the bracelet from his arm. These I have brought to you."

David felt crushed with sorrow. He tore his clothes, and the men who were with him did the same. In anguish David said, "These mighty men of Israel have fallen! Do not let the Philistines know it, for they will rejoice in their triumph. During their lives Saul and Jonathan were close to each other. In their death they are not divided. I shall miss Jonathan so much, for he was my best friend."

And David prayed, "Shall I return to Judah?" When the Lord told him to return, David asked, "To which place shall I go?" The Lord told him to return to Hebron.

David took his men and their families to Hebron to live.

David reigns as King

David Becomes King

2 Samuel 2:4—6:18

After David went to live at Hebron, the men of Judah made David their king. For a few years the other tribes of Israel were ruled by Ishbosheth, Saul's son.

When Abner, captain of Saul's army, and Ishbosheth were dead, the other leaders of Israel came to David with this message: "We are all your brothers, and we know God has chosen you to be our ruler." They made him king over all the land.

David wanted to make Jerusalem the chief city. First he drove out the Jebusites, a strange people who had lived around Jerusalem for many years. On Mount Zion he had his royal palace built.

The Philistines were still ruling many places throughout the land of Israel. Because they knew David would make trouble for them, they gathered their armies and came near Jerusalem to fight against David.

David did not run out to meet them. He asked God, "Shall I march against the Philistines? Will you go with me?"

David did as the Lord commanded, and his soldiers won a great victory over the Philistines. Their enemies ran off in such a hurry that they left their idols behind. David and his men gathered the idols and burned them.

Soon the Philistines marched back into the same valley for another battle. Again David prayed. God told him, "Do not rush into battle, but station your forces under the mulberry trees. When you hear the wind in the tops of the trees, that will be your signal to go into battle."

David did exactly as the Lord commanded, and God helped him drive all the Philistines out of the land. Never again did they come back to bother Israel while David was king.

David wanted to bring the ark of God to Jerusalem. He knew about God's plan for the ark to be kept inside the tabernacle, and so he built a new tabernacle for it. Then he sent word to the people throughout the land telling them that the ark was to be moved to Jerusalem.

An army of thirty thousand men came to see the ark moved. A new cart had been built to carry the ark. David and a company of musicians walked in front. They played on harps and other instruments and sang praises to God. Everyone rejoiced.

Suddenly the music stopped and everyone halted. As the oxen pulled the cart over a rough place in the road, the ark rocked as if it might fall off. When the driver saw that, he put his hand on the ark to steady it. When his hand touched the ark, he fell dead. God had commanded that no one but the priests should ever touch the ark, but the people had forgotten God's command.

"What can this mean?" everyone wondered. David was frightened too. He did not want to take the ark any farther. He left the ark at the home of a man who lived nearby. Then David and all the people went back to their homes.

Later David sent priests to carry the ark on their shoulders to the tabernacle at Jerusalem. Again David and the other musicians went before the ark, singing and playing on their musical instruments. When the ark was safely inside the tabernacle, they offered sacrifices to the Lord.

The Lame Prince

2 Samuel 4:4; 9:1-13

Mephibosheth is a very long name for a very small boy. But Jonathan, the prince of Israel, thought it was a very good name for his little son.

One day Jonathan kissed his little boy good-bye and went away to battle at Mount Gilboa. Jonathan never returned, for he was killed in that battle against the Philistines. Even his father, King Saul, and many other soldiers of Israel were killed in battle that day.

When this news was brought to the city of Gibeah, everyone was panic-stricken. The king's household knew their lives were in great danger. Even the servants were afraid. So the servants and all the people who lived in the palace ran away.

Mephibosheth was not big enough to run very fast or very far, for he was only five years old. He could not understand why everyone was in such a hurry.

His nurse picked him up in her arms and ran. But as she ran she stumbled, and the little prince fell to the ground. Both his feet were hurt so badly that he was never able to run again. With a kind man Mephibosheth lived in safety across the Jordan River.

After Jonathan's death David missed him very much. When David went to Jerusalem to live, he remembered his promise to show kindness to Jonathan's children.

David asked Ziba, who had been a servant in Saul's palace, "Are any of Jonathan's family still living?"

Ziba said, "Jonathan has a crippled son."

David found out where Mephibosheth lived and sent for him. Mephibosheth, now a young man, was afraid when he knew the king wanted to see him. What could the king want?

When Mephibosheth was brought to David, he knelt to the ground. He said, "I am your servant."

How glad David was to see Jonathan's son! He said, "Mephibosheth, do not be afraid of me. I want to show you kindness for your father's sake. I want to give you all the land that once belonged to your grandfather, King Saul. You are welcome to live in my palace and eat at my table every day."

Mephibosheth was surprised, for he had not expected such kindness. David called Ziba and made him overseer of all the lands and fields that were now Mephibosheth's.

The lame prince brought his wife and little son to Jerusalem to live. For Jonathan's sake David was kind to Mephibosheth as long as he lived.

David's Sin

2 Samuel 11:1–12:25

David was a wise man who loved God, but he was often tempted to do wrong. One day he saw a beautiful woman named Bathsheba, and he wanted to marry her. When David inquired about Bathsheba, he found out she was already married to a soldier named Uriah.

David welcomes Mephibosheth

How much David wanted Bathsheba for his wife! At his command Uriah was stationed at a dangerous place in the battle line so he would be killed. When Uriah was dead, David married Bathsheba.

Then Nathan, the prophet, came to see David and told him a story. He said, "A rich man and a poor man were neighbors. The rich man had many flocks and herds, but the poor man had only a pet lamb. One day the rich man had company. Instead of killing one of his own sheep, he killed his neighbor's pet lamb and roasted it for his guest."

How angry David was at the rich man! He thought the rich man should be punished severely.

Nathan answered, "That was a story, but you are just like that rich man. Because you wanted to marry Uriah's wife, you made sure he would be killed in battle."

Now David realized what a terrible thing he had done. He said, "I have sinned against the Lord." He knew he deserved to be punished for this great wrong. Although God forgave David's sin, he did not take away the punishment that the sin caused.

David and Bathsheba's first baby died. Later God gave them another child. They named the boy Solomon. God told David that someday Solomon would be king of Israel.

Absalom Tries to Become King

2 Samuel 15–17

Absalom was the most handsome prince who lived in the palace at Jerusalem. He did not act like his father, David. As he grew to manhood, he dreamed about the time his father would die and he could be king of Israel. Perhaps he did not know that God had already chosen his younger brother Solomon to be the third king of Israel.

As time passed Absalom got tired waiting for his father to die. He did not want to wait to become king. First he became very friendly with all the people who visited Jerusalem.

Absalom stood by the gate. When any man came to the king with any trouble, Absalom would ask, "Where do you come from?" As he talked with the stranger, he would find out what the stranger's trouble was and say, "Your claims are good and right, but the king has no one to listen to your troubles. If only I were king, every person could come to me and I would help."

Such kindness won the hearts of the people. Also they liked Absalom because he was so young and good-looking. They began to feel he would make a great king.

While this was happening, David was busy with his work. He did not know what Absalom was doing. One morning Absalom said to David, "Let me go to Hebron to worship God."

David said, "Go, my son." He was glad Absalom wanted to worship God.

But Absalom was only tricking his father. He had just given his father an excuse. Now he could leave Jerusalem easily and gather all his followers at Hebron. There they would make him king. Then he would return, take Jerusalem and rule in his father's place.

Perhaps Absalom planned to take his father by surprise, but a messenger hurried to tell David what was happening at Hebron. Quickly David called his faithful servants and told them, "Let us get away from the city as fast as possible. If Absalom and his followers find us, they will kill us and take the city."

And the servants told the king, "We will do whatever you say."

How disturbed David was! His own son wanted to kill him and take his place. He left the palace and Jerusalem a disappointed, broken man. And David's servants wept with him when they thought about Absalom's terrible plans.

The priests took the ark of God and started to follow David too, but David ordered them to return to Jerusalem. They could stay in the city and let David know what was going on. The priests obeyed.

The wise man Hushai hurried to join David. He tore off his coat and covered his head with dust to show the people how sorry he felt for David.

David said, "Hushai, I want you to go back to Jerusalem. Pretend to be Absalom's friend so you can find out about his plans. Tell the priests any news you want me to know. They will send me messengers with the news."

Hushai started back to Jerusalem. David and his followers traveled toward the wilderness near the Jordan River.

When Absalom and his friends came to the palace at Jerusalem, they discovered that David and his servants had run away. Absalom was so surprised to find Hushai that he said, "Is this the way you show kindness to your friend David? Why didn't you go with him?"

Hushai answered, "I want to befriend the man the Lord and the people choose to be king. Why shouldn't I serve you just as I served your father?" And because Hushai was a very wise man, Absalom was glad to have him.

At once Absalom and his friends began to plan how to capture David and win all his followers. They decided to send out an army that very night to find David and kill him.

But Hushai said, "Your plan is not good. David is a mighty soldier, and his soldiers know how to fight bravely. They will defeat your few men. First you should get a large army and be their leader. Then go after the king."

Absalom thought Hushai's advice was best. He sent messengers to call the soldiers of Israel together. While the army gathered, Hushai sent word to David to cross the Jordan River at once.

As the messengers hurried to tell David, someone reported them to Absalom. Absalom sent soldiers to catch them, but the messengers hid in a well until the soldiers returned to the city. Then they hurried to David. When David heard their news, he took his company and crossed the Jordan River.

Absalom Loses His Life

2 Samuel 18–19

Absalom thought his soldiers would be braver and more fearless if he led them into battle, but Absalom had not been trained as a warrior. Yet, as all kings did, he led his men out of the chief city to meet the enemy. Many, many armed men followed him to fight against David's experienced soldiers.

Meanwhile kind friends cared for David in the city of Mahanaim. David wanted to go with his men into battle, but they said, "Do not go with us. If we run from Absalom's men or even if half of us are killed, it won't make much difference. But you, O King, are worth ten thousand of us. It is better for you to stay here."

David promised, "I will do what you think best." Then he divided his soldiers into three companies and sent them to meet Absalom's forces in the woods of Ephraim.

As the men started out David told them, "For my sake be kind to my son Absalom if you should meet him face to face." Even though Absalom had tried to take his kingdom, David still loved his son. When the men were gone, he sat by the gate and waited to hear the first news of the battle.

David's men were victorious in battle. Many of Absalom's soldiers were killed and others ran off through the thick woods and got lost. Absalom, too, tried to escape through the woods on his mule. At one place the mule ran under an oak tree that had low branches. The branches caught Absalom by his head. Because the mule did not stop running, Absalom hung by his head in mid-air.

One of David's men saw what happened, and he remembered David's words, "For my sake be kind to my son Absalom." The man ran quickly to tell Captain Joab about the young prince.

Joab asked roughly, "Why didn't you kill Absalom when you saw him?"

The soldier replied, "Because David commanded us to spare Absalom's life."

As chief captain of David's army, Joab was not always careful to obey David's orders. He was a cruel man who sometimes did things David did not approve. This time Joab hurried to the oak tree and found Absalom still alive. Joab killed the prince. Joab's men threw Absalom's body into a deep hole and covered it with a mound of stones.

When Absalom's soldiers heard that their leader had been killed, all of them turned and ran. They had nothing left to fight for, and they were afraid of David's men. They crossed the Jordan River and returned to their homes as fast as they could go.

Joab told Cushi, "Go, tell the king what you have seen."

As soon as Cushi was gone, Ahimaaz, son of one of the priests, begged permission to carry a message to David.

Joab said, "You have nothing to tell. I have already sent Cushi."

Still Ahimaaz begged permission to go, and Joab gave in. Ahimaaz ran so fast that he was the first one to reach David. He told the king, "All is well. The men who fought against the king have been defeated."

"And is Absalom safe?" David wanted to know.

Ahimaaz answered, "When Joab let me come, there was much excitement, but I cannot tell you what it was about."

In raced Cushi with the news, "Tidings, my lord the king." And Cushi reported the victory.

Again David asked anxiously, "Is young Absalom safe?"

Cushi knew how much David loved his son, and it was hard to tell him the bad news. Finally he said, "May all your enemies and those who turn against you be as that young man is." Then David knew Absalom was dead.

Instead of rejoicing about the victory, King David covered his face and cried aloud because his son was dead. Over and over he cried, "O my son Absalom! My son! My son! I wish I had died instead of you." When the people heard David weeping, they were sad too.

Finally Joab came to David and said, "The people will think you love your enemies more than you love your friends. They have risked their lives to save you from danger. Now all you do is weep because your enemies have been killed. You do not thank the people who saved you. Do you want them to leave you too?"

David knew Joab was right. He stopped weeping and went to the gate to speak to his followers.

Not long afterward David and his followers returned to live in Jerusalem. David showed much kindness to those who helped him during his trouble.

David Counts His Soldiers

2 Samuel 24; 1 Chronicles 21—22

Under David's rule Israel grew from a weak, oppressed nation to a very powerful one. The heathen nations round about believed that God had made Israel powerful.

God wanted his people to trust in him instead of in their own strength as the other nations did. Yet when Israel grew so strong that the other nations were afraid to oppose it, David began to trust in the strength of his army just as other kings did. More and more he began to wonder how many soldiers he had in his kingdom. "How large an army could I raise in case of war?" he wondered.

God knew David trusted the army more than he trusted the Lord, and God was not pleased.

David commanded his chief captain, Joab, "Go count the soldiers in Israel and Judah."

Joab did not approve of David's plan. He asked, "Why do you want to do this?" Still David insisted. Joab took men with him and went throughout the land to count the soldiers.

When the counting was finished, a great sickness came upon the land, and many people died. Everywhere there was sorrow and death. David's heart was heavy for his people.

God sent an angel to the city. When David saw the angel, he cried out, "I have sinned and done wrong, but my people have not turned away from God. Let me die, but do not let trouble come to these innocent people."

God heard David's prayer. He told David to build an altar where he had seen the angel. At once David called his nobles and hurried to obey God's command.

The place where David saw the angel was at Araunah's threshing floor. Araunah was busy threshing his grain when he saw the king and his nobles coming. Leaving his work, he ran and bowed before David.

David said, "I want to buy your threshing floor and build here an altar to the Lord. Then all this sickness will leave the people."

"Make your altar here," Araunah said, "and offer up oxen. May the Lord God approve of you."

David wanted to pay for the threshing floor. At first Araunah refused the payment, but David insisted.

After building the altar, David laid offerings upon it and prayed to God. And God answered David's prayer.

At once David prepared for the building of the temple there on Mount Moriah. He began to get things ready so his son Solomon could build the beautiful place. And God was pleased with David's plan.

Solomon Becomes King

1 Kings 1:1—2:12

David was now an old man. He could no longer go among his people. Day after day he lay on his bed in the beautiful palace at Jerusalem. For many years he had ruled Israel and God had blessed him with honor and riches.

The people knew David could not live much longer, and they wondered who would take his place. David's oldest son Adonijah thought he should become king in his father's place. Adonijah was proud, and his parents had always given him everything he wanted. Perhaps he knew God had chosen Solomon to be the next king, but Adonijah wanted to be king more than anything else.

Adonijah took chariots, horses and fifty drivers to ride before him through the streets of Jerusalem. He thought people who saw him would think of him as a great ruler. Because he had always had his own way, he thought it would be easy to become king.

One day Adonijah called his friends to a valley outside the walls of Jerusalem for a great feast. Joab, the captain of David's army, and Abiathar, the high priest, came too. They planned to make Adonijah king after the feast was over. During the feast the guests ate, made merry and had a good time.

But God's prophet Nathan was troubled. He knew God had chosen Solomon to take David's place as king. David did not know what Adonijah was doing.

Nathan told Bathsheba, Solomon's mother, "Adonijah is about to have himself made king. If you want to save your own life and Solomon's, you had better tell David."

Bathsheba was upset when she heard the news. She had always believed Solomon would become king because David had promised it. Quickly she went to David's bedside. "Didn't you promise that Solomon would one day rule in your place?" she asked. "Now Adonijah is setting himself up to be king. All Israel waits for you to say who the next king will be."

While Bathsheba talked to David, Nathan came to see the king. Nathan asked, "Did you ever promise that Adonijah could be king?

Solomon prays for wisdom

Right now he and his friends are having a feast. They are saying, 'God save King Adonijah.'"

David remembered all the trouble Absalom had caused in trying to be king. He did not want Adonijah to do the same thing, so now, before he died, David planned to have his son Solomon anointed king.

He told Nathan, "Take my mule and have Solomon ride it. Go with him to Gihon and have the priest Zadok anoint Solomon as king. Then have all my servants blow their trumpets and shout, 'God save King Solomon!' Bring Solomon back to the city and have him sit upon my throne." Nathan did as David commanded.

When the people saw Solomon riding his father's mule and the servants going ahead blowing their trumpets, they knew Solomon had been made king. At once they shouted for joy.

Joab, the captain of David's army, heard the trumpets and said, "There is an uproar in the city." As a brave soldier, he wanted to go at once and find out what was happening in Jerusalem.

While Joab was still talking, a messenger came with the news, "King David has made Solomon king."

Now Adonijah and his guests were afraid. The guests left the feast and hurried home. But Adonijah was afraid to go back. He knew Solomon would find out what he had been doing. Maybe Solomon would want to kill him. At once he ran to the tabernacle and held onto the altar of God.

When Solomon heard that Adonijah had run to the tabernacle for safety, he said, "If Adonijah will do what is right, he will always be treated kindly."

Solomon sent for Adonijah. When Adonijah arrived he bowed before the king. Solomon let him go back to his home in peace.

David did not live long after that. Before he died he called Solomon to him and said, "When I am gone, be sure you obey all the Lord's commands. Then you will prosper. Be strong and prove you are manly."

Altogether David had reigned forty years. At his death he was buried in Bethlehem, which became known as the city of David. One of his descendants would be Jesus of Nazareth, the Savior God had promised.

God Gives Solomon a Gift

1 Kings 3—4

Solomon was not like his proud, selfish, ambitious brothers Absalom and Adonijah. Instead of wanting people to think he was great, Solomon knew he did not know how to rule the people wisely. He remembered that God had helped his father David. Now Solomon knew he, too, needed God's help.

Solomon took one thousand burnt offerings to Gibeon and sacrificed them upon the altar. All day he watched them burning. As the smoke drifted upward, he prayed earnestly for God's help. When night came he lay down to rest, but in his heart he was still praying for God's help.

While he slept Solomon had a wonderful dream. He saw God standing nearby. God said, "I will give you anything you ask for."

At once Solomon thought about how much a good ruler needed to know. Because Solomon felt he was not wise and understanding, he answered, "O Lord, my God, you were with David my father. You taught him how to follow your ways. You gave him a son to be king in his place. You have let me follow my father David as king, but I do not know how to be king. I rule so many people that I cannot count them. Give me, I pray you, an understanding heart. Then I shall be able to judge the people. Then I shall be able to tell the good from the bad."

God was well pleased with Solomon's request. He said, "Because you have asked for wisdom instead of a long life or riches or power over your enemies, I will give you what you ask for and these things as well. No king in all the land will be as wise and rich and honorable as you."

When Solomon awoke he knew he had been dreaming. But he believed God had spoken to him while he slept. He went back to Jerusalem and gave more offerings before the ark of God. Then he gave a feast for all his servants. From that time on Solomon judged the people wisely. They knew that God had blessed their king with great understanding.

Solomon Builds the Temple

1 Kings 5: 1—9:9

While David was king, he wanted to build a beautiful house for the Lord near his own palace in Jerusalem. He planned this to be a temple, designed just like the tabernacle Moses had made in the wilderness, only this temple was to be made of wood and stone.

God did not want David to build the temple. God said, "You have been a man of war, and you may not build my house. Your son Solomon will be a man of peace. He shall build the temple."

David obeyed the Lord. He did not begin the building, but he gathered some of the material and worked on the plans. He gave these plans to Solomon.

When Solomon became king, he began work on the temple. First he sent a letter to King Hiram of Tyre, a country by the sea. On the mountains of Lebanon in that country grew many beautiful cedar and fir trees.

Solomon told Hiram, "You know my father David could not build a house for the Lord because he was a man of war. Since we no longer have enemies to bother us, I plan to build the temple. Command that cedars of Lebanon be cut for me. I will be glad to pay your servants for their work, and my servants can help."

Hiram had been a close friend of David's. Now he was glad to help David's son. He answered, "My servants can cut down the trees. They will drag them to the sea and float them to a place where you can get them. You may pay us in food for this work."

Solomon agreed, and the men went to work. On the coast not far from Jerusalem, Solomon's men pulled the wet logs out of the sea and sawed them into boards. And Hiram and Solomon worked together and lived in peace.

Meanwhile Solomon had other men dig great stones out of the ground and cut them into the right shape for the foundation of the new building. He ordered that every stone should be cut to fit in place. When all the stones were ready, they were to be brought to Jerusalem.

Building the temple was such a big job that it took thousands of men to do the work. Every part of the building was fitted together

238

Solomon directs building of the Temple

without using a single hammer or nail. It took seven years to finish the building.

The temple stood on top of Mount Moriah where David had seen an angel and built an altar to worship God. At the same place where David's altar had been, the great altar of the temple was built.

Only the priests were allowed to enter the inner court and the rooms of the temple. Around these was a wide outer court where the people walked. Only Israelites were allowed inside the great court that surrounded the temple.

When the building was finished, Solomon called all the men of Israel to come to Jerusalem for the dedication. He took them to the house of God and offered many sacrifices upon the great altar of brass.

From Mount Zion they brought the ark of God and placed it in the inner room where only the high priest could go. Other furniture that had been in Moses' tabernacle was placed in the temple as God had commanded. When the priests carried the ark of God and the other furniture into the building, God's presence filled the temple with a cloud just as it had the tabernacle many years before. By this sign all the people knew that God was pleased with the house that Solomon had built.

Solomon knew that God was greater than the house he had built for him. He knew that God's presence was everywhere and not just in one place.

At the dedication Solomon prayed and asked God's blessings always to rest upon the temple. He asked that God always hear each prayer for forgiveness that was said there. When all the people had worshiped, he dismissed them and sent them back to their homes.

After the temple was finished, God spoke to Solomon in a dream. He said, "If you will follow my ways as your father David did, if you will keep my laws and do my commands, I will bless you and your children forever. If you or your children turn away from me to worship other gods, then I will despise this house you have built. And I will allow other nations to take the kingdom, and much sorrow will come to the people."

The Queen of Sheba Visits Solomon

1 Kings 10:1-13

As Solomon ruled he became famous throughout the region for his great wisdom. Even in Egypt where there were many wise men, none were as wise as the king of Israel. Visitors came from every land to hear him speak words of wisdom and to listen to the beautiful songs he wrote. Many of his proverbs and songs are found in the Bible books of Proverbs, Ecclesiastes and the Song of Solomon.

The Queen of Sheba heard that Solomon had received great wisdom from the Lord. She wanted to find out if he were as wise as people said. She traveled many miles across the sandy desert in a slow camel caravan. In her baggage she brought rich gifts for the king of Israel.

As the caravan came near to Jerusalem, she saw the great temple high on Mount Moriah. What a splendid city Jerusalem was!

When the queen talked with Solomon, she asked him many hard questions. And Solomon answered every one of them. There was nothing he could not explain.

Solomon showed the Queen of Sheba his beautiful palaces and the wonderful temple. She enjoyed the good food and noticed the rich clothing Solomon's servants wore. She watched Solomon as he went up to the house of the Lord.

When she saw all these things and heard Solomon's answers to her questions, she was glad she had come. She told him, "I did not believe all the things I heard about you, but now I know only half of your greatness and wisdom has been reported. Your men and servants must be very glad they can hear your wisdom. Blessed be the Lord your God who loves you and has made you king of Israel. Because he loves the people of Israel, he has made you their king."

Before she left the Queen of Sheba gave Solomon rich gifts—gold, spices and precious stones. And Solomon gave the queen the things she wanted most from the land of Israel. Then she returned to her own country.

Solomon's Last Days

1 Kings 11

For forty years Solomon ruled Israel. His fame was told far and wide, and his kingdom became very powerful. But Solomon's last days were not his best.

When he first became king, Solomon loved to serve God like David his father. As Solomon grew older, he married daughters of other kings and brought his wives to live in the royal palace at Jerusalem. These strange young princesses worshiped idols. Instead of learning to worship and serve the true God, they brought their idols to Jerusalem.

Solomon loved his wives and he tried to do what they asked. When they wanted temples for their gods, he granted their wish. He even went with them to their heathen temples and bowed down to their idols.

Solomon seemed to forget how much God had given him. No wonder God was displeased. God told Solomon, "Since you have not obeyed my laws and commands, I will take your kingdom away and give it to your servant. For your father's sake I will not do it as long as you live, but I will take it away from your son. For David's sake I will let your son have one of the twelve tribes to rule over."

During Solomon's reign he planned and erected many great buildings besides the temple. In different parts of his kingdom, he had large storehouses built. Here the people stored the grain and fruit they had grown.

It cost a great deal of money to build these beautiful places throughout the land. To get the money for these projects, Solomon required heavy taxes from his own people and from the nations his father had defeated in war. No wonder the people became restless and dissatisfied.

Among Solomon's servants was young Jeroboam. He was such a good worker that Solomon made him foreman of some of the building projects.

One day as Jeroboam left Jerusalem, God sent the prophet Ahijah to speak to the young man. Outside the city Ahijah

Solomon becomes wealthy and powerful

stopped Jeroboam. The prophet took off his new coat and tore it into twelve pieces.

To Jeroboam he gave ten pieces and said, "Take these, for the Lord God will take the kingdom away from Solomon and will give you ten tribes. Solomon is losing his kingdom because he has worshiped idols and disobeyed God's commands. Solomon's son will have one tribe because David obeyed the Lord as long as he lived. You shall be king over ten tribes of Israel. If you walk in God's ways and keep his commands, he will be with you."

When Solomon heard about this, he tried to kill Jeroboam. But Jeroboam ran away to Egypt and stayed until Solomon was dead.

THE DIVIDED KINGDOM
1 and 2 Kings; 1 and 2 Chronicles; Jonah; Jeremiah

Revolt Against Rehoboam
1 Kings 12:1-24

Young Prince Rehoboam grew up in the palace at Jerusalem when the kingdom of Israel was in its greatest glory. Was not his father, Solomon, one of the wisest kings of all time? Rehoboam had always lived in the midst of royal wealth and splendor. He had grown up in sight of the beautiful temple and had watched people from all parts of the land come to worship.

When Jeroboam heard that Solomon was dead, he returned to the land of Israel. He went with the men of Israel to Shechem where Rehoboam came to be crowned king.

Before the crowning the people of the ten tribes asked Jeroboam to say to Rehoboam, "Your father made us do heavy work and pay high taxes. If you will lighten our load, we will serve you."

Rehoboam was not ready to give his answer to this request. He said, "Give me three days to think about it. Come back then and I will tell you what I have decided."

Rehoboam was not a wise young man. Because he had always lived in wealth and luxury, he did not understand what it was like to be poor and have to work too hard.

First he called the old men who had advised his father. "What do you think I ought to tell the people?" he asked.

They said, "If you will give the people their request and deal kindly with them, they will serve you forever." The old men knew how restless the people had become under Solomon's rule. If the people were not satisfied, they might make trouble.

But Rehoboam did not like their advice so he called in his rich young friends and asked them. They told him to speak roughly to the people and threaten to make their work harder because they had dared ask to have things easier. Because Rehoboam liked their advice, he acted on it.

At the end of three days, the people returned with Jeroboam to hear Rehoboam's answer. Rehoboam spoke harshly, "My father made your yoke heavy, but I will make it heavier. I will use whips far worse than my father used."

Instead of fearing Rehoboam, the people said, "Then we will not have you for our king. We will go back to our homes, and we will fight before we will become your servants." Only the men of the tribe of Judah stayed to anoint Rehoboam as their king.

Rehoboam thought the ten tribes would soon change their minds and make him their king too. As his father had done, he sent one of his officers to collect taxes from the Israelites. This made the people so angry that they threw stones at the officer and killed him. Rehoboam was afraid the people might stone him, too, so he fled in his chariot to Jerusalem.

Back in Jerusalem Rehoboam decided to send soldiers from the tribe of Judah to fight against the men of the other tribes. After winning the battle, he would make himself king of all Israel.

God sent a prophet to Rehoboam. He told the young king, "Do not fight against the children of Israel. Let every man go back to his home, for this thing is of God." And Rehoboam obeyed.

Idol Worship Under Jeroboam

1 Kings 12:25–13:32

The ten tribes that refused to have Rehoboam for their king gathered at another place and chose Jeroboam as their ruler. He made Shechem his chief city.

When Jeroboam became king, he knew the words of the prophet Ahijah had come true. Now Jeroboam remembered that Ahijah had promised, "If you walk in God's ways and keep his commands, he will be with you." Jeroboam remembered, but he did not obey.

He was afraid to let his people go to Jerusalem to worship at the temple. He thought, "If the people go there to worship, they may decide they want Rehoboam for their king instead of me. Then they will kill me." He did not call on God for help or advice. He tried to work everything out for himself.

Jeroboam worships an idol

In Jerusalem Jeroboam had seen the idol temples Solomon had built for his heathen wives. In Egypt Jeroboam had seen the Egyptians worshiping animals with sacrifices. There the people had large temples for sacred oxen. Since Jeroboam was afraid to let his people go to Jerusalem to worship, he decided to make another place or two where his people could bow down.

First he collected much gold. When this was melted, he had it molded into two golden calves. He brought the people to see what he had made and explained, "It is too far for you to go all the way to Jerusalem to worship God. You can worship here in your own land. I will build two places of worship. The people who live in the south may worship at Bethel, and the others may go to Dan. I will set one of these golden calves in each place."

As the people looked at the calves, Jeroboam said, "Behold your gods, O Israel. These were the gods that brought your fathers out of slavery in Egypt."

As he had promised, Jeroboam built houses for the golden calves at Bethel and at Dan. At each place he built an altar on which to offer sacrifices to the gods. Since the Levites would not serve as priests for idol worship, Jeroboam had to get other men to be priests.

Jeroboam had the same feast days for idol worship as Judah had for worshiping the true God at Jerusalem. In this way Jeroboam made sure his people did not go to Jerusalem to worship.

In leading the people away from God into idol worship, Jeroboam sinned greatly. Because God was much displeased with Jeroboam, he sent a prophet to warn the king.

When the prophet came, Jeroboam was burning incense on the altar before the idol. The prophet said, "A new king, Josiah, a descendant of David will reign in Judah. He will tear down these places of idol worship and get rid of your ungodly priests. So that you may know these are the words of the Lord, this altar will suddenly fall apart and the ashes will cover the ground."

Jeroboam was so angry at the prophet's words that he commanded his servants, "Seize him!" As Jeroboam spoke he reached out his hand to grab the prophet, and his arm became so stiff he could not move it. At that moment the stones of the altar fell apart, and the ashes rolled to the ground.

How afraid Jeroboam was! He begged the prophet, "Pray for me, and beg the Lord to make my arm well again."

The prophet did pray, and Jeroboam's arm became well. He was so thankful that he said, "Come home with me. You can rest, and I will reward you for healing my arm."

"I would not go home with you," the prophet said, "if you gave me half of all you own. The Lord commanded me not to eat or drink anything until I got home." Then the prophet started home. On the way he was tricked into breaking his promise, and he lost his life.

Even after the prophet warned Jeroboam, he did not change his ways. Instead he made more men priests of idol worship.

Jeroboam's Wife Visits Ahijah

1 Kings 14:1-20

Jeroboam's son Abijah was ill. Everyone was worried about him. Nothing seemed to make him any better. Jeroboam was so worried about his son that he decided to ask God's prophet if the boy would ever be well again.

Jeroboam told his wife, "Disguise yourself so no one will know you are the queen. Then go to the prophet Ahijah who first told me I would be king of Israel. Take ten loaves of bread, some cakes and a bottle of honey as a present for the prophet. Ask him if our child will live." The queen agreed to go.

The king was afraid to go to Ahijah himself. He knew he had displeased God by leading the people into idol worship. He did not want Ahijah to remind him of his sins.

By this time Ahijah was old and blind. He would not have recognized Jeroboam's wife without the disguise.

The Lord told Ahijah, "Jeroboam's wife is coming to ask you about her son who is ill. When she comes she will pretend to be another woman." And the Lord told Ahijah what would happen to Jeroboam's son.

When Ahijah heard footsteps at the door, he called out, "Come in, wife of Jeroboam. Why do you pretend to be someone else? I have bad news for you."

How surprised the queen was that Ahijah knew her! Both she and Jeroboam had forgotten that God could speak to his prophets. She came into the room and gave her offering to the blind old man. Then she listened while he told her the words of the Lord.

"Go home to your husband," he said, "and tell him that he must be punished, for he has not followed God's ways or obeyed his commandments. Jeroboam has made idols of gold and set these up for the people to worship. No wonder they have turned their backs on the Lord. Great sorrow will come to your house. Your sick child will not get better. He will die about the time you reach home."

Ahijah said that the kingdom would be taken away from Jeroboam's family because Jeroboam had caused the people of Israel to sin. The words of the prophet came true. Great was the punishment for Jeroboam's sin.

Rehoboam Turns to Idols

1 Kings 14:21–15:8; 2 Chronicles 12–13

After three years as king of Judah, Rehoboam turned to idol worship. His mother had been a heathen princess before she married Solomon, and she had never given up her idols. Rehoboam knew as much or more about idol worship than he did about the true God.

Even though Solomon had built a great temple where the people could worship the true God, they did not use it much after Rehoboam bowed down to idols. Instead the men of Judah built altars and set up idols on every high hill and under every green tree. And God was greatly displeased.

Great trouble came during the fifth year of Rehoboam's reign. Shishak, king of Egypt, took twelve hundred chariots and sixty thousand horsemen and warred against Judah. They captured several fortified cities and went on to Jerusalem.

The prophet Shemaiah told Rehoboam and his princes, "You have forsaken the Lord. Your lives will be in the hands of Shishak."

Then Rehoboam and his princes bowed down and said, "The Lord is righteous." Because they humbled themselves before the Lord, their lives were saved. But Shishak plundered the temple and the palace. He took all the treasures he could find, even the golden shields that had belonged to Solomon.

This was not the only trouble that came to the land of Judah, for there was war also between Rehoboam and Jeroboam.

After seventeen years as king, Rehoboam died. His son Abijah became king. The three years of his reign were filled with constant war against Jeroboam.

Asa Follows God

1 Kings 15: 9-15; 2 Chronicles 14—15

Unlike his grandfather Rehoboam and his father Abijah, Asa was a good king who followed God. From the very first he ruled his people wisely. Asa believed that the people had done wrong in turning to idols. He wanted them to worship the one true God.

He commanded the people of Judah, "Seek the Lord God of your fathers. Keep the law and the commandments." And Asa ordered his servants to take away the altars for idol worship, smash the idols and cut down the groves where the idols had been placed.

When the king's servants had done this, he put them to work fortifying the cities of Judah. He said, "Let us build these cities, and around them put walls with towers, gates and bars. Because we have sought the Lord, he has given us rest from war these few years." And the country prospered.

The Ethiopians noticed how prosperous Judah was, and they decided to make war on that country. They marched against Judah with a great army.

Asa called his small army together, but they were no match for the Ethiopians. Then Asa prayed to the Lord, "Lord, you can give power to a few men just as easily as you can give it to a great company. Help us, O Lord, our God. We rest on Thee. O Lord, Thou art our God."

When the men of Judah met the mighty warriors of Ethiopia in battle, the Ethiopians turned and ran. They did not even stop to get their belongings. After the victory the men of Judah found many valuable things the enemy had left behind.

When Asa returned from battle, Azariah, a man of God, came to see him. Azariah said, "O King, listen to me and have all the people obey. The Lord is with you while you follow him. If you seek him, you will find him, but if you forsake him, he will forsake you. For a long time Israel had not followed the true God. They did not even have true priests to remind them of God's ways. Yet when they sought the Lord, they found him. In those times there was peace. Be strong in the Lord, Asa, and your work will be rewarded."

The people realized that the Lord God was with Asa and many came to Jerusalem to worship. From Judah and Benjamin and from Ephraim, Manasseh and Simeon, the people came. They offered many sacrifices to the Lord and pledged to seek the Lord God with all their hearts and with all their souls.

How happy they were to return to the worship of the true God! There was shouting among the crowd. Trumpets and cornets announced their joy.

About this time Asa discovered that his own grandmother, the queen mother, still worshiped her idol. He decided, "This will never do. My grandmother shall be queen mother no longer, for she sets the wrong kind of example for the people." Asa tore down the idol, broke it in pieces and had it burned outside the city.

Trouble Between Israel and Judah

1 Kings 15:16-24; 2 Chronicles 16

Baasha, king of Israel, grew jealous. Some of his people had gone to live in Judah, and many more were taking trips to Jerusalem to worship God. He decided to fortify Ramah, a city in the southern part of Israel. Here he would station soldiers to keep his people from crossing the border. Also his soldiers would keep the people of Judah from entering Israel. Baasha did not want anyone to teach his people to love God, for then they would want to go to Jerusalem to worship.

King Asa was much displeased when he heard about Baasha's plan. He tried to think of a way to keep Baasha from fortifying Ramah. This time he did not ask God's help. Instead he took silver and gold from the temple and sent it to the king of Syria with this message:

"There is a treaty between us and between our fathers. Look, I have sent you silver and gold so you will break your treaty with Baasha and make war on him. Then Baasha will not have time to build a fort on our border."

The king of Syria did as Asa requested. As soon as the Syrians marched against Israel, Baasha left his work and went to drive the enemy away. Baasha had already begun to fortify Ramah on the border between Israel and Judah. While he was fighting the Syrians, Asa and his soldiers tore down all Baasha's work at Ramah.

God sent a prophet to Asa. The prophet said, "You have done wrong because you relied on the king of Syria instead of on the Lord your God. Didn't the Lord deliver you from the Ethiopians even though you had only a small army? The Lord shows his power to those who trust him. You have been foolish. You will have wars for the rest of your life."

How angry Asa was! He did not believe the prophet. At his command the servants threw the prophet into prison.

As Asa grew older, he trusted God less. In his old age Asa had a painful disease of the feet. Even though the doctors could not cure him, he did not ask for God's help. About two years later Asa died, and the people buried him in the city of David. Asa had ruled Judah longer than any other king.

Elijah Is Fed by Ravens

1 Kings 16:29–17:9

Things were not going well in the kingdom of Israel. The people worshiped golden calves instead of the true God. Each new king worshiped idols and did wrong. Then Ahab became king of Israel in the last years that Asa ruled Judah.

Now Ahab was not fit to be king. He was worse than all the other kings of Israel. Not only did he worship the golden calves, but also he married Jezebel, a wicked princess. She brought her heathen religion and heathen priests into Israel. Ahab built temples for her gods and worshiped with her.

One day Ahab was much surprised to see a strange-looking man standing before him. The man wore a coat of camel's hair. He was the prophet Elijah who had come to give the king God's message.

Before the king had time to ask the man what he wanted, Elijah said, "As the Lord God of Israel lives, there shall not be dew or rain throughout the land until I announce it." Then Elijah turned and walked away as suddenly as he had come.

At first Ahab paid no attention to Elijah's words. But when the dew did not appear and the rains stopped, he remembered what Elijah had said. Through the entire kingdom, he sent men to look for the prophet, but Elijah could not be found.

Ahab became alarmed. He knew there would be a famine if there was no rain for the crops. Ahab sent word everywhere, even to other kings, asking each one to help find Elijah.

Now God told Elijah to hide by the brook Cherith. Here Elijah had water to drink. Each morning and evening the ravens brought him bread and meat just as God had said.

Finally the brook dried up because there had been no rain in all the land. Then Elijah wondered what to do.

God told him, "Go to Zarephath. There I have commanded a widow to give you food."

At once Elijah started across Israel to Zarephath.

A Widow Feeds Elijah

1 Kings 17:10-24

Near the gate of Zarephath Elijah saw a woman gathering sticks. He could tell by her clothing that she was a poor widow. He thought, "Perhaps this is the widow the Lord has sent me to."

First he asked her for a drink of water. When she turned to get the water, Elijah added, "Please bring me a little food, too, for I am very hungry."

At that the widow stopped and looked at him strangely. She said, "I have no bread to give you. I have only a handful of meal and a little oil at home. I am picking up sticks to make a fire. Then I will bake the last bit of food for my son and myself before we die of hunger."

"Do not be afraid," said Elijah. "Do just as you planned, but first make a little cake for me. Then bake cakes for you and your son. The Lord God of Israel has said that your barrel of meal and your bottle of oil will not be empty throughout the famine."

The widow hurried into the city and did as Elijah commanded. How surprised she was to find there was enough meal and oil for three cakes instead of just two.

Every day thereafter there was still a handful of meal and a little oil left for the cakes. Always there was just enough to feed the three of them. For several months Elijah stayed with the widow and her son.

One day the boy became very sick and died. The woman was brokenhearted.

Elijah said, "Give me your son." He picked up the breathless body and carried it to his room. Laying the child on the bed, Elijah prayed to God. "O Lord, my God, let this child be restored to life." Three times he asked God to do this.

And the Lord heard Elijah's prayer. Elijah picked the boy up in his arms and carried the child to his mother. "See," he said, "your son lives."

How happy the widow was! She said, "Now I know for sure that you are a man of God and that your words are true."

Elijah Comes Out of Hiding

1 Kings 18:1-16

After Elijah's visit to King Ahab, there was no rain or dew in Israel and the nearby countries for over three years. There was no grass on the hillsides, and the fields looked like wastelands. The farmers could not raise crops, and the people suffered from hunger. Many animals died. Even the king's horses and mules were gaunt, hungry-looking beasts.

By this time Ahab was sure there would never be rain until Elijah announced it. He wanted to find Elijah and bring him back to the palace. Perhaps he planned to force Elijah to announce rain.

Ahab sent messengers everywhere to look for the missing prophet. Always they returned with the same report, "We can find no trace of him." Elijah seemed to have disappeared completely.

Obadiah, Ahab's chief servant, was a man who feared God. One day the king told Obadiah, "We must find pasture somewhere for these horses and mules or they will die. Let us divide the land. You go one way while I go the other, and we will look for water and grassy spots." So the two separated and went in opposite directions.

Obadiah had not gone far when he met a man wearing a camel's-hair coat. He knew at once that this was Elijah. In surprise and fear he fell on his face before the prophet.

Elijah said, "Go tell the king I am here."

Obadiah asked, "Why have you come to me after the king has searched for you in every nation and kingdom? Now you want me to tell him you are here. Then when I tell the king, you will leave. The king will not find you, and I shall suffer. Already I am in disfavor because I hid a hundred of the Lord's prophets when Jezebel tried to kill them. If the king comes here and you are gone, he will think I hid you just as I did the other prophets. Then he will kill me."

Elijah quieted the excited servant. Again he said, "Go tell the king I am here. I will wait until he comes."

Finally Obadiah turned and ran to find the king. When Ahab heard that Elijah had been found, he did not bother to look any farther for pasture. Right away he wanted to see the man who had brought so much trouble on him and on his people. At once he hurried back with Obadiah to see Elijah.

Elijah and the Prophets of Baal

1 Kings 18:17-40

Because Elijah knew God had sent him to speak to the king, he was not afraid. At once King Ahab asked, "Are you the man who has been causing all this trouble?"

Elijah answered, "No, I am not the man who has troubled your country. You and your family are the guilty ones. You have forsaken the Lord God and disobeyed his commandments. You have worshiped the idol Baal. That is what has caused all this trouble. Now have the people of Israel and Jezebel's prophets of Baal meet me at Mount Carmel."

This was one time the king did not give the orders. Instead he did just as Elijah commanded.

When the crowd of curious people gathered at Mount Carmel, they saw Elijah for the first time in three years. They listened quietly while he spoke to them.

"How long are you going to serve first one god and then another?" he asked. "If the Lord is God, follow him, but if Baal is the true God, then choose him."

Elijah did not ask the people to choose right then. Instead he wanted to prove to them who was the true God. He said, "I and the prophets of Baal have met with you here. I am only one man, but there are four hundred and fifty prophets of Baal. Bring two bullocks for sacrifices. We will build two altars and lay a bullock on each altar. The heathen can call on their gods, and I will call on the Lord God. Let the one who answers by fire be your God."

The people liked this plan. Quickly they brought the offerings for the sacrifices. "What will happen next?" they wondered.

Elijah told the prophets of Baal to choose the bullock they wanted, and he took the one that was left. He said, "Since there are so many of you, you offer your sacrifice first and call on your god. Ask him to send fire."

In a short time the heathen prophets had their sacrifice ready. From morning until noon, they prayed, "O Baal, hear us," but there was no answer. They jumped up and down around the altar. Still nothing happened.

Elijah knew their god could not send fire from heaven. At noon he made fun of them saying, "Cry louder! Maybe he is talking or gone on a trip. Perhaps he is sleeping and cannot hear you."

The prophets cried louder than ever. They cut themselves with knives so Baal would feel sorry for them and answer their prayer. Still Baal did not answer, and no fire fell from the sky.

When it was time for the evening sacrifice at the temple in Jerusalem, Elijah told all the people to gather around him. As they watched he rebuilt the altar of the Lord that had once stood on this spot. He chose twelve rough stones and piled them together for the altar. Then he dug a ditch around it. On top of the altar, he placed the wood.

Elijah prepares the sacrifice

Elijah wanted to make sure the people would realize God's great power. He commanded, "Bring four barrels of water and pour them on the sacrifice and wood." When this was done, he said, "Do it a second time." A third time he said, "Do it again."

Twelve barrels of water had been poured on the altar. The wood and meat were drenched. The water filled the trench up to the brim.

When everything was ready, Elijah said, "Lord God of Abraham, Isaac and Israel, let it be known this day that you are God, that I am your servant, that I have done this to obey you. Hear me, O Lord, hear me that these people may know you are the Lord God and return to worship you."

At once fire fell from the sky and burned up the sacrifice and the wood. Even all the water in the ditch was licked up by the fire.

How amazed the people were! They had never seen anything like this before. Now they were sure Elijah's God was the true God. They fell on their faces and cried, "The Lord, he is God! The Lord, he is God!"

Making sure they would not be tempted to worship Baal again, the people killed all the sinful, heathen prophets.

Elijah, the Little Cloud and the Great Rain

1 Kings 18:41-46

What a day this had been for Ahab! He had seen God's fire fall from heaven upon Elijah's sacrifice. He had seen the people kill the prophets of Baal. While this was happening, Ahab looked on in silence. He did not know what to do. He could not save the heathen priests when all the people believed Elijah's God was the true God. What would his wife Jezebel do when she heard about it?

While these thoughts were going through Ahab's mind, Elijah told him, "Go up on the mountain and enjoy the feast the people have made. Now the famine is over and soon there will be rain."

Ahab looked at the sky, but there was no sign of rain. Yet at Elijah's word he went to join the feast.

Elijah climbed to the top of Mount Carmel and knelt to pray. Only his servant was with him. Bowing his face to the ground, Elijah prayed earnestly for God to send rain. Then he told his servant, "Go and look toward the sea."

The servant obeyed, but he saw nothing. Again Elijah prayed. Again the servant went and looked toward the sea. Still he reported, "There is nothing."

Seven times Elijah prayed, and seven times he sent his servant to look for a sign from God. The seventh time the servant came back and said, "A little cloud about the size of a man's hand is rising out of the sea."

At once Elijah believed God had answered his prayer. Rain was on the way. Immediately he sent his servant to tell Ahab, "Get your chariot and hurry back to your home in Jezreel before the rain overtakes you."

Elijah wrapped his hairy coat around his body and ran down the mountain to Jezreel. How happy he was that God had shown such wonders to Israel that day! Surely now the people of Israel would worship the true God and forsake Jezebel's idols!

As Elijah ran the winds became strong and the sky grew dark with the coming storm. Soon the rain fell in torrents. The dry thirsty ground drank in the fresh water, and the brooks overflowed their banks. Because he was so thankful that God had sent the rain, Elijah did not mind getting wet.

As Ahab rode back to Jezreel, he saw Elijah running ahead. The king hurried to his palace to tell Jezebel everything that had happened on Mount Carmel.

If Ahab was displeased with what Elijah had done, he did not try to punish the man of God. Perhaps he believed his wicked wife would take care of punishing Elijah. If that was what Ahab thought, he was not mistaken.

Elijah Under the Juniper Tree

1 Kings 19:1-8

Jezebel flew into an angry rage when she heard that her priests were dead. She sent a messenger to tell Elijah, "Tomorrow at this time if you are not as dead as my priests, let the gods kill me too."

When Elijah heard these words, he got up quickly and ran with his servant out into the dark stormy night. They must escape from the queen.

How afraid Elijah was! He did not call on God in his trouble as he had the day before. Perhaps he had thought Jezebel would leave him alone when she heard how powerful God was. Instead Jezebel did not pay the slightest attention to God. She planned only to get even with Elijah.

"Where can I hide?" Elijah wondered as he ran out of the gate of Jezreel. It would not be safe to go back to the widow's home in Zarephath. He could not hide in Judah, for the king of Judah was Ahab's friend. Elijah and his servant ran southward. On and on they went. When they went through Judah, Elijah's servant left him. Still Elijah fled.

Finally he came to a great wilderness and stopped to rest under a juniper tree. Elijah was so discouraged that he threw himself on the ground and prayed to die. Soon he fell asleep.

While he slept an angel came. "Get up and eat," the angel said.

There were cakes baking on coals of fire and a bottle of water to drink. Elijah ate, but he was so tired that he lay down and went to sleep again.

A second time the angel awakened Elijah and said, "Get up and eat, for you have a long way to go."

After eating the angel's food, Elijah was not hungry again for forty days. The food gave him strength to climb the mountain where God first spoke to Moses from the burning bush. Here Elijah found a cave. Because he was still discouraged and afraid of Queen Jezebel, he crept into the cave to hide.

Elijah hides under a juniper tree

Elijah and the Still Small Voice

1 Kings 19:9-21

While Elijah hid in the cave on Mount Horeb, the Lord asked him, "What are you doing here?"

Elijah told the Lord all that had happened in Israel. "The people have forsaken your law, thrown down your altars and even killed your prophets. I am the only one left," Elijah said sadly, "and now they want to kill me."

God answered, "Come out of the cave and stand on the mountain." And Elijah obeyed.

God caused such a strong wind to sweep across the mountain that even the rocks crumbled. But Elijah knew God was not in the great strong wind. Then God sent an earthquake, and the ground trembled beneath Elijah's feet. Still Elijah knew God was not in the earthquake. When the ground was steady again, fire broke out on the mountain and burned many trees. But Elijah knew God was not in the fire.

When everything was quiet after the fire, Elijah heard a still small voice. At once he knew this was the voice of God. Wrapping his coat about his face, Elijah stood in the door of the cave to listen.

Again God asked, "What are you doing here, Elijah?" And Elijah answered the question just as he had before. But God said, "You are wrong, Elijah. There are seven thousand people in Israel who have never worshiped Baal."

How surprised Elijah was! He began to take heart.

Then God said, "Go back to Israel and anoint Elisha to take your place when you die."

Now Elijah was not afraid to go back to Israel. He did as the Lord commanded.

He found young Elisha plowing with oxen in his father's field. Elijah threw his coat over the young man's shoulders. This was a sign that Elisha was to assume Elijah's work as a prophet of God.

Elisha killed the oxen and gave a farewell feast for the people. After the feast he went with Elijah.

Ahab and the King of Syria

1 Kings 20

King Ahab had an enemy named Benhadad, king of Syria. More than anything else Benhadad wanted to make the people of Israel his slaves.

Benhadad did not try to take Israel by himself. He had thirty-two other kings help him. They brought their armies, chariots and horses into the land of Israel. Near Samaria, Ahab's capital city, the enemy made their camp. They planned to capture the city and take Ahab prisoner.

Benhadad and the other kings thought they could defeat Ahab easily. They were so sure that they spent much time eating and drinking before the battle.

Meanwhile a prophet came to Ahab with a message from the Lord. He said, "The Lord has seen this great enemy gathered against you, but he will help you."

Ahab had only a very small army. "How can we win against such great forces?" he asked.

The prophet told Ahab what to do, and soon the king called his small army and marched against Benhadad and his men. They found Benhadad and the kings drinking. Soon the entire enemy army with all its drunken leaders was driven away. Many were killed.

Again the prophet told Ahab, "Strengthen yourselves and get ready, for the Syrians will attack you again about a year from now."

Ahab believed the prophet quickly this time. He prepared his army for another attack.

At the end of the year, the Syrian army came again, and it looked just as large and powerful as before. This time they did not pitch their tents on the hills near Samaria, but in the plains to the north.

The Syrians said, "They defeated us last year because the God of Israel is a god of the hills. This time we will fight in the valley, and their God cannot help them." How little the Syrians knew about the God of Israel!

Ahab formed his battle line and went out to meet the enemy. His soldiers looked like only a handful against the great Syrian army. The prophet told Ahab what the Syrians thought about God.

Because Ahab knew the God of Israel was everywhere, he was not afraid to meet Benhadad on the hills or in the valleys.

Again the men of Israel were victorious. Some of the Syrians ran with Benhadad to the nearby city of Aphek. They thought they would be safe from the men of Israel inside the city walls, but the walls crumbled and many were killed.

Benhadad was not hurt, and he ran to hide in the middle of the city. If he were captured, he feared Ahab would treat him harshly.

Finally some of his servants found him and said, "Listen, we have heard that the kings of Israel are merciful. If we go to him dressed in sackcloth and rope, Ahab may save your life."

Benhadad's servants dressed themselves in sackcloth with ropes on their heads. They went to Ahab and bowed humbly as if they would be willing to be Ahab's servants. They begged Ahab to save Benhadad's life.

Ahab treated the Syrians kindly and seemed glad to hear that Benhadad was still alive. When they brought Benhadad to Ahab, the Syrian king acted very humble. It was hard for Ahab to believe this was the proud king who tried to take Israel. Ahab felt so sorry for Benhadad that he invited him into his chariot. After they talked Ahab let the enemy king go back to Syria.

The prophet knew Ahab had done wrong. The prophet put ashes on his face and dressed like a soldier who had fought in the battle. No one would recognize him as a prophet. Then he waited by the roadside for Ahab to pass by in his chariot. When the king came along, the prophet called out. Ahab stopped to see what this poor soldier wanted.

The man said, "During the battle a man brought a prisoner to me and told me to watch him closely. He said if the prisoner escaped, I would lose my life. But in the heat of the battle, the man got away, and I cannot find him. What shall I do?"

"You must pay with your life," answered Ahab.

At this the prophet took the ashes off his face, and Ahab recognized him. The prophet said, "Because you have not punished Benhadad for the wrong he did, you will be punished severely."

When the king heard this, he bowed his head and returned to the palace with a heavy heart.

Naboth's Vineyard

1 Kings 21

In the town of Jezreel, Ahab had a summerhouse. Around it were wide grassy lawns and gardens of beautiful flowers and trees. Every time Ahab came to his summerhouse, he thought of some way to make it even more beautiful.

One day when the king walked through his gardens, he noticed the vineyard beyond his fence. Ahab thought, "I would like to have that vineyard for my own! Since Naboth owns it, I will speak to him about it. I will find him an even better vineyard or pay him for his land."

But Naboth did not want to sell. He said, "My father owned this vineyard, and my grandfather before him and even my great-grandfather. This land has always been in our family, and we want to keep it that way. I cannot let you have it."

Even when Ahab offered to find Naboth a better vineyard or pay him a good price, Naboth refused. The vineyard was his prized possession.

When Ahab realized that Naboth would not change his mind, the king turned and walked away. Over and over he told himself, "I want Naboth's vineyard." And the more Ahab thought about it, the unhappier he became. By the time Ahab reached his palace in Samaria, he was very disturbed because he could not get what he wanted.

As soon as Ahab reached the palace, he went straight to bed and turned his face to the wall. Ahab, the king of Israel, was pouting. He would not eat, and he refused to talk to anyone.

At last Jezebel came to the king's room and asked, "What is wrong, Ahab? Why are you so upset that you won't eat?" And Ahab told his wife how much he wanted Naboth's vineyard.

"Aren't you the king of Israel?" Jezebel asked. "Get up, eat and be glad. I will see that you get Naboth's vineyard."

Jezebel wrote letters to the rulers of Jezreel and put the king's seal on them. She said, "Announce a fast and bring Naboth to trial. When all the people have gathered, have two men accuse Naboth of wrongdoing. Even though the two men speak falsely, the people will be so excited that they will kill Naboth."

The rulers of Jezreel carried out the instructions in the royal letter. When Jezebel learned that Naboth was dead, she went to Ahab. "Now you can have Naboth's vineyard," she said. "He refused to sell it to you, but now he is dead."

At once Ahab went to Jezreel to look at his new property. As he walked between the long rows of grapevines, he planned the changes he would make. Just then Elijah came to the king. Ahab stopped short. He did not like to see Elijah.

The prophet said, "I have found you. God knows you are responsible for Naboth's death. Now you are taking his vineyard. Because you have done this, you, too, will lose your life."

Ahab trembled as he heard the prophet's words. No longer did he enjoy the sight of Naboth's vineyard. To show his sorrow he tore his kingly robes and dressed in sackcloth. Because he was sorry for the wrong he had done, he refused to eat. When the Lord knew Ahab was really sorry, he lessened the punishment.

Ahab's Son Becomes King

2 Kings 1

After Ahab died his son Ahaziah became king of Israel. Ahaziah was no better than his father. He did not try to please God. Instead he worshiped the idol Baal that his mother had brought to Israel. Like his mother Ahaziah hated those who served God.

Ahaziah was not king very long. Soon after he began to rule, he fell through a lattice in his beautiful palace at Samaria. In the fall he was painfully injured. For days and days he lay on his bed suffering.

"Shall I ever be well again?" Ahaziah wondered. Finally he called messengers to his bedside. "Go down to the land of the Philistines and find out from their god whether I shall get well."

Even though Elijah, a true prophet of God, lived in Israel, the king did not send to him for help. But the true God knew all about Ahaziah and about the messengers the king had sent to the Philistines.

The Lord sent an angel to tell Elijah what Ahaziah had done. The angel said, "Get up, Elijah, and go to meet the king's messengers. Tell them that Ahaziah will never get better."

Elijah did as the angel said. As he walked the road toward Samaria, he saw the king's messengers hurrying to carry out their orders. Elijah asked them, "Is there no God in Israel, that you have to go to an idol in the land of the Philistines to find out whether the king will get well? Go back and tell him that the Lord God has said the king will never be able to leave his bed again." With that Elijah turned and went away just as suddenly as he had come.

The messengers were so surprised and bewildered that they did not know what to do. Finally they decided to go back and tell the king what the strange-looking man had said.

As soon as they entered the sickroom, Ahaziah said, "Why have you come back so soon?"

"A strange-looking man met us," they answered, "and he asked if there is no God in Israel that you had to send to the Philistines to find out about your injury. He said you will never get well because you trust in false gods."

At once the king knew that the strange-looking man must have been Elijah. How angry Ahaziah was! He even sent soldiers out to capture Elijah, but God protected the prophet.

Later Elijah came to the palace. He walked boldly into Ahaziah's room. He was not afraid of the king. Again Elijah told Ahaziah that he would not recover from his fall. Not long afterwards Ahaziah died and his brother Jehoram ruled Israel.

Elijah and the Chariot of Fire

2 Kings 2

Elijah the prophet was now old. He had worked hard to destroy idol worship in Israel and help his people serve the true God. Now his work was over, and he was ready to go to heaven.

God had already chosen Elisha to be the next great prophet. For some time Elisha went everywhere with the old prophet. Elisha knew the time had come for God to take Elijah.

Elijah, too, knew that he would soon go to heaven. He made his last visit to the schools at Bethel and Jericho where the young prophets studied about God. At both places the young prophets asked Elisha, "Do you know that the Lord is going to take Elijah today?"

Both times Elisha said, "Yes, I know it."

At both places Elijah told Elisha, "Stay here, for the Lord wants me to go on."

Always Elisha insisted, "I will not leave you." So the two went on together. The prophets from the school at Jericho followed as far as the Jordan River.

When Elijah and Elisha reached the Jordan River, the old prophet took off his coat, wrapped it together and hit the water with it. At once the waters parted, and there was a dry path through the river. Then the two walked across to the other side. Soon the young prophets lost sight of Elijah and Elisha.

Elijah asked young Elisha, "What do you want me to do for you before I am taken away?"

Elisha said, "Let me have a double portion of your spirit."

Elijah knew that only God could give such a gift. So he said, "If you see me when I am taken away, then you will know that God will give you a double portion of my spirit."

On and on the two men went. Suddenly a chariot and horses of fire separated them. In a great whirlwind Elisha saw his dear old friend leave this world. He knew Elijah would not be with him any more. Looking upward, he called, "My father! My father!"

The chariot and Elijah soon disappeared in the clouds, and Elisha could not see them any more. When Elisha looked down, he saw the old coat that Elijah had worn. He picked up the coat and started back to the land of Israel. When he reached the Jordan River, the prophets were still standing on the other side.

Just as Elijah had done, Elisha wrapped the coat together and hit the water. He said, "Where is the Lord God of Elijah?" And the waters parted just as they had before.

When the young prophets saw what Elisha had done they said, "The spirit of Elijah is with Elisha." They hurried out to meet him and bowed at his feet. Now he was their master and teacher.

The young men wanted to send fifty of their group across the Jordan to look for Elijah's body. They thought they might find it on top of one of the mountains.

Elisha said, "Do not do this. You cannot find Elijah's body." But the young men coaxed and pleaded until finally Elisha let them go.

For three days they searched everywhere for Elijah's body. Nowhere could they find a trace of it. On their return they told Elisha they had found nothing.

He said, "Did I not tell you it was no use to go?"

For a time Elisha stayed with the young men at the school of the prophets in Jericho. One day the men of the city came to him and said, "You can see that our city is built in a pleasant place, but we do not have good water to drink. The water here causes many people to get sick and die. Even the land does not produce good crops because the water is not good."

Elisha said, "Bring me a bottle of salt." When this was done, he took the salt to the springs where the people got their water. Throwing the salt into the water he said, "From now on no one will die from drinking this water, for God has healed it." After that the water was always pure and sweet.

Elisha Saves Two Boys from Slavery

2 Kings 4:1-7

In the land of Israel there were both rich and poor people. Elisha, the prophet, visited both. He listened to their troubles and helped them as much as he could. Many people loved him and looked forward to his visits.

In one home where Elisha sometimes visited, there were two fun-loving little boys. Their father had been one of the young prophets who loved and served the true God. Since their father's death, their mother had not been able to make a living for them.

One day a stern man stopped at the door to collect all the money the family owed. Because the poor widow had no money to give him, the man said, "I will return later. If you do not have the money then, I will take your two sons to be my slaves."

The poor woman did not know what to do. She had no money, and it would be impossible to earn that much money. She did not know anyone who would lend her what was needed. As she tried to decide what to do, she remembered the prophet Elisha. At once she hurried to him with her story.

Elisha listened as the woman said, "You know my husband loved and served the Lord. Now that he is dead, we have no money to pay the bills. Unless I can get the money right away, my sons will be taken as slaves."

How much Elisha wanted to help! He asked, "What do you have in your house?"

The woman answered, "I have nothing but a pot of oil."

The prophet knew that would be enough if she followed his advice. He said, "Go home and borrow from your neighbors all the jars and pots and bowls they will lend you. Take these containers home. After you have closed your door, pour oil from your pot into all these you have borrowed. When one is full, set it aside and fill another."

The widow ran to her neighbors as fast as she could and borrowed many jars, pots and bowls. The boys carried them to their house. Then she closed the door just as Elisha had said.

The boys looked at the roomful of jars and asked, "Mother, what are you going to do with all these?"

She told them what Elisha had said. They brought her one jar after another, and she filled each container from her small pot of oil. They lifted and carried, lifted and carried.

Finally their mother said, "Bring me another jar."

"All the jars are full," the boys told her.

Every container was full of oil, but the widow's pot of oil was just as full as it had been when she started.

At once the widow hurried to tell Elisha what had happened. She said, "I have filled every jar, pot and bowl I could borrow. Still I have oil left."

"Go and sell the oil and pay your bills," Elisha told her. "You and your sons will be able to live on the money that is left over."

How thankful the woman was! The boys and their mother were very happy. Now they would not have to be separated. They knew

God had taken care of them in their need. More than ever they loved God and wanted to serve him.

A Room for Elisha

2 Kings 4:8-17

Elisha went from one place to another, teaching people to love and serve the true God. One day as he traveled he came to the little city of Shunem. Here a rich woman and her husband lived. They had many servants but no children.

When the woman saw Elisha and his servant, she invited them to stay for dinner. She knew Elisha was God's prophet.

From that time on Elisha stopped at her home whenever he came through Shunem. There Elisha and his servant rested, and the woman prepared food for them.

One day after Elisha's visit the woman said to her husband, "Since the prophet Elisha comes this way so often, let's build a room for him. We could put a table, a candlestick, a bed and a chair in it. Then he could rest in his room whenever he wished." The husband liked the idea, and so they had a special room built for Elisha and his servant.

The next time Elisha came, he was surprised and pleased with the room they had made for him. He wanted to repay them for their kindness. To the woman he said, "You have been so kind to us that we would like to do something for you. Is there anything you want me to tell the king or his chief captain?"

The woman told Elisha that she did not need anything, for she was happily living among her own people.

Still Elisha was not satisfied. Later he asked his servant, "What can we do for this Shunammite woman?"

"They are old, and they have no children," the servant said.

This time as Elisha and his servant were leaving, Elisha told the woman she would have a son as a reward for being so kind.

How hard it was for the woman to believe Elisha's words! Time passed and she did have a son. What a happy family they were!

Elisha and the Shunammite's Son

2 Kings 4:18-37

The Shunammite woman and her husband were very happy with their baby boy. The little fellow grew strong. A few years passed and the boy was old enough to follow his father about.

One day he went with his father to watch the servants cut the ripe grain. What fun he had running and playing in the fields. Suddenly the boy became very sick. He put his hand to his head and cried, "My head! My head!"

"Carry the boy home," the father told the servant.

When the mother saw the servant carrying her son, she was frightened. What could be wrong? The servant put the boy on his mother's lap. How still and quiet the boy was! The mother did not want to disturb him. About noon he stopped breathing. The mother was heartbroken.

She carried her son's body to Elisha's room and laid him on the prophet's bed. With a servant she started out to find Elisha.

It was a long ride to Mount Carmel, but the woman did not think about the distance. As she hurried she must have prayed that God would help her find the prophet.

When Elisha saw the woman coming far down the road, he told his servant, "Here comes the Shunammite woman. Run to meet her. Ask if everything is well with her, her husband and her son."

The servant did as Elisha commanded, but the woman did not pay much attention to the servant. She wanted to see Elisha. When she reached him, she fell at his feet. Elisha knew at once she was very troubled, but God had not shown him what the trouble was.

"Did I ask for a child?" the woman cried.

The prophet knew something was wrong with the little boy. He told his servant, "Take my staff and hurry to Shunem. Do not stop to speak to anyone. When you get there, lay the staff across the child's face."

But the woman was not satisfied. She said, "I will not go back with just the servant. You must come too, Elisha."

Elisha's servant reached Shunem first. He found the child's body on his master's bed. He put Elisha's staff across the child's face, but

274

A room is prepared for Elisha

there was no sign of life. He left the room and started back to meet Elisha and the woman. When he reached them, he said, "I obeyed your words, but the child did not awaken."

Elisha hurried on. When he saw the little boy's body, he understood the mother's grief and sorrow. How much he wanted to help her! He closed the door of his room and prayed earnestly that God would restore the child's life.

After praying he put his face on the child's face and his hands on the child's hands. Soon the child's body grew warm. Then the child sneezed several times and opened his eyes.

Elisha called his servant and said, "Tell the Shunammite woman to come here."

When she came to his room Elisha said, "Pick up your son."

How thankful she was to see her child alive again! She bowed thankfully at Elisha's feet before carrying the boy to his father.

The School of the Prophets

2 Kings 4:38-44; 6:1-7

Food was scarce in the land of Israel, and the poor people had little to eat. During this time Elisha went to visit the young prophets who lived at Gilgal.

Elisha told his servant, "Put a large pot on the fire and prepare food for the prophets to eat."

One young man gathered vegetables and greens to cook for dinner. By mistake he picked poisonous wild gourds and cooked them with the other vegetables.

They began to eat, and someone discovered the poisonous gourds in the food. They cried to Elisha, "O man of God, there is death in the food!"

Elisha was not alarmed. He asked for some meal and threw it into the pot full of food. No longer was the food poisonous. Then he commanded, "Serve the food so the people can eat."

While Elisha stayed with the prophets, a man brought him twenty loaves of barley bread and some ears of grain. Elisha knew how much the young prophets would enjoy the bread and grain. He told a servant to give the bread and grain to the prophets for their dinner.

In surprise the servant asked, "How can one hundred men be fed with these few small loaves? There is not enough grain to pass around."

Again Elisha said, "Give this food to the people so they can eat. The Lord will bless the food so there will be enough for all."

Then the servant obeyed. Every man had all he wanted to eat and there was some left over.

Some time later the prophets told Elisha, "This place is too small for us. Let us move down by the Jordan and build new homes."

Elisha approved of the plan and went with the young men. They cut down the trees along the riverbank for their new homes. While they worked the ax head flew off one man's ax and dropped into the river.

As the man saw it plop into the muddy water, he cried out, "Oh, what shall I do? It was a borrowed ax."

Elisha asked, "Where did it fall?"

The man showed him the place. Then Elisha cut a stick and threw it into the water there. As the men watched they saw the ax head rise from the bottom of the river and float like a piece of wood.

Elisha said, "Reach out and get it."

The man did, and the young men marveled at the mighty power of God that was shown by Elisha.

A Little Slave Girl Helps Naaman

2 Kings 5:1-14

In the country to the north of Israel lived the Syrians. They had never been taught about the true God, so they worshiped an idol called Rimmon. In their cities they built temples for Rimmon.

While Elisha was the prophet in Israel, the Syrians sometimes attacked the cities of Israel. The invaders took from these cities anything they wanted. Sometimes they even took people and children for slaves.

In one raid on an Israelite city, a little girl was captured. With others she was taken to Syria and sold as a slave. Naaman, the rich captain of the Syrian army, saw the little girl and bought her to serve his wife.

The little maid was treated kindly. She learned how to wait on her mistress. After a while she began to like her new home. As time passed she began to think of Naaman and his wife as her family.

Then trouble came. Naaman had a serious disease called leprosy. Already there were white spots on his skin. Unless he was cured, the skin would decay and drop off.

At first he did not have pain, but Naaman knew he would eventually suffer greatly. Even his fingers and toes would drop off. Perhaps he would lose other parts of his body. Finally he would die.

The king of Syria was sorry that the captain of his army had leprosy. Naaman was a brave captain. He had led the Syrians to victory many times. The king thought so much of Naaman that he chose the captain to go with him to the temple of Rimmon to worship their idol.

The little slave girl, too, was very sad when she found out her master had this terrible disease. How much she wanted to comfort Naaman and his wife! She told her mistress, "If my master Naaman would go to God's prophet in Samaria, the prophet would make him well."

Naaman's wife was interested at once. She hurried to tell her husband what the little girl had said. Naaman ran to tell the king.

The king smiled when he heard it, for he loved Naaman and wanted to see him cured of his leprosy. "I will write a letter to the king of Israel and ask him to cure you of this disease. You will go to Samaria at once and take the letter with you," the king said.

The king of Syria knew nothing about the true God. He thought surely the king of Israel would be the most powerful person in all that country. To repay the king of Israel for this favor, he sent gold and silver and beautiful clothing. The servants loaded these gifts onto their horses. With Naaman they started for Samaria.

Naaman's prancing horses and great chariot stopped before the palace in Samaria. A messenger delivered the letter to the king of Israel. Anxiously Naaman and his servants waited outside the gate for the king's answer.

A slave girl helps Naaman

How distressed the king of Israel was when he read the letter! He said, "Does the king of Syria think I am God that I can kill and make alive? Why has he sent this leprous man to me? How can I make him well? It must be that the king of Syria is only using this as an excuse to make war against us."

He was so troubled that he tore his clothes, for he did not know what to do. If he had loved and served the true God instead of idols, he would have known about God's prophet Elisha.

Outside the gate Naaman and his servants wondered why the king was so slow. Little did they know the excitement and trouble their letter had caused.

While they waited Elisha sent to the king and asked, "Why have you torn your clothes? Send the leprous man to me so he can know there is a prophet in Israel."

The king was relieved to get Elisha's message. Quickly he sent Naaman and his servants to Elisha's house.

When Naaman and his servants came, Elisha did not go out to meet them. Instead he sent a servant who told Naaman, "My master Elisha says, 'Go and wash in the Jordan River seven times. Then your skin will become new and the leprosy will be gone.'"

Naaman felt insulted. Not only had Elisha refused to come out to see him, but he had told Naaman to bathe in the muddy Jordan. Angrily Naaman stalked away from Elisha's house and started back to Syria. "Why should I bathe in that muddy river when I can bathe in the clear waters of our rivers at home?" he asked.

Naaman's servants knew that bathing alone would never cure their master of leprosy. They wanted him to do as the prophet said. If he did not, he might never be well again.

One servant said to Naaman, "If this prophet had come to you and told you to do something hard, would you have done it?" Naaman nodded his head. Then the servant asked, "Then why not do this little thing and be cured of your leprosy?"

Naaman knew the servant had spoken wisely. He ordered the driver to turn toward the Jordan. When they reached the river, he went down into the muddy water. He dipped his body one time. Still the spots of leprosy were there. Again he dipped, but he could see no change. Three, four, five, six times he dipped, but nothing happened. When he came out of the water the seventh time, he could not find a single trace of the disease anywhere on his body.

How happy Naaman was! He must go to the prophet at once and tell him what had happened.

When Elisha came out, Naaman said, "Now I know there is no God in all the earth but in Israel." He was thankful to be well again.

Elisha's Foolish Servant

2 Kings 5:15-27

Naaman was so glad to be cured of leprosy that he said to Elisha, "Let me give you a present to show you how thankful I am to be well again."

But Elisha would not take a present. He wanted Naaman to know that God's gifts could not be bought with money.

Then Naaman asked, "Let me take back some earth from the land of Israel. I want to make an altar and worship the true God."

Naaman thought God would not be pleased with an altar that was built from the soil of a heathen country. No longer did the Syrian captain want to worship idols. He knew now that idols could not see or hear or help in times of need.

When Elisha's servant, Gehazi, saw the fine gifts Naaman had offered, he was very disappointed that Elisha did not take them. He watched Naaman and his servants as they started back to Syria. He thought about all the things a person could buy with the silver and gold. He pictured in his mind the beautiful clothes Naaman had brought. The more Gehazi thought about these presents the more he wanted to have them.

When Elisha went back into the house, Gehazi ran after Naaman. Soon Naaman saw the servant running after them. He stopped his chariot and turned to meet Gehazi.

Gehazi said, "After you left two young prophets came to Elisha. He has sent me to ask you to give these young men some silver and some new clothes."

Naaman believed Gehazi. He gave even more than Gehazi had asked for. It took two servants to help carry the gifts.

When Gehazi got back to Elisha's house, he was careful not to let Elisha see him and Naaman's servants with the gifts. He hid the things and sent the servants back to Naaman. Then he went to Elisha.

"Where have you been?" Elisha asked.

Gehazi answered, "I haven't been away."

Elisha knew his servant had not told the truth. He said, "My heart went with you when you followed Naaman and brought back gifts. Because you wanted riches more than you wanted to please God, you will be a leper instead of Naaman."

And Gehazi's skin became as white as snow. Now the servant realized the great wrong he had done.

Joash, the Boy King

2 Chronicles 22:11—24:3

Joash was only seven years old when he became king of Judah. As a little prince he was never allowed to run and play like other children. He was seldom allowed out of doors. Most of the time he hid in the temple. Always there was someone to watch and protect him. If his grandmother, Queen Athaliah, had known about Joash, she would have had him killed to make sure he did not become the ruler of Judah in place of her.

Little Joash was an orphan. After his father's death, Queen Athaliah ordered all his brothers and sisters to be killed. Then she thought there was no one left to rule the country but her. The queen did not know about the baby prince, Joash. His aunt had hidden him with his faithful nurse in a safe place.

For six years Queen Athaliah ruled the people. Many, many of them did not want her to be their queen. They knew that only David's descendants should sit upon the throne. Athaliah was not one of David's family. She was a heathen. Never did she go to worship in the beautiful temple of the Lord even though it was close to her palace. Instead she worshiped in an idol temple. Because she wanted to make her temple more attractive, she ordered her sons to tear out the beautiful parts of the temple of the Lord and put them in her place of heathen worship. The sons obeyed.

The boy Joash becomes king

While Athaliah went on ruling the people, the high priest Jehoiada was busy planning a way to crown Joash king of Judah. Jehoiada was Joash's uncle. Jehoiada's wife had rescued little Joash as a baby. They had kept Joash safe all these years.

When Joash was seven years old, his uncle called the leaders from all parts of the country to the temple at Jerusalem. Jehoiada brought Joash to them and said, "Look at the king's son. He is one of David's descendants. He should rule Judah because the Lord chose David's descendants to be our rulers."

The men agreed, but how could they make Joash king while Queen Athaliah ruled so cruelly? Jehoiada explained, "We will divide into three groups. One group will guard the doors of the temple, another, the king's palace and a third, the gate. No one will be allowed in the temple but the Levites. The people will fill the temple courts. Here are swords and spears for those who guard the doors. They must not let Queen Athaliah or her forces enter."

And they did just as Jehoiada said. On the Sabbath Joash was brought out where all the people could see him. How glad the people were that one of David's descendants was still alive and would become their ruler! How excited they were as they watched Jehoiada and his sons anoint little Joash king and place the crown on his head. With a glad cry they shouted, "God save the king!"

When Queen Athaliah saw the crowds of people going to the temple and heard the shouts of joy, she was afraid things had gotten out of control. At once she ran to the temple and dashed through the crowd. There she saw the little king standing by the pillar with the crown on his head. "Treason! Treason!" Athaliah shouted as she tore her clothes.

Jehoiada commanded the guards to carry the queen away. They took her outside the city gate. There she was killed. When the idol worshipers heard about the queen's death, they were so afraid that they did not dare stir up trouble for the high priest and the new king.

Joash Repairs the Temple

2 Chronicles 24:4-11

Seven-year-old Joash was not old enough to rule the people himself. Until he grew to manhood, his uncle Jehoiada did that. Jehoiada taught Joash how to be a good ruler. He taught the boy to love and serve God.

When Joash became a man, he wanted to repair the temple of the Lord. Many, many years had passed since Solomon had built it. Now the temple was old. While Athaliah was queen, many of the beautiful decorations had been taken out and put in the temple of her idol Baal. Joash wanted to redecorate the temple.

Joash called all the priests and Levites. He told them, "Go to all the cities of Judah each year and collect money to repair the house of God. Take care of this matter right away, and we can begin work on the temple."

But the Levites did not begin at once, and the money came so slowly that Joash grew impatient. He commanded that a large box be placed at the door of the temple. Then everyone who came to worship would see the offering box. In the lid was a hole through which people could drop their money for repairing the temple.

The people were glad to help make the house of the Lord beautiful again. They brought much money. Soon the workmen were busy repairing every worn-out part of the great building. They even made new ornaments of gold and silver. From that time on the people came regularly to the temple to worship.

Jehoiada, the high priest, lived to be a very old man. As long as he lived, Joash ruled wisely and worshiped the Lord. After Jehoiada died the idol worshipers grew very friendly with the king. They persuaded Joash to do wrong. Then they caused him to forget God.

In his last days Joash did many things that displeased God. He even commanded Jehoiada's son, God's prophet, to be stoned.

Great trouble came to Joash after he forsook God. The Syrians invaded the country and robbed the people. In the battle many of the idol worshipers were killed, and King Joash was wounded. Finally some of his servants killed him while he slept.

285

God Protects Elisha

2 Kings 6:8-23

The king of Syria looked at the little country of Israel to the south. He wished Israel belonged to him. So he planned to attack one city at a time until he had taken the country from King Jehoram.

The Syrian soldiers attacked one city. How surprised they were to find Jehoram had the city strongly guarded! How could he have known that he should guard the city?

When the Syrian soldiers returned home, their king sent them to attack another city of Israel. Again Jehoram had a strong guard protecting the city and waiting to drive the Syrians away.

Several times the Syrians tried to capture cities in Israel, but every time the forces of Israel were waiting to drive them back. How strange that Jehoram always knew just which city the Syrians were going to attack!

The king of Syria decided that someone was telling Jehoram his military secrets. "I must find the guilty man and punish him," he thought. Calling all his soldiers together he said, "Show me which man is giving our secrets to the king of Israel."

None of the Syrian soldiers were being untrue to their king and their country, but one of them knew how Jehoram found out which cities to fortify. He said, "O King, I know who your enemy is. None of us are telling your plans. It is the prophet Elisha. He tells the king of Israel where you are going to attack. Then Jehoram sends his soldiers to protect that city."

The king of Syria knew he could never win the battles so long as Elisha was telling the Israelites his plans. He told his men, "Go and find out where Elisha is. Then I will capture him."

The men returned to tell the king that Elisha was at Dothan. To make sure they captured Elisha the king sent a large army after the prophet. The Syrian chariots and horses and soldiers surrounded the city where Elisha lived.

When Elisha's servant saw soldiers coming from every side, he ran to Elisha. In fear he cried out, "O my master, what shall we do?"

Elisha answered quietly, "Do not be afraid, for there are more with us than with the Syrians."

The servant could not understand. There were only two of them, but there were thousands of Syrians coming from every direction to take them prisoners.

Elisha prayed, "O Lord, open the eyes of my servant that he may see."

And the servant saw the mountains full of horses and chariots of fire to protect Elisha. Now he knew God was caring for them. He was not afraid any longer.

When the Syrians reached Dothan, all of them became blind. Then Elisha went out to them. He said, "Follow me, and I will take you to the man you want."

The Syrians followed, and Elisha led them to the city of Samaria. When all were inside the city gates, Elisha prayed, "O Lord, open the eyes of these men so they can see."

The men opened their eyes and looked around. How afraid they were! Here they were inside the walls of Samaria. This was King Jehoram's city. No wonder they were afraid!

Jehoram looked on all the Syrians. How surprised he was to have them all in his city without the least bit of trouble. He thought Elisha wanted him to take the Syrians prisoners. "Shall I kill them?" he asked the prophet.

Elisha answered, "No. You must give them bread and water, for they are hungry. Then you must send them on their way."

Jehoram was not a good man. Yet he respected Elisha and obeyed his words. He had much food cooked and gave it to the Syrians. When they finished eating, he sent them back to their own land. Never again did the Syrians try to harm Elisha.

Food for a Starving City

2 Kings 6:24–7:20

Great trouble came to the people of Israel. Benhadad, king of Syria, led his great army into Israel and surrounded the city of Samaria. Day after day the Syrians waited for the Israelites to open the gate, but the Israelites did not. They would do almost anything to keep from being captured by the Syrians.

Benhadad knew the people of Israel would starve if he waited long enough. All their fields were outside the city. Now that the city gates were locked there was no way for the people to get food. The Syrians were in no hurry. They camped about the royal city and waited.

Inside the city walls, the people became hungrier and hungrier. Those who were rich offered to pay a lot of money for even a handful of food. Finally there was nothing to eat except horses or donkeys.

Soon even King Jehoram had only a few horses left.

As Jehoram walked through the streets of Samaria, he saw how bad things were. In terror he tore his clothes and dressed in sackcloth. "Elisha, the prophet, is to blame for this famine," he said. "I am going to kill him for this."

Elisha knew Jehoram was sending a man to kill him. He told his friends to keep the man at the door until the king arrived. They waited and Jehoram did come with one of his officers.

Boldly Elisha told the king, "Tomorrow about this time there will be food for all the hungry people in the city. The food will be sold at the gate for a small price."

The king's officer did not believe Elisha. He said, "Even if the Lord made windows in heaven, could this be true?"

"You will see the food with your own eyes," Elisha said, "but you will not eat it." And the king decided to give Elisha one more day to see if his words came true.

That night four lepers came to the gate of Samaria and sat down. They were tired and hungry. Because they had this serious disease called leprosy, they could not live among their own people.

The lepers wondered what to do. If they entered the city, they would starve. If they gave themselves up to the Syrians, they might be killed or taken prisoners. If they were taken prisoners, they would be fed. Because they felt they had nothing to lose, these four lepers decided to give themselves up to the enemy.

That same evening God caused the Syrians to hear strange noises. It sounded like a mighty army coming through the darkness. They listened in fear. Then they said to one another, "Listen, the king of Israel has hired many kings and their armies to attack us."

The Syrians knew they were not prepared to fight a strong army, and they did not want to be defeated. Up they jumped and ran toward their homeland as fast as they could. Their tents, food and possessions were all left behind. Even as they ran they dropped treasures they had planned to take home. There were fine clothes and other things all along the road.

None of the people inside the walls of Samaria knew that the Syrians had fled. The four lepers did not know it either. They hoped the Syrians would take them prisoners and feed them.

When they reached the Syrian camp, there was not a soldier anywhere. But there was plenty of food, and the four ate hungrily. When their stomachs were full, they gathered treasures of gold, silver and fine clothing.

At first they planned to hide these things in a safe place. Then they thought about all the starving people inside the city. "It would be wrong not to tell the people what we have found," they decided. So they hurried to the city gate and told the gatekeeper the good news.

Soon the lepers' message was being told in every part of the city. Even King Jehoram was awakened to hear the news. At first he thought the Syrians were only trying to trick them into opening the gate. Finally his servants persuaded him to send out a scouting party.

Jehoram's men returned with the news that they could find none of Benhadad's army. "But we found their things dropped all along the road. They must have been in a great hurry to get away. They did not even stop to pick up the things they dropped."

When the people heard this, they went out to the Syrian camp to see what was left behind. They found much food and brought it to the gate of the city to sell.

The officer who had gone with Jehoram to see Elisha sat at the gate where the food was being sold. The starving people were so eager to get the food that they pushed and shoved and crowded.

The officer could not keep order. When the crowd pushed against him, he fell down and was trampled to death. As Elisha had said the day before, the officer saw the food, but he did not get to eat it.

Jonah Disobeys God

Jonah 1–2

God spoke to Jonah and said, "Get up and go to Nineveh. Preach to the people of that great city and warn them to turn from their wickedness."

But Jonah did not want to go to Nineveh, the capital city of Assyria. The Assyrians had a strong army that was conquering many of the nearby small countries. Israel was afraid it would be captured next.

Jonah knew the Ninevites worshiped idols. They had done this for hundreds of years. They did not know about the true God, and each year they became more wicked. Jonah could go and teach them about the true God. Instead he decided, "I'll not go to Nineveh. I'll go down to the Great Sea and take a ship going in the opposite direction. Then maybe I can get far enough away from God that he will not remind me to go to preach to the wicked Ninevites."

Down by the seaside Jonah found a ship ready to sail. He paid his fare and climbed aboard. The ship was bound for Tarshish, a city far from Nineveh. Jonah felt greatly relieved to be going somewhere else instead of Nineveh. He went down into the ship and soon fell asleep.

The ship set sail. When it got out into the sea, a great storm arose. The sailors were afraid. They called on their gods to quiet the winds, but the winds only blew harder than ever. What should they do? It looked as if the boat would be torn to pieces and all of them drowned.

To lighten the ship they threw all the cargo overboard. Even this did not help. As the captain paced the deck, he thought of Jonah. The captain found Jonah lying deep in the boat sound asleep. He shook Jonah and said, "Get up! Call on God. If God doesn't save us, we shall all die."

Jonah did not feel like calling on God for help. He knew he had run away from the work God wanted him to do. When he saw the mighty waves dash against the ship and toss it like a chip on the water, he was afraid he would never see dry land again.

The sailors ask Jonah how to calm the storm

Claire Upton

The storm continued to rage. The sailors decided that someone on board the ship was to blame for this trouble. They decided to cast lots and find out who the person was. They did this, and the lot fell on Jonah.

At once the sailors gathered around him and asked, "Who are you and what is your business? Why are you on this ship? What country do you come from?"

Jonah answered, "I am a Hebrew. I serve the Lord God who made the heaven and the sea and the dry land."

When they heard this, the sailors were even more afraid, for they did not know there was such a great God. Surely Jonah's God must be very angry. Jonah told them that he had run away because he did not want to preach to the people of Nineveh.

"What shall we do to you to calm this storm?" the men asked. They knew the ship would not hold together much longer.

"Throw me overboard and the storm will end," Jonah told them.

First the sailors tried to row toward land, but it was no use. Finally they picked Jonah up and threw him into the water. Then the waves grew quiet, the wind calmed and the storm was over.

When Jonah fell into the water, a great fish that God had made swallowed him. For three days and three nights, Jonah lived inside the fish.

During that time Jonah prayed to the Lord. He was sorry he had disobeyed. He would go to Nineveh gladly and preach to the people.

The Lord heard Jonah's prayer and had the fish cast Jonah up on the shore.

Jonah Preaches at Nineveh

Jonah 3—4

When Jonah entered the city, he cried out: "Nineveh will be destroyed within forty days because it is so wicked!" And he went throughout the city telling the people they would suffer because they had sinned against God.

As Jonah stood on the street corners and preached, the people stopped to hear his strange message. They had never seen a prophet of God before. Some ran to tell their king what Jonah had said.

Even the king was frightened. He left his throne and took off his rich robes. He dressed in sackcloth and sat in ashes to show how sorry he was for his sins.

Not only did the king repent, but he commanded, "Let everyone dress in sackcloth and cry earnestly to God. Let everyone turn away from evil. Perhaps God will have mercy on us and spare our lives."

After Jonah finished preaching, he went outside the city walls and waited to see fire fall on Nineveh. Although Jonah had obeyed God by telling the people of their sins, he did not want them to repent. The Assyrians and the Israelites were enemies, and Jonah hoped this Assyrian city would be destroyed. Then perhaps the Assyrians would not trouble Israel.

For forty days Jonah waited and no fire fell. Because the people believed Jonah's message and repented of their sins, God did not destroy the city. How unhappy Jonah was! He even prayed to die.

In the night God caused a gourd vine to grow up. It grew fast and soon shaded Jonah from the burning sun. The next night a worm attacked the vine. The green leaves withered and died. Again Jonah wished he were dead.

God said to him, "You were sorry to see the plant die even though you did not make it grow. Should you not feel more sorry for the people of Nineveh than you do for a plant?"

At last Jonah understood that God loves all people.

Isaiah and Hosea, Two Great Prophets

Isaiah; Hosea

Once when Isaiah was a young man, he went to the temple to worship. There he had a vision of the Lord sitting on his throne while the angels sang, "Holy, holy, holy is the Lord of hosts: the whole earth is full of his glory."

When Isaiah thought about how great and holy God is, he felt small and unworthy. He prayed, "Woe is me, for I am lost. I say wrong things, and I live among people who speak falsely."

Isaiah's lips were touched, and his sin taken away. Then the voice of the Lord asked, "Whom shall I send? Who will go for me?"

To this Isaiah answered, "Here I am; send me."

From that time on Isaiah spoke God's words boldly. He lived in Jerusalem and was well acquainted with the king's family and the other rulers. During his life four different kings reigned—Uzziah, Jotham, Ahaz and Hezekiah. Isaiah tried to persuade each of them to trust in God instead of heathen princes. His advice was more respected by Hezekiah than by the others.

While Isaiah was speaking God's words to the people of Judah, Hosea was warning the people of Israel that their unfaithfulness to God would bring punishment. Hosea tried to help the Israelites to understand what would happen if they did not obey the Lord.

Israel Is Enslaved

2 Kings 17

Though the Ninevites had listened to Jonah and asked God to forgive their sins, the people of Israel ignored the Lord's prophets. Of course a few believed, but most people did not. Their kings worshiped golden calves instead of the true God.

Many years passed. Finally God decided that the Israelites would never turn to him with all their hearts. Nineteen kings had ruled the land, and many times God had helped them out of trouble. Still they did not lead their people back to God.

God allowed the Assyrians, whose capital city was Nineveh, to capture some of the Israelites and take them as slaves to a strange land. For a while Hoshea, king of Israel, paid heavy taxes to the Assyrians.

One year Hoshea refused to pay. Again the king of Assyria sent his army. He took Hoshea and many of his people to Assyria. Only the poorest Israelites were left in the land. Those who were taken away were never again allowed to return to their homeland.

Since he had conquered the country, the Assyrian king ruled the land of Israel. He decided it was not good to leave the Israelite cities empty, and so he brought heathen people from the east to live in Samaria. He told them, "You can work the fields and care for the vineyards. Each year when you sell your crops, you can pay me for letting you use the land."

The heathen who came to live in the cities of Israel did not know about the true God. They sent a messenger to tell the king of Assyria, "We do not know how to worship the God of this land, and we are afraid of him."

The king of Assyria commanded, "Send back one of the priests that we captured. He can teach the heathen there to worship the God of Israel."

A priest of the Israelites taught the heathen about the true God, and the heathen tried to worship the God of Israel. Because they still worshiped their own idols, the right and wrong got mixed up.

Good King Hezekiah

2 Kings 18–19; 2 Chronicles 29:1–32:23

Of the twelve Israelite tribes, only the tribe of Judah was not carried into captivity. When young Hezekiah became the king of Judah, the kingdom was very weak. It had been ruled for many years by men who did not serve the true God. These rulers had even closed up the temple of the Lord.

Hezekiah wanted his people to worship the true God. He called for the priests and the Levites to come to Jerusalem and clean the temple.

The Feast of the Passover had not been held for many, many years. When God's house was ready for worship, Hezekiah invited everyone in the land of Judah and Israel to come to the Feast of the Passover.

Some of the people laughed when they received Hezekiah's invitation. They had worshiped idols for so long that they did not want to go to Jerusalem to worship the true God. Still many, many people from the land of Judah came gladly to the feast. Together they rejoiced in the Lord.

King Hezekiah ordered that all the idols in his land be destroyed. Because the people even worshiped the brass serpent that Moses had made in the wilderness, Hezekiah had it torn down and thrown into the fire. He tried to teach the people to do what was right, and his country became stronger.

Before Hezekiah came to the throne, the king of Assyria had gained power over Judah. Every year the people had to pay heavy taxes to him. Hezekiah did not want his people paying taxes to a heathen king, and so he refused to pay. He knew the king of Assyria would bring an army to try to force him to pay. To get ready for the attack, Hezekiah built up the walls of Jerusalem until they were very strong. Then he gathered an army and prepared to fight.

Even when Hezekiah had his men trained for battle, they were only a handful compared to the mighty Assyrian army. The enemy marched into the land of Judah and took one city after another. On toward Jerusalem they came.

At last Hezekiah knew his soldiers could not keep the Assyrians away, but it was too late to do anything about it. Finally poor Hezekiah sent word to the king of Assyria that he would not fight any longer.

When the king of Assyria got the message, he thought, "Now is my chance to ruin this little country of Judah." He demanded a heavier tax than ever before.

Hezekiah did not know how they could ever get all the money the king of Assyria demanded. He took all the gold and silver that was in his palace. Added to this was all the gold and silver he could get from the people. Still it was not enough. Finally he even had to take the silver and gold from the temple of the Lord.

Still the king of Assyria was not satisfied. He sent this message to Hezekiah: "I will destroy your city and take you and your people to a far country just as I have done to the people of Israel. When I fought against other nations, their idols did not help them. Your God won't be able to save you either."

How afraid Hezekiah was when he heard this message! What could his little army do against the powerful Assyrians? Hezekiah took the king's letter and went to the temple. He spread the letter before the altar and prayed. He asked God to help him and his people out of their trouble. Then he sent several princes to the prophet Isaiah to find out God's will.

Isaiah answered, "The Lord says that the king of Assyria will not enter Jerusalem, nor will he even shoot an arrow against it. He will go back to his country the way he came. There he will be killed."

That night the Assyrian soldiers became so ill that many of them died. Among the dead were all the leaders of the army. In fear the king gathered his troops and hurried back to his own land. Never again did he return to fight against Hezekiah, for God had heard and answered Hezekiah's prayers.

God Spares Hezekiah's Life

2 Kings 20

Hezekiah was sick, very sick. No one knew how to help him get better. When Isaiah came to visit the king, the prophet said, "The Lord wants you to get your business taken care of, for you are going to die."

Hezekiah was not afraid to die, but he felt his people needed him. When he heard what Isaiah said, he turned his face to the wall. "O Lord," he prayed, "I have followed you with all my heart. I have always tried to do right and please you." At the thought of leaving his people, Hezekiah wept sorrowfully.

God heard Hezekiah's prayer. As Isaiah was on his way home, God told him, "Go back to the king and tell him I have heard his prayer and seen his tears. I will add fifteen years to his life. In three days he will be able to go to the temple to worship."

How glad Hezekiah was to hear this! Still he wanted Isaiah to give him some sign that he was really going to be well.

Isaiah asked, "Would you like to have the shadow on the sundial go backward or forward ten degrees?"

"Have it go backward," Hezekiah said. "The shadow always goes forward. It would be a sign from God if it went backward."

Isaiah prayed and asked God to move the shadow backward ten degrees. Then Hezekiah believed the Lord would heal him.

Just as God had promised, Hezekiah was healed, and he lived for fifteen years more. He built up his kingdom and became very rich. For a time he was proud of his riches, but God taught him to be humble again.

When Hezekiah died all the people mourned. He had been a good king, and they loved him.

Josiah and the Forgotten Book

2 Chronicles 34—35

The king of Judah was eight-year-old Josiah. Since he was not old enough to rule the land, the high priest Hilkiah governed until Josiah was sixteen years old. During this time the king sought the Lord and did what was right.

While Josiah was still a young man, he proclaimed a house cleaning in the temple of the Lord. After Hezekiah's death the temple had been neglected. It had even been misused. One king had set up altars to his idol Baal right in the courts of the Lord's house. Josiah decreed that the temple be repaired so all the people could worship God there.

Many skillful workmen were hired to make the temple beautiful again. The heathen altars were torn away, carried outside the city and burned. Men worked in wood and stone to get the temple in readiness.

While the repair work was going on, the high priest cleaned the rooms of the temple. There, hidden away beneath some rubbish, he found a strange scroll. He looked at it carefully, then unrolled it and began to read.

Hilkiah soon recognized this scroll as the book of the Law. Long before, God had given Moses the words, and Moses had written them in a book. Moses had commanded that the book of the Law be read to all the people once each seven years, but the people had not kept his command. Then the book was forgotten.

Carefully the high priest removed the dust from this precious book. How excited he was! Finding this book was like finding a treasure. He called to Shaphan, the scribe, "I have found the book of the Law in the house of the Lord!"

The high priest placed the precious book in Shaphan's hands and sent him to King Josiah. Josiah, too, became excited. He had never heard the words of God's law. "Read to me from the book," he told Shaphan.

Shaphan read the strange words. He read about God's promise to bless the people if they served him faithfully. Then he read God's promise to punish the people if they forsook him and worshiped idols.

Josiah reads from the Law

Josiah was alarmed. His people had disobeyed God's law. Surely God would punish them as he had said. The king tore his clothes and wept bitterly. What would happen to his people?

Josiah told the priest, "Go, ask of the Lord about the words in the book. Great is the punishment in store for us because our fathers have not kept the word of the Lord."

Hilkiah went to Huldah, the prophetess, to ask her about God's plan to punish the people for their sins.

The prophetess said, "God will send great punishment to those who forsake his law and worship idols. But because Josiah has humbled his heart and wept tears of sorrow for the sins of his people, God will not let the people be punished while Josiah lives."

Josiah did not want to forget the words of God's law. The people must hear these words too. Throughout all the land messengers were sent to call the people to Jerusalem.

When the people came, Josiah read to them from the book. That day the king promised to keep the Law and to serve the Lord with all his heart. He commanded the people to make the same promise, and they obeyed.

Later Josiah prepared for the Passover Feast. From every part of the land, the people came. From his own flocks, the king gave many lambs for the Passover supper. The people rejoiced together and kept the feast for seven days. Not since the days of the prophet Samuel had there been such a great Passover.

For thirty-one years Josiah ruled the people. At the end of his reign, the king of Egypt marched through the land of Judah to fight against the Assyrians. Josiah did not want this army going through his country, so he got ready to attack them.

The king of Egypt did not want to fight with Josiah. He sent word for Josiah to go back home, but Josiah would not go. Instead he dressed like an ordinary soldier and went out to battle. During the fight an arrow wounded him. His servants brought him back to Jerusalem in a chariot. Josiah died, and the people buried him among the honorable kings of Judah.

Five Other Prophets

Amos; Micah; Nahum; Habakkuk; Zephaniah

Men who taught God's will were called prophets. Such men were specially chosen by God to tell the people his words. The Spirit of God helped them know what to say, and they were commanded to proclaim it.

Much of their work was warning the people to turn from their sins and follow God's way. By God's Spirit the prophets were often able to tell what would happen in the future if the people did not obey God.

The shepherd Amos came from Tekoa, a small town of Judah. But Amos did not speak God's words to his own people. God called him to preach in Israel.

Most of Amos' life was spent out of doors, either as a shepherd or as a tender of sycamore trees. It is probable that Amos sometimes took sheep, wool or hides as far as Egypt or Damascus.

Wherever he went or whatever he did, Amos never forgot he was one of God's prophets. He spoke out boldly against the sins of the king and the people. Most often Amos spoke about justice. How much he wanted to see the poor treated fairly!

In Judah Micah attacked the way the poor were wronged by noblemen. He was plainspoken in denouncing these evils. The prophet Micah is remembered as a man of the people who sympathized with those who suffered. Nahum, a later prophet, is remembered for his warnings to the people of Nineveh.

Zephaniah was a descendant of King Hezekiah. As one of God's prophets, Zephaniah spoke God's words to the people of Judah. He warned them that God was going to judge and punish the nations for their evil ways. He said the time would come when idolatry would be overthrown in Jerusalem. He begged the people of Judah to repent of their sins so they would not have to be punished.

The people did not listen. Finally Zephaniah told them a small group would follow God's ways in spite of their trouble and sufferings. This group would trust in the Lord and become a praise in the earth.

God's prophet Habakkuk was one of the temple singers. How disturbed he was because the world was so wicked! As the Chaldean nation grew in strength, it took the small countries around about. Habakkuk warned the people of Judah that this would happen to them, too, because they had turned away from God.

Jeremiah Answers God's Call

Jeremiah 1—6

Before Josiah became king of Judah, a son was born to a priest named Hilkiah. The boy was called Jeremiah. With his family he grew up in the small town of Anathoth near Jerusalem. Few people knew anything about Jeremiah, for he was shy and quiet.

When Jeremiah was twenty years old, God said to him, "I want you to be my prophet to the nations."

How frightened Jeremiah was when he heard this! How could he speak to kings and rulers about God? "O Lord God," Jeremiah said, "I don't know how to speak, for I am very young."

God did not want Jeremiah to make excuses. He said, "You will go to every person I send you to, and you will speak my words. Do not be afraid of anyone, for I am with you." Then the Lord touched Jeremiah's mouth and said, "I have put my words in your mouth, and I have set you over the nations to do a great work for me."

No longer was Jeremiah afraid to obey God. He knew prophets were often mistreated because they spoke out against the sins of the people, but Jeremiah was brave and courageous. He would follow the Lord.

While Josiah was king, Jeremiah was treated kindly. After Josiah died the people began worshiping idols again. They did not care for the true God. Jeremiah went throughout the land reminding the people of their sins and of the punishment that would come. The people paid no attention to him.

Trouble came to the land of Judah. The king of Egypt took their new king into captivity and placed another one of Josiah's sons on the throne. Then Egypt demanded heavy taxes from the people of Judah every year.

Josiah's sons were not good men like their father. They forsook God and allowed idols to be set up throughout the land. Because Jeremiah warned them of the punishment for their sins, they treated him roughly.

Jeremiah Warns the People

Jeremiah 7—35

God told Jeremiah, "Go stand in the gate of the Lord's house. Proclaim my words to the people as they enter the gates to worship."

Jeremiah obeyed. He took his place by the gate of the temple and called out to the people as they came to worship. Above the din of the crowd Jeremiah shouted, "The Lord God of Israel says to you: 'Mend your ways and your doings, or this land will not always be your home. Coming to the temple will not help you unless you live right. You must be fair to one another. You must not make life hard for the traveler, the orphans and the widows. You must not worship other gods.'"

Perhaps the people laughed at Jeremiah or thought he was a little crazy. They did not turn from their wicked ways. Jeremiah decided, "I must get the people to listen, or our country will be destroyed because the people have turned away from God."

Jeremiah put a heavy wooden yoke on his shoulders and stood where all the people would see him. It was so strange to see a man wearing a yoke that the people stopped to look at him. Then Jeremiah called out, "Unless you listen to God's warning and turn to him, you will someday wear the yoke of your enemies."

Another time he took the priests and those who would follow him to a place beside the Pottery Gate. To show them how the country would be broken to pieces unless they repented, Jeremiah dashed a piece of pottery to the ground and the chips flew everywhere.

The people did not like to be reminded of their sins. Even the men of Jeremiah's hometown turned against him and wanted to kill him. But Jeremiah was not afraid. He went on preaching. He even went to the king with this message: "The Lord says you must be just and fair. You must see that none are mistreated and robbed. Unless you do what is right, your kingdom will be destroyed."

It seemed that Jeremiah's warnings did no good, but God sent him to the temple again. This time he said, "The Lord says if you will not listen to his prophets and keep his laws, this temple will be destroyed and this city will be ruined."

The people had heard enough of Jeremiah's warnings. Now they were angry. "Traitor!" they cried. "He wants the Babylonians to capture us. He says the temple is not as important as what is in a man's heart."

Boldly Jeremiah answered, "I am in your hand. Kill me if you wish, but you will suffer for it, for God has sent me."

Some of the princes and people became afraid. They did not let anything happen to Jeremiah that time. Jeremiah left the temple safely, but he was never allowed to enter it again.

Jeremiah Writes God's Words in a Book

Jeremiah 36

While Jehoiakim was king, this word came to Jeremiah from the Lord: "Take a roll of a book and write in it all the messages I have given you for the people of Israel and Judah and all the nations. Perhaps the people will seek forgiveness for their sins when they hear this book read."

Jeremiah called Baruch to help him. Jeremiah spoke the words God had given, and Baruch wrote them on the scroll. The two men worked for a long time. Finally the scroll was finished.

Jeremiah said, "You know I am not allowed in the temple anymore, so I cannot read this book to the people there. You take it and read it in the temple on a special day when there will be many people to hear. You tell them that these are the words of the Lord. When they hear this, maybe they will repent of their sins."

Baruch obeyed. One of the priest's sons was so impressed with the book that he hurried to the palace to tell the princes. He told all he could remember that Baruch had said. The princes were so excited that they sent for Baruch to come and read the book for them.

Eagerly the princes listened to every word. How frightened they became when they heard that their country would be captured because the people had forsaken God! They believed God's message. "We must tell the king all these words," they decided.

The princes were not sure the king would obey Jeremiah's words. He might even be angry with Jeremiah and Baruch. In times past the king had been very harsh with Jeremiah for speaking out against the sins of the country.

"Take Jeremiah and hide," the princes told Baruch. "Let no one know where you are. Then we will tell the king about God's message in this book."

The princes brought the book to King Jehoiakim as he sat before his blazing fireplace. Jehoiakim commanded that the book be read aloud. As soon as three or four columns had been read, the king took his penknife, cut them off the scroll and threw them into the fire.

Except for the princes those who watched did not seem the least bit afraid. They did not take the words of the Lord seriously. "Don't burn the roll," the princes begged, but their pleading did no good. Finally the entire book had been burned.

When Jeremiah learned what had happened, he told Baruch, "Take another roll and write in it all the words that were in the book Jehoiakim destroyed."

The second book was longer than the first because Jeremiah wrote about Jehoiakim's punishment. And the words that Jeremiah wrote were true. Not long afterwards the great king of the Chaldeans came and took many people of Judah away to be slaves in Babylon. King Jehoiakim was put in prison for many years.

Jeremiah in the Dungeon

Jeremiah 37–52

Even with the changes in kings, Jeremiah's troubles did not end. While Zedekiah was king, the Chaldeans returned to besiege Jerusalem again. Jeremiah went among his people warning them that the Chaldeans would win. The princes became so angry with Jeremiah that they had him thrown into a dungeon.

Enemy armies came nearer and nearer Jerusalem. The city was in great danger. The king was afraid. Secretly he sent for Jeremiah. When Jeremiah came the king asked, "Tell me, is there any word from the Lord?"

If Jeremiah's words pleased the king, the prophet would be free again. Jeremiah knew he must tell God's message faithfully even if he did have to stay in a dark dungeon.

Bravely he said, "You and your armies will be captured by the king of Babylon." Then Jeremiah wanted to know, "What have I done against you or your servants that you have put me in prison? Where are your own prophets who told you the king of Babylon would never war against us? Please do not send me back to the dungeon, or I shall die there."

The king listened carefully. This time he sent Jeremiah to the home of a prison guard. There the prophet would have better treatment.

With this little bit of freedom, Jeremiah again began to warn the people of the terrible things that were going to happen to them. The people became so angry that they threw Jeremiah into an old well that had deep mud in the bottom.

Jeremiah would have died, but Ebedmelech, a kind Ethiopian, went to the king and pleaded for the prophet. He said, "O King, these men have done wrong by throwing Jeremiah into that pit. He will die there without food or water."

The king ordered, "Take thirty men and get Jeremiah out." Ebedmelech found old clothes and rags and tied them together to make ropes. These they let down into the pit for Jeremiah to fasten under his armpits. Then they pulled him out.

And Jeremiah told the king, "The army will capture the city, break down its walls and even destroy the beautiful temple of the Lord. But God will not let the Chaldean king, Nebuchadnezzar, kill the people of Jerusalem if they will offer to become his servants. Then they will not need to starve to death inside the city."

Now Jeremiah was kept in the court of the prison and treated more kindly. But he was not allowed to go through the city or talk to the people.

The people of Jerusalem and their king did not want to give themselves up to Nebuchadnezzar. So weary months passed by. They stayed inside the walls of Jerusalem and suffered from hunger and thirst. Jeremiah suffered with them.

At last when all the food was gone, the king decided to slip away from Jerusalem during the night. He thought he could get away

Jeremiah is put in a dungeon

unnoticed. But King Zedekiah had not gone far when his enemies captured him. They led him to Babylon. Most of the people of Judah were taken with him, and only the old and the weak and the very poor were left in the land. Because Ebedmelech had rescued Jeremiah from the pit, God protected him and he was not captured.

Nebuchadnezzar and his army broke down the walls of Jerusalem. They took all the gold and silver vessels from the temple and carried them back to their own land. Then they burned the city.

What became of Jeremiah? The Chaldeans treated him kindly. Finally the captain of the guard said, "You may go to Babylon with the captives or you may stay here."

Jeremiah chose to remain in his own land. His work was not yet finished. After the people had been taken captive to that strange land, Jeremiah felt very sorry for them. He grieved for his people. For that reason he is sometimes called "the weeping prophet."

God told Jeremiah, "Write a message of comfort and hope to the people in captivity." And Jeremiah wrote the comforting words that God gave him.

STORIES ABOUT THE JEWS
Ezekiel; Daniel; Nehemiah; Haggai; Ezra; Esther; Malachi

Captives in a Strange Land

2 Chronicles 36:14-21; Ezekiel

After the city of Jerusalem was destroyed, the Chaldean army started the long journey back to Babylon, taking their prisoners with them. Even King Zedekiah was a captive. With him were most of his people—able-bodied men and women, young people and even children. The Chaldeans called their prisoners from Judah, Jews.

Day after day the great company of people walked on and on. They stopped only at night to camp by the roadside and rest from their weary journey. Each night as they made camp, the prisoners knew they were farther away from their homeland.

When they finally reached Babylon, the Jews found that their new ruler treated them more kindly than they had hoped. After giving them fields and houses, he let them work for themselves just as they had done in their own country. He even took some of the Jews to his capital city and trained them to become his nobles.

God did not forget the Jews after they were carried away to Babylon. He sent them messages from his faithful prophet Jeremiah. God promised to bring the Jews back to their own country if they would try to please and serve him while they lived in Babylon.

The people listened to these messages. They longed for the time when they could return to their homeland.

Even though the Chaldeans worshiped idols, the Jews refused to do the same. They knew how God hated idol worship. Now they wanted to please God. Often they met in small groups to talk about the land of Judah and the beautiful temple of the Lord that had been destroyed. They wept with homesickness.

Sometimes the Chaldeans asked the Jews to sing for them. They knew the Jews were skillful musicians. But the captive people hung their harps on the willow trees and refused to sing.

"How can we sing the Lord's song in a strange land?" they asked. David's beautiful songs of joy and victory would sound out of place in this strange country. And in their hearts they felt too sad to sing.

The Jews carefully taught their children about the true God. They welcomed the priests and the Levites when they came to talk about the Law of Moses. As the days and years passed they did not forget the hope Jeremiah had given them—the hope of returning to Jerusalem if they served the Lord.

In Babylon another man began to hear messages from God and to speak those messages to the people. This man was Ezekiel, one of the captives. He had been among the first to be taken prisoner. And afterwards he warned the people left in Judah about God's punishment for disobedience. Ezekiel saw wonderful visions from God. He encouraged the people to believe that the time would come when they would return again to their own land.

Daniel in the King's Court

Daniel 1

When the captives from Judah arrived in Babylon, King Nebuchadnezzar commanded his chief officer, "From our captives choose the best young men. Look for those who are strong and healthy, wise, trained and able. Bring them to the palace and teach them our language."

The chief officer obeyed. The king explained that the young men were to eat food from his own table. That would help them to grow strong, he thought. At the end of three years these young men were to be brought to the king.

Among those chosen from the captives were Daniel, Hananiah, Mishael and Azariah. Now Daniel and his three friends wanted to keep the law God had given to the people of Israel. According to that law, there were some kinds of food they could not eat. When the food was brought from the king's table, Daniel saw food that Israelites were not allowed to eat.

What should he do? Daniel and his three friends decided they must do what seemed right. Bravely Daniel told the officer, "It would

311

Hebrew boys refuse the King's food

be wrong for us to eat the king's meat and drink his wine. Do not force us to do this."

At first the officer was afraid the king would be displeased if the boys refused to eat his food. He said, "When you stand before Nebuchadnezzar, he will be very angry with me if you do not look as strong and healthy as the other young fellows. The king might even kill me for not taking good care of you."

"Try us for ten days," Daniel bargained. "Let us eat good vegetables and drink pure water. Then see if we do not look as strong and healthy as the other young men."

Daniel's offer seemed fair enough, so the officer agreed. For ten days he brought them vegetables and wholesome food instead of rich food and wine from the king's table.

At the end of ten days the officer noticed that Daniel and his three friends looked even healthier than the others. From that time on Daniel and his friends were given the wholesome food they wanted.

And God blessed Daniel and his friends with wisdom. In a short time they learned the language and wisdom of the Chaldeans.

Three years passed. Then the king ordered, "Bring the young men to me." When they came he talked with them and asked hard questions. He discovered that Daniel and his three friends were ten times wiser than the wisest men of his kingdom.

No wonder Nebuchadnezzar was pleased with these young Jews! He gave them places of honor in the kingdom, and they lived in Babylon for many years.

Daniel and the King's Dream

Daniel 2

One night King Nebuchadnezzar had a very strange dream. When he awoke he was so troubled that he could not go back to sleep. The dream was so unusual he decided it must have a deep meaning. "In the morning I'll call the wise men and have them explain the dream," he decided.

Morning came at last, but when Nebuchadnezzar got up, he could not remember his dream. Now he was even more troubled than before. The dream was too important to forget.

At once he sent for his wise men. When they came he said, "I have had a very strange dream, and I'm anxious to know what it means."

"O King, live forever," the wise men said. "Tell us your dream and we will tell you what it means."

"But I have forgotten the dream," the king answered. "If you do not tell me what I dreamed and what it means, you shall all be killed. If you tell me my dream and explain its meaning, I will give you rich gifts and great honor."

How puzzled the wise men were! Surely the king was being unfair. How could any person know what someone else had dreamed and forgotten? A second time the wise men said, "But you must tell us the dream before we can explain it to you."

Nebuchadnezzar became very angry. After accusing them of putting off answering in order to gain time, he decreed that all the wise men of Babylon should be killed. At once he sent Arioch, the captain of the guard, to get all the wise men.

Daniel and his three friends had heard nothing of the king's decree until Arioch came to take them. When Daniel heard what had happened, he asked to see the king.

At the palace he told Nebuchadnezzar, "If you will give me a little time, I will find out what the dream was and explain its meaning." The king agreed.

At once Daniel hurried back to his three friends and told them about his agreement. Even though no person was wise enough to tell the king's dream, God knew about it. Earnestly the four prayed for God's help. That night God showed Daniel the king's dream and its meaning.

How thankful Daniel was! He prayed, "Blessed be the name of God forever and ever. Wisdom and might are his. He changes the times and the seasons. He removes kings and sets them up. He gives wisdom to the wise and knowledge to those of understanding. He reveals the deep and secret things. He knows what is in the darkness and what is in the light. I thank you and praise you, O God of my

fathers! You have given me wisdom and might. You have answered our prayer, for you have made me know about the king's dream."

Quickly Daniel went to Arioch, the captain of the guard, and said, "Do not kill the wise men, but take me to the king. I can tell him his dream."

Arioch, too, was glad. As he brought Daniel before the king, he said, "I have found a man among the captives of Judah who will tell you about your dream."

Daniel told Nebuchadnezzar, "The secret you want to know is one that no man could tell you, but there is a God in heaven who knows all secrets. He has told me about your dream."

The king listened closely, and Daniel said, "O King, when you went to bed, you wondered what would happen in the future. Then you fell asleep, and God showed you what would happen. You saw a great bright image of a man. The head was made of gold, the chest and arms of silver, the waist and hips of brass, the legs of iron and the feet were part clay and part iron.

"You saw a stone, not moved by hands, roll against the feet of this great image. The stone broke the feet, and the whole image fell to the ground and broke into pieces. The pieces were as fine as dust, and the wind blew them away. While you watched, the stone grew bigger until it became a mountain and filled the whole earth."

The king nodded. Now he remembered his dream. Daniel had told it exactly right.

"Now I will tell you what this dream means," Daniel said. "God wants to teach you through this dream. The great image represents the four great kingdoms of the earth. Your kingdom is first, the head of gold. After you will come a lesser king, represented by the chest and arms of silver. The third kingdom is shown by the parts of brass and the fourth by the iron legs and feet. At first this fourth kingdom will be very strong, but it will become weaker as shown by the iron and clay feet.

"In the days of these kings," said Daniel, "God will set up a kingdom that will never be destroyed. His kingdom is represented by the stone, not moved with hands, that rolled against the image. God will increase his kingdom until it fills the whole earth, and every other kingdom will be broken into pieces. This, O King, is the meaning of your dream."

Daniel offers prayer

Nebuchadnezzar was amazed! How wise Daniel was! Perhaps the king thought Daniel was a god, for he bowed on the floor to worship him. Daniel reminded the king that it was the God of heaven who had told Daniel the dream and its meaning.

Nebuchadnezzar said, "Surely your God is a God of gods and a Lord of kings and a revealer of secrets."

To Daniel the king gave many great gifts and made him ruler of all the province of Babylon. From that time on Daniel was the head of all the wise men in the kingdom. Because Daniel had told the king's dream, none of the wise men were killed.

At Daniel's request his three friends were made governors of the land. These young men were given Chaldean names. The king knew them as Shadrach, Meshach and Abednego.

The Fiery Furnace

Daniel 3

Nebuchadnezzar grew in power until he was the greatest king in the world. Year after year he added new countries to his kingdom. In every land he was greatly feared. No wonder Nebuchadnezzar became proud of his success.

At his order an idol was made. It was ninety feet tall and was covered with gold. It stood on the plain of Dura where all could see it easily.

When the idol was finished, the king ordered all the officials of his kingdom to come and worship it. Princes, governors, captains, judges, treasurers, counselors, sheriffs and rulers were commanded to come to the plain of Dura. No one dared disobey. The crowd of officials gathered. Among them were Daniel's three friends, Shadrach, Meshach and Abednego. For some reason Daniel was not there.

King Nebuchadnezzar felt even prouder as he looked over the great crowd that had gathered before the idol. At the king's order a herald called out, "O people of all nations and languages, when you hear the music you must fall down and worship the king's idol. If you refuse you must be thrown into a fiery furnace."

The music sounded, and the people fell to their knees. They were afraid to disobey, for none wanted to be killed. All bowed to the ground except three young men. These three stood up boldly. They were Shadrach, Meshach and Abednego.

Because Nebuchadnezzar had made these three young men governors, some of the Chaldeans were jealous. As the music sounded, they watched to see whether Daniel's friends would kneel before the idol. When they saw the young men standing bravely alone among all the kneeling princes and nobles, they hurried to tell Nebuchadnezzar.

They said, "O King, you have decreed that every man should fall down before the idol when the music sounded and whoever refuses would be thrown into the fiery furnace. When the music sounded the three governors, Shadrach, Meshach and Abednego did not obey. They will not worship or serve the golden idol you have set up."

How angry the king was! At once he ordered that Shadrach, Meshach and Abednego be brought to him. When they came he asked, "Is it true that you did not bow down?"

The king knew these three were good rulers, and he thought perhaps they had not understood his command. He would give them another chance. "Be ready," he said, "to bow down when you hear the music. If you do not worship this idol, you will be thrown into the fiery furnace. Then what god will save you?"

Bravely the three Hebrews said, "O King, we do not want another chance. We will not bow down before your idol, for we worship only the one true God. Our God is so great that he can deliver us from your fiery furnace. But even if he does not, we will not worship any idol."

Now the king was furious! He had even offered to give these young men a second chance to save their lives, but they had insulted him. He would be kind no longer. At his command the furnace was made seven times hotter. His bravest soldiers tied up the three so they could not even move.

Shadrach, Meshach and Abednego were not afraid. While the soldiers tied the strong ropes around them, they stood quietly. They did not even cry out when the men picked them up and carried them to the furnace.

When the three were thrown into the fire, the flames leaped out and killed the soldiers. Nebuchadnezzar saw it happen. He watched the furnace. His eyes grew wide in astonishment. The three who had dared disobey his command were walking about in the fire. Their ropes were gone. The king looked closer. He could not believe his own eyes. He called to the nobles, "Did we not throw three men into the fire?"

"Yes, O King," they replied.

"But now I see four men walking freely about in the middle of the flames!" he cried out. "They seem to be unhurt. The fourth one looks like the Son of God."

Nebuchadnezzar jumped up from his royal chair and ran to the door of the furnace. Loudly he called, "Shadrach, Meshach and Abednego, you servants of the most high God, come out! Come to me at once!"

In amazement the princes and nobles and rulers gathered around and watched as the three men walked out of the fire to Nebuchadnezzar. The fire had not burned them at all. The flames had not even singed a hair, and there was no smell of smoke on their clothes. Yet the strong ropes that had been tied about them had burned off.

The king was afraid to be angry with Shadrach, Meshach and Abednego now. He believed they were great men, and he must honor them. Surely they served a great God, one who had all power. Nebuchadnezzar said, "Blessed is your God. He took care of you because you trusted in him. Because you have not worshiped an idol, you have changed my command."

The men round about listened carefully. The king said, "I decree that anyone in any nation who speaks against the God of Shadrach, Meshach and Abednego shall be killed and his house destroyed." Then Nebuchadnezzar gave these three brave men higher places in his kingdom.

Nebuchadnezzar Loses His Mind

Daniel 4

Again Nebuchadnezzar had a dream. This time he did not forget it when he awoke. Again he sent for the wise men and told them the dream that troubled him.

The wise men listened carefully, but they did not know what the dream meant. The king sent them away and called for Daniel. Nebuchadnezzar believed God's Spirit was with Daniel to help him understand deep mysteries.

When Daniel came the king told his dream. "I saw a tree grow up in the earth. It became so great that the top of it reached up to the sky. Underneath its branches animals found shelter. In its branches the birds made their nests. People came from all over the earth to eat its fruit. Then a holy one came down from heaven and ordered, 'Cut down the great tree. Cut off its branches, shake off its leaves and scatter its fruit. Leave the stump of the tree with its roots in the ground for seven years. Then all who live will know there is a God in heaven who rules over the kingdoms of the earth.'"

God made Daniel understand what the dream meant, but Daniel was afraid to tell the king. For a whole hour Daniel sat quietly, wondering what to do.

Finally Nebuchadnezzar said, "Do not be afraid. Do not let the dream or its meaning trouble you."

Daniel took courage and said, "The great tree in your dream is you, for you have become a great king throughout the earth. The voice ordering the tree to be cut down means that you will lose your kingdom for seven years. During that time you will live like an animal in the field. You will eat grass like an ox, and the dew of heaven will be upon you. When you acknowledge that the most high God rules over all the earth, then you will live among men again and be restored to your kingdom."

Because Daniel knew God was merciful, he urged, "O King, listen to my advice. Leave your sins and do what is right. Be helpful to the poor that your days of peace may be lengthened."

The king did not take Daniel's advice. A year passed and nothing unusual happened. Perhaps Nebuchadnezzar almost forgot the strange dream. He grew even prouder of his great kingdom, the beauty of his palace grounds and the famous city of Babylon.

One day as he walked through the palace to admire it, he said, "Is this not great Babylon that I have built by my power for my glory?"

From heaven a voice answered, "O King Nebuchadnezzar, to you it is spoken: The kingdom is taken from you."

The king lost his mind and thought himself a wild animal. Because the people were afraid, they drove him out of the city. The king lived in the fields and ate grass like the oxen. His hair and nails grew so long that he even looked more like an animal than a man.

After seven years God restored Nebuchadnezzar's mind. Then the king lifted up his eyes to heaven and thanked God. He praised the Lord for his greatness.

When the people of Babylon saw that their king was now in his right mind, they welcomed him back. They honored and served him just as they had done before. Then Nebuchadnezzar knew that God is greater than any man. He praised and honored the King of heaven.

The Handwriting on the Wall

Daniel 5

Belshazzar, king of Babylon, gave a great feast and invited a thousand nobles and their many wives. The city was filled with merriment. The palace rang with talking, laughing and singing.

When the wine was served, the king remembered the beautiful gold goblets that Nebuchadnezzar had taken from the great temple in Jerusalem. At once he commanded his servants to bring these goblets to the palace so the guests could drink from them.

The servants obeyed. The goblets were brought, filled with wine and passed to the guests. As they drank they praised their idols of gold, silver, wood and stone.

Belshazzar's heart was merry. He liked giving big parties. Suddenly he turned pale and the laughter stuck in his throat. Great fear swept over him and his knees shook. There on the wall of the palace he saw the fingers of a man's hand writing strange words. The words were so strange that the king could not read them.

Daniel explains the handwriting

At once a terrible silence filled the banquet hall. Everyone was afraid, for no one could read the strange words the hand had written.

In a loud voice the king cried out, "Bring me the wise men." When they came he promised them a rich reward if they would read the words on the wall. Even the wise men did not know what the words meant.

Throughout the palace everyone talked about the strange writing. The queen mother heard about it and was told that not even the wise men could read the words. She went to the banquet hall where the king sat trembling among his frightened guests.

"O King," she said, "in this city there is a very wise man that you have forgotten. When Nebuchadnezzar was king this man was the master of all the wise men. This man is great because the spirit of the holy gods rests on him. Send for him and he will tell you the meaning of those words on the wall."

The king was glad to hear of someone who could help. He sent for Daniel right away. Daniel was now an old man. For a long time he had lived in Babylon, but he was little noticed by the kings who followed Nebuchadnezzar.

When the old wise man was brought into the banquet hall, Belshazzar asked excitedly, "Are you the Daniel my fathers captured from the land of the Jews? I have heard that the spirit of the holy gods is with you and that you have understanding and wisdom. My wise men could not tell me what the handwriting means. If you will tell me, I will give you rich gifts and much honor."

Daniel was not interested in the king's gifts, but he promised, "I will read the writing and explain its meaning."

First Daniel reminded Belshazzar of the punishment God had sent to Nebuchadnezzar because of his sin and pride. Even though Belshazzar knew this, he, too, was very proud and despised the God of heaven. He even dared to drink wine from the goblets from the Lord's temple while his guests praised their idols.

Daniel said, "Because you have done these things, God has written on the wall. The words are MENE, MENE, TEKEL, UPHARSIN. They mean this:

"Mene: God has numbered the days of your kingdom and brought it to an end.

"Tekel: You are weighed in the balances and found wanting.

"Upharsin: Your kingdom is divided and given to the Medes and Persians."

Belshazzar commanded that Daniel be clothed in a royal robe. Then he fastened a gold chain around Daniel's neck. Before all the guests the king proclaimed him the third highest ruler in the kingdom.

That very night the kingdom of Babylon was destroyed. The Medes and Persians captured the city, killed Belshazzar and put Darius upon the throne.

Daniel in the Lions' Den

Daniel 6

King Darius, the new ruler, chose one hundred and twenty princes to help him govern the kingdom. Over these princes he appointed three presidents. Because Daniel was so very wise, the king made him the first president.

The princes and the other two presidents were jealous of Daniel. They watched him carefully. They wanted to catch him doing something wrong so they could report him to the king. As hard as they tried, they could not find anything to report. Finally they decided, "The only way we can find fault with him is in the way he obeys the laws of his God."

When the princes and the presidents had decided on a way to trick Daniel, they went to the king. "King Darius, live forever," they said. The king asked why they had come and they replied, "All the presidents, princes, governors, counselors and captains of the captains have met and decided on a law you should make. For the next thirty days have every person make his requests only to you. Anyone who makes a request of any god or man except of you, O King, shall be thrown into the lions' den. Make this law so it cannot be changed."

Daniel had not helped plan this new law. He was not even with the group that stood before the king, but the king did not realize this. He liked being the most important person in the entire kingdom and so he signed the law. Then it was announced among all the people.

323

Daniel heard about the law, but he did not obey it. Just as before he knelt three times every day and prayed by his window opened toward Jerusalem. Here the nobles found him on his knees thanking God.

At last they had a way to get rid of Daniel. Quickly they hurried to the king and reminded him, "Have you not signed a decree that for thirty days every person who asks a request of god or man except of you shall be thrown into the lions' den?"

"That's right," the king answered, "and that law cannot be changed."

Then the nobles told the king, "That Daniel who was captured out of Judah is not loyal to you, O King. He has not obeyed your decree. Three times today he has prayed to his God."

How disturbed the king was! Now he was very sorry he had listened to the nobles and made such a law. All day he tried to think of some way to save Daniel. All day he studied the laws of his country. He hoped to find some way he could release Daniel.

When the sun went down, the nobles hurried to the palace and reminded the king that his new law had to be obeyed. Darius knew now that he could not save Daniel. He ordered him brought and thrown into the lions' den.

The king told Daniel how sorry he was to do this. "The God you serve so faithfully will surely save you from the lions," the king said.

A stone was rolled over the lions' den. The king put his seal on the stone so no one would dare move it without his permission.

With a heavy heart the king returned to his palace. He refused to eat any food or listen to music. Darius was so troubled that he could not sleep all night long. He kept thinking about Daniel.

At daybreak he hurried to the lions' den. In a troubled, anxious voice he called out, "O Daniel, servant of the living God, has your God saved you from the lions?"

The king listened. From the deep pit he heard Daniel answer, "O King, live forever. My God has sent his angel. The angel shut the lions' mouths, and they did not harm me. God knew I had done no wrong."

How glad the king was! He called his servants to pull Daniel out. Then he commanded that those who had plotted against Daniel be thrown into the den.

Daniel is thrown to the lions

Darius wrote letters to the people of every nation. He said, "Peace be with you. I make a decree that in every part of my kingdom men shall fear Daniel's God. He is the living God, steadfast forever. His kingdom shall never be destroyed, and his rule shall not end. By his power he has delivered Daniel from the lions."

From that time on Daniel was treated well by the kings of Babylon.

Daniel Prophesies

Daniel 7–12

From his youth Daniel had lived in Babylon and helped several kings rule the people. During those many years, he had never forgotten his childhood home in Jerusalem or the temple of the Lord.

Daniel had read the letters the prophet Jeremiah wrote to his captive people. Like all Jews Daniel liked to remember Jeremiah's promise that the Jews would return to their own land after seventy years. The seventy years would soon be up. How Daniel longed to see his people return to their land and rebuild the temple of the Lord!

Sometimes Daniel prayed all day long for himself and his people. Sometimes he could not eat. He even dressed in sackcloth and sat in ashes to show God how sorry he was for his sins and the sins of his people.

God heard Daniel's prayers. One evening an angel came to comfort him. The angel said, "O Daniel, you are greatly loved by the Lord. You shall be told what will happen in the years to come." And the angel told Daniel about the coming of the Savior.

Even though Daniel was very old, he still worked in the government. When Darius died King Cyrus took Daniel as an adviser to his capital city in Persia. Daniel still prayed earnestly for his people.

One day when Daniel was down by the river, an angel appeared to him. Around the angel shone a great brightness. Daniel fell to the ground. The men who were with him did not see the angel, but they felt the earth trembling beneath their feet. In fear they ran away.

As Daniel lay on the ground, the angel touched him. Daniel got up, and the angel spoke to him. At first Daniel could not answer, but the angel touched his lips. The angel talked for a long time. Later Daniel wrote all that the angel said in a book.

Daniel was both a great statesman and a great prophet. By his courage and loyalty to God, he helped several heathen kings respect the one true God. Daniel lived to see the time when King Cyrus allowed the Jews to return to their homeland.

The Homecoming of the Jews

Ezra 1:1–3:7

King Cyrus sent a proclamation throughout all the land. The people gathered to hear his message. These are the words they heard: "The Lord God of heaven has given me all the kingdoms of the earth. Now he has ordered me to build him a temple at Jerusalem. Who are there among his people, the Jews, who will return to Jerusalem and build this house for God?"

How happy and excited the Jews were when they heard this! At last they could return to their homeland. How proud they would be to help rebuild the temple of the Lord in Jerusalem! More than forty thousand Jews began to prepare for the trip at once.

On the appointed day the great company gathered in the valley along the Euphrates River. There were grandmothers and grandfathers, mothers and fathers, young people and children. Most of the people carried bundles or baggage for their long journey. These Jews were all ready to start back to the land of their fathers.

Zerubbabel, a brave young man from the family of David, was made leader of the returning Jews. When they reached Jerusalem, Zerubbabel was to rule the Jews as a prince under the command of King Cyrus.

Not all the Jews wanted to return to Jerusalem. Many had become so rich and prosperous that they did not care to go back. Instead they sent precious gifts to help in building the temple. How glad they were that many of their own people were returning to build up the temple of the Lord.

Daniel was too old to make the long journey back to Jerusalem. Perhaps, too, King Cyrus felt that he could not get along without Daniel.

The last good-byes were said, and the long journey began. The people moved slowly up the highway that a few of them had traveled seventy years before. This time they were happy, for they were no longer captives in a foreign land.

Many walked, some rode on horses and others on camels or donkeys. As they moved on they sang songs of joy. In their hands were beautiful harps. How eager they were to play sweet music in the house of the Lord!

Cyrus had sent with them all the gold and silver vessels Nebuchadnezzar had stolen from the temple. These vessels would be used in the new temple.

Nor was this the only gold and silver the returning Jews carried. Cyrus had commanded their neighbors and friends to give them money and rich gifts. The Jews had come to Babylon empty-handed captives. Now on their return they were laden with rich gifts.

As the journey neared its end, the people saw the crumbled walls of Jerusalem. Those who remembered how the city looked before Nebuchadnezzar destroyed it were very sad. Most of these pilgrims had never seen Jerusalem, for they had been born in the land of captivity. All were glad to come back and build their homes in the land Nebuchadnezzar had taken away from them.

In the ruins of Jerusalem the people found the place where the temple of the Lord had stood. They found the rock where the altar had been. Here the priests and the Levites cleared away the rubbish and gathered stones for a new altar. From the very first they offered sacrifices to God each morning and evening just as they had been commanded in the Law of Moses.

Trouble in Rebuilding the Temple

Ezra 3:8—4:24

The returning Jews did not begin to rebuild the temple of the Lord at once. Since winter was coming on, they built houses for themselves first. When spring came they started to work on the temple.

Zerubbabel and Jeshua, the high priest, hired carpenters and masons for the new building. Every man who was over twenty years old worked on the temple.

How happy the people were when the foundation was laid! The priests and the Levites and the musicians praised the Lord. The people sang together for joy. Everyone was happy that the great work had begun so well. Many people shouted, but some wept. Those who remembered how beautiful the first temple had been could not help shedding tears.

The Samaritans and some other people who lived near Jerusalem did not like having the Jews back. They did not want the temple rebuilt. They wanted this land for themselves. To trick the Jews they told Zerubbabel, "Let us help you build the temple, for we worship the same God as you."

Zerubbabel replied, "You shall have nothing to do with building the house of God. We will build it ourselves as King Cyrus commanded us."

This reply angered the Samaritans. Next they hired people just to make trouble for the Jews as they rebuilt the temple.

When Ahasuerus became the new king of Persia, the Samaritans wrote to him and complained about the Jews at Jerusalem. They said, "You should know that the Jews who returned to Jerusalem are building a rebellious city that will cause you trouble. They are finishing the walls and repairing the foundations. When the Jews have finished, they will no longer bother to pay you any more taxes.

"Because we are loyal to you, O King, we want you to search the records and find out all the trouble this city caused in times past. If the Jews are allowed to finish it, the land on this side of the Jordan River will be lost to you."

King Ahasuerus did not want his kingdom endangered. He thought the Samaritans had written the truth. No wonder he ordered that the building be stopped. And the temple was left unfinished as long as Ahasuerus ruled.

Beautiful Esther Becomes Queen

Esther 1—2

Esther was only a little girl when both her parents died. Her cousin Mordecai took her to live with him, and Esther became like a daughter to him. He worked in the king's household to earn their living. Both Mordecai and Esther were Jews.

Esther was a young woman when Ahasuerus gave a great feast in his palace. All the nobles and rulers of the kingdom were invited. The feast lasted for a week. While the king entertained his guests, Queen Vashti gave a great party for the women.

Toward the end of the week, the king invited all the men of the royal city to come to the palace and enjoy the feast. Perhaps Mordecai was there too.

By the last day the king had drunk so much wine that he was feeling reckless. He wanted all the men to see and admire his beautiful wife, the queen. Ahasuerus sent a servant to get her.

The servant returned, but the queen was not with him. She had refused to come because she knew the king's request was unwise. It was contrary to the customs of the people.

The king was angry when his wife disobeyed him. The advisers noticed the king's embarrassment. Turning to them he asked, "What is to be done with Queen Vashti for disobeying the king?"

One adviser said, "O King, the queen has wronged you and your guests and all the people in your kingdom. When the women of the land hear about this, they will no longer respect their husbands and obey them, as wives should do. Then there will be trouble throughout the kingdom. Let Vashti be queen no longer. Find someone better to take her place."

Ahasuerus was pleased to take this advice. He did not see Vashti again, and she was no longer the queen.

Now the king decided to choose another beautiful queen. He sent commands throughout the kingdom that the most beautiful young women should be brought to his palace. Then he could choose the one he liked best for his queen.

Mordecai knew Esther was very beautiful. He believed she would make a good queen. When the young women came from all parts of the kingdom to the palace, Mordecai sent Esther too. He advised her, "Don't tell anyone we are related or that you are a Jew."

At the palace the young women were taught the manners of court life. The king took a long time to decide which one was to be the queen. When Esther was brought to him, he knew at once that she was the one he wanted.

Ahasuerus placed the royal crown of Persia on Esther's head. He gave her rooms in his palace and servants to wait on her. In her honor he gave a great feast. Throughout the kingdom people knew that Esther had been chosen to be the new queen.

Mordecai saw very little of Esther after that. Every day he walked by her window and then returned to guard the king's gate. Faithful servants brought him messages from Esther.

One day Mordecai overheard two men planning to kill the king. He sent word to Esther at once. She sent a servant to tell the king. "Mordecai has discovered that two men are planning to take your life."

The king investigated and found that the report was true. At his order the two men were put to death. A record was written of how Mordecai had saved the king's life.

Ahasuerus must have forgotten Mordecai's kindness, for he did not promote the loyal gatekeeper. The king never suspected that Mordecai the Jew was his wife's relative.

Haman Plans to Kill the Jews

Esther 3:1—4:3

Among the princes at the royal palace in Shushan was proud Haman. He was very rich and so clever that he knew just how to please the king. The king put Haman in charge of all the princes and commanded the servants to bow before this proud man.

331

When Haman passed through the king's gates, all the servants except Mordecai bowed with their faces in the dust. Mordecai refused to bow before any man and give him the honor that belonged to God.

The servants were afraid when they saw that Mordecai did not bow before the honored prince. They asked, "Why do you disobey the king's command?"

"I am a Jew," Mordecai said.

The servants knew that Jews bowed only to God. Perhaps they feared they might be punished with Mordecai for not honoring Haman. Perhaps they thought Haman would promote them for reporting Mordecai, so they did.

The next time Haman passed through the king's gate he watched Mordecai. How angry he was that this man did not bow and show him reverence! He must find some way to punish him. Haman decided not to punish Mordecai only, but to have all the Jews in the kingdom killed. Little did he know that Queen Esther was a Jewess.

Because Haman helped rule the great kingdom of Persia, he was often with the king. Haman planned carefully how he would get the king's consent to have the Jews killed.

One day he told Ahasuerus, "O King, there are certain people scattered throughout your countries who obey their own laws instead of yours. This is not good for your kingdom. Let a law be made that these people be killed. I will even pay the soldiers who do it."

Ahasuerus did not know much about the Jews or their strange religion. He did not even know that his own wife was a Jewess. Because he trusted Haman's judgment, the king gave his consent.

Under the king's seal Haman had letters written to the rulers of every part of the kingdom, announcing that all Jews of every age were to be killed on a certain day. Royal messengers carried these letters throughout the kingdom. Haman thought he would surely get even with Mordecai now.

When the Jews heard about this letter, they could hardly believe their ears. Why was the king displeased with them? They had always lived peacefully and never caused any trouble. Because they worked hard, many of them were very rich. Now they were about to be killed, and everything they owned would be taken.

Esther receives a message

Why had the king passed such a law? Throughout the land the Jews tore their clothes, dressed in sackcloth and cried aloud. Many sat in ashes, fasted and prayed.

Mordecai was among the first of the Jews to hear about the new law. He knew at once that Haman was responsible for it. If the law were carried out, even Queen Esther would be killed.

Mordecai tore his clothes, wrapped himself in sackcloth and threw ashes on his body. He went through the streets crying bitterly. Because he was dressed in sackcloth, he could not go near the palace. If only he could get a message to Queen Esther, she might be able to think of some way to save their lives.

Queen Esther Is Troubled

Esther 4:4-17

Esther always watched for Mordecai to pass her window each day. Then one day he did not come. What could be wrong? Later in the day her servants said Mordecai was dressed in sackcloth and was going through the city streets crying aloud.

"What could have happened?" Esther wondered. Hurriedly she gathered some new clothes for a servant to take to Mordecai. How she longed to run and comfort him herself, but now that she was queen she could not do everything she wished.

Soon the servant returned with the clothes. Mordecai would not take them. Now Esther knew that something terrible had happened. Quickly she called for the adviser the king had given her. She sent him to find out what was wrong with Mordecai.

Mordecai told the adviser about Haman's plan to kill all the Jews. He gave the king's servant a copy of the letter Haman had written. "Tell Esther to go to the king and plead for her people," Mordecai said.

The adviser brought the letter to Esther and gave her Mordecai's message. Esther told the king's servant to take this answer to Mordecai. "You know that anyone who goes to the king without being called will be killed unless the king holds out his scepter to that person."

Esther was afraid to take such a risk. The king had not called for her all month. How could she go to the king unless he called for her?

Mordecai sent back this answer: "Esther, do not think you will escape death just because you live in the palace. All Jews will be killed. If you do not go to the king, who knows what will happen? Who knows, perhaps you have come to the kingdom for such a time as this!"

Esther was still afraid, but she longed to help her people. She would try. She commanded Mordecai to gather all the Jews of the royal city together. They were to fast and pray to God for three days that he would help her find favor with the king. If the king did not send for her during that time, she would go to him even against the laws of the palace and plead for herself and her people.

Esther Goes to the King

Esther 5

On the third day Esther dressed in her most beautiful robes and went to see the king. How surprised he was to look up and see Esther standing in the court before his throne. He knew she would not have come without an important reason. Because he loved her, he held out the golden scepter that was in his hand.

Esther knelt before the throne and touched the scepter.

"What is your request, Queen Esther?" he asked. "I will give you anything you ask up to the half of my kingdom."

Esther did not tell him about the great sorrow that clouded her life and the lives of her people. Instead she said, "O King, if it pleases you to grant my request, let the king and Haman come tomorrow to a special dinner that I will have for you."

The king promised to come. Esther left the court, and Ahasuerus sent word to Haman about the dinner.

How honored Haman felt to be the only guest invited to eat dinner with the king and queen! He hurried home to tell his wife and friends about this great honor. His gladness turned to anger as he passed through the king's gate and saw that Mordecai did not bow with the other servants. How he longed to be rid of Mordecai! Since

Mordecai would die with the other Jews when the law was carried out. Haman tried to control himself.

When Haman reached home, he bragged, "I am the only guest invited to have dinner with the king and queen tomorrow. But such an honor means nothing as long as I see Mordecai the Jew sitting at the king's gate."

Haman's wife and friends advised him, "Build a high gallows and ask the king for permission to hang Mordecai. Then you will have a light heart when you go to dinner with the king and queen."

The idea sounded good to Haman, and he had the gallows built.

The King Honors Mordecai

Esther 6

That night King Ahasuerus could not sleep. As he tossed restlessly on his soft pillows, he commanded the servants to bring the book of records. Then he ordered them to read the things he had done since becoming ruler of all Persia. In the records was Mordecai's warning about the two men who were plotting to kill the king.

"What honor has been given to Mordecai for doing this?" the king asked.

"Nothing has been done for him," the servants answered.

By now it was early morning and the king thought he heard someone in the court. "Who is it?" he asked. The servants looked and reported that Haman had come. "Let him come in," the king said.

Proudly Haman entered, wondering what he could do to please the king. He had come early intending to get the king's permission to hang Mordecai on the gallows he had made.

The king asked Haman, "What shall be done for the man the king delights to honor?"

Haman thought surely he was the man the king planned to honor. After a few moments he said, "Let the man you are glad to honor be dressed in your royal robes. Let him ride on your horse and wear your crown. Let one of the most noble princes put the royal robe and crown on the man. Then have the prince go before the honored one through the streets of the city and cry out for all to hear, 'This is done to the man the king delights to honor.' "

The king was pleased with Haman's answer. He said, "You are my noble prince, so I command you to take my royal robes and crown and put them on Mordecai at once. Then have him mount my horse and lead him through the city, proclaiming to all, 'This is done to the man the king delights to honor.' Be sure you do everything you have mentioned to honor this man."

Haman turned pale and hurried out of the court! How he hated to go through the city streets announcing the king's honor upon Mordecai! Haman did it, but only because he did not dare disobey the king's command.

As soon as this terrible ordeal was over, he ran home and covered his head in shame and sorrow. Now he could never get the king's permission to hang Mordecai.

"You must be careful," Haman's wife told him. If Mordecai gets promoted above you, your own life may be in danger."

Haman was so upset that he completely forgot about the invitation to have dinner with the king and queen. The king had to send a messenger to bring Haman to the palace.

Esther Pleads for Her People

Esther 7—10

The king and Haman came to the dinner Esther had arranged. Again the king asked, "What would you have, Queen Esther? I will give you anything you ask up to the half of my kingdom."

With courage the queen answered, "If I have found favor with you, O King, and if it pleases you, save my life and the lives of my people. It is not as if we were being sold as slaves, but we are all about to be killed."

Ahasuerus was astonished to hear this. Who would dare threaten the queen's life? He asked, "Who is he and where is he who would dare do such a thing?"

"The man is Haman," the queen answered.

337

Now Haman was more frightened than he had ever been in all his life. He did not know what to do. Never had he guessed that the beautiful queen was a Jewess. Nor did he know she had been brought up by Mordecai. Haman sat speechless.

The king stormed out of the room, and Haman fell at Esther's feet begging for mercy. The king walked in the garden wondering how to punish Haman. When he returned and found Haman pleading for his life, the king called the servants. He ordered, "Hang Haman on the gallows he prepared for Mordecai."

After Haman's death the king made Mordecai a man of great honor in the kingdom. To make sure the Jews were not killed on the day Haman had ordered, the king sent new letters to every part of the land. He decreed that the Jews should not be killed. If they were attacked, they were to defend themselves.

The Jews were saved. To celebrate the day of their great victory, an important feast was held. They called it the Feast of Purim. Even to this day the Jews keep this feast and tell the story of beautiful Queen Esther who saved the lives of her people.

The Temple Is Finished

Ezra 5–6; Haggai 1–2

When Ahasuerus, king of Persia, refused to let the Jews finish the temple, they built comfortable homes for themselves and worked in the fields around Jerusalem.

Then another Darius became king of Persia, but the Jews did not ask him for help. They had given up trying to finish the temple. But the prophet Haggai went among the people and told them the words of the Lord.

The people heard Haggai say, "Why should you live in fine houses when the house of the Lord is still in ruins? God wants you to consider your ways. You have worked hard at farming the land, but you do not have enough to eat, drink or wear. God says for you to go up to the mountain and get wood for his house. Then he will be pleased. You cannot expect God's blessings until you finish his house.

338

The new Temple is dedicated

The people listened to Haggai's message from the Lord and obeyed. Again they began work on the temple. They had only begun when the Samaritans came to see what was going on. The Samaritans asked, "Who gave you orders to do this?"

The people of Jerusalem answered, "Cyrus, the king of Persia, commanded us to build the house of God."

The Samaritans did not believe this, so they wrote to Darius who was now the king of Persia and told him what the Jews had said. Darius searched the records that had been written when Cyrus was king.

When Darius found that the Jews had spoken truly, he decreed, "You Samaritans are to let the men at Jerusalem alone. Let them build this house of God. From now on you shall send your taxes to be used in rebuilding the temple instead of sending them to me. Also you shall send sacrifices for the altar. Anyone who refuses to obey this decree will be killed." After the decree went forth, the Jews were not troubled by their enemies any more.

When the temple was finished, all the people gathered with great joy to dedicate the house of the Lord. Many sacrifices were offered. The people gave thanks because God had helped them and given them a friend in the new king. With glad hearts they praised the Lord.

Ezra Teaches God's Law

Ezra 7–10; Nehemiah 8

Years passed and Artaxerxes became king of Persia. From his capital city of Shushan, he governed the people of many lands. The Jews who had returned to rebuild the temple at Jerusalem were also a part of his kingdom.

During this time a Jew named Ezra served God faithfully in Babylon. Because he wrote the words of God in books, he was called a scribe. More than anything else Ezra wanted to teach Jews everywhere the laws God had given to Moses.

King Artaxerxes sent out a decree that Ezra and all the Jews who wanted to do so could go up to Jerusalem. They were to take silver and gold for the temple. The people in the countries through which they passed were to give them anything they needed. Ezra was to teach God's laws. Those who would not obey God's laws and the king's laws were to be punished.

When Ezra heard the king's decree, he said, "Blessed be the Lord who has put it in the king's heart to beautify the temple at Jerusalem."

By the riverside Ezra met with the Jews who were going with him. Before they started out, they fasted and prayed for God's protection. They would have to travel through many dangerous places, and they did not have soldiers with them. Ezra explained to his friends, "I was ashamed to ask the king for soldiers because we have told him how the Lord cares for those who serve him."

With God's blessing Ezra and his friends started on their journey. For four months they traveled. At last they reached Jerusalem safely and very thankful they were that God had protected them. With great joy they worshiped in the temple that Zerubbabel had built. They presented the gifts of gold and silver the king had sent.

Soon Ezra discovered that things were not going well in Judah. The Jews there had become discouraged. Some of the young people had married their heathen neighbors. They were not teaching their children the law God gave to Moses. They had not rebuilt the city of Jerusalem. The walls still lay in ruins.

Ezra was deeply troubled. He knew his people had done wrong by marrying heathen. He prayed earnestly that God would forgive their sins.

And the prophets Zechariah and Haggai also ministered to the people. They urged the leaders to rebuild the city of Jerusalem.

Nehemiah, the King's Cupbearer

Nehemiah 1:1—2:18

In the palace was a noble young man who waited on King Artaxerxes. His name was Nehemiah, and he was a Jew.

One day Nehemiah's brother returned from the land of Judah. How eager Nehemiah was to hear news from the land of his fathers. As soon as his work was done in the palace, he asked eagerly about Jerusalem and the people who had gone back to rebuild the temple of the Lord.

341

Clive Upton

Nehemiah's brother and his friends shook their heads sadly. They said, "Things are not going well in Jerusalem. The walls of that great city have never been repaired. The place is still in ruins. It is a shame that such a glorious city lays waste. The people who live there are now poor and greatly troubled by their enemies."

When Nehemiah heard this, he was so disappointed that he wept. He longed to see Jerusalem and its people get along well. How much he longed to help them!

For several days Nehemiah fasted and prayed to the Lord. He said, "O Lord, I beg you, listen to my prayer and the prayer of my people. Help me this day to find favor before the king."

Nehemiah returned to his work in the palace. As he poured the king's wine, the king asked, "Nehemiah, what makes you look so sad? Are you sick? Is there nothing but sadness in your heart?"

And Nehemiah was afraid. Was the king angry because his servant looked sad? Nehemiah answered, "Let the king live forever. I am sad because the great city of my people lies in ruins."

"And what do you ask for?" the king said.

Nehemiah prayed that God would help him say the right words. Then he answered, "If it please the king and if I have found favor in your eyes, I ask that you send me to Jerusalem to rebuild the city of my fathers."

Both the king and queen listened carefully. The king wanted to know how long Nehemiah would have to be gone to do this.

Nehemiah explained it would take a long time to go so far and rebuild the walls. Taking courage he asked, "If it please the king, give me letters to the governors beyond the river so they will help me on my journey. Then give me a letter to the keeper of your forest, so he will give wood for this work."

The king agreed. With Nehemiah he sent captains and soldiers from his army. The company made the journey on horseback.

After many days they came to the countries near Judah. Nehemiah showed the rulers of these countries the letters from the king. These rulers did not like the people at Jerusalem, and they did not want the city strengthened. But because Nehemiah had royal orders, they dared not stop him.

Nehemiah directs the wall building

When Nehemiah and his men came to Jerusalem, they rested for three days. Then one night Nehemiah took a few soldiers and rode around the broken down walls. He found the broken stones lying in heaps. In some places his horse could not even find a path.

In the morning Nehemiah told the rulers and the priests why he had come. When he told how God had answered prayer in letting him come to Jerusalem, the leaders said, "Let us arise and build the wall."

The Walls of Jerusalem Are Rebuilt

Nehemiah 2:19—6:19

The news of Nehemiah's coming was told throughout Jerusalem. How glad the people were that God had sent Nehemiah to help them rebuild the city!

Work on the walls was begun at once. Almost everyone wanted to help. Of course a few only wanted to find fault, but this did not bother the busy workers. Even the women wanted to help. Some of the rich women hired workers to build a part of the wall.

The people cleared out the rubbish and gathered huge stones. While some worked on long stretches of the wall, others repaired the wall that was in front of their homes.

What a busy crowd of workers they were! Nehemiah rode around the walls on his horse and directed the building.

Now Sanballat and Tobiah were enemies of the Jews. When these two heard what was going on in Jerusalem, they were very angry. If the city were strengthened, they would not be able to get in and oppress the people. Together the two planned every way they could to bother the workers.

At first Sanballat and Tobiah made fun of the Jews. They said, "Your wall is so weak that it would fall down if even a fox tried to walk on it."

Nehemiah and his workers paid no attention to their enemies. They went on working and did not even stop to answer.

Then Sanballat and Tobiah had to think of some other way to hinder the work. They wrote letters to Nehemiah, saying, "You have come to rebuild Jerusalem and make yourself king over the city. Then you plan to rebel against the king of Persia."

"I have not come for such a purpose," Nehemiah replied and went on with his work.

This only made the enemies angrier. They planned next to attack Jerusalem. When Nehemiah heard about their plan, he armed his men with swords and spears. Some worked on the wall with one hand and held a spear in the other. Night and day guards stood on the wall to watch for the enemy. Because the enemy heard that the men of the city were armed, they did not attack.

At last the walls were finished, but the doors had not been put on the gates. Now Sanballat and Tobiah decided to act friendly toward Nehemiah and get him out of the city. They sent a messenger to tell Nehemiah, "Come and meet with us in one of the villages on the plain."

Nehemiah decided this was only a trick. "This work is important, and I cannot stop to meet with you," he said.

After fifty-two days of hard work, the entire wall was finished. How thankful the people were for Nehemiah! He had encouraged them and helped them to rebuild the wall of their ruined city.

The People Worship God

Nehemiah 7–13

For twelve years Nehemiah stayed in Jerusalem and governed the city. Then he returned to King Artaxerxes in Shushan. He appointed Hanani and another man to rule in his place.

Nehemiah was in Shushan only long enough to get the king's permission to go back to Jerusalem and stay there. On his return he helped the people obey the commands God had given Moses. Because he wanted the people to worship God with all their hearts, he called them to hear Ezra read the law of the Lord.

When the people gathered, Ezra stood up before the congregation. He opened the book before all the people, and the people stood up to listen. Ezra praised the Lord and all the people answered, "Amen, amen." They lifted their hands and bowed their heads to worship the Lord.

Ezra read the Law so everyone could understand it. Even though he read from morning till noon, the people listened carefully. They were so moved by the words of the Law that they wept.

When Ezra had finished, the leaders said, "This day is holy to the Lord. Do not weep. Go, eat and rejoice, for the joy of the Lord is your strength."

On the second day they listened to the reading of the Law again and heard about the Feast of the Booths. The people were so impressed that they sent this message throughout the land of Judah: "Go to the mountains and get branches of olive, pine, myrtle and palm to make booths."

Everywhere the people obeyed. With great gladness they celebrated the Feast of Booths. They kept the feast for seven days and each day they listened to the reading of the Law.

Because Ezra and Nehemiah taught so faithfully, the people paid more attention to obeying God's law. They refused to worship idols any longer.

Before Nehemiah died Malachi, the last of the prophets, came to speak God's word to the people. He told the Jews about the coming of the Savior. Later he wrote these words in a book. The Jews kept the book of Malachi with the books Ezra had written. And Malachi's writings are the last words of the Old Testament.

Ezra leads in worship

THE YEARS BETWEEN THE
OLD AND THE NEW TESTAMENT

The Years Between the Old and the New Testaments

More than four hundred years passed between the latest stories of the Old Testament and the stories of the New Testament. During those years there were many changes.

Although God let the Jews return to their homeland and rebuild Jerusalem, they did not become a separate kingdom at once. Instead, they were subjects of the king of first one country and then another.

Once during these years the Jews freed themselves and chose one of their own people to rule over them. This man was not a descendant of David, but the son of a priest. After his death his sons ruled until the Roman army conquered the little Jewish nation. From that time on the Jews were ruled by the Romans.

Because the capital of the Roman government was so far from Judah, the Roman emperor sent Herod to be king of the Jews. Herod made Jerusalem his home and governed the Jews in a way that pleased the Romans. He did not care what the Jews thought of his rule.

After eighteen years as king, Herod found out he had many enemies among the Jews. Because he wanted to make friends with them, he planned to rebuild their temple. Several hundred years had passed since Zerubbabel had built it. Herod had that old temple torn down, and in its place he put up a white marble building. Parts of it were covered with silver and gold.

The new temple took several years to finish. During that time Herod hired more than ten thousand men to do the work. The great temple could be seen towering above all the other buildings of Jerusalem. It reflected the dazzling glory of the morning sunlight.

This new temple pleased the Jews greatly and they were proud of it. In this temple the priests, descendants of Aaron, offered sacrifices to God each morning and evening just as God had commanded Moses on Mount Sinai.

STORIES OF THE NEW TESTAMENT
in Two Parts

STORIES ABOUT JESUS
Matthew; Mark; Luke; John; Acts 1:1-14

An Angel Visits the Temple
Luke 1:1-23

While the people prayed in the temple, the priest Zacharias entered the holy place to burn incense on the golden altar. Zacharias did not always serve in the temple. Since there were so many priests, they divided into twenty-four groups. Each group took its turn at serving in the temple.

Zacharias had left his home in the hill country of Judah to serve with the Abia group of priests. All the men in Zacharias' family had been priests, for they were descendants of Aaron, the first priest of Israel. Even his wife Elizabeth came from a family of priests.

Both Zacharias and Elizabeth loved and served the Lord. Like all their people, they looked forward to the coming of the Savior.

When the two were younger, they had prayed much that God would give them a baby. No child had been born. Even though they were old now and childless, they continued to serve God faithfully.

Twice each day, in the morning and in the evening, Zacharias took the censer of burning coals from the great altar. Then he went into the holy place alone to offer incense upon the golden altar of God.

This time as Zacharias entered the holy place he saw an angel. Zacharias was so afraid that he fell to the ground.

"Do not be afraid, Zacharias," the angel said, "for your prayer is heard. You and your wife will have a son. You will name him John. Many will rejoice with you when he is born. He will never drink wine or strong drink. God's Spirit will be in him. He will have the spirit and power of Elijah to make the people repent of their sins and serve God."

Zacharias listened eagerly, yet the angel's promise seemed too wonderful to be real. He asked, "How can I know this is true? I am an old man, and my wife is getting up in years."

The angel answered, "I am the angel Gabriel who stands in the presence of the Lord. He has sent me to tell you this good news.

355

Because you did not believe what I told you and asked for a sign to prove my words true, you will not be able to speak another word until the child is born." Then the angel disappeared as suddenly as he had come.

The people standing in the court of the temple wondered why Zacharias stayed in the holy place so long. At last, he came out. The people waited for him to speak, but he could not say a word. He made motions to show them he could not talk. The people believed Zacharias had seen a vision from God.

When the Abia group of priests had finished their turn at serving in the temple, Zacharias returned to his home in the hill country of Judah. He had not been able to say a word since the angel visited him in the holy place. Now Zacharias believed the angel's promise.

The Angel Visits Mary

Matthew 1:18-25; Luke 1:26-56

God sent the angel Gabriel to visit Mary in the city of Nazareth in Galilee. Mary was a young woman who was engaged to marry Joseph, a carpenter of Nazareth. Both Mary and Joseph were descendants of King David.

The angel spoke to Mary and told her, "The Lord is with you and you are greatly favored."

Mary was troubled. She did not know what the angel meant. Then he said, "Do not be afraid, Mary, for you have favor with God. You will have a son, and you shall call his name Jesus. He will be great. He will be a king who will rule forever."

How surprised Mary was! She did not understand what the angel meant. "How can this be?" she asked.

The angel answered, "The child who will be born to you will be the Son of God. Elizabeth, too, will have a son although she is old. Nothing is too hard for the Lord."

And Mary believed the angel. "Let it be as you have said," she answered simply.

Mary thought about the many years her cousin Elizabeth had wanted a child. How happy she must be! Although it was a long way to Elizabeth's house, Mary went to see her.

As soon as Mary entered her cousin's house, God caused Elizabeth to know that Mary would be the mother of the Savior. Mary and Elizabeth spent many happy days together.

The angel of the Lord told Joseph, too, about the coming of Jesus. He said, "Mary will have a son, and you shall call his name Jesus: for he will save his people from their sins."

How glad Joseph must have been to know the Savior was to be born! He and Mary eagerly awaited the coming of the baby Jesus.

A Baby Named John

Luke 1:57-80

In a little home in the hill country of Judah, there was great rejoicing. A son had been born to Zacharias and Elizabeth, just as God had promised. The neighbors and relatives were almost as happy about the baby as Zacharias and Elizabeth were.

According to the Jewish custom, babies were named when they were eight days old. On the eighth day neighbors and relatives came. They advised, "Call him Zacharias after his father."

How surprised they were to hear Elizabeth say, "No, do not call him Zacharias; his name is John."

"Why do you want to call him John?" they asked. "You have no relatives by that name." Because Zacharias had been speechless since the day the angel spoke to him in the temple, they made motions to ask him what he wanted his son named.

Zacharias understood what they wanted. He motioned for a writing tablet. When they brought it, he wrote in plain letters for all to read, "His name is John."

"How strange!" the people thought. Then all at once Zacharias was able to speak again. He praised God for giving them this wonderful baby.

News of the baby's birth spread throughout the hill country, and people often talked about him. "What kind of child will he be?" they wondered. They had heard how the angel told Zacharias that the child would be born. And the people talked about how Zacharias had been unable to speak from the time he saw the angel until the baby was named John. Surely all these things were very strange.

Zacharias was filled with wisdom from God, and he told his neighbors and friends about his little son. Zacharias praised the Lord.

To the little baby he said, "You, my child, shall be called the prophet of the Highest, for you will go before the Lord and prepare his ways. You will teach the people of salvation by the remission of their sins, through the tender mercy of our God."

And Zacharias said many other things about John. Later his words came true, for the Spirit of God had put these words in his heart.

As long as Zacharias lived, he cared for his son. How proud he was to see the boy grow tall and strong! As John grew he liked best to be out of doors.

A Wonderful Baby's Birth

Luke 2:1-39

The people of Nazareth were excited! The Roman emperor had commanded everyone to enroll in the town or city from which his family had come. No one dared disobey his command.

Soon travelers were going in every direction. Joseph and Mary were going to Bethlehem, for they were both of the family of David.

From Nazareth a company of people started toward the south. The road led through Samaria and over the Judean hills to Jerusalem. From Jerusalem Joseph and Mary went farther south until they came to Bethlehem. Some of their company left them in cities along the way, while other people joined them.

When they reached Bethlehem, it was crowded with people. No place could be found for new arrivals. The journey from Nazareth had been long and hard. How much Mary wanted a place to rest! Joseph could find only the stable of the inn. That night Baby Jesus was born. Mary wrapped him in soft cloths called swaddling clothes and laid him in a manger.

Shepherds were watching their flocks that night near Bethlehem. Suddenly the angel of the Lord came near, and a great light shone through the darkness. The shepherds were afraid. Why had the angel come to them?

The angel said, "Fear not, for I bring you good tidings of great joy, which shall be to all people. For unto you is born this day in the city of David a Savior, which is Christ the Lord. And you shall find the baby wrapped in swaddling clothes, lying in a manger."

What wonderful news! Many angels sang, "Glory to God in the highest, and on earth peace, good will toward men." Then the angels returned to heaven, and the light faded into the still darkness of the night.

The shepherds said to each other, "Let us now go to Bethlehem and see this thing which the Lord has made known to us."

Leaving their flocks, they hurried to Bethlehem. There in a stable they found Mary, Joseph and the infant Savior. Kneeling before the manger, they worshiped the little babe who lay quietly sleeping on the hay.

They told Mary and Joseph, "An angel of the Lord told us the news and an angelic choir sang praise to God." On the way back to their flocks, they told everyone they met about the angel's visit and the Savior's birth.

When the baby was eight days old, Joseph and Mary named him Jesus, the name the angel had chosen. The name Jesus means salvation.

According to Jewish law, each family had to make an offering to the Lord for their first baby boy. Rich people gave a lamb; poor people, two young pigeons. When Jesus was forty days old, Joseph and Mary took him to the temple at Jerusalem. They offered two young pigeons to the Lord, for they were poor.

Old Simeon was in the temple. God had promised him, "You shall not die until you have seen the Savior." When Mary brought Baby Jesus to the temple, God's Spirit made Simeon know that this child was the promised Savior.

Simeon came eagerly to meet Mary and took the baby in his arms. "Now may God let me depart in peace, for I have seen with my eyes the salvation which he has sent," Simeon said.

Mary loves the baby Jesus

Anna was an old woman who had served God faithfully all her life. When she saw Jesus, she too gave thanks to God.

Mary never forgot what Simeon and Anna said about Jesus, nor did she forget the story the shepherds told. She thought about these strange things and wondered how her son Jesus would finally become the Savior of the world.

The Wise Men Follow a Star

Matthew 2

Far to the east of Judea lived certain Wise Men who studied the stars. One night they discovered a new star. By this God made them know that Christ had been born.

These Wise Men feared God, and they wanted to see the child who was to be the Savior of the world. At once they planned to take rich gifts to the newborn king and to worship him as their Savior.

Many days they traveled across the desert to Judea. They hurried to Jerusalem, for surely the wonderful child would be in the most beautiful and famous city.

Herod, the ruler, was troubled. Why were these strangers riding on camels into his city? Why did they ask, "Where is he that is born king of the Jews? We have seen his star in the east and have come to worship him."

Herod knew nothing about the newborn king. What can this mean? he wondered. Calling the chief priests and scribes, he demanded, "Where is the Savior to be born?"

The chief priests and scribes remembered what the prophets had written long ago. They answered, "The Savior is to be born in Bethlehem. He is to rule his people."

Now Herod was more worried. What if this newborn king should take away his throne? Secretly he called the Wise Men and asked, "When did you see this star?" When they told him, he said, "Go to Bethlehem and search diligently for the young child. When you have found him, let me know that I may come and worship him."

Wise Men bring gifts

Outside the city gates, the Wise Men saw the same bright star they had seen in the east country. It seemed to lead them. Surely God was helping them find Jesus.

At Bethlehem the star stood still over the place where Jesus was. At last they had found the newborn king! Falling to their knees, they worshiped him. Opening their treasures, they gave him rich gifts—gold, frankincense and myrrh.

Before the Wise Men left Bethlehem, God told them in a dream not to go back to Herod. So they returned to their own country by another road.

Not long afterwards, an angel of the Lord said to Joseph in a dream, "Arise, and take the young child and his mother, and flee to Egypt. Stay there until I tell you to return, for Herod will look for Jesus and try to kill him." Joseph got up, took Mary and Baby Jesus and hurried out of Bethlehem. They traveled until they came to the country of Egypt.

Herod waited a long time for the Wise Men to return from Bethlehem, but they never came. Maybe they had guessed why he had been so eager to see Jesus. Now Herod was angry! He had not found the newborn king!

Herod sent his soldiers to kill every child two years old or less in Bethlehem and the country round about. Surely, this would get rid of Jesus!

But Jesus was safe in Egypt. When Herod died, an angel told Joseph, "Arise, take the young child and his mother and go back."

Back to Bethlehem they started. In Judea Joseph learned that Herod's son was now ruler. What if the new king were like his father? Because Joseph was afraid, they went on to Nazareth. Here they made their home, and Joseph opened his carpenter's shop.

When Jesus Was a Boy

Luke 2:40-52

As a little boy, Jesus loved to watch Joseph work and to play with the shavings that fell from his bench. Of course Jesus liked to run and play outdoors with his friends too.

Jesus learns in the Temple school

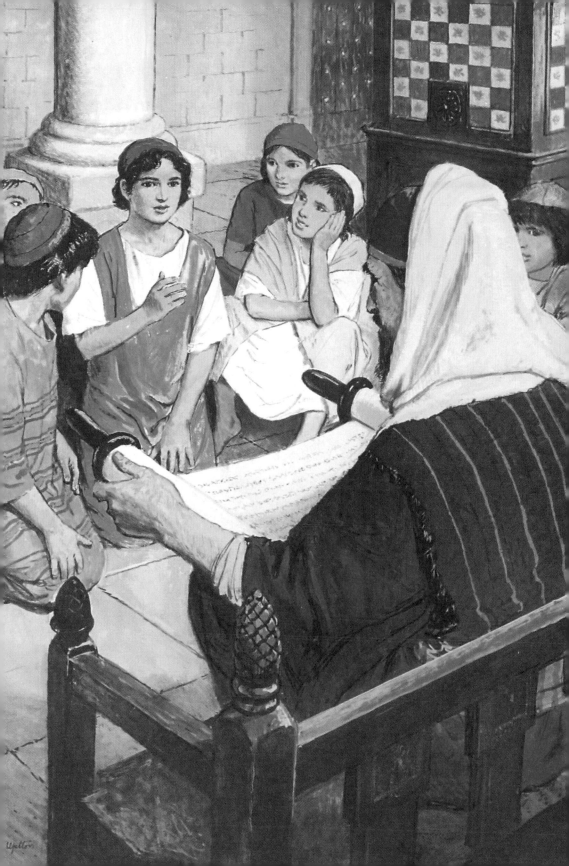

Nazareth, Jesus' hometown, was nearly seventy miles from Jerusalem. The people could not go every week to worship God at the temple in Jerusalem. Instead they built a synagogue in Nazareth. Here they heard the reading of books written by Moses and the prophets.

When Jesus was old enough to go to school, Mary and Joseph sent him to the synagogue. It was here Jewish boys learned to read and write. They studied the psalms and the writings of Moses and the prophets. Like other Jewish boys, Jesus learned many Scripture verses by memory, for no one had a Bible of his own.

One spring morning a company of Jews left Nazareth for the Feast of the Passover at Jerusalem. Joseph and Mary had gone to this feast every year since their return from Egypt. But the feast would be different for them this year. They were taking Jesus for the first time. Now that Jesus was twelve, he would be going every year.

As the company moved slowly down the road, people from other cities and villages joined them. At Jerusalem they met people from every part of the land. What an exciting time this was! How wide Jesus' eyes must have been when he saw the beautiful temple!

Jesus began to understand that God was his Father and that he must work with God. Each day at the temple he listened to the chief priests and scribes and asked them questions.

After the feast the people of Nazareth started home. Mary did not see Jesus, but she thought he was with their friends and relatives.

Evening came and still Mary did not see Jesus. Joseph and she began to search for him. All through the company they asked, "Have you seen Jesus?" Always the answer was the same. No one had seen him that day.

Now Mary and Joseph were very worried. They turned back to Jerusalem, hunting for Jesus.

On the third day they found him. He was not playing with other boys in the streets or learning to swim in the Pool of Siloam. Jesus was at the temple with the wise teachers, listening to them and asking questions.

How surprised Mary was to find Jesus there! She said, "Son, why did you stay here when we were starting for home? Your father and I have been so worried! We've looked everywhere for you."

Jesus goes to Jerusalem

Jesus answered, "Why did you look for me? Didn't you know that I would be at my Father's house?"

Mary did not understand. What did Jesus mean?

Jesus had surprised the teachers in the temple. He asked questions they could not answer.

As the years passed Jesus grew to be a noble young man. He learned to explain the Scriptures and to talk with God. By helping Joseph with his work, Jesus also became a carpenter. When Joseph died, Jesus worked to care for Mary and his brothers and sisters. His kind, thoughtful ways won him many friends. Jesus lived in his Nazareth home until he was about thirty years old.

John Preaches in the Wilderness

Matthew 3:1-12; Mark 1:3-8; Luke 3:1-20; John 1:15-28

When John was about thirty years old, he left his home and went throughout the hill country of Judea. He preached, "Repent, for the kingdom of heaven is at hand." Instead of going to the cities to preach God's message, John stayed in the country near the river Jordan.

People came from every part of the land to hear him speak. For more than four hundred years, no great prophet had arisen to speak God's words to the people. No wonder they were eager to hear John!

When the people gathered to hear this strange desert preacher, they saw a man dressed in rough clothing made of camel's hair. About his waist was a leather girdle. Because he spent all his time preaching in the country, his food was dried locusts and wild honey.

Many who heard John's preaching repented of their sins. Some found fault, but all were impressed. News of this strange preacher spread to the farthest corners of the land. Everywhere people wondered, "Who is this man?"

The Jews at Jerusalem sent priests and Levites to ask John, "Who are you?"

John said, "I am not the Christ."

"Are you Elijah?" they asked. When John said he was not, they wanted to know, "Are you a prophet?" Again John's answer was no.

Finally the priests and Levites asked, "Then who are you? Tell us so we will know what to report to the people who sent us."

To this John said, "I am the voice of one crying in the wilderness, 'Make straight the way of the Lord.'"

Still the priests and Levites had another question. "Why do you baptize people if you are not Christ, Elijah or a prophet?"

"I baptize with water," John explained. "There is a great one coming whose shoes I am not worthy to unloose. He will baptize you with the Holy Spirit."

In the crowds to whom John preached were all kinds of people. Usually there were a few Pharisees and Sadducees, the religious rulers of the Jews. They seemed to be very religious, but in their hearts many of them were proud and sinful. They thought they were more righteous than other people.

One time some Pharisees and Sadducees came to John to be baptized. He said to them, "Who has warned you evil men to flee from God's anger? You will not be ready to enter God's kingdom."

Those who believed John's preaching and repented of their sins asked him, "What should we do now?"

He answered, "The person who has two coats should give one to the man who has none. He who has more food than he needs should share with those who are hungry."

The tax collectors listened closely. Then they wanted to know what they should do. John told them, "Do not ask for more tax money than you are supposed to."

Soldiers, too, wondered what they should do now that they had repented of their sins. "Do not hurt or falsely accuse any man. Be content with your wages."

In the Jordan River John baptized those who confessed their sins. For that reason the people called him "John the Baptist."

John Baptizes Jesus

Matthew 3:13-17; Mark 1:9-11; Luke 3:21-22; John 1:29-34

Jesus was thirty years old when he left Nazareth and went to the Jordan River where John preached and baptized the people. When John saw Jesus in the crowd he called, "This is the Lamb of God that takes away the sin of the world. This is the one who is greater than I."

But Jesus had not come to be introduced to the people; he wanted to be baptized. John said, "Why have you come to be baptized? You are much greater than I." John felt unworthy to baptize the Son of God.

Jesus answered, "I must be baptized because it is God's plan. Baptize me now." And John took Jesus into the river and baptized him there.

When the two were coming out of the water, a strange thing happened. The heavens opened and the Spirit of God in the form of a dove came down upon Jesus. A voice from heaven said, "This is my beloved Son in whom I am well pleased."

Jesus Is Tempted

Matthew 4:1-11; Mark 1:12-13; Luke 4:1-14

After Jesus' baptism the Spirit of God led him into the wilderness. Jesus knew the great work God wanted him to do. Now he spent many days thinking and praying about it.

After forty days in the wilderness, the tempter came to Jesus. Because he knew Jesus was weak and hungry, he said, "If you are the Son of God, command that these stones become loaves of bread."

Even though Jesus was very hungry, he refused. He would not use God's great power just to please himself. Instead he trusted his heavenly Father to care for his needs. To the tempter he said, "It is written, 'Man shall not live by bread alone, but by every word of God.'"

When this temptation failed, the devil tried another. Taking Jesus to the roof of the temple he said, "If you expect people to believe that you are really God's Son, you must show some great signs. Now jump off and trust God to protect you from getting hurt.

371

Jesus comes to be baptized by John in the Jordan River

In the Scripture he has promised that his angels will not let any harm come to you."

Satan tempted Jesus with an easy way to get followers. Even though Satan had used words of Scripture, Jesus did not do this foolish thing. He knew the Scriptures forbid a person to do anything foolish and then expect God's angels to help him. He reminded the devil, "It is said, 'Thou shalt not tempt the Lord thy God.'"

Finally on a high mountain the devil showed Jesus all the kingdoms of the world. "These great kingdoms are mine," the tempter said, "and I can give them to anyone I choose. I will give them to you if you will fall down and worship me."

Jesus did not weaken. He answered, "Get away from me, you evil one! For it is written, 'Thou shalt worship the Lord thy God, and him only shalt thou serve.'"

At last Satan left Jesus alone, and angels came from heaven to care for Jesus' needs. He had won a great victory over the devil. Now he was ready to do his Father's work.

Jesus Makes Five New Friends

John 1:35-51

Many people believed the message John preached. With new eagerness they awaited the coming of the King from heaven. How glad they would be to hear that their King had arrived! In their hearts they believed he would set up a kingdom like David's, and the Jews would be his favored people.

One day John the Baptist saw Jesus walking along the road near the river. John cried out, "Behold the Lamb of God!"

Two of John's disciples had heard John say so many wonderful things about Jesus that they turned and followed him. When Jesus saw the two men coming after him, he asked, "What do you want?"

They answered, "Master, where do you live?"

"Come and see," Jesus said. Jesus took the two with him and they talked all day.

Jesus is tempted

Never had they heard a man speak as Jesus did! Andrew, one of the two, got so excited about what he heard that he ran to find his brother Simon. Simon, too, must hear. Both Andrew and Simon believed that John the Baptist was a prophet of God. They listened to him often and followed him wherever he went.

Already Andrew was sure that he had found a teacher even greater than John. When Andrew found Simon, he called out, "Come with me, for we have found the Messiah!" And the two hurried back to Jesus.

When Jesus saw the brothers, he looked at Simon and said, "You are Simon, the son of Jonah, but you shall be called Peter."

How surprised Simon was! How did Jesus know his name? Jesus seemed to know all about him. As Simon listened he too believed that Jesus was the Christ. Now he was just as eager to follow Jesus as Andrew was.

The next day Jesus started back to his home in Galilee. With him were his three new friends. As they walked along, they met a man named Philip. He lived in the same town as Simon and Andrew.

To Philip Jesus said, "Follow me." And Philip did.

As Philip walked with Jesus and the other three, he marveled at the wise words Jesus spoke. Surely this was the promised Savior and king. Philip was so thrilled that he ran to find his friend Nathanael. Philip told him, "We have found the one Moses and the prophets wrote about, Jesus of Nazareth."

Because Nathanael knew the Scriptures well, he remembered that the prophet had written that the king of the Jews would be born in Bethlehem. So he asked Philip, "Can any good thing come from Nazareth?"

Philip did not waste a minute trying to convince his friend. Instead he said, "Come and see."

Because Philip was so eager, Nathanael went along. When Jesus saw Nathanael, he said, "Look, an Israelite in whom there is no deceit!"

Nathanael was astonished. "How do you know me?" he asked.

"Before Philip called you," Jesus said, "I saw you under the fig tree."

How could Jesus have known where he was and what he was doing? At once Nathanael believed that Jesus came from God.

Jesus calls, "Follow me."

With joy he exclaimed, "Master, you are the Son of God! You are the King of Israel!"

Jesus said, "Do you believe just because I said I saw you under the fig tree? You shall see greater things than these."

The Wedding at Cana

John 2:1-11

A family in Cana of Galilee gave a feast. One of the family was to be married, and they had invited many people to the wedding. Among the guests were Jesus, his mother and his followers.

The wedding feast lasted several days. Perhaps these people were poor, or maybe they had not expected so many friends to come. The feast was not over, but the wine was all gone.

When Jesus' mother found out about this, she called her son aside. "They have no more wine," she explained. Wouldn't he help their friends at a time like this?

Mary called the servants. Pointing to Jesus, she said, "Do whatever he tells you."

And Jesus told them, "Fill the water pots with water."

And the servants filled the huge jars to the brim. Then Jesus said, "Pour out some and take it to the governor of the feast."

Again they obeyed. But instead of water, wine came out of the great stone jars. How surprised they were! Quickly they carried some to the governor of the feast, for he had to taste everything before it was served to the guests.

The governor took the wine without knowing what had happened. When he tasted it, he was surprised that this was much better than the wine that had already been served.

At once the governor called the bridegroom and told him, "At other wedding feasts the best wine is served first, but you have kept the best until the last."

This was Jesus' first miracle. By it he had helped people who were in need. The men who were with Jesus marveled at what he had done. Surely no man could do such miracles!

Jesus Keeps the Passover

John 2:13-25

At the time of the Passover, people from every part of the land went up to Jerusalem to keep the feast. Among those who went were Jesus and his friends—Andrew, Simon, Philip and Nathanael.

When Jesus entered the temple court, he found it crowded, noisy and busy. Nothing about it made a person feel like praying. It looked more like a market than a house of prayer. Men had brought live oxen, sheep and doves into the temple to sell for sacrifices. These animals only added to the noise and confusion.

In one corner money-changers sat at small tables. Every Jew over twenty years old had to give a piece of silver money called a half shekel to the priests. This money was used for sacrifices and for the temple.

Those who came from distant countries brought the kind of money used in their homeland. Since half shekels were the only coins the priests would take, all other coins had to be changed for half shekels to pay the priests. Every person had to pay to have his money changed into temple coins.

How angry Jesus was when he saw people making a market place out of God's house! Taking small cords, he tied them together and made a whip. With the whip he drove out all the animals and their keepers. Then he upset the money-changers' tables. To those who sold doves he said, "Take these things away. Do not make my Father's house a house of selling."

Many Jews were angry at Jesus for doing this. They asked, "What sign do you show that you have a right to do such things?"

Jesus knew they would not believe him even if he showed them a sign. He answered, "Destroy this temple and in three days I will raise it up." Jesus meant the temple of his body. He knew the Jews would help to kill him. Then in three days he would rise from the dead.

The Jews did not understand. They thought Jesus meant the great temple Herod had rebuilt on Mount Moriah. They scoffed, "It took forty-six years to build this temple and you say you can rebuild it in three days!" Shaking their heads doubtfully, they walked away.

During the feast Jesus began to teach the people and to do miracles among them. Many believed in him when they heard his words and saw the great works that no other man could do.

Nicodemus Comes to Jesus

John 3:1-21

One man who believed in Jesus was a ruler among the Jews. He was Nicodemus, a rich Pharisee. Most of the Pharisees were very proud. They did not believe that either John the Baptist or Jesus were teachers sent from God.

Nicodemus was not like the other Pharisees. He heard Jesus teach the people who had come to worship at the Passover. "Surely Jesus is very great," Nicodemus thought.

While other Pharisees were finding fault with Jesus, Nicodemus wanted to hear more of his teachings. One night he went to the place where Jesus stayed to talk with him.

Nicodemus said, "Master, we know you are a teacher from God. No man could do the miracles you do unless God was with him."

Jesus wanted Nicodemus to know about the kingdom of God. He said, "Unless a man is born again, he cannot see the kingdom of God."

Nicodemus was puzzled. He asked, "How can a man be born after he is grown up? Can he become a tiny baby again?"

Jesus did not mean that a man would be born again in body but in heart. He said, "Unless a man is born of water and of the Spirit, he cannot enter the kingdom of God. Do not be surprised when I say that you must be born again. The wind blows. You hear it and you see what it does. Yet you do not see the wind itself. You cannot tell where it comes from or where it goes. That is the way it is with those who are born again."

Nicodemus thought about Jesus' words. No one could see the Spirit. Yet a person whose heart was changed, born again, would act as if he had the Spirit of God in his heart.

Finally Jesus said tenderly, "God so loved the world that he gave his only begotten Son, that whosoever believeth in him should not perish, but have everlasting life."

378

The Woman at the Well

John 4:1-43

Jesus decided to return to Galilee. He and his disciples took the shorter road that led through Samaria. Not many Jews went this way because they hated the Samaritans. Although both the Jews and the Samaritans worshiped God, the Samaritans had built a temple in their own country instead of going to Jerusalem to worship.

In many ways Jesus was not like most other Jews. For one thing he did not feel bitter towards the Samaritans. He knew that God loved the people of every land.

When they had traveled as far as the little city of Sychar, Jesus was tired. He sat down to rest by a well Jacob had dug hundreds of years before. Here his disciples left him and went into the city to buy food.

Soon a woman from Sychar came to get water. She knew at a glance that the strange man sitting there was a Jew. Since Jews paid no attention to Samaritans, she passed by him and lowered her water jar into the deep well. When the water jar was full, she pulled it up again.

Just as the woman was ready to start back to the city, Jesus said, "Give me a drink."

The woman was so surprised at his request that she said, "Since you are a Jew, why do you ask a Samaritan woman for a drink? You know the Jews have nothing to do with the Samaritans."

Jesus replied, "If you knew who asks you for a drink, you would ask him to give you living water."

The woman did not understand. She said, "Sir, this well is deep and you have nothing to draw the water up with. How could you give me living water? Are you greater than Jacob who gave us this well?"

"Whoever drinks of this water becomes thirsty and returns again and again for more," Jesus answered. "Whoever drinks the water that I give will never be thirsty again. The water that I give springs up into everlasting life."

Now the woman was really interested. She did not know that the living water was Jesus' free gift of salvation to all people. So she said, "Sir, give me this water so I won't have to come here to get water any more."

And Jesus told the woman things about herself that she thought no one knew. He told her about the wrongs she had done.

The woman wondered how this stranger could know all about her. Then she decided, "Sir, I believe you are a prophet." Because she did not want to be reminded of her sins, she tried to start an argument about religion. She said, "We Samaritans worship here, but you Jews say people should go to Jerusalem to worship."

Jesus did not argue. Instead he explained that God planned to bring salvation through the Jews. "God is not found in only one place," he said, "for God is Spirit. Those who worship him must worship in spirit and in truth."

The woman had never heard such wonderful words. She said, "I know the Messiah, the Christ, is coming from God. When he comes he will tell us everything."

How surprised the woman was when she heard Jesus say, "I am he!" Before she could ask him more, the disciples returned with food. Leaving her water jar by the well, she ran to tell her friends about this wonderful stranger.

When the disciples saw Jesus talking with the Samaritan woman, they wished they could ask him, "What did she want? Why did you talk with her?" Instead they offered him food. "Master, eat," they said.

Jesus refused. He said, "I have food to eat that you know nothing about."

And the disciples whispered to one another, "Did someone bring him food while we were away?"

Jesus knew their question so he said, "My food is to do the will of my Father who has sent me into the world."

Back in the city, the woman ran through the streets telling the people about Jesus. "Come see a man who told me all the things I ever did," she said. "Is not he the Christ?"

The people were so curious that they decided to see this man for themselves. They went back to Jacob's well with her.

Jesus talked with the Samaritans about the things of God. They invited him to stay and teach them more, and Jesus agreed.

For two days Jesus taught the people of Sychar. Many believed. They said to the woman who first met Jesus at the well, "Now we believe. Not because of what you told us, but because we heard for ourselves, we know this man is the Christ, the Savior of the world."

Jesus took his disciples and went on to Nazareth.

Jesus Heals the Nobleman's Son

John 4:45-54

Many people of Galilee were eager to see Jesus. It was told throughout the country that Jesus had turned the water to wine at Cana. Since then word had come about his teachings and his miracles in Jerusalem during the Passover. When Jesus entered Galilee from Samaria, news of his coming spread rapidly from one city to another. Everywhere people hoped Jesus would come to their cities and work miracles.

One man could not wait for Jesus to come to his city. He went looking for Jesus. He was a nobleman, an honored ruler of the city of Capernaum. How worried he was because his little son lay sick with a burning fever! The doctors could not help the little boy. How much the father wanted to see his son well again!

As soon as the nobleman heard about Jesus, he hurried to find him. When he found Jesus, he pleaded with the Master to come and heal his son. Without Jesus' healing touch, the child might die.

So many people were following Jesus just to see him work miracles that Jesus said, "Unless you see signs and wonders you will not believe that I am sent of God."

Again the nobleman begged, "Sir, if you do not come at once, my son may be dead before we reach him."

Jesus looked kindly at the distressed father. He said, "Go back home. Your son lives."

Because the nobleman believed Jesus' words, he started back to Capernaum. No longer was he afraid for his son. Jesus had said the boy was well.

As the nobleman approached Capernaum, his servants came running to meet him. He could tell by their faces that they had good news. "Your son lives. He is well," they said.

"At what time," asked the nobleman, "did he begin to get better?"

And the servants replied, "His fever left him yesterday at the seventh hour."

That was the very hour Jesus had told the nobleman, "Your son lives." Not only the nobleman but also all his household believed in Jesus when they heard how the sick boy had been healed.

Jesus Speaks at Nazareth

Luke 4:16-32

"Jesus is home. Jesus is back in Nazareth." The news spread quickly from one person to another.

The people of Nazareth had heard about Jesus' teachings and miracles in other cities. Now they wanted to hear for themselves what Joseph's son would say. Jesus stood up in the synagogue to read, and the leader brought him the book the prophet Isaiah had written long years before. Jesus read these words about the promised Savior:

"The Spirit of the Lord is upon me,

Because he has anointed me to preach the gospel to the poor;

He has sent me to heal the brokenhearted,

To preach deliverance to the captives,

And recovering of sight to the blind,

To set at liberty them that are bruised,

To preach the acceptable year of the Lord."

After reading these words, Jesus closed the book, gave it back to the leader and sat down. The speaker in the synagogue always stood up to read God's words and sat down to explain their meaning.

Among those who listened were people who had known Jesus nearly all his life. They were proud men, unwilling to learn new truths. They had heard of Jesus' miracles in Cana and Capernaum, but they did not believe he was the promised Savior. Jesus was only a poor man. They expected the Savior to be rich and powerful.

Everyone watched and waited for Jesus to speak. How surprised they were when they heard his words! They did not know he could speak so well. Little did they know that Jesus was the world's greatest teacher.

His words pleased them until he said, "Today Isaiah's words have come true. I am the one who is to preach the gospel to the poor and the captives, to heal and to help as Isaiah promised."

"How could this be true?" they asked each other. "Is not this Joseph's son?"

Jesus knew they would not believe him. No prophet is honored by his own people. Jesus said, "One time Elijah the prophet ran away from Israel to hide in the home of a poor widow in a heathen land. Because this poor widow cared for God's prophet, God took care of her. God healed Naaman, the heathen leper, when he obeyed Elisha's words. Yet many Israelites had leprosy and never were healed."

The proud men of Nazareth were angry. Was Jesus telling them that God cared for other people besides the Jews? They would not listen to such words! The leading men ran to Jesus, grabbed him and pulled him outside the synagogue. An angry mob followed.

The mob led Jesus to the top of the high hill on which Nazareth was built. They planned to throw him over the edge upon the sharp rocks far below. Strangely enough, Jesus walked quietly through the excited mob, and they did not see him go.

Jesus went to Capernaum, the city by the Sea of Galilee. Here he taught the people about God, and the people were glad to listen.

Many Fish

Luke 5:1-11

After some time Jesus returned to Capernaum to teach the people, and his disciples went back to their work as fishermen. One day Jesus walked to the seashore where Simon Peter, Andrew, James and John were washing their nets.

Many people had seen Jesus leave the city, and they followed. Soon a great crowd gathered on the shore. How eager they were to hear Jesus preach!

Jesus stepped into Peter's boat and moved it just out from shore.

There Jesus spoke to the people. After teaching them he told Simon, "Move out into the deep and let down your nets for a catch."

Simon replied, "Master, we have fished all night, and we have caught nothing." Then he added, "But if you say so, we will try again."

Simon and Andrew rowed out from the land and let down their nets once more. This time many, many fish swam into their nets and were caught. The net became so heavy that Simon and Andrew could not pull it out of the water. Quickly they motioned to their partners in the other ship to come and help them. Simon, Andrew, James and John pulled with all their might. Never had they seen so many fish. Soon both ships were full of fish—so full that the boats began to sink.

Falling at Jesus' knees, Simon cried out, "Leave me, O Lord! For I am a sinful man."

Jesus did not intend to leave Simon. He answered, "Do not be afraid. From now on you will catch men."

Fishermen Leave Their Nets

Matthew 4:18-22; Mark 1:16-38

As Jesus walked by the Sea of Galilee, he saw Andrew and Simon fishing. He called to them, "Follow me and I will make you fishers of men." Immediately they left their boats and followed him.

As the three walked along the shore, they saw two other fishermen mending their nets. These brothers, James and John, were partners with Simon and Andrew in the fishing business. Jesus called James and John to follow him also. At once they left their ship to follow Jesus.

With the four fishermen, Jesus returned to Capernaum. On the Sabbath they went to the synagogue. Many people came to hear Jesus. When he spoke they felt as if God were talking to them.

In the crowd was a man who had a very bad spirit. The bad spirit made the man call out, "Let us alone! What do we have to do with you, Jesus of Nazareth? I know you are the Holy One from God."

Jesus said to the bad spirit, "Hold your peace and come out of him." And the bad spirit came out.

Jesus teaches the people from a boat

How surprised the people were! Never before had they seen anyone with such power. They said to one another, "What is this? What new teaching? Jesus even commands evil spirits and they obey him!"

Jesus and the four fishermen left the synagogue and went to the home of Simon and Andrew. There they learned that Simon's mother-in-law was sick with a fever. They brought Jesus to her. Taking hold of her hand, he lifted her up. The fever left at once. She got up and helped get the meal.

For the Jews the Sabbath ended at sunset, and they began their work again. When the sun set on this Sabbath, Simon and Andrew saw many people coming toward their home. Some came with crippled friends leaning on their arms. Others led the blind or carried the sick. All wanted Jesus to make their friends and loved ones well.

What a busy time followed! Jesus was glad to help the people. He healed many that night.

When the last group left Simon's house, Jesus lay down to sleep. He must have been very tired, but after sleeping only a few hours, he got up quietly and left the city. He found a place where he could be alone to talk with his heavenly Father. Jesus prayed for strength and help to do the great work he had to do.

At daylight more people came to Simon's house, asking for Jesus. Simon and his friends found Jesus was not there. They went to look for him and found him at his place of prayer.

"Everyone is looking for you," they said.

Jesus answered, "I must preach the kingdom of God in other cities also, for I am sent to do this great work." So the disciples went with him to other cities in Galilee. Jesus taught in the synagogues and healed the sick. Many believed in him.

Jesus Calls Matthew

Matthew 9:9-13; Mark 2:14-17; Luke 5:27-32

In the land where Jesus lived, there was one group of Jews who were hated and despised. They were the publicans, the tax collectors who worked for the Roman government. The Jews wanted to be an independent nation with their own ruler. They resented the Romans and anyone who worked with the Roman government.

The publicans' job was to collect from the Jews the taxes levied by the Roman government. Often the publicans took more money than the government charged. In this way they stole from the people and became rich themselves.

Not all publicans robbed the people by taking too much tax money. Because some did, the people thought all tax collectors were dishonest. For that reason the people called them sinners.

One day Jesus walked along a street in the city of Capernaum. There he saw Matthew sitting at a publican's table, collecting tax money from the people. Even though many Jews hated Matthew, Jesus knew that Matthew had a good heart, that he would make a good disciple. To Matthew he said, "Follow me."

Gladly Matthew left his money table and followed Jesus. As Matthew walked away, he thought about his many friends who would like to see Jesus. How much Matthew wanted them to hear Jesus' words!

At his home Matthew gave a great banquet. He invited many friends who were also tax collectors. Jesus and his disciples were the guests of honor.

Even though they had not been invited, the proud scribes and Pharisees gathered in the courtyard of Matthew's house. They watched the dinner party and talked to each other about what they saw. They criticized Jesus for being with these publicans and sinners. No good Jew would do such a thing.

Finally the scribes and Pharisees called Jesus' disciples aside and asked, "Why does your Master eat and drink with publicans and sinners?"

Jesus heard what the proud Jews had said. He answered, "Those who are well do not need a doctor, but the people who are sick. I have not come to call the righteous people, but I have come to call sinners to repent."

The scribes and Pharisees thought they were too righteous to need repentance. The publicans and sinners admitted they had done wrong. Many of them listened to Jesus' words and repented of their sins.

Matthew, the publican, became a true disciple. One of the books in the New Testament is called the Gospel According to Matthew. It records more of Jesus' words than does any of the other Gospels.

The Cripple at the Pool of Bethesda

John 5:1-18

In Jerusalem was a pool called Bethesda. At times the waters of this pool were strangely moved. The people believed that the first person to step into the water when it was moved would be healed.

No wonder so many sick, crippled and blind came to wait for the water to move. Five porches had been built beside the pool so these people could rest in the shade while they waited. Some had been coming here for a long time, hoping to be healed when the water was troubled.

Perhaps many were too sick to move quickly when they saw the water bubble up. Perhaps they got so tired watching that they did not see the action when it began. Since only the first person in was made well, many people were always disappointed.

One Sabbath Jesus walked through the porches beside the pool. He saw all the people who had come for healing. Lying on a mat was a crippled man who had not walked for thirty-eight years. Jesus looked down at him and asked gently, "Would you like to be made well?"

The man answered, "Sir, I have no one to help me into the water when it is troubled. Before I can crawl down, someone else steps in."

"Rise up," Jesus said. "Take your bed and walk!"

The surprised man felt strength filling his weakened body. He stood on his feet. At first it was hard for him to believe that he was really well again. Then he stooped down and rolled up his mat. When he turned to speak to Jesus, Jesus was gone. Picking up his mat, the man started home. How happy he was!

As he walked along carrying his bed mat, people looked at him strangely. The Jews believed it was a sin to carry anything on the Sabbath. Some stopped and reminded him, "This is the Sabbath. It is not right for you to carry your bed."

The crippled man waits to be healed at the pool of Bethesda

The man answered, "The one who healed me said, 'Take up your bed and walk.'"

His answer excited the people. Quickly they asked, "Who told you to do this?" How angry they were that someone told this man to break the Sabbath! Because the poor man did not know who Jesus was, he could not answer.

Not long afterwards, the man who had been healed went to the temple to worship God. There Jesus found him and said, "Now you are well. Sin no more lest something worse happen to you."

At once the man knew it was Jesus who had made him well. He felt so happy and thankful that he told everyone how Jesus had healed him at the pool of Bethesda.

This only made the leaders angrier! Not only had the man carried his bed, but he had been healed on the Sabbath. They thought it was more important to keep the Law than for a crippled man to be made well again.

Jesus answered, "My Father is at work and I work."

The Jews were furious when they heard this. They wanted to kill Jesus. Not only had he broken the Sabbath, but he said God was his Father.

And that day Jesus taught all those in the temple about the heavenly Father.

Jesus Heals a Withered Hand

Matthew 12:1-15; Mark 2:23-3:6; Luke 6:1-11

After Jesus had angered the Pharisees by healing a crippled man on the Sabbath, they became Jesus' enemies. From that time on, they followed Jesus just to find fault.

One Sabbath Jesus and his disciples walked through a grain field. The disciples were so hungry that they picked a few ears and ate them. When the Pharisees saw this, they said to the Master, "You and your disciples have broken the Sabbath law by gathering food to eat."

392

Jesus reminded them of the time David went to the tabernacle and ate the bread that belonged only to the priests. God knew David and his men were hungry, so he did not punish David. "Even the priests and the Levites work on the Sabbath, offering sacrifices in the morning and the evening," said Jesus. "The Son of man is Lord even of the Sabbath." And he went on to the city to teach in the synagogue.

As he stood up to teach the people, he saw a man who had a withered hand. The Pharisees watched him closely. They hardly knew what this Jesus would do next. The people followed him so willingly that the Pharisees were afraid. They tried to think of clever questions to trick Jesus.

"Is it lawful to heal on the Sabbath?" they asked.

Jesus answered, "If any of you have a sheep and it falls into a pit on the Sabbath, do you not get it out? A man is much more valuable than a sheep! Why then is it not lawful to do good on the Sabbath?"

The Pharisees said no more, but their faces showed how angry they were. Jesus was sorry their hearts were so hard. To the man with the withered hand Jesus said, "Stretch out your hand."

The man obeyed and immediately his hand was healed. The Pharisees were so outraged that they left the synagogue and met to plan a way to kill Jesus.

Jesus knew what the Pharisees were planning. He went out and great crowds followed him. He healed all the sick among them.

The Twelve

Matthew 10:1-4, Mark 3:13-19; Luke 6:12-16

Many people besides the four fishermen and Philip, Nathanael and Matthew followed Jesus. His teachings were so wonderful that many wanted to be his pupils or disciples. They followed his company from one place to another.

Finally Jesus felt he needed to choose twelve of these men for special training so they could help in his great work. He wanted to send these men to places where he had never gone. They would preach to the people about the kingdom of God.

Even though Jesus knew the hearts of all men, he felt he needed God's help in choosing the Twelve. One night he slipped away quietly and climbed the mountain to pray. There in the quietness he prayed all night for help and wisdom and for strength to do his work.

When morning came Jesus was ready to choose his helpers. Leaving his place of prayer, he joined the company of followers who were waiting in the valley.

From them he chose Simon, whom he called Peter, and Andrew, the brother who first brought Simon to Jesus. Then he chose James and John, the brothers who had been partners with Simon and Andrew in the fishing business. Afterwards he chose Matthew, the publican; Philip, of Bethsaida; Thomas and Bartholomew; another James, who was the son of Alpheus; another Simon, also called Zelotes; Judas, the brother of James; and last of all Judas Iscariot, who finally sold his Lord.

To these twelve men Jesus gave the power to heal. He told them to preach the kingdom of God. These twelve he called apostles, which means, "those who are sent out." And Jesus sent out the Twelve to preach to others.

The Sermon on the Mount

Matthew 5—7; Luke 6:17-49

After Jesus had chosen his twelve disciples, he wanted to teach them how to do his work. Up the mountainside they climbed. Then Jesus sat down, and they gathered near to hear him. Many others gathered to hear Jesus too.

Jesus said, "Blessed are the poor in spirit: for theirs is the kingdom of heaven." Perhaps he thought about the proud scribes and Pharisees. The proud will never believe his words and learn how to enter the kingdom of God. Humble people who feel they need God's help to live right are the ones Jesus called the "poor in spirit." They are blessed because they shall be given the kingdom of God.

He also said, "Blessed are they that mourn: for they shall be comforted." These words sounded strange. Who ever thought that blessings belong to the troubled and sad? The people did not understand how God loves to comfort his children.

"Blessed are the meek," said Jesus next, "for they shall inherit the earth." He meant that gentle people who control their temper, who try to do what is right, would enjoy God's blessings.

Then Jesus said, "Blessed are they which do hunger and thirst after righteousness: for they shall be filled." Perhaps he thought again of the proud Pharisees who believed they were so good that they did not need to repent of their sins and seek God's help. Those who want God's Spirit as much as they want food and drink will be blessed.

"Blessed are they who show mercy to others," said Jesus, "for mercy shall be shown to them. And blessed are they who have pure hearts, for they shall see God. And blessed are those who make peace among men, for they shall be called the children of God." These words the disciples understood, for they knew that God will surely bless people who show understanding love, who do not allow sin to enter their hearts and who make peace where trouble is.

Then Jesus said, "Blessed are they who are persecuted for the sake of righteousness; for theirs is the kingdom of heaven." People who are persecuted are greatly wronged. After Jesus had been crucified and had risen from the dead, the disciples and other followers learned what it means to be persecuted for righteousness' sake. Jesus said to those who are persecuted, "Rejoice, and be exceeding glad; for great is your reward in heaven."

In this wonderful sermon, Jesus taught how Christians should live, how they should pray, how they should treat their enemies and their friends, how God loves and cares for them.

At the close of his sermon, Jesus said, "Those who hear my words and do them are like a wise man who built his house upon the rock. When the rain fell, the floods came and the winds blew, the house stood strong. But those who hear my words and do not obey them are like a foolish man who built his house upon the sand. When the rain fell, the floods came and the winds blew, the house fell. Great was the fall of it."

The people looked at each other in surprise. Surely Jesus was the greatest teacher of all. But how could they obey his teachings? "Love your enemies. Pray for those who mistreat you. Do good to those who hate you." They knew these words sounded like the words of God. Those who loved God wanted to live by these words. God would help them.

Jesus Heals a Leper

Matthew 8:1-4; Mark 1:40-45; Luke 5:12-16

When Jesus and his twelve disciples came down from the mountain, a great crowd followed him. Most of the people had come from the cities and villages in Galilee, but some had even come from Jerusalem and other places in Judea.

Nearby stood one poor man who did not dare press into the crowd. How much he needed to be healed of leprosy! He was not allowed to live among his friends and relatives for fear they would catch the disease. He was not allowed to get close enough to touch anyone who was not a leper. What an unhappy life!

The poor leper thought, "I wonder if this Jesus will heal me." Before anyone could stop him, he ran to Jesus, knelt at his feet and worshiped him. Looking up at Jesus, the man said, "If you are willing, I know you can heal me."

Jesus looked down at the man kneeling at his feet. Great pity and love filled his heart. Jesus knew this man was dying by inches. No doctor could cure this dreaded leprosy. Jesus knew the many unhappy days this poor man had spent away from his home and loved ones. He knew how lonely a leper was.

Jesus was not afraid to touch this poor man. Kindly he laid his hand on the leper and said, "I am willing. You are healed now."

Quickly the man jumped to his feet. The weary look was gone from his eyes. The man's face was all smiles. Now he was well! How thankful he felt! At first it was hard to believe he had been healed, but when he looked at his skin, there was no sign of leprosy.

In God's law that Moses gave to the people, the Lord commanded lepers to offer sacrifices of thanksgiving when they were healed. Jesus reminded the man, "Do not tell anyone about this, but go and show yourself to the priests and offer the sacrifice that Moses commanded."

The man was so happy and thankful for what Jesus had done that he could not keep quiet about it. He had to tell his friends. His friends told their friends, and so the news spread far and wide.

Everyone talked about this great miracle. Many left their homes to follow Jesus. So many people flocked to see and hear him that he could no longer enter the cities. From then on he spent much of his time in the country, and the people came to him there.

A Roman Captain Shows Great Faith

Matthew 8:5-13; Luke 7:1-10

Jesus returned with his disciples to Capernaum, where he had healed many sick people at the close of one Sabbath. News of his coming reached the city before he arrived. Friends were glad to hear this news.

Other people besides those who knew him were glad to hear of his coming. One of them was a Roman centurion, a captain over one hundred Roman soldiers.

This captain was friendly toward the Jews. He had even built a synagogue for them, perhaps the very one in which Jesus had often taught the people on the Sabbath. Because of his kindness, the Jews honored him.

One day a servant of the centurion became sick. On the next day, he grew worse until it seemed that he could not live much longer. The centurion loved his servant.

Now the centurion had heard about the sick people whom Jesus had healed. He knew Jesus could heal his servant, but he felt too unworthy to go to Jesus. So he sent the Jewish teachers in the synagogue to ask Jesus to heal the sick servant.

When these Jewish teachers came to Jesus, they told him about the centurion's servant. They told him also about the kindness of this Roman captain and how he had built their synagogue. "He is a worthy man," they said, "for he loves our nation."

Jesus went with them. As they neared the centurion's home, they saw men coming to meet them. These friends had been sent to tell Jesus that he need not come into the house to heal the sick man. The centurion did not feel worthy to have Jesus enter his house, and he felt himself too unworthy to go out to meet Jesus. So he sent his friends to carry this message: "Lord, do not trouble yourself to come into my house, for I am not worthy to receive so great a man as you are. Just speak the word and my servant will be made well. I know you have the power to command sickness to depart, just as I have power to command my soldiers to obey me."

When Jesus heard these words, he was greatly pleased. There was a crowd of curious people following, hoping to see another miracle. He turned to them and said, "Nowhere among the Jews have I found such great faith in me as this captain has shown."

When the friends returned to the house, they found the servant healed.

Four Men Tear Up a Roof

Matthew 9:2-8; Mark 2:1-12; Luke 5:18-26

Wherever Jesus went, crowds followed him. They gathered around him in the streets and in the homes where he stayed. Some of these people were his friends; others were merely curious to hear him speak and to see him do some miracle; others followed to find fault with him.

One day while Jesus was in Capernaum, many people came to the house where he was staying. Disciples, friends, curiosity seekers and faultfinders crowded the house until not another person could get inside the door.

Jesus healed those who were sick and preached about the kingdom of God. As the people listened, they heard strange noises overhead. Presently the roof began to part, and the people saw a man lying on a cot being lowered from the ceiling.

From the roof the crippled man's four friends looked on anxiously. Would Jesus heal their crippled friend? He was not able to move about. Day after day, he had lain weak and helpless on his bed. His friends had tried to bring him to Jesus, but they could not get through the door because of the crowd. They had to find another way.

398

Friends bring a crippled man to Jesus

When the four carriers could not get through the door, they took the crippled man up onto the roof. Laying down the bed mat, they got down on their knees and began lifting out the tiles of the roof. Soon they could see Jesus preaching below. They tied ropes about the sick man's bed and lowered him very carefully into the room before Jesus.

The people in the room wondered what was happening. They wondered what Jesus would do. Perhaps some of them knew the sick man. How surprised they were to hear Jesus say, "Son, be of good cheer, for your sins are forgiven!"

Now the people did not watch the sick man any longer. Instead, they looked at Jesus in surprise. He had dared to say, "Your sins are forgiven." They knew God could forgive sins, but they did not know that Jesus was the Son of God.

The scribes and Pharisees who had come to find fault said in their hearts, "Who is this Jesus who pretends to forgive sins? None except God can do that!"

Jesus knew their thoughts and said, "Why do you think evil of me in your hearts? Is it easier to tell the man that his sins are forgiven, or to tell him to rise up from his bed and walk? But that you may know I have power on earth to forgive sins too"—Jesus said to the man—"Arise, take up your bed, and return to your own house."

Immediately all the stiffness left the sick man's body and his strength returned. He got up, rolled up his bed and lifted it up onto his shoulders. The people were so surprised that they made way for him as he walked through the room and into the street to join his happy friends.

The people did not know what to think. Some were afraid; all were amazed. They glorified God. As they hurried home, they said to each other, "Surely we have never seen anything like this before!"

A Widow's Son Is Raised to Life

Luke 7:11-17

In the city of Nain in Galilee lived a widow. She had only one child who was now a young man. Proudly the widow had watched her son grow! She thought of the time when he would be able to earn their living.

One day the young man became ill. How worried his mother was! Day after day, she sat at his bedside watching for some sign that he was getting better. Tenderly she nursed him, but in spite of all her loving care, he grew worse. Then one day he died.

Now the widow was alone. Both her husband and her son were dead and she was very sad and lonely.

Neighbors and friends came to weep with her and plan for the funeral. They wrapped long strips of linen cloth around the lifeless body and placed it on a frame called a bier.

The funeral procession started. In front were the men carrying the bier. Many people followed. The mourners wept aloud as they slowly walked toward the burial place. Suddenly the funeral procession stopped outside the gate. Everyone wondered what had happened. Then they saw a great crowd coming toward them. Walking in front of the crowd were Jesus and his twelve disciples.

When Jesus saw the widow's great sorrow, he wanted very much to help her. He knew the deep ache and loneliness that filled her heart. "Do not weep," he said kindly. Then going over to the bier he said, "Young man, I tell you to arise!"

The young man who had been dead sat up. He began to talk. In amazement, the mourners unwrapped the long linen strips from the young man's body. Then Jesus took him to his mother.

At once the cries stopped and a great silence fell over the people. They could hardly believe their own eyes. Soon they were sure that Jesus had raised the young man to life again. How they rejoiced! "A great prophet is come among us!" they exclaimed. Others cried, "Surely God has visited his people!"

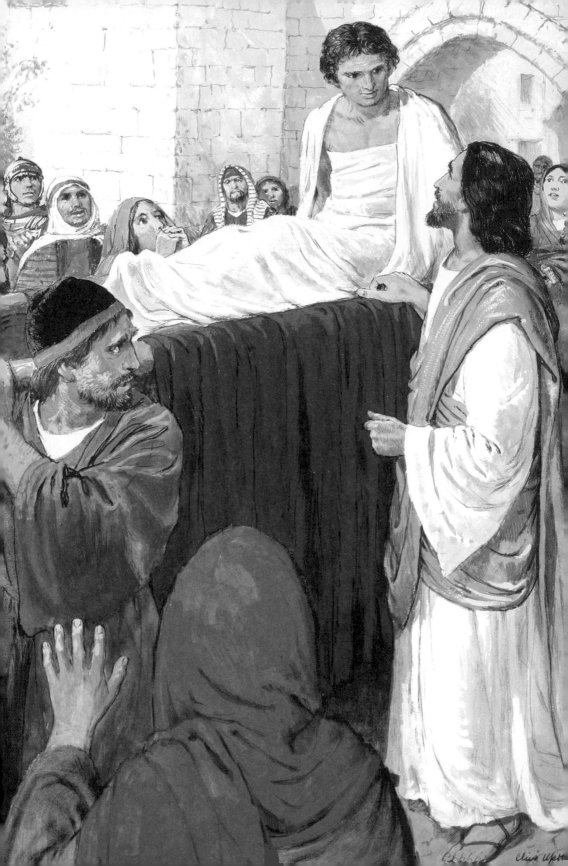

John the Baptist in Prison

Matthew 11:1-6; Luke 3:19-20; 7:18-23

After John baptized Jesus, he continued to preach fearlessly. John even reminded Herod the ruler of his sins, and Herod was very troubled. Herod's wife did not like John the Baptist or his preaching. She wanted her husband to kill this wilderness preacher. To please her Herod had John the Baptist put in prison.

News of how Jesus raised the widow's son from the dead spread through the country quickly. Even in prison, John the Baptist heard about it. John longed to see and know more about these things. Calling two of his disciples, John said, "Go to Jesus and ask him, 'Are you the one who is to come, or should we look for another?' "

The two hurried to Jesus with John's question. While they waited for Jesus' answer, many people gathered around the Master and begged for healing. There were cripples, blind, lepers, deaf and people with all kinds of sicknesses. One by one, Jesus healed them.

Turning to the two men who had come from John the Baptist, Jesus said, "Go back and tell John what you have seen. Tell him how the blind see, the lame walk, the deaf hear, the lepers are cured, the dead are raised to life and the evil spirits are cast out. To the poor the glad news of the kingdom is preached."

The two took this message back to John. How glad he was to hear about the wonderful works of Jesus! Not long afterward, Herod commanded that John be killed. Friends who had comforted John in prison came and buried his body. Then they went to tell Jesus what Herod had done.

A Woman Anoints Jesus' Feet

Luke 7:36-50

While Jesus taught the people in Galilee, a Pharisee named Simon came to listen. Like many other Pharisees, Simon tried to find fault with Jesus. Because he could find none, he decided to ask Jesus to dinner. During dinner Simon planned to watch Jesus closely to see whether the Master might do something wrong.

Jesus raises the widow's son to life

Jesus accepted Simon's invitation and went to his house. Others went too. Some were invited, and some were not. All came into the dining room where the food was spread on the table. The guests took their places around the table, and those who were not invited stood back and looked on.

As was the custom Jesus and the other guests lay on couches facing the table. While they ate, an uninvited woman entered the room. She looked from one guest to another until she saw Jesus. At once she knelt at his feet and wept sorrowfully for her many sins. With her hair she wiped away the tears that fell on his feet. She poured costly perfume on his feet and kissed them.

Simon, the Pharisee, watched the woman. He knew she was a great sinner. Why did Jesus let such a woman weep at his feet? Imagine his surprise when he saw the woman anoint Jesus' feet with costly perfume. In his heart Simon said, "If Jesus were a prophet, he would not allow this woman to come near him. He would know what a sinner she is."

Jesus knew Simon's thoughts. Looking at the proud Pharisee, Jesus said, "Simon, I have something to tell you."

Simon answered very politely, "Master, what is it?"

Then Jesus told him this story: "There was a rich man who loaned money to two poor men. To one he loaned five hundred pence. To the other he loaned fifty. When the time came to pay back the loan neither man had any money. They came to the rich man, and he forgave them both. Which of these two men will love the rich man more?"

"I suppose," answered Simon, "that the man who was forgiven the more will love more."

"You are right," said Jesus. Then he turned to the sinful woman still weeping at his feet and said, "Simon, when I came into your home, you did not treat me like an honored guest. You did not give me water to wash the dust from my feet, but this woman has washed my feet with her tears and dried them with her hair.

"You did not give me a kiss of welcome, but this woman has kissed my feet. You did not anoint my head with oil as you anoint the heads of your friends, but this woman has poured costly perfume on my feet. I tell you that her many sins are forgiven, for she has loved much. Those who have little forgiven love little."

To the woman Jesus said, "Your sins are forgiven. Your faith has saved you. Go in peace."

Those who looked on said in their hearts, "Who is this man that forgives sins too?"

The Story of the Sower

Matthew 13:1-23; Mark 4:1-20

One day Jesus walked with his disciples beside the seaside outside Capernaum. Great crowds followed along the beach. They thought Jesus was leaving their city, and they wanted to go with him. They crowded so close around Jesus that he stepped into a boat and sat down to teach them.

And Jesus began to teach them by parables. These parables were short stories to show the truths of the gospel. As Jesus sat in the boat, he told them about a farmer who went out to sow seeds in his field. This is the story:

"One day a sower took a bag of grain and went out to his field. He walked back and forth across the field scattering handfuls of seed on the ground. As the grain fell, the breeze helped scatter it.

"Some seeds blew onto the road. When the birds saw the seeds lying there, they flew down and ate them. Other seeds fell on stony places and began to grow, but the soil was so shallow that the plants soon withered and died. Some seeds fell in thorny places, and the thorns grew so fast that they choked out the good seed.

"But not all the seeds were wasted. Many of them fell on good ground. There they sprouted and sent their roots into the rich soil. After a time they grew into stalks of grain. The stalks produced many more seeds than were first scattered on the ground. Some fields produced thirty times more, others sixty times more and some even one hundred times more."

The disciples wondered what the story meant. Why was Jesus telling stories instead of preaching sermons? When they climbed back into the boat, they asked him, "Why are you teaching the people with parables?"

405

Jesus answered, "Because I know you will try to find out what the stories mean. Others who hear the stories will not try to understand the meaning because their hearts are not open to God's message."

Then Jesus explained to the disciples what the story of the sower meant.

"The sower," he said, "is the person who speaks the words of God. The different kinds of soil represent the ways people act when they hear God's message. Those who hear it but do not try to understand are like the roadside where the seeds fell. Just as the birds flew down and ate those seeds, the evil one comes and the people forget the message they have heard.

"Those who listen gladly to God's words but do not obey them are like the stony places. The seeds fell but did not grow because they could not take deep root in the stony soil.

"Those who believe God's word in their hearts but allow trouble, money, or pleasure to crowd it out are like the soil where the thorns choked out the good seeds.

"But those who hear and obey God's word are like the good ground. Here the seeds fell, sprouted, grew into stalks and produced much grain."

Stories About the Kingdom of Heaven

Matthew 13:24-52; Mark 4:21-34

Jesus told another story to the people. This time he said: "The kingdom of heaven is like a man who sowed good seeds in his field. At night when everyone was asleep, his enemy came and scattered weed seeds everywhere. Both the good seeds and the weed seeds sprouted and grew.

"When the servants saw the weeds, they came to the man and asked, 'Didn't you sow good seeds in your field? Where did all these weeds come from?'

"The man answered, 'An enemy has sown the weeds.'

"'Shall we pull out the weeds?' the servants asked.

"'No,' said the master, 'wait until the time for the harvest. If you pull up the weeds now, you will pull up the wheat with them. When the wheat is ripe, I will send reapers to gather the weeds, tie them in bundles and burn them. Then they will gather the wheat and put it in my barn.'"

Next Jesus said, "The kingdom of heaven is like a grain of mustard seed. A man planted it in his field, and it became the tallest thing there. Even the birds came and made nests in its branches."

The women listened more closely when they heard Jesus say, "The kingdom of heaven is also like leaven or yeast that a woman puts into the dough when she is mixing bread. The yeast works through all the dough and causes it to rise."

At last Jesus sent the people away. Then the disciples asked, "Tell us the meaning of the story about the weeds and the good seeds."

Jesus said, "The good seeds are the people of God, and the weeds are the evil people. Someday God will separate the evil from the good, just as the farmer separates the weeds from his wheat."

Jesus Calms the Storm

Matthew 8:23-27; Mark 4:35-41; Luke 8:22-25

Jesus spent all day teaching the people by the Sea of Galilee. When evening came he said to his disciples, "Let us cross over to the other side." The disciples and Jesus went in one boat. Some who saw them leave the shore got into their own little boats and followed.

When they were far out from shore, a storm came up. Great waves dashed against the boat. The disciples pulled at the oars with all their might, but it did no good. If the boat were broken to pieces, they would never see land again.

Several disciples knew the sea well. They had seen it rage before, but this time they were completely helpless in the power of the storm.

What should they do? Just then a great wave swept over the boat and flooded it with water. Now the boat would sink. How afraid they were!

Jesus was so tired from teaching the people all day that he had fallen asleep. The storm did not seem to bother him a bit.

At first the disciples did not want to wake him. They knew how tired he was. Now that the boat was about to sink, they ran to him and cried out, "Master, don't you care if we die in this storm?"

Jesus opened his eyes and looked into their frightened faces. He asked, "Why are you so afraid? Don't you have any faith?"

As the disciples watched, Jesus stood up and spoke to the wind and the sea, "Peace, be still." At the sound of his voice, the storm stilled. The sea became quiet and calm.

How amazed the disciples were! They asked one another, "What kind of man is he that even the wind and the sea obey him?" And they thought much about the Master's great power.

Jesus Heals a Wild Man

Matthew 8:28-34; Mark 5:1-20; Luke 8:26-39

After the storm was stilled, Jesus and his disciples went ashore in the country of the Gadarenes. Nearby was a cemetery where a wild man lived. No chains were strong enough to hold him. Night and day, he wandered in this lonely place, crying and cutting himself with stones.

From a distance the wild man saw Jesus. At once he ran, fell at Jesus' feet and worshiped him. The evil spirits that troubled him as with one voice called out to Jesus, "What have I to do with you, Jesus, Son of the most high God? I beg you, do not torment me."

Jesus knew the man could never be well so long as he was filled with evil spirits. Jesus said, "Come out of the man, you unclean spirit." Then he asked the man, "What is your name?"

The evil spirit replied, "My name is Legion, for we are many."

On a mountainside nearby was a herd of two thousand hogs with the servants who took care of the animals. The evil spirits said to Jesus, "Send us into the hogs."

"Go," Jesus answered.

At once the great herd ran down the mountainside, plunged into the sea and all the hogs were drowned. How frightened the servants were when they saw this! Away they ran to the city to tell what had happened.

Jesus calms the storm on Galilee

Soon a crowd of curious people gathered. They were much surprised to see the wild man sitting at Jesus' feet, wearing clothes and acting perfectly well. A peaceful look was on his face, and he had the right use of his mind again.

The people were afraid. What kind of man was Jesus? A whole herd of hogs had been drowned on account of him. What if he did more things like that in their country? They did not even think of bringing their sick for him to heal. Instead they begged him to go away and leave them alone.

Jesus and his disciples returned to their boat, and the man who had been healed followed. He wanted to go with them, but Jesus said, "Go back to your home and tell your friends what great things the Lord has done for you."

Gladly the man obeyed. From city to city he went, telling people about the wonderful power of Jesus.

Jesus Answers Calls for Help

Matthew 9:18–10:42; Mark 5:22-43; Luke 8:41–9:6

Jesus and his disciples had just returned by ship to Capernaum. An eager crowd waited on the shore to welcome them. And again Jesus taught them and healed the sick.

A man came running to Jesus. He fell down at Jesus' feet and cried, "My daughter is dying, but if you will come and lay your hands on her, she will be made well."

This man was Jairus, a ruler of the synagogue in Capernaum. Perhaps Jesus knew Jairus, for he had taught often in the synagogue. At once Jesus started to go with the man to heal his daughter. The disciples went too, and the crowd followed, eager to see another miracle. As they went the people pressed close to Jesus.

In this crowd was a poor woman who had been ill for twelve years. She had spent all her money on doctors, yet they did not help her. Now she had no more money. Hearing about Jesus' power to heal, she decided to go to him and be made well.

The sick woman is healed when she touches Jesus' garment

How hard it was to reach him! But she pressed her way through the crowd till she came very near. In her heart she thought, "I need not ask him to make me well; if only I can touch the hem of his coat, I shall be healed." So she edged her way closer, until she could reach out her hand and touch Jesus' clothes. Immediately she was healed, and she stepped back into the crowd.

But Jesus knew what the woman had done. Turning around he asked, "Who touched me?"

Amazed, the disciples asked, "Why do you ask who touched you when the people are pressing against you from every side?"

But Jesus answered, "Someone has touched me, for I felt healing power go from my body."

The woman came trembling and fell down before him. Jesus spoke to her kindly, "Daughter, your faith has made you well; go in peace."

Jairus stood by waiting impatiently for Jesus to come to his house. What if his daughter died before they reached her bedside? And sure enough, a servant came with the sad news, "Do not trouble the Master any longer, for it is too late."

Jesus heard the message and knew how Jairus felt. He said, "Do not be afraid; only believe, and she shall yet be made well." So on they went.

At the ruler's house, many friends and neighbors had gathered to weep with the sorrowing mother. Jesus asked, "Why do you weep? The girl is not dead but sleeping." They laughed at him, for they knew the girl was dead.

Then Jesus sent everyone out of the room except the father and the mother and Peter, James and John. Taking the girl's hand, he said, "Little girl, get up!" At his command she opened her eyes, got up and walked about the room.

Jesus told her parents, "Give her food to eat." He asked that they tell no one what he had done. News of this miracle would only draw greater crowds than ever.

When they left the home of Jairus, two blind men followed Jesus, crying, "O Son of David, have mercy on us!" They followed him into the house where he was staying.

Jesus asked, "Do you believe that I am able to open your blind eyes?"

Quickly they answered, "Yes, Lord."

Touching their eyes, Jesus said, "Let it be done to you just as you believe." And their eyes were opened.

So great were the crowds that came to hear Jesus he could not teach them all. Sending his twelve disciples to other cities, he told them to preach the gospel and heal the sick. The work was too great for Jesus to do alone.

A Boy's Lunch Basket

Matthew 14:13-23; Mark 6:30-46, Luke 9:10-17; John 6:1-15

The disciples returned to Jesus, telling about the people they had healed and taught in Galilee. Now more and more people heard about Jesus. They came from everywhere to hear and see him.

The people were so eager to hear Jesus and have their loved ones healed that they were always with him. He did not have time to rest or even to eat. So Jesus called his twelve disciples to him and said, "Come with me to a quiet place, for we must rest awhile."

They sailed to the other side of the sea and went into a desert place. But they did not find much time to rest, for soon a great crowd gathered. The people had followed them. Perhaps the disciples were disappointed because the people had found them again, but Jesus looked at the people lovingly. "They are like sheep that have no shepherd," he said. Jesus sat down to teach them again. He healed the sick and taught the people about the kingdom of heaven.

Evening came. Still the people stayed. They seemed to forget they could not find food or shelter in the desert. The disciples wanted Jesus to send the people away. "Send the people away," said the disciples, "so they can buy food in the towns and villages as they go home."

But Jesus answered, "We must feed them before sending them away." Turning to Philip, he asked, "Where shall we find bread that all these people may eat?"

Philip looked at the people and shook his head. "If we should buy two hundred penny worth of bread," he answered, "there would not be enough for each one to have a small piece."

In this great crowd were five thousand men besides all the women and children. When they left home, they did not know they would have to go so far to find Jesus. One boy, however, had not forgotten his lunch basket. In it were five little loaves of barley bread and two small fish.

The boy heard Jesus and the disciples talking about what to do. He went up to Andrew, showed his lunch basket and offered to give the food to Jesus. Andrew told Jesus about the boy's offer.

"How many loaves are there in the basket?" asked Jesus.

"Only five and two small fish," Andrew said. "But what will that be among so many people?"

"Bring it to me," Jesus replied. To the disciples he said, "Make the people sit down in groups of fifty and a hundred."

Jesus took the loaves and fish, gave thanks and broke the food into small pieces. He filled a basket for each disciple to pass among the hungry people.

When the crowd had eaten all they wanted, Jesus had the disciples gather up the food that was left. There were twelve baskets full.

This miracle excited the people. They wanted Jesus to become their king. How wonderful it would be to have a king who could feed them by working miracles!

Jesus would not allow the people to make him king. He had not come to the earth to rule an earthly kingdom. He commanded his disciples to enter the ship and return to the other side of the sea. Sending the people away, he went alone up the mountainside to pray.

Jesus Walks on the Water

Matthew 14:23-36; Mark 6:47-56; John 6:16-29

After spending the day with Jesus, the people walked along the northern shore of the sea to their homes. The disciples climbed into their boat and started to row toward Capernaum. Jesus went up the mountain to pray alone.

After nightfall a strong wind blew across the sea and beat against the little boat. The disciples rowed with all their might, but they could not make much progress against the wind. Higher and

A boy gives his lunch to Jesus

higher, the waves dashed and rolled. The little boat could not plow through them.

How tired the disciples became! They must have remembered the time Jesus was with them and stilled the storm. If only he were with them now!

Far away on the mountain, Jesus had prayed for several hours. When the storm came up, he knew how much his disciples needed him. He would go to them at once. Out across the water he walked, just as easily as if it had been land. Nearer and nearer he came to the tossing ship.

The disciples looked up and saw a person walking on the waves. How frightened they were! Each disciple thought he had seen a spirit, for surely no man could walk on the water. In fear they cried out.

When Jesus heard their cry, he said, "Do not be afraid, for it is I."

The voice was familiar, but still the disciples could scarcely believe it was Jesus. Finally Simon Peter called out, "Lord, if it is you, tell me to come to you walking on the water."

And Jesus answered, "Come."

With a bound Simon Peter leaped over the side of the ship and started to Jesus. The other disciples looked on in amazement. What great power Jesus had!

A strong wind blew against Peter, and he was afraid. He looked at the waves and began to sink. "Lord, save me!" he cried out.

Jesus reached out his hand and caught Peter. "O man of little faith, why did you doubt?" Jesus asked.

The two climbed into the boat, and the others rejoiced. At once the wind stopped. Again the disciples marveled at the Master's great power. They worshiped him, saying, "Surely you are the Son of God."

When morning came the people who had been with Jesus the day before went to find him again. They had seen the disciples leave in their boat. But Jesus had stayed behind. The people looked everywhere, but they could not find him. Finally they sailed across the Sea of Galilee to Capernaum in their search for Jesus.

417

Jesus walks on the water

At Gennesaret near Capernaum, they found the Master. Here, too, crowds of people from this region gathered around him. They brought with them those who were sick.

Wherever Jesus went, in villages or cities or in the country, the people laid the sick in the road he would travel. They believed the sick would be healed if they could even touch the hem of his robe. And those who did were healed.

A Gentile Mother Comes to Jesus

Matthew 15:21-28; Mark 7:24-30

Near Galilee was the small country of Phoenicia. The people who lived there were Gentiles. Many of them worshiped idols. Since they lived so close to Galilee, they knew about the Jewish religion too.

So many people followed Jesus that he could not find time to be alone with his disciples. Perhaps he would have more time to teach his friends if he left Galilee. And so Jesus took his disciples and went to the neighboring country of Phoenicia.

But even the Phoenicians had heard about Jesus. They were eager to see him. News of his coming spread throughout the region. Even in a strange land, Jesus could not hide himself.

In this region a poor Gentile mother was very sad. An evil spirit tormented her little girl. This worried mother had heard that Jesus could cast out evil spirits and restore people to their right minds. As soon as she learned that Jesus was nearby, she left her work and ran to find him.

When she reached Jesus, she pleaded, "Have mercy on me, O Lord, Son of David, for my daughter is very ill."

Jesus did not seem to hear the woman. He paid no attention to her request. Still the woman followed, begging for his help. The disciples were annoyed at her. Scorning her, they told Jesus, "Send her away, for she calls after us."

Perhaps the woman was afraid Jesus would do that. At once she fell at his feet and worshiped him. "Lord, help me," she begged.

The loving heart of Jesus was touched. He wanted to help this poor woman. To test her faith he answered, "I am not sent to the Gentiles, but to the lost children of Israel. It is not right to take the children's bread and throw it to dogs."

The proud Jews called the Gentiles "dogs." The woman understood that Jesus referred to the Jews and the Gentiles. She did not mind being called a dog if only her daughter could be healed.

She said, "I know the children's bread should not be given to the dogs, but the dogs eat the crumbs that fall from the children's table." As a Gentile the woman wanted a crumb of healing for her child.

Jesus did not make the woman wait any longer for his answer. He was so pleased with her faith and her wise words that he said, "O woman, you have great faith. Go back home, for your daughter is well."

Gladly the woman jumped to her feet and obeyed Jesus. She was sure her child was well. When she reached home, the little girl was lying on the bed, resting quietly. The evil spirit was gone.

Jesus Heals and Feeds the Crowd

Matthew 15:29-39; Mark 7:31—8:10

Leaving Phoenicia, Jesus and his twelve disciples passed through the country where Jesus had once healed a wild man called Legion. When Jesus healed him, the evil spirits entered a herd of hogs that was nearby. The hogs ran down the mountainside, plunged into the sea and were drowned. Because of this the people had begged Jesus to leave.

On this second visit, things were different. The man who had been made well had returned to his home and told everyone about Jesus. Everywhere he told people that the power of Jesus had cured him. They listened with interest. Before they had been afraid of this man Legion, but now he was changed. The people were sorry they had sent Jesus away.

When Jesus returned the people flocked to see and hear him. They followed him into the country. For three days they listened to his teachings. They brought to him their lame, blind, dumb, crippled and sick. Jesus healed every one of them.

Among those that were brought for healing was a man who could not hear or talk. Jesus took the man aside from the crowd. Putting his fingers in the man's ears and touching his tongue, Jesus looked up to heaven and said, "Be opened!"

Immediately the man could hear and speak. He was so happy and thankful that he could not keep from telling what Jesus had done. Jesus asked him and the people who saw him not to tell about the healing. The people were so astonished that they said, "Jesus does all things well. He makes both the deaf to hear and the dumb to speak."

The evening of the third day Jesus called his disciples aside and reminded them, "I feel sorry for all these people. They have been with me three days and they have nothing to eat. If I send them home now, they will faint by the way. Many live far away."

The disciples agreed, but they asked, "How can we feed such a crowd out here in the desert?"

"How many loaves do you have?" Jesus asked.

And they told him, "Only seven and a few small fish."

Jesus turned to the people and commanded them to sit down. When they had obeyed, he gave thanks for the loaves and fish.

Just as when he fed the five thousand from the boy's lunch, these few loaves and fish became enough food for everyone. More than four thousand people were fed. Seven baskets of food were left over.

Now Jesus dismissed the crowd. They started home. Among them were the sick that had been made well. How glad the people were that Jesus had visited their country this second time!

In a boat Jesus and his disciples crossed to the other side of the Sea of Galilee.

The Blind Man of Bethsaida

Mark 8:22-26

Near Bethsaida, a town by the Sea of Galilee, lived a blind man. He had never been to Jesus, but he had heard that the Master healed all who were brought to him. The blind man wished that he too could be healed.

One day someone told the blind man that Jesus and his twelve friends were in Bethsaida. "I must go to Jesus at once," the blind man said. And friends led him to the place where Jesus was staying.

Jesus did his best not to attract any more crowds. He knew the time of his ministry was growing short. He must train the disciples so they could carry on his work after he was gone. He needed to spend time alone with them.

Friends of the blind man asked Jesus to heal his eyes. Jesus took the man by the hand and led him outside the town. When the two were alone, Jesus touched the blind eyes and asked, "Can you see?"

At first things looked blurred to the man. He answered, "I see men that look like trees walking."

Again Jesus touched the man's eyes and his sight was restored. The man saw everything clearly.

Jesus said, "Do not go into the town or tell any of the townspeople what I have done for you."

And the man who had been blind went on his way rejoicing.

Peter's Great Confession

Matthew 16:13-28; Mark 8:27—9:1; Luke 9:18-27

Jesus and his disciples traveled north to the city of Caesarea Philippi. On the way Jesus questioned the disciples. First he asked, "Who do people say that I am?"

The disciples answered, "Some say you are Elijah, the prophet, come back to earth. Some think you are John the Baptist risen from the dead. Others believe you are Jeremiah or another prophet who taught long ago."

Next Jesus asked, "But who do you say that I am?"

Boldly Simon Peter answered, "You are the Christ, the Son of the living God."

Jesus rejoiced to hear this. At least his disciples understood who he was. Jesus charged them not to tell this to anyone.

Then Jesus talked about the troubles and sorrows that would come to him at Jerusalem. He would be arrested and cruelly treated. Because the elders, chief priests and scribes would reject him, he would be killed. After three days he would rise again.

The disciples did not understand what Jesus meant. They believed he would soon be their king, and they would have important places in his kingdom. Why should he talk about dying now?

Simon Peter, who often spoke for all the Twelve, took Jesus aside and said, "These terrible things must never happen to you."

Jesus turned and looked sadly at his disciples. To Peter he said, "You talk like Satan, the tempter. You do not understand the things of God; you understand only the things of men."

How much easier it would have been for Jesus to accept a throne and an earthly kingdom than to suffer and die! But Jesus did not want to do anything just because it was easy. He wanted to do his Father's will.

Later Jesus gathered the people and his disciples around him and told them what it meant to be his follower. "If anyone wants to follow me, he must not live his own way but my way. He must not be selfish and try only to take care of himself. If he will let his life be used entirely for my sake and for the gospel's, he will be saved. What is a man profited if he gains the whole world and loses his own soul? Or what will a man give in exchange for his soul? God will reward every man for what he does."

The people marveled at Jesus' teachings.

The Mount of Transfiguration

Matthew 17:1-13; Mark 9:2-13; Luke 9:28-36

After a long hard climb up a rough mountain slope near Caesarea Philippi, the three disciples were tired. Far above the quiet valley, Simon Peter, James and John looked for a place to rest. These fishermen were more used to rowing a boat than climbing a mountain. Jesus had asked them to go with him to the mountain to pray.

When the three disciples reached the top, they were too tired to pray. They fell asleep, and Jesus prayed alone.

While they slept, a great change came over the Master. His face shone as bright as the sun, and his clothing gleamed whiter than anything on earth. Two men came from heaven to talk with him. One was Moses who had written down God's law, and the other was Elijah who had spoken God's words to Israel. The three talked of Jesus' coming death.

The three were still talking when the disciples woke up. How amazed they were to see their Master clothed in such glory! In astonishment they watched as he talked with Moses and Elijah.

As Moses and Elijah were leaving, Simon Peter exclaimed, "Lord, it is good for us to be here! If you are willing, let us build three tabernacles—one for you, one for Moses, and one for Elijah."

While Peter spoke, a cloud overshadowed the disciples and they were afraid. From the cloud a voice said, "This is my beloved Son, in whom I am well pleased. Hear him."

The disciples fell to the ground, trembling with fear. Jesus came near, laid his hands on them and said, "Get up. Do not be afraid."

The disciples looked around and saw only Jesus. The cloud and the heavenly visitors were gone. Now they believed surely that Jesus was the Son of God.

The next day they climbed down the mountain. Jesus told them not to tell anyone about what had happened until after he had risen from the dead. Still the disciples wondered why he talked about pain and death when he, the Son of God, had been in such heavenly glory on the mountain.

Later when all the disciples were together, they asked, "Why do our teachers say that Elijah must come before the Messiah appears?"

Jesus answered, "Elijah has already come but they did not know him. They went on doing just as they pleased. They will make the Son of man suffer also."

The disciples understood that Jesus was referring to John the Baptist who had been imprisoned and killed. Meanwhile a crowd gathered in the valley to see Jesus.

Jesus Heals an Epileptic Boy

Matthew 17:14-21; Mark 9:14-29; Luke 9:37-43

Jesus and his three disciples left the Mount of Transfiguration and started back to the valley. They found the other nine disciples surrounded by a questioning crowd.

When Jesus came near, a man ran out of the crowd and fell at his feet. "Lord, have mercy on my only son," he pleaded. "He has spells and falls down. Sometimes he has fallen into the fire or into the water. I brought him to your disciples, but they could not help."

Jesus was greatly disappointed that his disciples did not have enough faith to heal the boy. "O faithless generation," Jesus said sadly, "how long shall I be with you? How long shall I put up with you?" Turning to the troubled father, Jesus said, "Bring your child to me."

As they brought him, the boy had an attack. He fell to the ground, lay in the dust and foamed at the mouth.

"How long has your son been this way?" Jesus asked.

The father answered, "Ever since he was a small child. Often he has almost lost his life when these attacks came upon him. If you can do anything, have mercy on us and help us."

Jesus knew the father did not have faith in his power to heal the boy. "If you can believe," Jesus told him, "all things are possible to him who believes."

At once the father cried out, "O Lord, I do believe; help me not to doubt."

Jesus commanded the bad spirit to come out of the boy and torment him no longer. The boy lay so quiet on the ground that the people said, "He is dead."

Jesus stooped down, took the boy's hand and lifted him up. The boy stood on his own feet and walked to his father. He was completely well.

As soon as the disciples could be alone with Jesus, they asked, "Why were we not able to heal the boy?"

"Because you did not have faith," Jesus said. "You cannot help such people unless you live a life of prayer." And he talked to them about their need for faith in God.

Who Is the Greatest?

Matthew 17:22—18:14; Mark 9:30-43; Luke 9:43-50

Leaving the north country near Caesarea Philippi, Jesus and his disciples started back to Capernaum. On the way Jesus told them, "The Son of man will be delivered into the hands of men. They will kill him, but he will rise again on the third day." The disciples did not understand what Jesus meant, and they were afraid to ask.

As they walked along some of the disciples began to argue about who would be greatest in the kingdom of heaven. They still thought Jesus would set up an earthly kingdom and honor them with high positions.

When they reached Capernaum, Jesus took his disciples to a private home. He did not want to attract the crowds and few people knew about his stopping place.

While they were in Capernaum, a man who collected tax money for the temple in Jerusalem stopped Simon Peter. He asked the disciple, "Does your master pay taxes?"

"Yes," Peter answered.

When Peter returned to the house where they were staying, he told Jesus about this. Jesus said, "Take your hook and line down to the sea. There will be a piece of money in the mouth of the first fish you catch. Take this and pay our taxes."

Peter obeyed and found the piece of money in the fish's mouth, just as Jesus had said. After paying the tax, Peter returned to the place where they were staying.

When all the disciples were together, Jesus asked them, "What were you arguing about on the way to Capernaum?"

No one answered. They were too ashamed to tell, but Jesus knew what they had talked about as they walked along the dusty road. Jesus said, "If anyone wants to be great, he must serve others." Taking a little child into his arms, he said, "No one can enter the kingdom of heaven unless he becomes like a little child. Whoever is as humble as a little child shall be the greatest in the kingdom of heaven. You must be careful not to do anything that will make a person lose faith in me."

To show the disciples how important each person was, Jesus said, "If a man has one hundred sheep and one goes astray, does he not leave the ninety and nine and go to look for the one that is lost? When he finds the lost sheep, he is happier over it than over the ninety-nine that are safe in the fold. In the same way your heavenly Father does not want to lose a single person from his kingdom."

Then John told Jesus that some of them had seen a man healing people in Jesus' name. "We told him to stop doing that because he was not one of us."

"You should not have done that," Jesus said. "Whoever does a miracle in my name is helping me in my great work." Jesus must have been discouraged that his disciples understood so little about him and his work.

Peter Learns about Forgiveness

Matthew 18:21-35

One day Simon Peter asked Jesus, "Lord, how often shall I forgive my brother if he sins against me? Shall I forgive him seven times?"

Jesus replied, "I do not say that you shall forgive him seven times only, but seventy times seven."

Peter was surprised. Could he ever forgive a man that many times?

Jesus told Peter a story about a king whose servant owed him much money. The king called this servant and asked him to pay the debt, but the servant could not. The king said, "Because you cannot pay the money you borrowed, I command that you, your wife and your children be sold, and that all you own be taken away from you. In this way I can get back some of the money you borrowed."

The servant fell on his face before the king, crying, "O King, have patience with me and I will pay every penny I owe!"

Because the king felt sorry for the man, he said, "I will forgive all the debt, and you need not try to pay it back."

When this servant left the king, he met a poor man who had borrowed only a few dollars from him. He asked the man to pay it back, but the man could not. The servant became so angry that he took the poor man by the throat and cried, "Pay back what you borrowed or I will throw you into prison!"

The lost sheep needs its shepherd

The poor man fell to his knees and pleaded, "Have patience with me, and I will pay every penny I owe."

The king's servant would not listen. Because the poor man had no money, the king's servant threw him into prison.

Other servants of the king felt sad when they saw how unkindly this poor man had been treated, and they told the king.

The king was surprised. Quickly he sent for the unkind servant. In anger the king told him, "O wicked man, I forgave all your debt because you could not pay. Should you not have been willing to forgive the small debt your poor neighbor owed even as I forgave you? Now you will go to prison until you pay all you ever owed."

When Jesus finished the story, he said to Peter, "If you do not forgive from your heart the wrongdoings of others, neither will your heavenly Father forgive you."

On the Way Through Samaria

Luke 9:51-56

Jesus and his disciples were on their way to Jerusalem. They planned to take the road through the country of Samaria. At one Samaritan village, Jesus planned to spend the night. He sent messengers ahead to find a place for them to stay.

But the Samaritans did not want Jesus and his disciples to stay overnight in their town. Jesus and his disciples were Jews. Because the Jews had often been unkind to the Samaritans, the Samaritans did not want anything to do with the Jews.

James and John were furious that they had been refused lodging for the night. They said, "Lord, why don't you call fire down from heaven on this village?"

Jesus answered, "How wrong you are! The Son of man is not come to destroy men's lives, but to save them." Jesus went on to another village, and his disciples followed.

The Ten Lepers

Luke 17:11-19

As Jesus and his disciples passed by, they met ten men who were lepers. These men had heard that Jesus healed the sick. Because they were lepers, they could not go near Jesus. From a distance they called loudly, "Jesus, Master, have mercy on us!"

Never did Jesus pass by and refuse to help one who called. When he saw the lepers, he said, "Go show yourselves to the priests." At once the lepers started to go to the priests for an examination. As they went the leprosy left their bodies, and they were made every bit well.

One of the lepers stopped and turned back when he knew he had been healed. Running to Jesus, he fell down before him, worshiping and thanking him for this miracle. The other nine hurried on their way, never stopping to thank the great healer. Now the man who gave thanks was not a Jew, but a Samaritan.

Jesus said to his disciples, "Were not ten lepers made well? But where are the nine? None turned back to give thanks except this stranger." Then Jesus said to the man kneeling at his feet, "Rise up and go your way, for your faith has made you well."

Would-Be Followers

Matthew 8:18-22; Luke 9:57-62

As Jesus and his disciples walked along the road, a man said to the Master, "Lord, I would like to follow you wherever you go."

Jesus explained that his followers had many hardships. "Foxes have holes in the ground for their homes, the birds of the air have nests, but the Son of man has no place of his own to lay his head."

They had not gone much farther when Jesus said to a man by the road, "Follow me."

"But my father is old," the man answered. "Let me wait until he dies. Then I will follow you."

"That will be too late," Jesus told him. "You should go now and preach the kingdom of God."

429

After they had gone on a little distance, another man told Jesus, "Lord, I want to follow you. But first let me go home and spend some time with my relatives."

Jesus answered, "No man who starts to do my work and looks back is fit for the kingdom of God."

None of these men would make good followers, for they did not put Jesus and his work first in their lives.

Jesus Attends the Feast in Jerusalem

John 7:2-53

Summer was over, and the cooler days of autumn had come. On the hillsides around Jerusalem stood groups of booths or huts made from branches. During the Feast of Tabernacles, the Jews lived out of doors. These booths were their only shelter. Visitors came from every part of the land for the feast.

On the first day as people talked together, they wondered if Jesus would come to the feast to teach them. Some told of things they had heard him say. Others talked about his miracles.

As the people talked and asked about Jesus, they expressed different opinions. Some said, "He is a good man." Others replied, "No, he deceives the people." Only in their small groups did the people talk about Jesus. No one dared speak of him publicly. They were afraid of the Jewish rulers.

The people looked for Jesus but he was nowhere to be found. "Where is he?" they asked.

About the middle of the week, Jesus came to the temple and taught. His enemies thought this would be a good time to catch him. They sent men to listen to his teaching. These men would find fault with what Jesus said and accuse him before the rulers.

And the men did as they had been ordered. Yet as they listened to the Master, they marveled. "How does this man know so much without having been trained?" they wondered.

Jesus answered, "My teaching is not mine, but his who sent me."

Day after day Jesus sat in the temple, teaching all who came to him. No one tried to send him away, and no one tried to arrest him.

Many Jews who lived in Jerusalem knew how much their leaders hated Jesus. They wondered why the leaders had not seized the Master and thrown him into prison. They said of Jesus, "Is not this the man they are after? Here he is speaking boldly, and they say nothing to him. Do the rulers believe he is the Christ?"

The rulers of the Jews—the chief priests, the scribes, the Pharisees and the Sadducees—did not believe Jesus was the Christ. They were jealous because he was the center of attention at the feast. They hated his teaching because he accused them of only pretending to be righteous. Finally they sent officers to take him.

As the officers listened to Jesus, they heard him say, "I will be with you yet a little while. Then I shall go to him who sent me. You will look for me, but you will not be able to find me. Where I am, you will not be able to come."

When the officers heard this, they asked one another, "Where could he go that we would not be able to find him? Would he go to the Jews who live abroad? Would he go to teach the Gentiles?"

The officers noticed how eagerly the people listened to Jesus. They heard some say, "Truly this is the Prophet," or, "This is the Christ." They heard others question, "Will Christ come from Galilee? According to the Scriptures he will come from Bethlehem and be of the family of David."

Even though the people differed in what they thought of Jesus, the officers were so impressed that they could not arrest him. They listened carefully to his words and wondered why he should be punished. So they returned to the rulers without Jesus.

The chief priests and Pharisees were angry that the officers had not obeyed orders. "Why have you not brought him?" they asked.

The officers replied, "No man ever spoke like this man," and they refused to harm him.

Then the rulers were all the more angry and excited. They asked, "Are you letting this man deceive you as he deceives the people? Have any of our rulers believed in him? Only the people who do not understand the Law believe him."

Among the angry rulers sat Nicodemus, the Pharisee who had come to Jesus one night. He loved Jesus and believed in him. In the hope of protecting Jesus, he asked, "Does our law condemn any man before he is given a hearing?"

The angry rulers turned on Nicodemus and replied scornfully, "Are you from Galilee? Don't you know that no prophet comes from that country?" After saying that, they dismissed the meeting and went to their homes.

A Sinful Woman Is Brought to Jesus

John 8:1-11

Early the next morning the scribes and Pharisees planned another way to get Jesus arrested. They would go to him themselves and ask a very tricky question about the Law of Moses. If he did not agree with the Law of Moses on this thing, the rulers would accuse him of disobeying the Law and making himself greater than Moses.

As Jesus taught in the temple, the scribes and Pharisees brought a sinful woman. They said, "Master, this woman is very wicked. We caught her committing sin. Moses commanded in the Law that such people should be stoned to death. What do you think we ought to do?"

Jesus knew his enemies were trying to trick him. At first he paid no attention to them. Instead he stooped down and wrote in the sand as if he had not heard their question.

How angry the men were that Jesus did not answer! So they asked him again and again.

Finally Jesus stood up and looked them straight in the eyes as he said, "Let the man among you who is without sin throw the first stone at her." Again Jesus stooped down and wrote in the dust.

At first the rulers looked from one to the other. Then as they remembered some of their own sins, they looked away. Some stared at the ground. Their consciences troubled them. One man became so uncomfortable that he left. Soon another followed. One by one, they turned and went away.

Jesus teaches in the temple

When Jesus looked up, he saw only the woman there. He asked, "Where are those who accused you? Did no man condemn you?"

And she replied, "No man, Lord."

Then he said, "Neither do I condemn you. Go and sin no more."

Questioned by His Enemies

John 8:12-59

As the people gathered in the temple, Jesus taught them again. "I am the light of the world," Jesus said. "The man who follows me will not walk in darkness. He will have the light of life."

When the Pharisees heard this, they accused him. "Your words are not true. You are just speaking for yourself."

Jesus answered, "It is written in your law that the testimony of two men is true. I witness for myself and the Father who sent me witnesses for me."

The Pharisees knew that Joseph the carpenter was dead, so they asked, "Where is your Father?"

"You do not know me or my Father," Jesus told them. "If you knew me, you would know my Father also."

Jesus continued to teach publicly in the temple. The Pharisees wanted to seize him, yet no one dared lay hands on him.

Later Jesus said, "I go my way, and you will look for me. You will die in your sins. Where I go, you cannot come."

The Jews did not understand what Jesus meant. They whispered to one another, "Does he plan to kill himself? He says where he goes we cannot come."

Knowing their thoughts, Jesus said, "You are from below. I am from above. You are of this world. I am not of this world."

To those who believed on him, Jesus said, "If you do what I command, then you are truly my disciples. You shall not die in sin, but have eternal life."

Angrily Jesus' enemies said, "Now we know you have an evil spirit. Abraham is dead, and all the prophets are dead. Yet you say anyone who obeys your commands will never die. Are you greater than our father Abraham? Who do you think you are?"

Jesus replied, "I do not honor myself, but my Father, God, honors me. You do not know my Father, but I know him. If I said I did not, I would be telling a lie. I know him and obey his words. Your father Abraham was glad when he saw my day, but you do not act like the children of Abraham."

At once the Jews cried out, "How could you have seen our father Abraham? You are not even fifty years old!"

"Before Abraham was, I am," Jesus answered.

"I AM" was the name by which God was known long ago. The Jews were struck with horror when they heard Jesus call himself by that sacred name. They picked up stones and would have killed him, but Jesus lost himself in the crowds.

Jesus Heals a Blind Man

John 9

One Sabbath day as Jesus left the temple, he saw a blind man begging by the roadside. This man had been blind since birth. He lived with his parents in Jerusalem.

The disciples had seen him before. They asked, "Master, who sinned that this man was born blind?"

"No one sinned," Jesus told them. "He is blind so the power of God can be shown through him."

The disciples watched as Jesus stopped in front of the blind man. Mixing a little clay, Jesus rubbed it on the blind man's eyelids. "Go, wash in the pool of Siloam," Jesus told the poor man.

Without a word the blind man arose and groped his way to the pool. Here he washed the mud from his sightless eyes. Immediately he could see, and he ran home to tell the good news.

Everyone was surprised when he told what had happened! Some who saw him asked, "Is this the man who sat by the roadside and begged?" Some replied, "This is he." Others said, "It looks like him."

The man who had been blind settled the question by saying, "I am he."

The excitement grew when the people heard that Jesus had opened the blind man's eyes. They gathered around him and asked, "What did Jesus do to you? How did he open your eyes?"

The man told how Jesus mixed a little clay, rubbed it on his eyes and sent him to wash in the pool of Siloam. "When I did as he commanded, I could see," he said joyfully.

"Where is this Jesus now?" the people asked. But the man did not know.

The neighbors took the man who had been blind to the Pharisees. There the rulers questioned him. Finally they said of Jesus, "This man is not of God because he does not keep the Sabbath."

Others standing by said, "How could a sinner do such miracles?"

And the people were divided. Some thought Jesus had the power of God. Others thought he deceived those who believed on him.

Turning to the man who had been healed, the Pharisees asked, "What do you say of the one who opened your eyes?"

The man replied, "I believe he is a prophet."

Jesus' enemies were much distressed by this miracle. They tried to find some way to prove it was not true. Perhaps the man had only pretended to be blind. The rulers called his parents and questioned them.

The parents were afraid. The rulers had already agreed that anyone who confessed Jesus as the Christ would be turned out of the synagogue. When asked to identify their son and tell how he was made to see, they answered, "We do not know how he was made to see or who opened his eyes. He is old enough. Ask him. He will speak for himself."

Jesus' enemies grew angry. Again they asked the man who had been blind, "What did Jesus do to you? How did he open your eyes?"

He said, "I told you once, and you would not listen. If I tell you again, will you also be his disciples?"

Scornfully they said, "We are Moses' disciples, for we know God spoke to Moses. As for this fellow we do not know where he came from."

Now the man Jesus had healed said boldly, "It is strange that you do not know where Jesus came from, since he opened my blinded eyes. If any man worships God and does his will, God hears that man. Since the world began, no one has opened the eyes of one who was born blind. If Jesus were not of God, he could do nothing."

The rulers were angry when they heard this. Because the man had dared to try to teach them, they threw him out of the synagogue. No longer would he be welcome to worship there.

When Jesus heard what had happened, he went to find the man. Jesus asked, "Do you believe on the Son of God?"

The man answered, "Who is he, Lord, that I may believe?"

And Jesus said, "You have seen him with your eyes. He is speaking to you right now."

"Lord, I believe!" the man said joyfully.

Little Children Are Brought to Jesus

Matthew 19:13-15; Mark 10:13-16

While Jesus was teaching the people, mothers brought their little children. These mothers wanted Jesus to put his hands on the children and pray for them.

When the disciples saw the mothers and children, they did not like it. Because they thought Jesus was too busy to be bothered with little children, they called the mothers aside and said, "You should not trouble the Master with your children. He has more important work to do."

How disappointed the mothers and children were! They wanted to see Jesus and talk to him. Perhaps some had come a long way.

Just then Jesus saw the mothers and children. He called the children to him. Jesus felt sorry for what the disciples had done. Looking at them he said, "Do not forbid the little children to come to me, for of such is the kingdom of God. Whoever of you does not receive the kingdom of God just like a little child can never enter into it." And he took the little ones in his arms to love them.

Jesus knew that children would gladly believe him and that many times they would lead older people to believe in him too. He knew their hearts were tender and quick to respond to his love. Older people were more ready to doubt and to question whether he was the Christ.

The Rich Young Ruler

Matthew 19:16-30; Mark 10:17-31

One day a young man came running to meet Jesus. This rich young man wore expensive clothing. Kneeling down in the dust before Jesus, he said, "Good Master, what good thing shall I do that I may have eternal life?"

"Why do you call me good?" asked Jesus. "There is none good but God. You know the commandments: Do not kill. Do not steal. Do not speak falsely. Honor your father and your mother."

"Yes, I know the commandments of Moses," answered the young man, "and I have kept them from childhood. But I seem to lack something yet. O Master, tell me what it is!"

Jesus looked into the young man's face and loved him. How Jesus longed to help him! Jesus said, "You lack one thing. If you would be perfectly happy, go home and sell all you have and give your riches to the poor. Then you will have riches in heaven. Afterwards you may come back and be my disciple."

What a change came over the young man's face when he heard these words! With bowed head he walked slowly away, for he loved his riches.

Jesus watched him go away. Turning to the disciples he said, "How hard it is for rich men to enter the kingdom of God!" The young man loved his riches more than he loved God. He could not be happy, for his heart was not right with God. Always he would feel something was lacking, something clouding his hope of life in heaven. But he turned away from Jesus, choosing rather to be rich in this world than to be a disciple of the Lord.

Seventy Other Disciples Sent Out

Luke 10:1-24

Jesus knew he did not have much longer to preach. Soon he must lay down his life. Many people still needed to hear the gospel and be healed. To do this work Jesus chose seventy other men who had followed him and knew his teachings. He gave them power to heal

438

the sick. Then he sent them out, two by two, to preach in the cities and villages east of the Jordan River.

Before they left Jesus told them not to take any money or any extra clothing. He said their needs would be taken care of. They were to eat whatever was served in the home where they stayed. Then he said, "Whatever city you enter, heal the sick that are there and tell them, 'The kingdom of God is come near to you.'"

Just as the twelve disciples had done, so these seventy went forth to heal the sick and tell people of the kingdom of heaven. When their mission was over, they hurried back to tell Jesus of their success. They rejoiced because they had been able to heal the sick.

Jesus said, "Do not rejoice in this, but rather be glad that your names are written in heaven." And he gave thanks for the work that was done. Jesus prayed, "I thank you, O Father, Lord of heaven and earth."

Turning to his disciples, Jesus told them, "Blessed are the eyes that see the things you see. I tell you that many prophets and kings wanted to see the things you see, but they did not see them. They wanted to hear the words you hear, but they did not hear them."

And Jesus rejoiced that his followers had preached the good news abroad.

The Good Samaritan

Luke 10:25-37

A lawyer came to Jesus and asked a question to trick him. He said, "Master, what shall I do to have eternal life?"

Jesus understood how well this man knew the Law of Moses. Instead of answering the question, he asked the lawyer, "What is written in the Law of Moses? Do you not know its teachings?"

The lawyer replied, "Moses wrote that we should love the Lord our God with all our heart, and with all our soul, and with all our strength and with all our mind. And he wrote that we should love our neighbors as ourselves."

"You have answered right," Jesus said. "Do this and you shall have life in heaven."

But the lawyer had another question. He asked, "Who is my neighbor?" To answer him Jesus told the story about the Good Samaritan.

"One day a man traveled the road from Jerusalem to Jericho. On the way robbers stopped him. They took his money, tore off his clothes, beat him and left him half dead by the roadside.

"Soon a priest came along. He saw the injured man lying there, but he did not stop to help. He did not even say a kind word to the poor man.

"Next, a Levite came by. He, too, saw the wounded man lying by the road, but he did not give him a second look. He hurried on, leaving the poor man to die.

"Perhaps the man would have died if a kindhearted Samaritan had not come along. The Samaritan saw the suffering man lying there. At once he stopped his mule, climbed down and bent over the stranger. The wounded man was a Jew. Even though the Jews were not friendly to his people, the Samaritan felt he must help this Jew who was in great trouble.

"First he poured oil on the man's wounds and bandaged them. Then lifting the man to his mule, the Samaritan took him to an inn. Here he cared for the wounded man.

"On the next day the Samaritan had to continue his journey. To the innkeeper he gave money and explained, 'Take care of this man until he is well. If you need more money, I will pay it when I come back.'

"Now," asked Jesus, "which of these three men was a neighbor to the one who was attacked by robbers?"

"The man who treated him kindly," answered the lawyer.

And Jesus said, "Go, and do the same."

Lazarus Is Raised from the Dead

John 11:1-54

Lazarus was a Jew who lived in the village of Bethany with his two sisters, Mary and Martha. Since their home was near Jerusalem, Jesus often stopped to visit them on his way to attend the feasts at the temple. Always Mary, Martha and Lazarus welcomed him. They loved him dearly and believed he was the Christ.

One day while Jesus taught the people in the country east of the Jordan, a messenger came from Bethany. Mary and Martha had sent the messenger to tell Jesus, "Lord, the one you love is sick." The anxious sisters thought Jesus would come at once and heal their brother. They knew his great power. How much they needed him now!

But Jesus did not go at once. He explained to his disciples, "Lazarus' sickness is for the glory of God."

The sisters were greatly disappointed when the messenger returned without Jesus! They watched their brother grow weaker and weaker. Then he died. They were grief-stricken. Why hadn't Jesus come?

Still they hoped he would come, for he had raised the dead to life. The day passed, but Jesus did not arrive. At last the neighbors and friends came to help wrap Lazarus' body for burial. They carried him to a burial cave.

Mary and Martha followed, weeping bitterly. They saw Lazarus laid in the cave and watched the great stone rolled over the opening. Still Jesus had not come.

Two days after receiving the message from Mary and Martha, Jesus said to his disciples, "Let us go back to Judea again."

The disciples did not like the idea. They answered, "Master, when you were there before some of the people tried to stone you. Why go back?"

"Our friend Lazarus sleeps," Jesus told them. "I go to awaken him." At first the disciples thought Lazarus must be getting better. Then Jesus told them that Lazarus was dead. He said, "For your sakes I am glad I was not there so you may believe."

Lazarus had been dead four days. The sisters thought it would be too late for Jesus to help them now even if he did come. Friends came from Jerusalem to comfort the sisters, but it was Jesus they wanted most.

At last word came that Jesus and his disciples were nearing the village. Martha ran to meet him. "Lord," she cried, "if only you had been here, my brother would not have died!"

To comfort her Jesus said, "Your brother will rise again."

"I know he will be resurrected in the last day," she answered.

That was not what Jesus meant. He explained, "I am the resurrection and the life. He that believes in me, though he dies, yet shall he live. And those who live and believe in me shall never die. Do you believe this?" he asked.

Martha answered, "Yes, Lord, I believe you are the Christ, the Son of God."

But Martha did not really understand what Jesus meant. She left him and hurried to call her sister Mary. "The Master wants to see you, Mary," she said.

Mary hurried to meet Jesus and found him resting by the roadside. Falling at his feet she sobbed, "Lord, if you had been here my brother would not have died!"

The Jews who had come from Jerusalem to comfort the sisters saw Mary leave the house in a great hurry. They thought she was going to Lazarus' grave, so they followed. When they saw her fall weeping at Jesus' feet, they wept aloud.

"Where have you laid Lazarus' body?" Jesus asked.

They took him to the cave. Jesus wept in sympathy when he looked at the sisters and their sorrowing friends.

The Jews whispered, "See how much he loved Lazarus! Surely this man who opened blind eyes could have healed Lazarus."

While they talked, Jesus commanded that someone roll the stone away from the front of the cave.

Martha exclaimed, "Lord, he has been dead four days. By this time his body is decaying!"

Jesus answered, "Did I not tell you that you would see the glory of God if you believed?"

The stone was rolled away. While the people watched, Jesus lifted his eyes to heaven and said, "Father, I thank you that you have heard me. And I know that you hear me always. I say this so the people who are here may believe you have sent me." Then Jesus looked into the door of the cave and cried with a loud voice, "Lazarus, come out!"

Speechless, the people watched. How astonished they were to see Lazarus get up and come out!

Jesus said, "Take off the burial clothes and let him go." And Lazarus went home with his sisters and Jesus.

The Jews who had seen this miracle believed that Jesus was the Christ. Soon the scribes, Pharisees and chief priests heard what had happened at Bethany. How excited they were! "What shall we do?" they asked. "If we let him go on, soon all men will believe in him. Then the Romans will take away our nation."

From that time Jesus' enemies planned how they would capture and kill him.

A Sick Man Is Healed

Luke 14:1-6

Jesus knew his enemies were plotting against him in Jerusalem. For that reason he and his disciples returned to the country near the Jordan River. Here Jesus preached and healed all the sick who were brought to him.

One Sabbath a Pharisee who lived nearby invited Jesus to his house for dinner. Jesus accepted. Many people gathered at the Pharisee's house. Among the guests were Pharisees and lawyers. Others had come without being invited. These stood around the dining hall and watched while the guests ate.

One man who looked on had a sickness called dropsy. He must have heard that Jesus would be here. The man wanted very much to be healed.

When Jesus saw the sick man, he felt sorry for him. Jesus, too, wanted the man to be well again. Turning to the Pharisees and lawyers, he asked, "Is it lawful to heal on the Sabbath?"

The men refused to answer. Then Jesus healed the man and sent him away. Jesus said, "If one of your animals should fall into a pit on the Sabbath, not one of you would wait until after the Sabbath to pull him out."

Because the Pharisees and the lawyers understood that Jesus was teaching them to be merciful to people as well as to animals, they could not think of anything to say to him. Perhaps they felt ashamed.

The Parable of the Supper

Luke 14:7-24

After they had finished dinner at the Pharisee's house, Jesus began to teach. He had noticed that when the guests had arrived, each one tried to get the best place for himself. Jesus wanted them to think more of others than of themselves.

He said, "When you are invited to a wedding, do not choose the most honored place for yourself. A person more important than you may come. Then you will be asked to give your place to him, and you will be embarrassed. Instead if you take the lowest place, you may be called up higher. Your friends will honor you."

Then Jesus turned to the Pharisee who had given the dinner and said, "When you prepare a feast, do not invite your friends and relatives and rich neighbors. They will return your invitation. If you want to be rewarded in heaven, invite the poor, the crippled and the blind to your feasts. Such people cannot repay you, and God will bless you for your kindness."

One of the guests who listened to these words said, "Blessed is he who will eat bread in the kingdom of God."

To all those present Jesus told a story about the kingdom of God. He said:

"A certain man gave a great supper and invited many guests. When everything was ready, he sent his servant to bring the guests. But each one made an excuse for not attending.

"The first man said, 'I have just bought a piece of ground, and I must go to see it. Please excuse me this time.'

"Another man said, 'I have just bought five yoke of oxen, and I want to try them out. I'd like to be excused this time.'

"A third said, 'I have just been married, and I want to stay home with my wife. Won't you please excuse me?'

446

"Everywhere the servant went the guests asked to be excused. The master was very angry when the servant returned alone. He ordered, 'Go quickly into the streets and lanes of the city. Bring the poor, the crippled, the old and the blind.'

"The servant obeyed, but still there was room for more. The master said, 'Go out into the country places and bring others.' And the house was filled with hungry people who enjoyed the good food."

A Crippled Woman Is Healed

Luke 13:11-17

Jesus went to teach in the cities and villages where the Seventy had preached and healed. On the Sabbath he went to a synagogue to worship. There he saw a woman who was badly bent over. For eighteen years she had not been able to straighten her back or shoulders. Jesus knew how hard it must be for the woman to get around. Calling her to him, he said, "Woman, you are no longer crippled." He put his hands on her bent back, and she was able to stand straight again.

The woman was very happy, and she praised God that she was well.

The ruler of the synagogue was angry that Jesus had healed on the Sabbath. He said, "There are six days in the week for men to work. Let the sick be healed on those days and not on the Sabbath."

But Jesus replied, "You are only pretending to keep the Law and please God. Do you untie your animals and lead them to water on the Sabbath? Then why should not this poor woman be loosed on the Sabbath from the thing that has crippled her for eighteen years?"

These words made Jesus' enemies feel ashamed. The other people praised God because they had seen his wonderful works.

Jesus Answers the Pharisees

Luke 13:31-35; 15:1-10

One day some Pharisees came to Jesus and said, "Leave here

quickly, for Herod wants to kill you." They hoped Jesus would be frightened and run away. Then they would be rid of him.

Jesus was not afraid of Herod. He knew his greatest enemies were among the rulers of the Jews. They hated him because he reminded them of their sins and because he taught the poor people.

To the Pharisees Jesus said, "Go to Herod and tell him I am at work healing the sick today and tomorrow, and on the third day I shall be made perfect. I must go on my way today, tomorrow and even the following day. It cannot be that a prophet should die outside Jerusalem." Jesus remembered how the Jews had killed God's prophets in other days. It was the Jewish leaders and not Herod who would condemn him to death.

Many tax collectors and sinners followed Jesus and listened to his words. That was why the Pharisees and scribes found fault with him. They said, "This man receives sinners and even eats with them."

Jesus knew what they were doing, so he spoke to the people in parables or stories. He saw many women in the crowd so he told a story they would understand well.

"What woman," he asked, "who has ten pieces of silver and loses one does not do everything she can to find it? She lights a candle and looks for it. Then she sweeps the house and looks everywhere. When she finds it she calls to her neighbors and friends, 'Rejoice with me, for I have found the money I lost.'

"In the same way," said Jesus, "there is rejoicing in heaven when one lost sinner comes to God."

The Prodigal Son

Luke 15:11-32

As the people listened eagerly, Jesus told them this story:

"A certain man had two sons. The younger said, 'Father, give me my share of the money that I am to have when you die.'

"So the father divided his wealth between his two sons. The younger packed his things and went on a long trip. He spent his money freely. He wasted most of it in having a good time. At first

there were many friends to enjoy the money with him. When the money was all spent, the friends were gone too.

"About this time there was a famine in the land, and the young man became hungry. He got a job tending hogs for a farmer. Even then the young man did not have enough to eat. He even wished someone would give him some of the food that was thrown to the hogs.

"How miserable the young man was! Finally he said to himself, 'My father has many servants who have plenty to eat, and here I am starving. I will go back to my father and tell him how I have sinned. I will tell him that I'm not worthy to be his son, and I would like to be one of his servants.' And the young man started home.

"The father missed his younger son. He worried about his boy. Every day he longed for his son to come home. Every day he watched for him.

"One day in the distance the father saw a man coming. As the man got nearer, the father could see that he was ragged. Soon the father recognized the young man as his son. Running to meet him, the father threw his arms around the boy.

"'Father,' the son said, 'I have sinned against heaven and against you. I am no longer worthy to be your son....'

"Before the son could finish, the father ordered the servants, 'Bring the best robe and put it on him. Put a ring on his finger and shoes on his feet. Prepare a feast. Let us eat and rejoice, for the son who I thought was dead is alive. He was lost, but now he is found.' The entire household rejoiced.

"While this was happening, the older son was working in the field. When he returned to the house and heard all the excitement, he asked, 'What has happened?'

"The servants said, 'Your brother has come back. Your father is giving a dinner because the boy has returned safe and sound.'

"The older brother was not happy. Indeed, he was angry. He would not even go into the house. The father came out and talked to his older son. The selfish older son could think only of himself. He said,

'I have served you faithfully all these years, but you do not rejoice over me. Now when my brother comes back after spending all his money on wild living, you celebrate.'

451

The prodigal son

"At once the father knew his older son was jealous. He said, 'Son, you have always been with me. Everything I have is yours. I thought your brother was dead, but he is alive. It is right to rejoice because he has come back. Though he was lost, now he is found.'"

The Rich Man and Lazarus

Luke 16:19-31

There was a certain rich man who thought only of himself. He wore expensive clothes. Every day he ate the best kind of food. His many servants were quick to do his bidding. He lived only to enjoy himself.

At the rich man's gate lay a beggar named Lazarus. He was too ill to work for a living, so he asked for the crumbs that fell from the rich man's table. He felt he had a right to ask for help, since both he and the rich man were descendants of Abraham. But the rich man would not help Lazarus at all. Even the dogs seemed sorry for Lazarus, but not the rich man.

Finally Lazarus died and the angels carried him to heaven. Here he was not a beggar. He could live in peace and happiness with Abraham and other good people who had left the world.

Later the rich man died. His friends buried him in a new cave and mourned for him. The rich man was taken to a place of torment. There he lifted up his eyes. Far, far away he saw Lazarus. How happy Lazarus looked with Abraham! The rich man cried out. "Abraham, have mercy on me. Send Lazarus that he may dip the tip of his finger in water and cool my burning tongue."

Abraham answered, "Remember the good things you enjoyed in your lifetime while Lazarus had only trouble and suffering. Now he is comforted and you are tormented. I can send nothing to you because no one can pass from this place to your place of torment."

The rich man remembered his brothers who were still living on the earth. He did not want them to come to this place. He said, "Please send Lazarus back to my father's house. He must warn my five brothers about this dreadful place."

Abraham answered, "They have the words of Moses and the prophets. Let them obey those words."

The rich man knew his brothers would never do that. He pleaded, "No, but if someone were to be sent from the dead, they would repent."

Finally Abraham said, "If they will not pay any attention to the words in God's book, they would not pay any attention to one who rose from the dead."

The Unjust Judge

Luke 18:1-8

God does not always answer prayer right away. Sometimes he wants to make sure people are really in earnest about what they pray for. He lets them come to him again and again before he gives the things they ask. To teach men to keep on praying until their prayers are answered, Jesus told the story of the unjust judge.

A poor widow had been wronged by an enemy. She could not punish her enemy or get back what he had taken, so she went to the city judge for help.

The judge was not a good man. He was not interested in helping the widow. At first he did not even pay any attention to her. But the woman kept coming to see him about her troubles.

Finally he got tired of her coming. He said to himself, "Even though I am not a good man, I will do what this widow wants so she will stop bothering me."

Then Jesus said, "Learn a lesson from this unjust judge. He did what the woman wanted because she came to him often. Shall God not grant the wishes of those who call on him day and night?"

The Pharisee and the Publican

Luke 18:9-14

In the crowd were people who were proud of their righteousness. They despised those who they thought were sinners. To teach them a lesson Jesus told this story:

Clive Upton

"Two men went up to the temple to pray. One was a Pharisee and the other a tax collector.

"The Pharisee stood and prayed loudly for all to hear, 'God, I thank you that I am not like other men—unrighteous, unjust, unfair in business dealings or even like this tax collector. I fast twice a week. I give a tenth of all I own.'

"But the tax collector stood by himself. He would not even lift his eyes toward heaven when he prayed. Bowing his head, he beat his breast and said, 'God, be merciful to me a sinner!'"

And Jesus said, "I tell you, this tax collector and not the proud Pharisee, went home with God's blessing. For whoever lifts himself up in his own sight is not pleasing to God, but whoever humbles himself shall be lifted up."

James and John Want to Be Honored

Matthew 20:17-28; Mark 10:32-45; Luke 18:31-34

It was time again for the Passover Feast at Jerusalem. Jesus knew this would be the last one he would attend. He wanted to prepare his disciples for the things that would happen. He said, "We go up to Jerusalem. The Son of man will be betrayed into the hands of the chief priests and scribes. They will condemn him to death. They will take him to the Gentiles. The Gentiles will mock, beat and crucify him. On the third day he will rise again."

But the disciples did not understand. They still believed he would become the earthly king of the Jews.

Then the mother of James and John came to him with her two sons. She knelt before him and asked a favor.

"What do you want?" Jesus asked her.

She said, "Let one of my sons sit on your right hand and the other on the left in your kingdom."

Jesus told James and John, "You don't know what you ask for. Can you drink from the cup that I drink of and be baptized with the baptism that I am baptized with?"

The Pharisee and the tax collector pray

"We are able," they answered.

Jesus said, "That is true, but it is not mine to give the places on my right hand and on my left. They shall be given to those for whom my Father has prepared them."

When the other disciples found out what James and John had wanted, they were angry. Why should James and John ask to be honored above them?

Jesus called his disciples and told them, "You know the rulers of the Gentiles have great authority. It shall not be the same among you. Whoever wants to be great among you, let him be your minister. Whoever wants to be chief among you, let him be your servant. Even the Son of man did not come to be ministered unto but to minister and to give his life a ransom for many."

As Jesus and his disciples left Jericho, a great crowd followed.

Blind Bartimeus

Matthew 20:29-34; Mark 10:46-52; Luke 18:35-43

Many people were on their way to Jerusalem for the Passover. A crowd traveled with Jesus and his disciples. Many of them had heard Jesus teach and had seen him heal the sick. The news of Jesus' coming was told throughout the country. Some stood by the roadside just to see him go by.

Outside the city of Jericho sat Bartimeus, begging from the people who passed. He heard the sound of many footsteps and wondered why such a crowd was passing. Someone told him, "Jesus of Nazareth is going by."

Bartimeus had heard of Jesus. Probably someone had told him how Jesus had healed the man who had been blind since birth. How much Bartimeus, too, wanted to receive his sight. He got up from his seat by the roadside and called out loudly, "Jesus, Son of David, have mercy on me."

Some who stood near Bartimeus tried to quiet him. Instead he called out the more loudly, "Jesus, Son of David, have mercy on me."

Jesus stood still. He commanded that the blind man be brought to him. Those who went to get the blind man told him, "Be of good comfort. Come, he calls for you."

How glad Bartimeus was! He threw off his cloak and went to Jesus.

Jesus asked, "What do you want me to do for you?"

"Lord, give me my sight," Bartimeus said.

Jesus answered, "Go your way. Your faith has made you well."

At once the blind eyes opened and Bartimeus could see as well as those who had never been blind. He followed Jesus, glorifying God.

When the people saw what had happened, they too praised God.

Zacchaeus Climbs a Tree

Luke 19:1-10

In Jericho lived a rich man named Zacchaeus, who was the head tax collector. When news came that Jesus was passing through Jericho on his way to Jerusalem, Zacchaeus wanted more than anything else to see this wonderful man.

Zacchaeus stood with the crowd gathered beside the road, but he could see nothing. He was too short to see over the heads of the people. Down the road he ran and climbed into a sycamore tree. Now he could surely see Jesus.

Soon travelers going to Jerusalem came along the road. The people of Jericho watched eagerly to catch a glimpse of Jesus. On the travelers walked until they came to the sycamore tree. Here Jesus and his disciples stood still. Jesus looked up and saw Zacchaeus.

"Zacchaeus," called Jesus, "come down at once, for today I must stop at your house."

How surprised Zacchaeus was! Now he could take Jesus home and talk with him.

Joyfully Zacchaeus led the way. As they went, others followed. Some found fault because Jesus was stopping in the home of a tax collector whom they called a sinful man. The Pharisees would not enter such a house. They hated sinners.

Zacchaeus' heart was changed by Jesus' kind words. He told Jesus, "Behold, Lord, I will give half of my goods to the poor. And if I have taken more from any man than I should, I will give back four times as much as I took."

Jesus was glad to hear Zacchaeus say that. Jesus answered, "Today salvation is come to your house, for the Son of man is come to seek and to save those who are lost."

The Parable of the Pounds

Luke 19:11-27

Because many people were listening, Jesus told a parable or story sermon. He knew the people were expecting the kingdom of heaven to be set up soon like an earthly kingdom. He hoped this story would help them understand what the kingdom of heaven is like. Jesus said:

"A certain nobleman went to a far country to receive a kingdom. Before leaving home he gave a sum of money, called a pound, to each of his ten servants. They were to use the money until his return.

"When the nobleman came back, he called the ten servants and asked how they had used the money.

"The first servant brought the money and said, 'I traded with the pound you gave me, and I have gained ten pounds.' The nobleman was pleased and said, 'Because you have done this, you are to rule ten cities in my kingdom.'

"Next came a servant who had gained five pounds by using the money wisely. To him the nobleman said, 'To you I will give the rule of five cities in my kingdom.'

"Then a third servant brought only the one pound the nobleman had given him. 'Here is your pound. I kept it wrapped in this napkin while you were away. I was afraid I might lose it, and I knew you were a harsh master.'

"The nobleman answered, 'If you knew I was a harsh master, why did you not put my money into a bank that I might have it and its interest on my return?' He commanded those who stood by, 'Take the one pound from the unfaithful servant and give it to the one who has ten.'

Jesus talks with Zacchaeus

"The servants asked, 'Lord, he has ten pounds, why give him more?'

"He answered, 'To every one who uses what he has, more shall be given, but he who does not use what he has shall have it taken away.'"

Mary Anoints Jesus

Matthew 26:6-13; Mark 14:3-9; John 12:1-11

"Jesus is coming! Jesus is coming!" the news spread through Bethany quickly. How glad his friends were to hear this! What could they do to welcome him and show him their love?

Simon, who had once been a leper, planned to have a supper at his house for Jesus. Martha at once busied herself helping to get the meal ready. She was very thankful to Jesus for raising her brother from the dead. Helping with this dinner was one way she could show her thanks.

Lazarus eagerly waited Jesus' coming too. When the people heard that Lazarus would be at this dinner, they wanted to see him. Was it really true that he had been raised from the dead? What did he look like? They would see for themselves. Although they were not invited, they would go and stand around the room to watch.

Mary, too, wanted to see Jesus again. No women were invited to eat this dinner with Jesus and his disciples, but that would not keep Mary from seeing him. She must find some way to show him her love.

At last Jesus and his disciples arrived. Simon welcomed them to his home. The guests were brought into the dining hall and the food was served. Curious onlookers crowded in.

While the guests ate, Mary brought a container of expensive perfume. It had taken a whole year's wages to buy it, but she wanted to give Jesus her very best. Mary made her way to the couch where Jesus reclined. She poured the rare perfume on his head and feet. Then she knelt and wiped his feet with her hair.

As soon as the container was broken, the scent of sweet perfume filled the air. People knew at once that this perfume was expensive. The disciples began to whisper among themselves, "Why has she done this?"

Judas Iscariot, who was treasurer for the disciples, said, "Why wasn't this perfume sold and the money given to the poor?"

Jesus knew what his disciples thought. He told them, "Let this woman alone. Why should you trouble her? She has done a good work. She has anointed my body for burial. You will always have the poor with you, but I shall not be with you much longer. By this anointing, Mary has shown her love for me. I tell you, wherever the gospel is preached throughout the world, it will be told that Mary did this for her Lord."

Judas Iscariot did not like Jesus' words, for he loved money. He hoped to be a rich ruler in the kingdom he expected Jesus to set up. After the supper was over, Judas went to Jerusalem to see the chief priests and scribes. He would turn Jesus over to them.

For many days Jesus' enemies had planned how they might capture the Master. After Lazarus had been raised from the dead, they were even more eager to get rid of Jesus because he had gained many new followers.

Jesus Rides into Jerusalem as King

Matthew 21:1-11; Mark 11:1-11; Luke 19:29-40; John 12:12-19

All Jerusalem was excited. People flocked out the city gate and hurried along the road to Mount Olivet. Many of them had come to Jerusalem for the Passover. They wanted to meet Jesus because they had heard so much about him.

As Jesus and his disciples came near to Jerusalem, he said to two of them, "Go to the village nearby. As you enter the village, you will see a colt that has never been ridden. Untie him and bring him to me. If anyone asks, 'Why do you do this?' say, 'The Lord has need of him.'"

The two disciples went to the village, found the colt and untied it. Some asked, "Why are you untying that colt?" When they heard that Jesus needed the colt, they let it go.

The disciples brought the colt to Jesus and spread their coats on its back. Then Jesus sat on the colt. Many people spread their clothes along the road for Jesus to ride over. Others waved palm branches. They shouted, "Blessed is the King who is coming in the

name of the Lord! Peace in heaven and glory in the highest!" All along the way, people were rejoicing and praising God.

In the crowd were Pharisees who had come to find fault. They said to Jesus, "Make the people stop shouting."

Jesus answered, "If they should be still, the stones would immediately cry out."

As Jesus rode up Mount Moriah to the temple, the people shouted, "Hosanna to the Son of David!"

The city people hurried into the streets to ask, "Who is this?"

The crowd answered, "This is Jesus, the prophet from Nazareth of Galilee."

Jesus Teaches in the Temple

Matthew 21:12-27; Mark 11:12-33; Luke 19:41—20:17

Early the next morning Jesus and his disciples left Bethany where they had spent each night during the feast. They were on their way to the temple at Jerusalem. As they walked along, Jesus became hungry. By the roadside he saw a fig tree. When he looked for figs on its branches, there were none. As he walked away, he said, "Never again will anyone eat fruit from this tree."

When they reached Jerusalem, Jesus and his disciples went to the temple. Here Jesus saw men buying and selling animals for sacrifices. Others were changing money into temple coins. Jesus knew they cheated the people. Once before he had driven these men out of the temple.

Again he drove them out. "In the Scriptures it is written, 'My house shall be called a house of prayer,' " Jesus said, "but you have made it a den of thieves."

When word spread through the city that Jesus was at the temple, the blind and lame were brought to him. Jesus healed them all. While the chief priests and scribes watched him do this, little children came singing, "Hosanna to the Son of David," as they gathered around Jesus.

In anger the chief priests and scribes asked him, "Do you hear what these children are saying?"

"Yes, I hear them," Jesus said. "Have you not read these words in the Scriptures, 'Out of the mouths of little children comes perfect praise'?"

How angry the chief priests and scribes were! They wanted all the more to get rid of Jesus, but they could find no way. They were afraid to do anything here, for all the people listened eagerly to his every word.

In the evening Jesus and his disciples walked back to Bethany to stay with their friends. When they returned to Jerusalem the next morning, they passed the fig tree they had seen the day before. Its leaves were all withered, dry and dead. How could this happen in one day?

Jesus told his disciples, "Have faith in God. If you have faith to believe that God hears your prayers, you will do greater things than this. When you ask anything of God in prayer and believe in your hearts that he hears you, it will be given you."

As they entered the temple this time, many people were already waiting to hear Jesus teach. Of course the chief priests and scribes were there too. Since they did not want Jesus to teach the people, they tried to start an argument. "By what authority do you teach and work miracles? Who gave you this authority?" they demanded.

Jesus said, "I will answer your question if you will first answer mine. Was the baptism of John from heaven or of men?"

The chief priests and scribes did not know what to say. They talked among themselves. "If we say John's baptism was from heaven, he will ask us why we didn't believe that John was God's prophet. We dare not say his baptism was of men, for all these people would rise up against us."

Because they were afraid to answer Jesus' question, they said, "We cannot tell whether John's baptism was from heaven or of men."

Then Jesus answered, "Nor will I tell you by what authority I do these things or who gave me this authority."

The Parable of the Two Sons

Matthew 21:28-32

Jesus told the people this story: "A certain man had two sons. He went to his older son and said, 'Son, go and work in my vineyard today.'

"The boy answered his father roughly, 'I will not go.' Afterwards he was sorry he had answered his father that way. Then he went and did what his father had asked.

"Of the second son the father made the same request. The young man replied, 'I will go, sir.' But the second son did not keep his promise.

"Now," Jesus asked, "which of the two obeyed his father?"

"The first son," the people answered.

Jesus explained, "Truly, I tell you that sinners will enter the kingdom of God before you who pretend to be righteous. John preached to you, but you did not believe him. The sinners believed his message. Even though you saw it, you did not repent and believe." Jesus wanted them to understand that God does not want promises but right living.

The Parable of the Wicked Farmers

Matthew 21:33-46; Mark 12:1-12; Luke 20:9-19

"Listen to another story," Jesus said. "There was a man who planted a vineyard and fenced it in. After digging a winepress and building a watchtower, he hired farmers to take care of his vineyard while he was in another country.

"When harvest time came, the owner sent servants to the farmers to get some of the fruit. The farmers treated the servants roughly. They beat the first one and sent him away without any fruit. They threw stones at the second one and injured him. They even killed the third servant.

"Later the owner sent other servants, and the same thing happened. At last the owner decided, 'I will send my son. They will respect him.'

465

"From the watchtower the farmers saw the son coming. They said to each other, 'The owner has sent his son. This vineyard will belong to him when his father dies. Let us kill the son and take this vineyard for our own.' And that is what they did."

Then Jesus asked, "When the owner returns, what will he do to those men?"

The people answered, "He will make them pay with their lives. Then he will hire better men to care for his vineyard. The new men will give him a share of the fruit that grows."

Jesus looked boldly at his enemies who were standing in the crowd. He told them, "The kingdom of God will be taken from you and given to another people who will show by their lives that they are the children of God."

The chief priests and scribes knew Jesus had accused them in the story he told. In their anger they would have seized him, but they were afraid of the crowd, for the people believed that Jesus was a prophet.

The Parable of the Wedding Feast

Matthew 22:1-14

To help the people understand what the kingdom of heaven is like, Jesus told them this story:

"A king gave a feast when his son was married. Many guests from a nearby city were invited. When everything was ready, the guests did not arrive.

"The king sent his servants to remind the people of the wedding feast. Still they would not come. They made fun of it and went on with their work. Some even mistreated and killed the king's servants.

"When the king heard what had happened, he was angry. He called out his army and ordered them to burn the city and destroy those who had killed his servants.

"Then he said to his servants, 'The wedding feast is ready, but those that were invited are not worthy to come. Go into the highways and invite everyone to the marriage.'

"The servants obeyed. Among these guests were the rich and the poor, the good and the bad. To each one the king gave a special robe to wear for the wedding.

"When the king came to welcome these guests, he saw one man dressed in dirty rags. This man had refused to put on the wedding robe the king had provided. The king asked, 'Friend, why did you not put on the wedding garment I gave you?'

"The man hung his head, for he had no excuse. Angrily, the king told his servants, 'Tie him up hand and foot and take him away.' "

Jesus wanted to help people understand that many who were counting on entering heaven because of good religious acts alone would be disappointed. The gates would be open only to those who truly repented of their sins.

Jesus' Enemies Come with Questions

Matthew 22:15-23:39; Mark 12:13-40; Luke 20:20-47

Jesus' enemies decided that the only way they could keep him from teaching was to interrupt him with many questions. First they sent Pharisees to ask if it was right to pay taxes to Caesar, the Roman ruler.

The Jews hated to pay these taxes. Jesus' enemies knew the people would no longer want to make Jesus their king if he said it was right for them to pay taxes. But if Jesus said it was wrong to pay taxes, his enemies would report him to the Roman government. Then the Romans would punish him.

When the Pharisees came to Jesus, they said, "Master, we know you are true. You teach God's way without caring whether people like what you say or not." The Pharisees did not believe this, but they wanted to flatter Jesus. Then they added, "Tell us what you think. Is it right or wrong to pay tax money to Caesar?"

The Pharisees had thought Jesus would answer either yes or no, but they were mistaken. Jesus knew the evil in their hearts. He paid no attention to their flattery. "Why do you tempt me, you hypocrites?" he asked. "Show me the money."

They brought him a penny. Jesus looked at the coin on both sides. "Whose likeness is this on the coin? Whose name is written here?"

The men explained that Caesar's name and picture were on the coin. "Then," said Jesus, "give to Caesar the things that belong to him, and give to God the things that belong to God."

How surprised the men were at his answer! Again they had failed to trick Jesus. Now they still had no reason to accuse him. Other enemies brought hard questions, and Jesus answered them all.

One who came to question Jesus was a lawyer. He asked, "Which is the greatest commandment of the Law?"

Jesus answered, "'Thou shalt love the Lord thy God with all thy heart, and with all thy soul, and with all thy mind, and with all thy strength;' this is the first commandment. And the second greatest is this: 'Thou shalt love thy neighbor as thyself.' No other commandments are so important as these."

The lawyer looked at Jesus and said, "Master, that is true. There is one God and no other but him. To love him with all one's heart, understanding, soul and strength while one loves his neighbor as himself is surely more pleasing to God than burnt offerings and sacrifices."

Jesus was pleased to hear the lawyer say this. Jesus told the man kindly, "You are not far from the kingdom of God."

After that no one dared ask Jesus any question.

Jesus' Last Hours in the Temple

Mark 12:41-44; Luke 21:1-4; John 12:20-36

During the feast the Greeks who had come to worship told Philip, "Sir, we would like to see Jesus." Because they were not Jews, they could not enter the part of the temple where Jesus was teaching. They had to stay in the outside court, called the Court of the Gentiles.

Philip told Andrew that men from Greece wanted to see Jesus. Together they went to tell Jesus.

Jesus told Philip and Andrew, "The hour is come that the Son of man should be glorified." The disciples did not understand what Jesus meant, for he was speaking of his death.

The widow gives her two mites

Jesus hated the thought of pain just as anyone does. He felt troubled that his time was so short. Prayerfully he said, "Father, save me from this hour." Remembering that his work would not be finished if he did not die for sinners, he added, "Father, glorify thy name."

At that instant a voice from heaven answered, "I have glorified it, and I will glorify it again."

The people who stood nearby heard the voice, but they could not understand the words. Some said, "It is thundering." Others replied, "An angel spoke to him."

When Jesus heard the voice from heaven, he felt strengthened. He found a place to sit down near the temple treasury. Here were the money boxes where the people gave their offerings. Jesus saw rich men give large offerings. Also he saw a poor widow stop to put in two small coins. Together these coins were worth less than a penny.

Turning to his disciples, Jesus said, "Truly, I tell you this poor widow has given more than anyone else. Others had plenty to give. She is poor, yet she gave all that she had."

With his disciples Jesus left the temple for the last time.

The Parable of the Ten Virgins

Matthew 25:1-13

On the Mount of Olives Jesus told his disciples another story about the kingdom of heaven. He said, "It is like ten young women, called virgins, who took their lamps and went to meet the bridegroom. Five of the young women were wise and five were foolish. All of them had been invited to the marriage of a friend.

"Together they started to meet the wedding party. Since the wedding was to take place at night, they took their lamps for light. The foolish five did not take oil for their lamps.

"The young women waited and waited. The wedding party was slow in coming. The young women became so tired that they fell asleep.

"About midnight someone called out, 'The bridegroom is coming. Go out to meet him.'

"At that the young women got up and trimmed their lamps so they would be ready to join the procession. The foolish five discovered that their oil was gone. 'What shall we do?' they cried. Then they turned to their friends and said, 'Please give us some of your oil, for our lamps have gone out.'

" 'We cannot give you oil,' the wise young women answered. 'If we do there will not be enough for us. Go and buy yourselves some oil.'

"The foolish young women had no choice. They went to buy oil. While they were gone, the wedding party came. The wise young women joined the party on the way to the bridegroom's house.

"When all the guests were inside, the door was shut. Now no one else was welcome. The foolish young women arrived after the door was shut. They knocked and called out, 'Open to us.' But the bridegroom would not let them in. They had come too late."

Jesus told this story to teach the disciples that they must always be ready for his coming. They would never know when he would call for them to leave this world and go to be with him. If they were not ready when he called, they too would be shut out.

Jesus Tells About the End of the World

Matthew 25:31-46

Jesus told his disciples that at the end of the world the Son of man will come in his glory with the angels. He will sit upon his throne. Before him all the nations of the earth will be gathered. Then he will divide the good from the evil. Those who have believed in him, he will place on his right. Those who have disobeyed, he will place on his left. The good and the evil will be divided just as the shepherd divides the sheep from the goats.

"Then shall the Son of man be King," said Jesus. "He will say to those on his right, 'Come, you who are blessed of my Father, and live in the kingdom which has been prepared for you. For I was hungry, and you fed me. I was thirsty, and you gave me drink. I was a stranger, and you took me in. I did not have clothes to wear, but you gave me some. I was sick, and you visited me. I was in prison, and you came to see me there.'

"And the ones on the right will reply, 'Lord, when did we see you in need and do all this for you?'

"And the King will answer, 'Whenever you helped one needy person, you helped me.'

"Then the King will turn to those on his left and say, 'Depart from me, you who are cursed, into the everlasting punishment that has been prepared for the devil and his helpers. For I was hungry, and you did not feed me. I was thirsty, and you gave me nothing to drink. I was a stranger, and you would not take me in. I was without clothes, but you did not help me. I was sick, but you did not visit me. I was in prison, but you did not come to me there.'

"And the ones on the left will reply, 'Lord, when did we see you hungry, or thirsty, or without clothes, or a stranger, or sick or in prison, and not help you?'

"And he will say to them, 'Whenever you refused to help anyone, you refused to help me.'

"And those on the right," said Jesus, "will go into life eternal but those on the left will have everlasting punishment."

The Last Supper with the Twelve

Matthew 26:17-30; Mark 14:12-26; Luke 22:3-39; John 13

"Where shall we go to prepare the Passover meal?" the disciples asked Jesus.

Jesus told Peter and John, "Go into the city, and there you will meet a man carrying a pitcher of water; follow him. When he goes into his house, say to him, 'Where is the guest room where Jesus is to eat the Passover with his disciples?'"

The two went their way. It was as Jesus had said. The owner of the house led them to an upstairs room. Probably he knew Jesus and was glad to have him use the guest room.

When evening came Jesus and the other ten joined Peter and John. A feeling of sadness crept over them when Jesus said that this was his last supper with them.

Would Jesus really be taken away from them? It seemed impossible to think men ever could kill him. And soon they were talking about other matters at the supper table. Some wondered who would be the greatest in Jesus' kingdom. They did not understand his teachings.

Jesus knew their thoughts and wanted to teach them more about his kingdom. He got up from the table, took off his outer coat and tied a towel around his waist. Taking a basin of water, he began to wash their feet.

The disciples looked at each other in surprise. Why should Jesus do this? They had washed their feet before coming into the upper room. Peter pulled his feet away from Jesus and exclaimed, "Lord, you shall never wash my feet!"

"If I wash you not," said Jesus, "you shall never have a part in my kingdom."

But Peter wanted a part in Jesus' kingdom! He said, "Lord, wash not only my feet, but also my hands and my head."

When the washing was over, Jesus laid aside the towel and put on his coat again. He explained, "You call me Lord, and Master, and so I am. If I, your Lord and Master, have washed your feet, you ought to wash one another's feet. For I have given you an example that you should do to each other as I have done to you. The servant is not greater than his master, and if you would be good servants, you will obey my words. If you know my commands, you will be happy when you obey them."

Being troubled, Jesus said, "One of you will betray me."

How could this be? The disciples began asking, "Lord, is it I?"

Jesus said, "It is the one to whom I shall give this piece of bread when I have dipped it." Jesus gave the bread to Judas Iscariot and said, "Whatever you do, do quickly." Immediately Judas left the room and went out into the night.

The disciples did not understand. Because Judas took care of the money, they thought he was going to do something for Jesus.

After supper Jesus took bread, offered thanks, broke the bread in pieces and gave each disciple a piece. "Take this bread and eat it, for it is my body which is broken for you." Then he took the cup. When he had given thanks, he passed it to them saying, "Drink this, for it is my blood, which is shed for you. I will never again drink

of the fruit of the vine with you until that day when I drink it new in the kingdom of God."

Jesus told them that he would soon die and leave them alone. They should not be afraid. "After I am risen, I will go before you into Galilee."

Peter said, "Lord, I'll never leave you!"

Jesus answered, "This night before the cock crows, you will deny me three times."

Then Jesus and his disciples sang a hymn together, left the upper room and went to the Garden of Gethsemane.

Two Disciples Fail Their Lord

Matthew 26:14-16, 36-75; Mark 14:10-11, 32-72; Luke 22:1-6, 39-71; John 18:1-27

Judas Iscariot went to the chief priests and asked, "What will you give me if I turn Jesus over to you?" And they promised him thirty pieces of silver.

After leaving the upper room, Jesus and the Eleven went to the Garden of Gethsemane. At the entrance Jesus told eight disciples, "Stay here while I go and pray." Taking Peter, James and John, he went into the garden to pray.

While he prayed the disciples fell asleep. They could not understand why he was so troubled, and they did not know how to comfort him. How he longed to have them near to pray with him! Twice Jesus awakened Peter, James and John. Then while he prayed in agony alone, God sent an angel to strengthen and comfort him.

Jesus knew he would die on the cross. He must bear the sins of the world in order to become the Savior of men. Because he had a body and mind like ours, he dreaded to suffer the pain of such a death and he dreaded to be left alone by those he loved. So he prayed, "O my Father, if it be possible, let this pass away from me. Nevertheless not my will but thine be done."

A third time Jesus roused the sleeping disciples, saying, "Rise, let us be going; my betrayer is near." They followed. At the entrance they saw men carrying torches. Judas, the untrue disciple, was

Jesus and his disciples in the Upper Room

with the men. Stepping forward he said, "Hail, Master!" and kissed Jesus on the cheek.

Jesus looked sadly at this disciple and asked, "Judas, do you betray the Son of man with a kiss?"

Judas had told the men he would kiss Jesus so they would know whom to take prisoner. Taking hold of Jesus roughly, the soldiers led him away.

At this Peter drew a short sword, struck one of the soldiers and cut off his ear. Jesus said to Peter, "Put up your sword." Then he healed the soldier's ear. Peter drifted into the shadows with the other frightened disciples.

The soldiers bound their prisoner and started for the assembly room where Jesus' enemies were waiting. Peter followed far behind, wondering what he should do and fearing that the soldiers might take him prisoner too.

The soldiers brought Jesus to the house of Annas, and here the trial began.

As Peter stood in the courtyard, a young girl said, "Are you not also one of his disciples?"

Peter was afraid and said, "No, I do not know the man." Peter went to the fire to warm himself. Around the fire stood other men, the high priest's servants and some soldiers. One turned to Peter and asked, "Are you not one of this man's disciples?" Again fear filled Peter's heart, and he replied, "No, I am not!"

A soldier standing by who had seen Peter use his sword said, "I saw you in the garden with him!" Peter cursed and said, "I know not the man!"

Meanwhile the high priest and others had been questioning Jesus and treating him shamefully. They led Jesus away. As he passed by, he looked sadly at Peter. Now Peter remembered Jesus' words, "Before the cock crows, you will deny me three times." Peter turned blindly away from the fire, rushed out and wept bitterly.

The Darkest Day in All the World

Matthew 27:1-54; Mark 15:1-39, Luke 23:1-47; John 18:28—19:30

As the trial went on, Judas became greatly troubled. He had hoped that Jesus would free himself from his enemies by some miracle, but Jesus was allowing himself to be helpless in their hands. Judas hurried to the chief priests and scribes, saying, "I have sold an innocent man! I have sinned!"

They looked at him scornfully and asked, "What is that to us? You yourself must answer for your sin." Turning away, they refused to take back the money they had given him for betraying Jesus. Judas threw it on the floor of the temple and ran out. Finding a lonely place, he hanged himself.

Soldiers led Jesus before the Roman governor, Pilate, who knew nothing about Jesus. Pilate took him into the judgment hall and talked with him. Afterwards he said, "I find no fault in this man." But the leaders stirred up the mob to shout, "Crucify him! Crucify him! He stirs up the people throughout the country, even from Galilee."

When Pilate heard this, he said, "This man belongs to the country that Herod rules." Herod was a son of the king who had tried to kill Jesus when he was a baby. Pilate sent Jesus to Herod at once.

When the soldiers brought Jesus bound with chains, Herod was glad. He hoped that Jesus would do a miracle before him, but Jesus would not answer even one of Herod's questions. With his soldiers Herod mocked Jesus, dressing him in rich robes and pretending to honor him as a king. Then he sent Jesus back to Pilate.

Now Pilate's wife was greatly troubled about Jesus, for that night she had dreamed about him. She pleaded with her husband to set Jesus free, saying, "He is a just man, not worthy of death."

Pilate, too, wanted to free Jesus. He told the mob, "Both Herod and I have examined this man and find no fault in him."

But the mob cried, "If you set this man free you are no friend of Caesar, and Caesar will not want you for our governor."

Pilate was afraid. He talked to the restless mob about another prisoner, a robber named Barabbas who had caused the Jews much trouble. Pilate asked, "Shall I release to you Barabbas, the wicked robber, or Jesus?"

With loud cries the mob answered, "Set Barabbas free!"

Pilate asked, "What shall I do with Jesus?" They answered, "Crucify him! Crucify him!"

Taking a basin of water, Pilate washed his hands before the Jews, saying, "I am not guilty of the death of this innocent man."

The Jews cried out, "We ourselves will bear the blame. Let his blood be on our heads!"

Because Pilate wanted to please the people, he called Roman soldiers and told them to lead Jesus away to be crucified. So the trial came to an end.

The Roman soldiers took Jesus and put a crown of thorns upon his head. They put a reed in his hand and bowed before him, saying, "Hail, King of the Jews!" They blindfolded him, spat upon him and hit him, saying, "Tell us who struck you!" Jesus said not a word. Finally the soldiers took off the purple robe, dressed him in his own clothes and led him away to be crucified. They gave Jesus and the two robbers heavy crosses to carry.

A crowd of curious people followed the soldiers to the crucifixion. Many in the crowd were Jesus' enemies, others were friends who longed to help but could not. As they went, Jesus fell beneath his heavy cross. The soldiers called a stranger from the crowd to carry the cross.

On the hillside of Calvary the crowd stopped. Soldiers removed the prisoners' clothing and fastened their hands and feet to the crosses. Then they raised the crosses high in the air and planted them firmly in the ground, leaving the prisoners to hang there until they died.

From the cross Jesus prayed, "Father, forgive them, for they know not what they do."

A sign above Jesus' head bore the words, "This is Jesus, the King of the Jews."

One of the thieves who was crucified with Jesus made fun of him. The other said, "We deserve to die, but this man has done no wrong." To Jesus he said, "Lord, remember me when you come into your kingdom."

Jesus answered, "Today you shall be with me in paradise."

Jesus is on trial before the Roman governor Pilate

Sorrowing friends were standing at the foot of Jesus' cross. Among them were his mother and John. Jesus asked John to care for Mary.

Jesus' enemies also stood around the cross. Some of them said, "If you are the King of the Jews, save yourself."

About noon the sky suddenly grew dark. For three hours the great darkness lasted. Then Jesus cried with a loud voice, saying, "It is finished!"

The Roman captain standing near the cross said to his soldiers, "Truly this man was the Son of God."

The Watchers at the Tomb

Matthew 27:55-66; Mark 15:42-47; Luke 23:50-56; John 19:31-42

After the crucifixion a rich man named Joseph came boldly to Pilate and asked to take the body of Jesus and bury it. Joseph loved Jesus. With Pilate's permission Joseph and Nicodemus went to Calvary, took Jesus' body down from the cross and wrapped it in fine linen with the sweet spices and perfumes that Nicodemus had brought. Then they laid it in a new grave that Joseph had bought for himself. The grave was cut out of a large rock and opened into a garden.

Jesus' enemies were afraid that his friends might disturb his grave. Hurrying to Pilate they said, "Sir, we remember that Jesus said, 'After three days I will rise again.' Order the grave made secure until the third day, lest his disciples come at night, steal him away and say to the people, 'He is risen from the dead.'"

Pilate answered, "You have a guard. Go and make the grave as secure as you can."

They went and made the grave secure by sealing the stone and setting a guard.

The women who had watched Joseph and Nicodemus lay Jesus' body away longed to show their love for him. After sunset the next day, when the Sabbath was ended, the women prepared sweet perfumes and planned to go early in the morning to anoint the body of Jesus.

But the eleven sorrowing disciples hid themselves. They had forgotten that Jesus had said he would rise again on the third day. Nothing seemed left for them now.

Jesus Rises from the Dead

Matthew 28:1-15; Mark 16:1-11; Luke 24:1-12; John 20:1-18

The hours dragged slowly for the Roman soldiers who guarded Jesus' grave. No one had come. Perhaps they laughed at the Jews for being afraid.

As dawn came the ground began to tremble. Another earthquake had come. The frightened soldiers saw a mighty angel come down, roll the stone from the grave and sit on it. The angel's face was like lightning and his garments were as white as snow. The soldiers fell to the ground, trembling and helpless, and lay there as if they were dead. As soon as they were able, they fled into the city to report to Jesus' enemies.

When the women came to the garden, they found the grave empty. At first they did not see the angel, and they wondered who had stolen the body of their Lord. Mary Magdalene ran to tell Peter and John that Jesus' body had been taken away.

After Mary had gone, the other women saw an angel in the tomb. They were afraid and bowed themselves to the ground.

The angel said, "Do not be afraid. Why are you seeking the living among the dead? Jesus is not here; he is risen as he said. Go quickly and tell his disciples and Peter that he is alive and will meet them in Galilee."

The women ran from the place, filled with joy, yet trembling with excitement and fear. The good news seemed too wonderful to be true. Still, they believed and hurried to tell the disciples and other friends.

The disciples could not believe the glad message. Peter and John ran to see for themselves. When they came to the tomb, they found no one, but they saw the grave clothes that Joseph had wrapped around Jesus' body. Peter and John were sure now that Jesus was alive once more.

Women come to the tomb early

Mary Magdalene had not stayed in the garden long enough to hear the angel's message. Now she returned, longing to find where her Lord had been taken. Entering the garden again, she stood by the empty grave and wept. Then she stooped down, looked into the grave and saw two angels. One was sitting at the head and another at the foot where Jesus' body had been.

They said to her, "Woman, why are you weeping?"

She replied, "Because they have taken away my Lord and I do not know where they have laid him." Then turning around she saw Jesus himself standing near. But tears blinded her eyes, and she did not know him.

He, too, asked, "Why do you weep?"

Supposing him to be the gardener, she said, "Sir, if you have carried away my Lord, tell me where you have laid him."

Then Jesus said, "Mary!" and she knew his voice. What joy filled Mary's heart! She fell at his feet and cried, "Master!"

Jesus said, "Go at once and tell my friends that I will ascend to my Father and your Father, to my God and your God."

While these things were happening, the soldiers were telling the chief priests what had taken place in the garden. The chief priests were greatly alarmed. They quickly called Jesus' other enemies, and all wondered what to do. They offered the soldiers much money if they would promise to tell no one that Jesus had risen or that an angel had opened the tomb.

The Roman soldiers cared nothing about the Jews and their religion. They gladly took the money and went away. And when they were questioned about the disappearance of Jesus' body, they said the disciples stole it while they slept.

The Stranger on the Road to Emmaus

Luke 24:13-35

The Passover Feast was over, and visitors at Jerusalem were returning home. Along the road leading to Emmaus, a village seven miles from Jerusalem, two men walked slowly with bowed heads. As they talked about Jesus' trial and crucifixion and about the

484

Mary Magdalene kneels at the feet of the risen Jesus

women's message that morning, a stranger joined them. He asked, "What are you talking about so earnestly? Why are you sad?"

Cleopas asked, "Don't you know what has been happening?"

"What things?" the stranger wanted to know.

They answered, "Concerning Jesus of Nazareth, a great prophet in word and deed before God and all the people. The chief priests and rulers condemned him to death and crucified him. We believed he was the Christ.

"This is the third day since it happened and this morning some women of our company astonished us. They had gone early to the tomb, but they did not find Jesus' body. They saw angels who said, 'He is risen.' Some of us hurried to the grave and found it empty, but we did not see the angels or our risen Lord."

The stranger talked to them about the Christ. He showed them by the Scriptures that Christ would have to suffer these very things and rise again the third day if he would really be the Savior.

When they came to Emmaus, the two said, "Stay with us, for it is almost evening." So the stranger went with them. When they sat down to eat, he took bread, blessed it and gave it to them. At once they knew he was Jesus, the risen Lord. Then he disappeared.

How happy they were! Back to Jerusalem they hurried to tell the disciples they had seen the Lord.

Doubting Thomas

Luke 24:36-48; John 20:19-31

The two disciples who had met Jesus on the Emmaus road hurried to Jerusalem to tell the other disciples. When they reached the room where the disciples were, they went in and closed the door. As the two told how Jesus had walked and talked with them, Jesus appeared in their midst.

"Peace be unto you," he said.

But the disciples did not feel peace and quiet in their hearts. They were frightened. Was this a spirit?

Jesus said to them, "Why are you so troubled? Why do you have such thoughts in your hearts? Look at my hands and my feet, and

Jesus meets with the disciples after his resurrection

you will see that it is I. Touch me and you will know that I am not a spirit. A spirit does not have flesh and bones.

The disciples looked at his hands and feet. It really was the Lord. They were so amazed that they didn't know what to do.

"Have you anything here to eat?" Jesus asked. And they gave him broiled fish and honey.

Then Jesus opened their understanding of the Scriptures. He said, "Christ had to suffer and to rise from the dead the third day. Now repentance and remission of sins must be preached to all nations, beginning at Jerusalem. You are witnesses of these things."

How the disciples rejoiced at their visit with Jesus! Thomas had not been with the disciples when Jesus came. Joyfully they told him, "We have seen the Lord."

But Thomas answered, "Unless I place my finger in the print of the nails in his hands and place my hand on his side, I will not believe."

Eight days passed. Again the disciples were together in a room, and the doors were shut. This time Thomas was with them. As suddenly as before, Jesus appeared to them and said, "Peace be to you!"

While the disciples marveled at Jesus' strange coming, he spoke to Thomas, "Put your finger in my hands and place your hand on my side. Do not doubt but believe."

Falling to his knees, Thomas said, "My Lord and my God!"

Jesus told Thomas, "Because you have seen me, you believe. Blessed are those who believe even though they have not seen me."

Jesus' Last Meeting with His Disciples

Mark 16:15-19; Luke 24:50-53; Acts 1:1-14

For forty days after Jesus rose from the dead, he often talked with his disciples about the kingdom of God. Each time they saw him they worshiped him. Still they did not understand that his kingdom would not be an earthly one.

At their farewell meeting, Jesus said, "All power is given unto me in heaven and in earth. Go ye therefore and teach all nations, baptizing them in the name of the Father, and of the Son and of the Holy Ghost."

As they talked together, Jesus said, "John the Baptist baptized you with water but you shall be baptized with the Holy Spirit in a few days. You shall receive power from heaven when the Holy Spirit comes upon you. You will witness boldly of me in Jerusalem, in Judea, in Samaria and in the farthest parts of the world. But do not go away from Jerusalem until the Holy Spirit is given you."

When he had said this, Jesus was lifted up into heaven. The disciples watched until he disappeared. As they stood looking upward, two angels clothed in white came to them. The angels said, "Men of Galilee, why do you stand looking into heaven? This same Jesus who is taken up into heaven will come again in the same way as he went away."

The disciples returned to Jerusalem. In the upper room they met with other friends of Jesus to wait and pray until the Holy Spirit should be given them. No longer were they sad. Great joy filled their hearts. They knew that Jesus was really the Christ, the Savior, the Son of God.

STORIES ABOUT THE APOSTLES
Acts, the Epistles, Revelation

~~~~~~

The Coming of the Holy Spirit
Acts 1:15—2:47

Before Jesus returned to heaven, he told his followers, "Now I must leave you and go to my Father. I will send the Holy Spirit to be with you. Stay in Jerusalem until you receive the Holy Spirit."

Back to Jerusalem his followers went. Just a few weeks before when Jesus was seized, they had been terrified. What if they were arrested too? In fear they had hidden or run away.

Now these followers were no longer afraid. They were changed men. They did what the Master said without question. They had seen the risen Lord! Joy and hope filled their hearts. How glad they were to be Jesus' followers!

Ten days after Jesus ascended to heaven the Jews celebrated the feast of the harvest, called Pentecost. All Jerusalem was filled with strangers from every part of the world. People of many languages gathered at the temple to thank God for their good harvests.

This time the followers of Jesus did not go to the temple to observe the feast. One hundred and twenty of them met in an upper room to pray and wait for the Holy Spirit.

Suddenly it happened. No one knows exactly how, but the Holy Spirit came upon them. They heard the sound of a mighty rushing wind and saw little tongues of fire on the head of each person.

At once they began to praise God. Every trace of fear was gone. They had a new boldness and courage to tell others that Jesus was really the Christ and that they were his followers.

Soon the noise of their rejoicing was heard in the street below. People stopped to listen and see what was happening. The followers of Jesus left the upper room and went into the street below. They had to tell others about the Savior. As they praised God even the foreigners understood, for each person heard his own language.

The foreigners looked at each other in amazement. "What does this mean?" they asked. "We hear these men speaking in our own languages, but they have lived in Galilee all their lives. Have they studied our languages?"

In the crowd were Jews from Jerusalem. They had been there when Jesus was crucified and when he rose from the grave. They recognized these happy people as followers of Jesus. Turning to the crowd that looked on, the Jews said, "These followers of Jesus must be drunk. We've never seen them act like this before."

Peter overheard. Boldly he stood up where all the people could see him. "Men of Jerusalem and all Judea," he said, "we are not drunk as you suppose, but we have received a great blessing from God." But Peter did not stop with that. He preached to them about Jesus.

The people listened as they had never listened before. They were hearing Peter with their hearts as well as with their ears. How sorry and ashamed they were to have had a part in crucifying Jesus! They felt so guilty that they cried out, "Men and brethren, what shall we do to be saved?"

Peter replied, "Repent for your sins, every one of you, and be baptized in the name of Jesus Christ. Your sins will be forgiven and you will receive the Holy Spirit. The gift of the Holy Spirit is not given just to us but to everyone who believes on the Lord."

And many people did repent and find forgiveness. That day three thousand were baptized. How happy they were! They rejoiced greatly because their sins had been forgiven.

By the power of the Holy Spirit the apostles worked many signs and wonders in Jerusalem. Fear fell on the people who saw and heard. Every day more believers were added to their number. Soon there was a great company of believers.

Those who believed on Jesus sold what they owned and divided their money with those who were poor. Each day they met to praise and worship God in the temple. Many people believed when they saw and heard these followers of Jesus, and the Lord added to the church daily those who were being saved.

That was the beginning of the first Christian church—the first of thousands that would be scattered around the world.

The Lame Man at the Gate Beautiful

Acts 3; 4:4

Just outside the gate of the temple called Beautiful sat a poor cripple who had never walked a step. Every morning friends carried him here. He begged from the people who passed him on their way into the temple. Many felt sorry for him and gave him money.

One afternoon Peter and John went up to the temple at the hour of prayer. As they approached the Gate Beautiful the crippled beggar called out to them. He wanted them to give him some money.

The two apostles stopped and turned to look at the beggar. They saw how crippled he was. Peter said to him, "Look at us!"

The cripple looked up, expecting to receive a coin. But Peter said, "Silver and gold have I none but what I have I give to you." Then he commanded, "In the name of Jesus Christ of Nazareth, rise up and walk!"

Peter reached down, took the surprised man by the hand and lifted him up. At once strength came into the feet and ankles that had always been useless. The man walked and jumped, praising God.

With Peter and John he entered the temple. He was so happy and thankful to be able to walk that he rejoiced aloud. The people were amazed when they saw him walking and leaping for joy. They knew this was the man who had always begged at the temple gate.

The happy man threw his arms around Peter and John and the astonished people gathered around. When Peter saw the people, he began to preach to them. "Men of Israel," he said, "why do you marvel at what has happened to this lame man? Why do you look at us so strangely—as though we had healed this man by our own power or holiness?"

Peter told the people that the God of Abraham, Isaac and Jacob had glorified his Son Jesus whom the Jewish people had refused to believe. "Even before Pilate, the Roman governor," said Peter, "you denied Jesus when Pilate wanted to let him go. You killed the Prince of life but God has raised him from the dead. We are his witnesses. Through faith in the name of Jesus this man who was crippled now walks. You can see that he is perfectly well."

The lame man is healed

Many of the people were saddened to think they had not believed Jesus while he was with them. Peter noticed their sorrow and said, "I know you did not realize what you were doing when you cried out, 'Crucify him!' Nor did your rulers know. But God told you in the writings of his prophets that these things would happen to his Son. And now, if you will repent of your sins, they will be blotted out. God will forgive you and free you from guilt."

Five thousand people who listened believed in Jesus and were saved.

Peter and John in Prison

Acts 4:1-31

When the priests and Sadducees heard Peter and John preaching that Jesus had been resurrected from the dead, they were very disturbed. They had paid the Roman soldiers to keep quiet about this. Now here were Peter and John telling it publicly. "This teaching must be stopped!" the rulers cried. Until they could decide what to do, they had Peter and John put in prison.

The next day Peter and John were brought before the same chief priests and rulers who had tried Jesus. These men began questioning Peter and John by asking, "By what power or in what name did you do this miracle?"

Peter was not afraid to answer. "By the power of the Holy Spirit," he said boldly. Then he asked the rulers, "Are we being tried because this crippled man has been healed? I declare to you that this man was healed in the name of Jesus Christ of Nazareth, whom you crucified and God raised from the dead."

The rulers looked on in amazement. They saw the man who had been crippled standing with Peter and John. His face beamed with joy and happiness.

Because the chief priests and rulers did not know what to do, they sent Peter and John out while they discussed the matter. "What shall we do with these men?" they asked one another. "This is a great miracle they have done, and all the people of Jerusalem know about it. We cannot deny it. But let us make sure this teaching does not spread among the people. We can threaten Peter and John so they will not speak to anyone in the name of Jesus again."

494

The prisoners were led back and commanded to teach no more in the name of Jesus, but Peter and John would not promise to obey. They said, "Judge for yourselves whether it is right for us to obey you rather than God. We cannot keep from telling about the wonderful things we have seen and heard."

Before letting the two go, the rulers threatened to punish them severely if they were caught teaching in Jesus' name.

At once Peter and John went to their friends and told them what had happened. Together they prayed, "Lord, you are God. You have made the heaven and earth and the sea and all that is in them. The rulers gathered against thy Son, Jesus. Now, Lord, they have threatened us. Grant us boldness that we may speak thy word. Give us thy power to heal and do wonders in the name of Jesus."

And the place where they met was shaken. Again the Holy Spirit came upon them, and they spoke the word of God with boldness.

Sharing in the Early Church

Acts 4:32—5:11

About five thousand people now worshiped with the apostles at Jerusalem. These believers worshiped God together in Solomon's porch in the temple. Among them were some who earned just enough to buy food and clothing. Others were in need. Still others had plenty and enough to spare. Those who had more than they needed shared until every one had enough. Their hearts were filled with love for one another.

Barnabas owned a piece of land. He sold it and laid the money at the apostles' feet. The apostles used the money to care for the poor and needy.

Those who had houses or lands or goods did the same. Among these followers none were hungry or without shelter.

Ananias and his wife Sapphira had a piece of land too. They sold it, intending to give the money to the apostles. After seeing the money, they did not want to give all of it. They decided to take most of it to the apostles and keep the rest for themselves. "But we will pretend to give it all," they agreed.

Ananias took his bag of gold to the apostles. Peter did not praise Ananias. Instead he looked at him and said, "Ananias, why have you let Satan tempt you to lie to the Holy Spirit and keep back part of the money? The land was your own, and after you sold it the money was yours. You did not have to give it unless you wanted to. Instead you pretended to give all. You have not lied to men but to God." When Ananias heard these words he fell dead.

Three hours later Sapphira came looking for her husband. Peter asked her, "Did you and your husband sell your land for this amount of money?"

"Yes," Sapphira answered when she saw the amount.

Then Peter asked, "Why did you and your husband agree to do this wrong?" And Sapphira, too, fell dead.

Great fear came upon the early church and upon those who were not believers. Everyone was afraid to pretend to be a believer unless his sins had been forgiven and he was doing what was right.

An Angel Opens Prison Doors

Acts 5:12-42

The apostles' teaching was talked about on every street in Jerusalem. Even in the cities round about, the people had heard that the apostles were filled with the power of God. Each day more believers were added to the church until it numbered many thousands.

The people were much impressed by the miracles that the apostles did in the name of Jesus. They even brought their sick and laid them in the streets where Peter walked. They believed in his power so much that they thought even his shadow would make the sick well. From many cities and towns, the sick were brought and the apostles healed them.

The Jewish rulers grew angrier every day. They watched the works of Jesus spread farther and farther. The Jewish people were honoring the apostles and Jesus Christ more than they were their rulers. "We must do something at once to crush this new teaching," the rulers decided. So they seized the apostles and locked them in prison.

Ananias brings his offering

Night came and the rulers went home to rest. They thought their worries were over since the apostles were behind bars.

While the rulers slept, an angel opened the iron doors of the prison and went inside to speak to the apostles. The angel told them, "Go back to the temple and teach the people all the words of life."

The angel led the apostles out of the prison into the cool night air of the quiet street. There he left them, and they went on to their homes. Early in the morning they went to the temple to teach the people.

That same morning the high priest and his council met for the apostles' trial. They sent officers to bring the apostles from prison, but the officers returned alone. "We found the keepers standing guard outside the locked doors," they said, "but when we went in, we could find no one."

What could this mean? The high priest and his council did not know what to do. While they were trying to find out what had happened, someone came from the temple with more news. The man said, "The men you put in prison are in the temple teaching the people."

Now what could the Jewish rulers do? The people would stone them if they tried to seize the apostles in the temple. Finally the rulers ordered their officers to take the apostles quietly and bring them to the council room.

When the apostles were brought in, the rulers asked angrily, "Did we not order you not to teach about Jesus? Then why have you filled this city with your teaching? Why have you told the people that we are guilty of Jesus' death?"

Peter and the other apostles stood up boldly and answered, "We should obey God rather than men. The God of our fathers raised up this Jesus whom you killed. And God has made this same Jesus a Prince and a Savior, to give forgiveness of sins. We are witnesses of these things and so is the Holy Spirit whom God has given to those who obey him."

When the rulers heard this, they were furious. They even wanted to kill the apostles. At that moment a well-known and respected teacher stood up. He was Gamaliel, a Pharisee. After asking that the apostles be dismissed from the room, Gamaliel said, "Men of Israel, be careful how you treat these men. Let them alone.

"We should obey God rather than men."

If their work is of men, it won't amount to anything. If it is of God, you cannot overthrow it. You cannot fight against God."

Because the rulers honored Gamaliel as a wise teacher of the Law, they decided to let the apostles live. Even so the rulers were still angry with the apostles. They commanded Peter and the others never to teach or speak in the name of Jesus again.

After being severely beaten, the apostles were allowed to go. Even though their backs were bleeding, they rejoiced that they were counted worthy to suffer for Jesus' sake. How light their sufferings were compared to what Jesus had to go through! They could not expect to be treated any better than he had been.

Again the apostles returned to the temple. Each day they taught there and in the people's homes about the Savior, Christ the Lord.

Seven Are Chosen

Acts 6:1-6

Of the thousands of people who believed in Jesus, some were Jews from many parts of the world. Those who lived in countries where the people spoke Greek were called Grecians or Hellenists. Other believers were called Hebrews because they spoke the Hebrew language and lived in Palestine.

For some time there had been an unfriendly feeling between the Grecian Jews and the Hebrews. The Grecians complained that their widows were not being cared for properly. They thought the poor and needy among the Hebrews were getting better care.

When the apostles heard about this, they called all the believers together. The apostles explained, "It is not right for us to spend all our time taking care of the poor. We must preach the gospel. There are other faithful men among you who can see that the needy ones are cared for. Choose seven wise men who are filled with the Holy Spirit and let them do this work. Then we apostles will have more time to pray and to preach."

The people liked this idea—both the Hebrews and the Grecians. They chose seven faithful men to handle the money and care for the poor. The first man they chose was Stephen. Another was Philip.

The seven are chosen

Both these men were preachers of the gospel. Little is known about the other five.

The seven men were brought to the apostles. Laying their hands on these men, the apostles prayed God's blessing upon their work. The new plan worked well.

Stephen Is Stoned

Acts 6:7–8:3

Now the number of believers increased greatly. Even many of the priests believed and obeyed the gospel. Everywhere throughout Jerusalem people talked about Stephen. Because he was full of faith and power, he did many wonders and miracles.

The foreign Jews met in their synagogue to study the Scriptures. Stephen went there to preach the gospel, but the leaders argued with him about his teachings. They tried to prove that Jesus was not the Christ. God gave Stephen such wisdom to speak about Jesus that the leaders were left without a word to say.

They were very angry that Stephen spoke so convincingly about Jesus. Since they could do nothing to stop him, they hired men to go among the Jews and accuse Stephen. Wherever these men went, they lied, "We have heard Stephen speak against Moses and against God."

The people were upset when they heard this. Some even believed it was true. As soon as the rulers and scribes heard it, they seized Stephen and brought him before the council.

The men who had been hired to tell lies about Stephen came to the council meeting too. They were called on to tell what they knew about Stephen. They said, "This man never stops saying terrible things about the temple and the Law. We have heard him say that Jesus of Nazareth will destroy the temple and change the customs that Moses gave us."

While the false witnesses spoke, the council watched Stephen closely. Even though his face shone like an angel's, they proceeded to accuse him.

Stephen makes his defense

The high priest turned to Stephen and asked, "Are these things true?"

Bravely Stephen stood up and answered them. He repeated the familiar story of their people, beginning with Abraham. He reminded them that their fathers had disobeyed God's laws.

The rulers became angry and their eyes flashed as he spoke.

Stephen knew his life was in danger. Still he was not afraid. Turning to the rulers, he said, "You stiff-necked people, you resist the Holy Spirit just as your fathers did. They killed God's prophets, and you killed Jesus Christ."

The men were furious that Stephen dared accuse them of doing wrong. Even though they made ugly threats, Stephen paid no attention to them.

To give him courage to face his enemies, God let him see into heaven. Looking up, Stephen said, "I see the heavens opened, and the Son of man standing on the right hand of God."

At once the rulers cried out loudly. They held their hands over their ears so they would not have to hear Stephen say another word. Suddenly they rushed at him, seized him and dragged him outside the city gate. Those who had lied about him took off their cloaks and laid them at the feet of a young Pharisee named Saul.

Stephen's enemies picked up stones and threw them at him. Even then Stephen's courage did not fail. He lifted his eyes to heaven and prayed, "Lord Jesus, receive my spirit!" As the stones struck his body he knelt down and cried out loudly, "Lord, do not blame them for this sin." Soon his body was silent and still. He was the first man to be killed for preaching about Jesus.

When Stephen's friends heard about his death, they took his mangled body and buried it tenderly. And they mourned greatly for this young man who had given his life for the sake of the gospel. From that time on the followers of Jesus were mistreated and tormented in Jerusalem. The Pharisee Saul went from house to house sending men and women to prison. Except for the apostles, all the believers left Jerusalem and went to live in other towns and cities. Perhaps they thought they could find safety outside Jerusalem.

Stephen is taken out to be stoned

Simon Tries to Buy the Holy Spirit

Acts 8:4-25

Simon lived in the city of Samaria, about thirty miles north of Jerusalem. The people of all that country thought Simon was a great person, for he did tricks and magic they could not understand. "This man has the power of God," they said.

Then Philip came to Samaria and preached about Jesus Christ and the kingdom of God. Philip was one of the seven men who had been chosen to care for the poor. Now that it was not safe for believers to live in Jerusalem, most of them had gone elsewhere. Wherever they went they told about Jesus Christ and the new religion spread fast.

Since Philip had little to do in Jerusalem now, he traveled about preaching the gospel. The Samaritans listened eagerly to his preaching. They had never heard the gospel story before. As they saw Philip work miracles in the name of Jesus, they marveled at the great power God had given him. Many men and women believed in Jesus Christ and were baptized.

Simon, too, heard about Philip and came to see and hear. He watched this preacher from Jerusalem heal the sick and make the lame walk. Simon knew he could not do these things. And he, too, believed and was baptized.

Because Simon was so impressed by the miracles that Philip did, he followed him everywhere. Perhaps he thought Philip had a new kind of magic. Perhaps he hoped to learn to do the same miracles Philip did.

News reached the apostles in Jerusalem that many Samaritans had accepted Jesus as Savior after hearing Philip preach. The apostles sent Peter and John to help. As soon as Peter and John arrived, they went to find Philip and the new believers. Peter and John laid their hands on the new believers and prayed. These people, too, received the Holy Spirit.

Simon was amazed. He wished he had the kind of power Peter and John had. Because he was used to buying the things he wanted, Simon offered the apostles money and asked, "Give me, too, this power that I may lay my hands on a person and he will receive the Holy Spirit."

Peter was indignant that anyone would try to buy the Holy Spirit. To Simon he said, "May your money die with you if you think God's gifts can be bought. You do not have any part in this, for your heart is not right with God. Repent of your sins and pray for God's forgiveness, for there is still sin in your heart."

Simon was frightened. He begged Peter, "Pray to the Lord for me that none of these things will happen."

After the apostles had testified and preached the word of the Lord, they returned to Jerusalem. Through each village they passed, they preached to all who would listen. All the way to Jerusalem, more believers were added to God's church.

Philip and the Ethiopian

Acts 8:26-40

The angel of the Lord said to Philip, "Get up and go south on the road that runs between Jerusalem and Gaza," and Philip obeyed.

Philip was not the only traveler on the road that day. A royal chariot was headed south toward Ethiopia. The head of the queen's treasury was returning home. He had been to Jerusalem to worship God. In his hands was a scroll of the Book of Isaiah. Only a man of wealth and position could buy such a book.

"Go slowly," the Ethiopian called out to the driver of the chariot. "I want to read." Then he drew out his precious possession—the Bible scroll. How he longed to know God better!

On and on he read, but the eager look on his face became a dark frown. What did these words mean?

When Philip saw the chariot, God's Spirit told him, "Go, and catch up with the chariot."

As Philip ran beside the chariot, he could hear the Ethiopian reading from the Book of Isaiah. Philip asked, "Do you understand what you are reading?"

The very disappointed Ethiopian answered, "How can I understand when I have no one to teach me?" He invited Philip to ride along and explain the meaning of the strange words:

"He was led as a sheep to the slaughter,
And as a lamb before his shearer is dumb,
So he opened not his mouth.
His story who can tell?
For his life is taken from the earth."

"Whom is the prophet writing about?" the Ethiopian asked. "Is he writing about himself or some other man?"

Philip used these verses to preach to him about Jesus. Jesus was made to suffer and to die. Just as a lamb is quiet before the shearer, so Jesus said nothing to those who wronged him.

The Ethiopian had not heard the story of Jesus before. He listened eagerly. Not only that, but he believed that Jesus was the Christ. How thankful he was that Philip had come along! At last he was learning the very thing he had longed to understand.

As they rode along, they came to a place where there was water. The Ethiopian said, "See, here is water. What keeps me from being baptized?"

Philip answered, "If you believe with all your heart, you may be baptized."

"I do believe that Jesus Christ is the Son of God," the man replied. He commanded the servant to stop the chariot.

The Ethiopian and Philip climbed out of the chariot and went down into the water. There Philip baptized him.

When they came out of the water, the Ethiopian saw Philip no more. All the way back to his homeland he rejoiced as a follower of Jesus. He was eager to tell the people of Ethiopia about Jesus.

Beginning at Azotus, Philip preached the gospel in all the towns until he came to Caesarea.

Saul on the Road to Damascus

Acts 9:1-8

As a boy Saul had left his home in Tarsus and come to Jerusalem to study the Jewish religion. When he grew older, he became a very strict Pharisee.

Philip rides with the Ethiopian

Saul believed in the Law of Moses. It seemed to him that Jesus and his followers dishonored the Law. Because he loved the Law of Moses so much, Saul hated those who did not honor every tiny part of it. He especially hated those who believed in Jesus and longed to find some way to get rid of them.

In Jerusalem Saul had mistreated and put in prison many who believed in Jesus. He had made life so miserable for the believers that many had fled to other cities for safety.

News reached Jerusalem that the religion of Jesus was growing and spreading through the whole country. The more the Jewish leaders tried to stamp it out, the faster it grew. What should they do?

Saul became angrier than ever. "I will stop this crazy religion yet!" he cried. Rushing to the high priest he asked permission to go to Damascus and search for followers of Jesus. Saul planned to kill them or bring them back to Jerusalem as prisoners.

The high priest wrote letters to the rulers of the synagogues in Damascus. He told them about Saul's coming and commanded them to help Saul find the believers in their city. Saul was to take these letters to the synagogues.

With a few friends he started at once on the long trip to Damascus. Other messengers hurried to Damascus too. They wanted to warn the believers that Saul was on his way to arrest them.

Saul and his company traveled north from Jerusalem and passed through many towns and villages. Finally they neared Damascus.

It was noon. Saul and his friends could see the great wall of Damascus ahead. Suddenly they stopped. A great light from heaven shone round about them, and Saul fell to the ground. The men thought they heard thunder but Saul heard a voice from heaven call out, "Saul! Saul! Why are you persecuting me?"

Saul was both amazed and terrified. He had thought he was protecting the true religion when he opposed those who believed in Jesus. He cried out, "Who are you, Lord?"

The voice answered, "I am Jesus of Nazareth whom you are fighting against. It is hard for you to oppose me."

Instantly Saul remembered how cruelly he had treated men who believed in this Jesus. How wrong he had been! Now he asked, "What shall I do, Lord?"

Saul is blinded by a bright light

"Get up and go into Damascus," Jesus told him. "There you will be told what you must do."

Saul got up, but he could not see which way to go. The great light had blinded his eyes. The men who were with Saul had not been blinded by its brightness. They led Saul, trembling with fright, into the city to the house of Judas.

Saul Becomes a Follower

Acts 9:9-19

Three days passed, and still Saul could not see. He sat alone in his darkness. In his heart he was so disturbed that he could neither eat nor drink. He had been so wrong!

Also in Damascus was a believer named Ananias, to whom God gave a vision. In the vision God called, "Ananias."

"Here am I, Lord," he answered.

The voice said, "Get up and go to the street called Straight. At the house of Judas ask for a man called Saul of Tarsus, for this man is praying. In a vision he has seen a man named Ananias coming in and laying his hand on him so he will receive his sight."

Ananias was surprised to hear this, and it was hard for him to believe what he had heard. Every believer knew and feared this man Saul.

"Lord," Ananias said, "I have heard many tell what this man did in Jerusalem. He persecutes those who believe. Now the chief priests have sent him here to capture all those who believe in you."

God answered, "Go, do as I have commanded. Saul is a chosen servant of mine to carry my name to the Gentiles and even to the kings of the earth, as well as to the Jews. I will show him that he must suffer great things for my sake."

No longer was Ananias afraid to obey. Because he believed God's words, he did just as he had been told. At the house of Judas he found the blind Saul. Gently he said, "Brother Saul, the Lord Jesus, who appeared to you on the road to Damascus, has sent me so you would receive your sight and be filled with the Holy Spirit."

When he placed his hands on Saul, something like scales fell from the blinded eyes. At once Saul could see. The first thing he wanted was to be baptized, for he was now eager to please God. No longer was his heart filled with hatred for anyone. Friends brought him food. After eating he felt stronger.

For several days Saul met with the believers at Damascus. From the very first he spent some of his time in the synagogue, preaching that Christ is the Son of God.

Saul Escapes in a Basket

Acts 9:20-31; 22:17-21; Galatians 1:17-24

The Jews of Damascus were amazed when they found Saul worshiping with the disciples of Jesus. But they were more astounded when they saw him stand up before all the people in the synagogue and preach boldly in the name of Jesus.

They looked at one another and asked, "Is this the man who put in prison and even killed many people in Jerusalem because they believed that Jesus is the Christ? Didn't we hear that he was coming to our city to arrest the believers and take them back to the high priest in Jerusalem?"

For a time Saul worshiped with the disciples and taught in the synagogues. Then telling his new friends goodbye, he went to Arabia. For three years he spent his time in prayer and in studying the Scriptures. He saw clearly now that Jesus of Nazareth, whom he once despised, was the Messiah.

Again Saul went back to Damascus and preached even more boldly than before. Even the Jewish teachers who did not believe in Jesus could not prove that Saul's teaching was wrong. Many Jews who listened came to believe in Jesus.

This made the Jewish rulers so angry that they planned to kill Saul. At each city gate they placed guards with orders to kill Saul if he tried to leave the city. They planned to get rid of him at all cost.

Saul heard about their plans. Believers hid him until night came. Then they took him to a building on top of the city wall. Saul climbed into a large basket and his friends lowered him to the ground outside the wall. This time he escaped.

Where could Saul go? The chief priests, scribes and Pharisees in Jerusalem were no longer his friends. Three years had passed since they sent him to Damascus to arrest the believers and he had not arrested a single one. Instead he had become a believer himself.

Some of the apostles were still in Jerusalem. Saul longed to tell them how the love of Jesus had changed his heart and life. With this in mind, he started for Jerusalem.

But the apostles did not welcome Saul when he arrived. They were afraid of him. What if this were only a trick to capture them? He had treated other believers roughly and even caused some to be killed. The apostles did not want to have anything to do with him. Saul must have been disappointed.

At last Saul found a friend in kindhearted Barnabas. Barnabas took Saul to the apostles. He told them what had happened to Saul on the road to Damascus, how the Lord had spoken to him, how he had preached boldly in the name of Jesus in Damascus.

After this the church in Jerusalem received Saul gladly. They were glad that God had changed their enemy into a true friend. For fifteen days Saul stayed in Jerusalem and met with the believers. He even went to the synagogues where he had once seized followers of Jesus. Here he taught boldly about the Christ.

When the chief priests and rulers heard that Saul was in Jerusalem they were vexed. How did Saul dare to speak in the name of Jesus? At once they began to plan to kill him.

While Saul was in the temple praying, the Lord told him, "Hurry, Saul! Get out of Jerusalem quickly, for the Jews will not believe your testimony of me."

Saul answered, "Lord, they know how I imprisoned and beat those who believed in you. They know that when Stephen was stoned for preaching in your name, I was there. I even kept their cloaks while they killed him."

Again the Lord said, "Go away. I will send you far from here to be my witness to the Gentiles."

When the apostles found out Saul's life was in danger, they took him to the city of Caesarea on the seacoast and put him on a ship bound for Tarsus, the city of his birth.

Saul escapes in a basket

After Saul left Jerusalem, things quieted down. The church continued to grow in every city and village where the gospel story was told.

A Man Is Healed of Palsy

Acts 9:32-35

In cities and villages throughout the land, there were many disciples or saints who met to worship the Lord. The apostles went from city to city. At each place they met with the disciples, preached to them and encouraged them to serve the Lord.

On one trip Peter came to Lydda, a city near the Great Sea, to visit with the saints. Here he saw a man named Aeneas who was sick with palsy. For eight years Aeneas had not been able to leave his bed.

Peter looked at the poor man with pity. Then he said, "Aeneas, Jesus Christ makes you well! Get up and make your bed."

In glad surprise Aeneas heard these words. Because he believed he was healed, he tried to rise up. At once strength filled his body and he was perfectly well.

Throughout the city and round about, it was told how Aeneas had been healed. Many people came to see Peter and hear him preach the gospel. And many turned to the Lord.

Dorcas Is Raised from the Dead

Acts 9:36-43

In the city of Joppa was another company of believers. Among them was a woman named Dorcas who spent all her time caring for the sick, the poor and the needy. No wonder she was loved dearly.

While Peter was in the nearby city of Lydda, Dorcas became ill. She grew worse, and in a short time she was dead.

Her friends were filled with sorrow. How could they get along without her? Lovingly they washed and dressed her, then laid her in an upper room.

When Dorcas' friends heard that Peter was at Lydda, they sent for him to come at once. And Peter did. They took him to the room where they had laid Dorcas' body. Many friends stood around weeping bitterly. Widowed mothers showed the clothes that Dorcas had made for their children.

Peter knew what Jesus would have done in a time like this. He knew how Jesus was touched with the sorrow of others. After telling everyone to leave the room, Peter knelt and prayed. Then he turned toward the body and said, "Dorcas, get up!"

The woman opened her eyes and when she saw Peter, she sat up. He gave her his hand and helped her up. Peter called to the believers and widows. How happy they were to see their dear friend alive!

News of this miracle spread throughout all Joppa very quickly. Many people came to see and hear Peter. And many believed in the Lord. For a long time Peter stayed in Joppa at the home of Simon, the tanner.

Peter and Cornelius

Acts 10:1–11:18

Thirty miles north of Joppa in the city of Caesarea lived Cornelius, a captain in the Roman army. Although a Gentile, Cornelius worshiped the true God and taught his household to do the same. Throughout the city he was known as a man who helped the poor and needy.

Every day Cornelius prayed earnestly to God. One afternoon while he was praying an angel came and said, "Cornelius."

When the captain looked up and saw the angel, he was afraid. "What is it, Lord?" he asked.

The angel said, "God has heard your prayers and seen your good works. Now send men to Joppa to the house of Simon the tanner who lives by the seaside. Simon Peter is staying there and he will tell you what to do."

As soon as the angel was gone, Cornelius called two of his household servants and one of his soldiers who served the Lord. He told them what the angel had said and asked them to go to Joppa to find Simon Peter.

The next morning the three started for Joppa. They neared the city about noon. At this hour Peter was on the housetop praying. He felt very hungry but dinner was not yet ready. While he waited, he fell into a strange sleep.

In his sleep Peter saw a great sheet let down from the sky. In it were several kinds of tame and wild animals. As the sheet was lowered, a voice from heaven said, "Get up, Peter! Kill and eat."

Peter looked at the animals in the sheet. Now the Jews ate only certain kinds of meat. Those that Moses had forbidden them to eat were called "common" and "unclean." When Peter saw such animals in the sheet, he answered, "No, Lord, I cannot, for I have never eaten anything that is common or unclean."

The voice replied, "What God has made clean do not call common."

The sheet was lifted back to heaven and lowered a second time and a third. Still Peter refused to touch the animals because he was a Jew. Finally the sheet disappeared and Peter awoke.

What could all this mean? Peter wondered. As he thought about it, the Spirit of God told him, "Three men are looking for you. Get up and go to meet them. Do not doubt but go with them for I have sent them."

When Peter reached the gate he saw the three men whom Cornelius had sent. He told them, "I am the man you are looking for. What do you want?"

The three told Peter about their master, Cornelius, and how the angel had commanded him to send for Peter. Peter said, "Stay with me tonight and I will go back to Caesarea with you in the morning." The men agreed.

Early the next morning Peter, with six believing Jews and Cornelius' three servants, started for Caesarea. When they reached Cornelius' house, it was full of people waiting to see Peter and hear his word.

Never before had Peter gone to the home of a Gentile. Strict Jews refused to be friends with Gentiles for they knew this was how idol worship had started among their people in the past.

Suddenly Peter understood his vision on the housetop. Without hesitating he entered the door to meet the Gentile family who waited so eagerly for his coming.

Peter meets Cornelius

When Cornelius saw Peter, he fell at his feet to worship him. Peter lifted him up and said, "Stand on your feet. I am a man like you." The two talked together and Cornelius led Peter into the crowded room where the relatives and friends were waiting.

Peter told them, "You know it is against the Jewish law for a Jew to be entertained by people of any other nation. But God has shown me I should not call any man common or unclean. For that reason I have come to you. Now I see that God accepts any people who fear him and do what is right and good, whatever their nation."

Soon Peter was telling Cornelius and his guests about Jesus who died to save people from their sins. He explained that whoever believed in the name of Jesus would be saved. As he spoke God gave the Holy Spirit to these Gentiles who listened.

The six men who came with Peter were amazed that God would give the Holy Spirit to Gentiles too. These six had always been strict Jews, even after they believed in Jesus. They thought that salvation was just for the Jews. Now they understood that God intended it for people of every nation.

Peter asked, "Can anyone forbid these Gentiles to be baptized since they have received the Holy Spirit just as we have?" And all were baptized as Jesus had commanded.

For several days Peter stayed and taught them. Then he returned to Jerusalem.

News about what had happened at Cornelius' house had already reached Jerusalem before Peter and his friends arrived. Some of the believers thought Peter had done wrong by going to a Gentile home.

When Peter came he told them about his vision on the housetop and about Cornelius' servants coming for him. God's Spirit had commanded him to go to Cornelius. There Peter and his friends had found eager listeners who believed in the true God. Gladly they received Peter's message, and God gave them the Holy Spirit.

When the Jerusalem believers heard Peter's story, they rejoiced that God's salvation was for people of every nation.

An Angel Lets Peter Out of Prison

Acts 12:1-23

King Herod wanted to be popular with the Jews, so he made friends with their chief priests and rulers. It did not take him long to find out how much the Jewish rulers hated those who believed that Jesus was the Christ. To please them Herod began to make trouble for the believers. First he had James, the brother of John, killed. The chief priests and rulers were so pleased about this that Herod ordered Peter put in prison.

The church felt the loss of James very keenly. They could not spare Peter too. Each day they met and prayed for his release. But the days passed and still Peter lay in the dreary prison. Finally the church met at Mary's home to pray all night.

It was midnight and Peter was fast asleep, chained to two soldiers. Outside the prison door other soldiers stood on guard. While Peter slept, an angel came and awakened him. The angel said, "Get up quickly." When Peter did this the chains fell off his hands.

Then the angel said, "Put on your sandals and dress yourself." Peter obeyed. Before they left the cell, the angel said, "Wrap your cloak around you and follow me."

Again Peter obeyed. Out of the cell and past the guards they walked. When they came to the great iron gate that led to the city, it swung open before them. Out they walked. As they started up the street, the angel disappeared.

Peter had thought he was dreaming but now he knew this was real. He said, "Now I know for sure that the Lord sent his angel to deliver me from Herod and the Jews who wanted to kill me."

At once he hurried to Mary's home where the church was praying. He knocked at the gate and Rhoda called out, "Who is it?" When she heard Peter's voice, she was so excited that she did not open the gate but ran to tell the good news. "Peter is here! Peter is here!" she called out.

Those who had been praying did not believe her. They said, "You are crazy." When she insisted, they said, "It must be his angel."

All this time Peter stood outside the gate, knocking. Finally they went to see for themselves. When they opened the gate, there he stood. They were astonished. Peter entered the room and motioned for them to be quiet while he told them how the Lord had answered their prayer.

Peter knew he was not out of danger yet. He bade his friends good-bye and said, "Be sure to tell James and the others about this." (This James was probably the brother of Jesus.) Then Peter went on to another place.

At daybreak there was much excitement at the prison. What had become of Peter? King Herod was very angry that his prisoner had escaped. He questioned the keepers but they knew nothing. Finally he commanded that the keepers be put to death.

Not long afterwards Herod died. After his death the disciples were not persecuted so bitterly in Jerusalem.

Barnabas and Saul at Antioch

Acts 11:19-30; 12:24-25

Many believers fled to other cities and nearby countries when life became dangerous for them in Jerusalem. Wherever they went they told about Jesus, and many who heard believed in Jesus too.

Some of the believers fled northward to the country of Syria. In the large city of Antioch, they made their homes. From the very first they preached about Jesus, both to the Jews and to the Gentiles. Many who heard believed and turned to the Lord.

When the church at Jerusalem heard about the believers at Antioch, they sent Barnabas to visit them. It took him several days to get to Antioch. As soon as he reached the city, he wanted to meet the believers. How impressed he was with the great number of Gentiles who now believed in Jesus! He rejoiced and encouraged them to serve the Lord with all their hearts.

The believers brought their friends and neighbors to hear Barnabas preach, and many more people were won to the Lord. The church at Antioch was growing so fast that Barnabas needed more helpers. He remembered that God had called Saul to preach to the Gentiles. Saul was now in his hometown of Tarsus, not far from Antioch. Barnabas decided to go to see Saul.

Barnabas and Saul were glad to see each other again. Barnabas did not return to Antioch alone, for Saul came with him. For a whole year the two preached the gospel there and encouraged the believers.

The townspeople noticed that people who believed in Christ acted differently from others. They began calling the believers Christians because they acted like Christ.

Prophets from Jerusalem came to visit the church at Antioch. They said God had showed them there was to be a great famine throughout all the lands.

Time passed, and a great famine did come. Word reached the church at Antioch that the believers in Judea were hungry and in need. At once the Antioch Christians wanted to help. Each man gave as large an offering as he could. Then the church chose Barnabas and Saul to take this offering to the saints at Jerusalem.

When Barnabas and Saul arrived in Jerusalem with the offering, they probably stayed at Mary's home. She was one of Barnabas' relatives.

When the two got ready to go back to Antioch, Barnabas and Saul invited Mary's son, John Mark, to go with them. This young man wanted very much to work for the Lord. Gladly he said good-bye to his friends and went with Barnabas and Saul.

Later John Mark became a fine gospel worker and carried the gospel to heathen lands. Finally he wrote the Gospel According to Saint Mark. You will find the stories he wrote in your Bible.

Barnabas and Saul, First Missionaries

Acts 13:1-13

The church at Antioch grew so large that it took several teachers to minister to the people. Often these teachers met with Barnabas and Saul to pray for the work of the church. One time as they prayed together, the Holy Spirit told them, "Release Barnabas and Saul for the work I have called them to do." And the teachers understood that God wanted Barnabas and Saul to go to faraway countries and preach the gospel.

The church at Antioch hated to see Barnabas and Saul leave, but they felt God had a special work for these two to do. Tender good-byes were said after they had prayed together, and the two set off on their first missionary journey. With them was Barnabas' nephew, John Mark.

The first stopping place was the island of Cyprus. They preached about Jesus in the cities of Salamis and Paphos. At Paphos the Roman governor Sergius Paulus sent for them. He, too, wanted to hear the word of God.

When the two missionaries came, the governor listened eagerly—so eagerly that a magician who was watching feared that Sergius Paulus was about to become a Christian. Because the magician did not want this to happen, he tried to turn the governor's attention to other things.

Saul, who from this time on was called Paul, noticed what the magician was trying to do. The Holy Spirit filled Paul and he looked straight at the magician and said, "You enemy of all righteousness, will you never stop trying to oppose the way of the Lord? Because you have tried to turn people away from the Lord, you will be blind for a time."

From that moment on the man could see nothing and had to ask for someone to lead him by the hand. When Sergius Paulus saw this, he was astonished. At once he believed in the power of God and in Jesus, his Son.

After the Roman governor believed in Christ, the missionaries took a ship for Perga in Asia Minor. Here John Mark left them and returned to his home in Jerusalem. Barnabas and Paul went on to another city called Antioch.

Paul and Barnabas at Antioch and Iconium

Acts 13:14—14:7

In Antioch in Asia Minor Paul and Barnabas found a Jewish synagogue. On the Sabbath they went there to worship with the Jews. When the rulers of the synagogue saw these strangers, they told them, "You men and brethren, if you have any word of encouragement for the people, speak to them."

At this invitation Paul stood up and told them about Jesus, how he died and was resurrected, that through him we might have forgiveness of sins. When Paul had finished preaching, the Jews left the synagogue. At once the Gentiles came and begged Paul to preach the same sermon to them on the next Sabbath.

Some of the Jews did not like what Paul had said, but others wanted to hear more. On the next Sabbath the whole city met to hear the missionaries tell about Jesus. When the Jewish leaders saw the crowds following Paul and Barnabas, they were jealous. To turn the people away they began to speak unkindly of the missionaries.

Paul and Barnabas knew what the Jewish leaders were doing. They told them, "It was necessary that the word of God should be preached to you first. We see that you refuse to believe, so we will preach to the Gentiles who are eager to hear the message. God has commanded us to take the light of salvation to the Gentiles, even in the farthest places of the world."

When the Gentiles heard this, they were glad. Afterward many of them believed in Jesus, and the word of the Lord was spread throughout all the region.

But the Jewish leaders did not want things to go so well with the Christians. They stirred up a bitter feeling toward Paul and Barnabas, and the city officials began to persecute the two. They ordered the missionaries to leave their city, and Paul and Barnabas went on to the city of Iconium. Nor did they go discouraged, for the Holy Spirit filled their hearts with joy.

At Iconium many Jews and Gentiles believed in Jesus and were saved. For a long time Paul and Barnabas stayed there and ministered to the people.

All the time the unbelieving Jews stirred up trouble. They told things about Paul and Barnabas that were not true. When people heard these stories, they turned against the missionaries. Soon the Jews and Gentiles were working together to get rid of Paul and Barnabas. They planned to stone them.

Paul and Barnabas found out about their plan and went on to Lystra to preach the gospel there.

Paul and Barnabas Mistaken for Gods

Acts 14:8-28

At Lystra Paul and Barnabas found idol worshipers who had never heard about the true God. The missionaries stood in the streets and preached to the people in Greek, a language everyone understood. How strange the gospel message sounded to these heathen people!

A man who had been crippled from birth listened eagerly. Paul noticed him and realized that the man had faith to be healed. In a loud voice Paul called out to him, "Stand up on your feet!" And the man jumped up and walked.

The people were amazed. They had never seen anything like this before. In wonder they crowded around to stare at the missionaries, and they talked excitedly to one another in their own language. Paul and Barnabas could not understand that they were saying, "The gods have come down to us in the form of men."

The excitement mounted. Soon Paul and Barnabas saw the heathen priest leading oxen to sacrifice and bringing wreaths of flowers. These people often made such offerings to their Greek gods, Jupiter and Mercury.

Suddenly the missionaries realized that these heathens thought they were gods and wanted to offer sacrifices to them. They called Barnabas Jupiter. Because Paul did the preaching, they called him Mercury.

A feeling of horror came over Paul and Barnabas. Tearing their clothes, they rushed among the people and cried out, "Sirs, why are you doing this? We are men like you. We preach to you that you should turn away from idols and serve the living God. He made the heaven, the earth, the sea and all things. He gives us rain from heaven and causes our food to grow in the fields."

It was all Paul and Barnabas could do to keep the people from offering sacrifices to them. Although the people understood the Greek words Paul spoke, their minds were so full of idol worship that they could not understand about the true God; however, a few people understood and received the gospel gladly.

Word reached Iconium that Paul and Barnabas were preaching about Christ in Lystra. At once the unbelievers in Iconium sent men

"We are men like you."

to Lystra to tell lies about the missionaries. The people were so stirred up when they heard these lies that they caught Paul and stoned him until they thought he was dead. After dragging his bleeding body outside the city, they returned to their homes.

The believers stood around Paul in fear and sorrow. As they watched they saw him move. Paul was not really dead. Soon he got up and walked back to the city with them.

The next day Paul and Barnabas went on to Derbe where they preached the gospel courageously. Here many people turned to the Lord.

After spending some time at Derbe, the missionaries started for home. On the way they stopped at the places they had visited before to encourage the Christians.

At last they reached Antioch in Syria and the church that had sent them out. When all the church had gathered, Paul and Barnabas told them all that God had done through them on their missionary journey. How happy the Christians were to hear such good news!

A Serious Problem

Acts 15:1-34

After Paul and Barnabas returned from their missionary trip, men came from the church at Jerusalem and told the Antioch Christians, "Unless you obey every part of the Law of Moses, you cannot be saved."

The Christians at Antioch were much disturbed. Many of them were Gentile Christians who believed they were saved even though they did not obey every part of the Law of Moses.

Paul and Barnabas were anxious. What if the Gentile Christians became discouraged and turned away from the gospel?

God had given Moses certain rules for the Israelites, or Jews. The Gentiles had never kept this law. Many of them did not even know its teachings. Keeping these rules did not save the people, but it did separate the people who worshiped God from those who worshiped idols. The Law of Moses had prepared the hearts of the Jews to receive the Messiah.

Paul and Barnabas had worked among many Gentile Christians. They had seen these people receive the Holy Spirit just as the Jewish Christians had. Paul and Barnabas told the men from Jerusalem, "You are mistaken. The Gentiles are saved without keeping Moses' law."

This was a serious problem. The Christian church could be torn in pieces by arguing about it. Finally the church at Antioch decided that Paul and Barnabas should take some of their teachers and talk this matter over with the apostles in Jerusalem.

So the group started out. On their way they visited other churches and Paul and Barnabas reported about their missionary trip and how the Gentiles had accepted the gospel. Everywhere the disciples rejoiced that the gospel was being spread.

When the group from Antioch arrived in Jerusalem, the apostles and the leaders met to talk over the serious problem that had come up. Men who had been strict Pharisees before they believed in Jesus said, "The Gentiles must keep the Law of Moses." They did not realize that Jesus' teachings help people to live pure and holy lives even when the people know nothing about the Law of Moses.

There was much tension and arguing about this matter. Peter rose to his feet and said, "Men and brethren, you know that some time ago I preached to the Gentiles and they believed. God gave them the Holy Spirit just as he gave it to us. He did not put any difference between them and us. Why should we set up a barrier? All of us believe that we are saved through the Lord Jesus Christ."

Everyone was quiet. Barnabas and Paul told about the miracles and wonders God did among the Gentiles on their missionary trip. Finally James said, "Men and brethren, we should not trouble the Gentile believers to do things the same way we do them. Instead we should warn them to keep away from idols and sin."

And everyone agreed with James. The Jerusalem church wrote a letter to the church at Antioch and sent it with Paul and Barnabas. They sent two of their own preachers, too, to visit the Antioch church.

Many eager people greeted those who came from Jerusalem. They listened carefully as the letter from the apostles was read. They rejoiced when they heard that they would not be expected to live like Jews in order to please God. And the church at Antioch continued to worship God and obey the teachings of the gospel.

Judas and Silas, the men who had come from Jerusalem with Paul and Barnabas, preached to the people and urged them to be faithful to Jesus Christ. After several days Judas returned to Jerusalem, but Silas stayed on with the church at Antioch.

Paul Begins a Second Journey

Acts 15:36–16:15

Paul said to Barnabas, "Let us go back to every city where we have preached the word of the Lord and see how our brethren are getting along."

Barnabas agreed, but he wanted to take his nephew John Mark with them. Because John Mark had gone only part way with them the time before, Paul did not want to take him again. The two missionaries could not agree on this matter, and so Barnabas took Mark and sailed to the island of Cyprus where they witnessed for the Lord.

Paul chose Silas, the preacher from Jerusalem, to go with him. They went to Asia Minor and visited the churches there. At Lystra, the town where Paul had been stoned, they met Timothy, a fine young man. Timothy's father was a Gentile and his mother was a Jewess.

Paul was much impressed with this young Christian. All the people of the region had good things to say about Timothy. Before leaving Lystra, Paul invited Timothy to go with him and Silas, and Timothy accepted gladly.

The missionaries did not preach at each place, for in many places the people were not ready to accept the gospel. Finally they came to Troas, a city on the seacoast. Ships came to Troas from places much farther away than Jerusalem. The people in those faraway countries had never heard the gospel preached.

One night while they were at Troas, Paul had a vision. In his dream he saw a man of Macedonia who begged him, "Come over to Macedonia and help us."

When Paul awoke he told Silas and Timothy about the vision. All three believed that God wanted them to preach the gospel in Macedonia.

531

Barnabas and Mark sail for Cyprus

Now another disciple, a doctor named Luke, joined the missionaries. Paul, Silas, Timothy and Luke sailed to Macedonia. Later Luke wrote two books of the New Testament—the Gospel of Luke and the Acts of the Apostles.

The first Macedonian city they visited was Philippi. Since only a few Jews lived in that city, they had no synagogue. Each Sabbath they met to pray outside the city by the river. On the Sabbath Paul and his friends left the city to find the place where the Jews met.

A few women had gathered by the river. Paul and his friends sat down and taught them about Jesus, God's Son. While Paul talked, he noticed that one woman, Lydia, listened most eagerly. She believed his words about Jesus and knew her sins were forgiven. Lydia and all her household believed and were baptized.

When the riverside service was over, Lydia told Paul and his friends, "If you think I am faithful to the Lord, come and stay at my house." The missionaries accepted her invitation, and while they were in Philippi, they stayed at the home of this rich woman.

The Philippian Jailer

Acts 16:16-40

An angry mob made its way down the streets of Philippi to the city prison. The leaders of the mob half dragged two men along. At the prison they turned the two over to the jailer.

The two men were Paul and Silas, the Christian missionaries. Because they had helped an unhappy slave girl, these heathen people were punishing them. This is how it happened:

Each day Paul and Silas and their friends walked through the streets on their way to the riverside to pray. Each day a slave girl saw them. Everyone heard her call out loudly, "These men are the servants of the most high God. They have come to show us the way of salvation!"

The slave girl was not herself, for she was filled with an evil spirit. By the power of this evil spirit she could tell about the future. Her masters made much money from her fortune-telling.

After several days Paul became annoyed because the evil spirit tormented this girl. Finally he turned and said to the evil spirit, "I command you in the name of Jesus Christ to come out of her."

Immediately the evil spirit departed, and the girl was herself again. No longer could she tell about the future, for the evil spirit was gone. When her masters discovered this, they were furious. She could not earn money for them now. They grabbed Paul and Silas and dragged them through the market place to the rulers of the city.

They told the rulers, "These Jews are causing a great deal of trouble in our city by teaching strange customs. It would be against the law for us Romans to accept or practice these customs."

The crowd shouted out against Paul and Silas. The officials ordered that Paul and Silas were to be beaten. This done, the officers ordered the jailer to put these dangerous prisoners in the inner prison and fasten their feet in stocks.

Paul and Silas found themselves alone in the dark, smelly room. How their backs hurt! But Paul and Silas were not like the other prisoners. They did not complain because they had been mistreated. Instead they talked to each other about God and his great love. At midnight they prayed and sang praises to God.

The other prisoners heard the prayers and the songs. Why were these two men so happy? Surely they had been beaten enough to make them sad!

Suddenly a great earthquake shook the foundations of the prison. The locked doors swung open. Even the stocks on the apostles' feet came unfastened.

The jailer awakened and saw the prison doors swing open. Terrified he ran to the prison. He knew the rulers would kill him if even one man escaped. Believing that the prisoners had all escaped, he drew his sword to kill himself.

Paul cried out in the darkness, "Do not harm yourself! We are all here."

The jailer called for a candle and rushed into the prison. There he saw all the prisoners, Paul and Silas among them.

Now the jailer knew Paul and Silas could not be dangerous men. They must be men of God just as the slave girl had said. Trembling, he fell at their feet, crying, "Sirs, what must I do to be saved?"

They said, "Believe on the Lord Jesus Christ, and you shall be saved." And everyone in the prison heard about Jesus Christ, the Savior of men.

The jailer believed and his heart was filled with joy. All of his household turned to the Lord. He took Paul and Silas to his house, washed their wounds and bandaged their backs. Then he brought food for them to eat. Instead of treating Paul and Silas like prisoners, he treated them like guests.

Before morning Paul and Silas baptized the jailer and his household. Together they rejoiced in the Lord.

In the morning the officials sent word to the jailer, "Let those men go!"

But Paul answered, "We are Romans. The rulers had us punished without a trial and put us in prison. Do they think they can get rid of us this easily? No, let them come and set us free."

When the rulers heard this, they were frightened. It could go hard with them for mistreating Roman citizens. Quickly they came to the jailer's house and begged Paul and Silas to leave the city.

Before leaving Philippi, the missionaries went back to Lydia's house and encouraged the Christians. After telling them good-bye, Paul and Silas went on to another place.

Years afterward Paul wrote a letter to the church in Philippi. That letter is in your Bible. It is called Philippians.

In Other Cities of Macedonia

Acts 17:1-15

Paul and Silas went to other cities to tell about Jesus. At Thessalonica they found a Jewish synagogue. Here they went each Sabbath to teach the people that Jesus is the Christ. Some Jews and many Greeks received the gospel gladly.

The Jews who did not believe were angry because so many people listened eagerly to Paul and Silas. To get rid of these two

"Believe on the Lord Jesus Christ."

missionaries, they had a group of rough men cause a riot in the city. When everything was in an uproar, they went to Jason's house to look for Paul and Silas. Because they could not find the missionaries, they dragged Jason and some others before the city officials.

The unbelieving Jews complained. "These men who have turned the world upside down have come to our city too. They are staying with Jason. What these men teach is against the laws of Caesar. They even say there is another king whom they call Jesus."

Both the rulers and the people were troubled when they heard this. They made Jason promise to keep the peace and let him go. Then the believers sent Paul and Silas on to the next town, for they were afraid of what might happen if the missionaries stayed in their city.

At Berea Paul and Silas found another Jewish synagogue and met with the Jews on the Sabbath. They told about the Savior whom the prophets had written about. These Jews listened carefully. Then they studied the books of the prophets to make sure Paul and Silas spoke the truth. Many believed. Among the believers were highly respected Greek men and women.

Word reached Thessalonica that Paul and Silas were preaching at Berea. Those who had caused so much trouble at Thessalonica came to Berea to do the same thing.

The believers knew Paul and Silas were in great danger. They had Paul set sail at once but Silas and Timothy stayed on. From Athens Paul sent word for Silas and Timothy to join him.

Paul Preaches on Mars' Hill

Acts 17:16-34

While Paul waited in Athens for Silas and Timothy, he looked over the city. He saw idols everywhere. How many different gods these people worshiped! There was even an altar to the Unknown God.

In this city was a Jewish synagogue also. Here Paul spoke to the Jews about Christ.

As he walked through the streets, sincere people asked him questions about the gospel. Soon he was teaching them about Christ each day. Others were curious and gathered to listen. It was hard

for them to understand about Jesus and his resurrection. They thought Paul spoke about a strange god from another land.

But Paul's listeners were so impressed that they wanted him to speak on Mars' Hill. At this place important matters were discussed. Some of the wisest men of Greece spoke here. And Paul's friends took him to Mars' Hill to speak about Christ.

Paul stood up before all the wise men and the curious crowd. He said, "I saw the altar you built to the Unknown God. I want to tell you about this God now. It is he who has made the world and all things in it. He is the Lord of heaven and earth. He does not live in temples made by men. He gives life and breath to all creatures. He has made the people of every nation.

"This God is not far from every one of us. He wants people of every nation to seek him. He is not like gold or silver or stone that man shapes into an idol. Now that you know about the true God he commands you to repent of your sins, for the day is coming when he will call all men to judgment." And he told them about Jesus whom God had raised from the dead.

When the wise men heard this, some laughed. Others shook their heads doubtfully and said, "Come back another time and tell us more about this strange thing."

But several came and asked to know more about Christ. One of them was Dionysius, an important man in Athens. Dionysius believed and was saved. A few others turned from their idols and believed in the true God and in his Son, Jesus Christ.

Many Believe at Corinth

Acts 18:1-23

From Athens Paul went to Corinth, another Greek city. Here he became acquainted with a man and his wife who had just come to Corinth. They were Aquila and Priscilla, Jewish tent makers.

Paul, too, knew how to make tents. While in Corinth he worked with Priscilla and Aquila during the week. On the Sabbath he preached in the synagogue.

Silas and Timothy joined Paul in Corinth. How glad he was to see them! About this time Paul was led by the Spirit to speak more boldly about Christ in the synagogue. Many of the Jews were stirred up at this, so Paul turned to preach to the Gentiles.

Among the Jews who believed was Crispus, the chief ruler of the synagogue. He and his household believed and were baptized in the name of Jesus. Because the Jews who worshiped at the synagogue would not accept the gospel, the believers worshiped next door at the home of Justus.

One night the Lord told Paul in a dream, "Do not be afraid. Speak boldly. I am with you, and no man will hurt you here. I have many people in this city who will believe on me when they hear your words."

And Paul obeyed the Lord. For a year and a half he preached the gospel in Corinth to all who would listen. Many believers were added to the church.

The Jews who did not believe were afraid to let Paul go on preaching. Too many people believed on Christ. The Jewish leaders seized Paul and took him before Gallio, the ruler of the city. They told Gallio, "This man persuades people to break the Law by the way they worship God."

Paul opened his mouth to speak. Before he could say a word Gallio said, "O you Jews, if it were a matter of right or wrong, I would listen to you. Since it is a question of your law, I will not be a judge in this case."

The crowd was so angry that they grabbed one of the leaders of the synagogue and beat him, but Gallio did not pay any attention to them.

Paul stayed on in Corinth for some time before deciding to return to Jerusalem. When he got ready to sail, Aquila and Priscilla went with him as far as Ephesus.

After attending the Feast of the Passover at Jerusalem, Paul went on to Antioch to visit the church where he had been one of the first pastors.

The Gospel Is Preached in Ephesus

Acts 18:24–19:20

The people of Ephesus, a large city of Asia Minor, worshiped the goddess Diana. Heathen people from many parts of the world had sent money to build a great temple for her. When the temple was finished, it was so beautiful that it was called one of the Seven Wonders of the World.

The heathen went to the temple of Diana to worship their goddess. In their homes they had idols of Diana to which they bowed down.

Not everyone in Ephesus worshiped Diana. The Jews who lived there had built a synagogue where they could worship the true God. On the Sabbath they met in the synagogue to hear the Old Testament scrolls read.

Apollos, a Jewish preacher, visited the Jews at Ephesus. He was an eloquent preacher, and the people listened eagerly to his words. Although Apollos followed the Lord with all his heart, he had never heard about Jesus. He knew about John the Baptist and believed that John was a prophet sent from God. He taught the Jews at Ephesus John's words.

Some who heard believed, and Apollos baptized them as John did to show they had repented of their sins.

As soon as Aquila and Priscilla heard Apollos preach, they invited him to their home and taught him about Jesus Christ. How glad he was to hear about Jesus! He believed at once.

Then Apollos preached that Jesus was the Christ. He was so convincing that many others believed. When he got ready to go to Greece, the believers wrote to the disciples there and told them about Apollos. In Greece, too, Apollos greatly encouraged those who believed.

Soon after Apollos left Ephesus, Paul arrived. He was happy to find so many believers in this city! He asked them, "Have you received the Holy Spirit since you believed?"

And the people answered, "We did not even know there was a Holy Spirit."

Paul wanted to make sure these believers knew the truth so he asked, "Into what were you baptized?"

And they said, "The baptism of John."

Then Paul taught them that John wanted them to believe in Jesus Christ. When they heard this, they were baptized in the name of the Lord Jesus. Paul laid his hands on these twelve believers and prayed. They were filled with the Holy Spirit.

For three months Paul taught in the synagogue, proving by the Scriptures that Jesus was the Christ. Many were not willing to believe in Jesus. They spoke harshly about Paul and the Christ he preached about.

Paul left the synagogue and took the believers to a school nearby. Here he taught them every day for two years. His teaching became known throughout all the city and the country round about. And many believed in Jesus and were baptized.

While Paul taught in Ephesus, he worked miracles in the name of Jesus. He healed many who were sick. Some were too sick to be brought to Paul. Their friends brought handkerchiefs and aprons for Paul to touch. Prayerfully they laid these on those who were sick, and the sick were made well.

The people marveled at God's great power. Seven brothers who were magicians watched Paul heal the sick and cast out evil spirits in Jesus' name. They thought they could do the same thing. When they found a man who had an evil spirit they said, "We command you to come out in the name of Jesus whom Paul preaches."

The evil spirit answered, "Jesus I know, and Paul I know, but who are you?" And the evil spirit caused the man to jump on these brothers and beat them terribly. In fear they ran out of the house to escape.

When people heard what had happened, they had even greater respect for the mighty power of Jesus. They praised God. Many who believed had once practiced magic. Now they confessed their wrong and turned away from their superstitions.

In those days books were very rare and expensive. A single book cost so much that few people could buy even one. But the people of Ephesus had saved their money to buy books about magic. When

they saw the mighty power of God, they brought their books, built
a great bonfire and burned the books in the streets.

Now that they believed in Jesus they would not need such books.
They did not want to be tempted by even having such books in their
houses. Because the books were full of magic instead of the power
of God, they knew it would be wrong for anyone to have them.
A crowd watched as these expensive books went up in smoke.

A Riot at Ephesus

Acts 19:21—20:3

Not all the people of Ephesus believed in Jesus when they
heard Paul's preaching and saw the miracles he did. Many still
preferred to worship at the temple of Diana. They believed their
goddess had fallen from the sky, so they worshiped her as if she
were a special gift from heaven. In their homes the heathen had
idols or images of Diana.

People who came to visit Ephesus liked to take home an image
of Diana as a souvenir. Diana was an ugly-looking image but the
people worshiped her.

Many silversmiths worked steadily at making small idols of Diana.
They grew rich selling the idols. One of the silversmiths was
Demetrius. He was distressed that so many people were leaving
their idol worship to serve Jesus Christ. Every day he heard
of more people who believed in Jesus Christ. Every day he grew
more restless, for he was afraid all the heathen would become
Christians. Then what would happen to the silversmiths?

Demetrius called all the silversmiths to a meeting. He told them,
"You men know we make a lot of money by our work. Not only at
Ephesus but also throughout the province of Asia this Paul has
turned many people away from Diana. He says there are no gods
that are made with hands. Soon we will have no business left. Not
only that, but people will no longer come to worship at the temple
of Diana. Finally they will hate her temple and destroy it."

These words excited and angered the silversmiths. At once
they began to shout, "Great is Diana of the Ephesians!" They went
through the streets shouting those words. Other people followed.

Soon the whole city was stirred by the excitement. Some seized two of Paul's companions and dragged them into the theater.

When Paul heard what had happened, he wanted to go to rescue the two, but his friends would not let him. They were afraid the people would tear Paul to pieces if they could lay their hands on him.

For two hours the city was full of excitement and confusion. Many people did not even know what it was all about, but they all joined in the cry, "Great is Diana of the Ephesians!"

Finally one of the city officials stood before the people and motioned for them to be quiet. He said, "Men of Ephesus, people everywhere know we worship the goddess Diana whose image fell down from heaven. Since that's how it is, you ought to be quiet. Don't do anything you will be sorry for.

"You have brought these men here. They have not robbed any temples or spoken evil about our goddess. If the silversmiths want to bring charges against these men, let them take it to court and have the trouble settled by law. All of you are in danger of being arrested for breaking the peace." And with those words the city official dismissed the people and sent them home.

Paul had been planning to leave Ephesus even before the riot started. He visited the churches in Macedonia and Greece before returning to Jerusalem. While in Greece, Paul discovered that the Jews were waiting to capture him as he set sail for Syria. To escape Paul went back by land the same way he had come.

On the Way to Jerusalem

Acts 20:5–21:17

From Macedonia Paul sailed across the sea to Troas. Here he stayed for several days getting ready for his trip back to Jerusalem.

On the night before he left, Paul met with the believers in a large room on the third floor. They broke bread together in memory of the last supper Jesus ate with his disciples before he was crucified. Then Paul preached until midnight. Paul knew he would never see these people again and his heart was full of things to tell them.

While Paul preached, a young man named Eutychus sat in an open window listening. Time passed and Eutychus got sleepy. His head began to nod. He should have known how dangerous it was to go to sleep in a third-story window. In his sleep he fell out of the window to the ground below.

Friends rushed down the stairs. They picked him up, but he was dead.

Paul threw his arms around the young man's body. "Don't worry," he told those standing near. "He is still alive." They took the lad away alive and were comforted.

Finally they climbed the stairs and ate again. Then Paul went on preaching. At daybreak he left the city.

Paul's next farewell meeting was with the leaders from Ephesus who had come to the seacoast to say good-bye. How much he loved them! This would be their last meeting.

He said, "You know how I have worked and lived among you. I have taught you publicly and in your homes. I have testified to both the Jews and the Greeks. I feel that I must go to Jerusalem but it is hard to tell what will happen there. In my heart I think chains and suffering await me, but this does not make me afraid. It does not matter how long I live, but that I finish with joy the work the Lord Jesus has given me. I know I shall see you no more, but I will pray for you. Take good care of the church of God over which the Holy Spirit has made you overseers."

Together they knelt and prayed. They threw their arms around Paul and wept. With heavy hearts they accompanied him to the ship and he set sail.

The ship stopped several days at Tyre. During that time Paul and his friends met with the Christians there. When the ship was ready to sail, the men, women and children walked to the shore with Paul. On the shore they knelt and prayed.

The next stop was at Caesarea. While Paul and his friends were here, Agabus came from Jerusalem. This old man was a prophet. He took off Paul's sash or belt and tied it around his own hands and feet. Pointing to the sash Agabus said, "So shall the man who owns this be bound and given to the Gentiles."

The Christians were much troubled when they heard this. They begged Paul not to go on to Jerusalem but he answered, "Why do you weep and break my heart? I am ready, not only to be bound at Jerusalem but also to die there for the name of the Lord Jesus."

When they discovered that they could not change his mind, they said, "The Lord's will be done."

A few days later Paul and his friends went on to Jerusalem with other Christians from Caesarea. At Jerusalem the elders of the church welcomed them with joy.

Paul Is Taken Prisoner

Acts 21:18—23:10

The day after Paul arrived in Jerusalem he went to the elders of the church to tell them about his work. He told how God had worked through him among the Gentiles.

The elders glorified God. Then they said, "You see, brother, many thousands of Jews believe in and still keep the Law of Moses. They think that you tell the Jews in other countries to pay no attention to the Law of Moses. What shall we do? The people will find out you are here."

Finally the elders decided that Paul should prove to the Jewish believers that he honored the Law of Moses. For this reason Paul went to the temple and performed the ceremony of cleansing as Moses had commanded.

About a week later Jews from Asia Minor recognized Paul, for he had taught in their synagogue about Christ. They had not accepted his teaching. They hated him because he taught that Gentiles could become the people of God without keeping all the Jewish rules.

To arouse the people, they shouted, "This is the man who teaches men everywhere against the Jews and the Law and the temple. He has even brought disgrace to the temple by bringing Greeks here."

Because they had seen Paul in the city with two Greeks, they assumed that he had brought them into the temple too. The old enemies of Jesus joined the mob and rushed to seize Paul. They pulled Paul out of the temple and shut the doors. While they beat him, someone ran to the Roman captain and reported the trouble.

The captain took soldiers and ran to find out what was happening. When he got through the crowd, he commanded that Paul be bound with two heavy chains. Then he asked the crowd, "Who is he and what has he done?"

Some cried one thing and some another. The captain could not hear in the noise of the angry mob. He led Paul away to the castle where prisoners were kept. The mob followed crying, "Away with him!"

Because the soldiers were afraid the people would tear Paul in pieces, they picked him up and carried him on their shoulders to the stairs of the castle.

At the top of the stairs Paul asked the captain, "May I speak to you?" Granted permission Paul said, "I am a Jew of Tarsus. I beg you, let me speak to the people." And the captain gave his permission.

Standing at the top of the stairs, Paul motioned to the angry crowd. When they were quiet, he spoke to them in Hebrew. The Jews loved this language, and they listened closely.

Paul began by telling them about himself. "I am a Jew born in Tarsus, but I was brought up here in Jerusalem. Gamaliel taught me the strictness of the Law. I was just as eager to follow God's way as you are. For a time I even persecuted the believers, binding them, putting them in prison and having some killed. The high priest and the rulers know this is true, for they gave me letters of permission to arrest the believers who had fled to Damascus.

"On the way to Damascus a great light from heaven shone around me. As I fell to the ground I heard a voice saying, 'Saul, Saul, why do you persecute me?' Then I answered, 'Who are you?' And the voice said, 'I am Jesus of Nazareth whom you persecute.' Those who were with me saw the light but they did not hear the words.

"The Lord told me to wait at Damascus until he showed me what I was to do. I could not see, but my friends led me into the city. There Ananias came to me and said, 'Brother Saul, receive your sight,' and my eyes were opened. Ananias said that I was chosen to be a witness of Jesus Christ to all men of what I had seen and heard. Then he baptized me in the name of the Lord.

"When the Jews at Jerusalem wanted to kill me for believing in Jesus, the Lord told me, 'Depart, for I will send you to the Gentiles.'"

When the people heard Paul mention the Gentiles, they would listen no more. They shouted, "Away with this fellow from the earth.

He is not fit to live." The mob waved their cloaks and threw dust into the air.

The chief captain commanded that Paul be brought into the castle and beaten so he would tell what he had done when they questioned him.

As they tied Paul for the beating, he asked, "Is it lawful for you to beat a Roman citizen who has not been found guilty?"

When the chief captain heard this, he was afraid. He asked, "Tell me, are you a Roman?"

"I am," Paul answered. The chief captain then told his soldiers not to harm Paul, but to give him special care.

The next day Paul was brought before the chief rulers of the Jews. The captain noticed that even the Jewish rulers did not agree about what to do with Paul. Some wanted to set him free and others insisted that he be put to death. The rulers caused so much excitement and uproar that the captain had his soldiers take Paul away.

A Young Man Saves Paul's Life

Acts 23:11-35

The second night Paul was prisoner in the castle, the Lord spoke to him, "Be of good courage, Paul. Just as you have spoken boldly for me in Jerusalem, you are to speak boldly for me in Rome."

And Paul was encouraged by these words. For a long time he had wanted to visit Rome, the capital of the Roman Empire, and preach the gospel there.

Paul's enemies were not satisfied to have him in prison. They wanted him killed. Forty of them vowed to eat nothing until they had killed him. They hurried to tell the chief priests and rulers their plan.

"You can help us," they said, "by asking the chief captain to send Paul here tomorrow so you can question him further. While the soldiers are bringing him from the castle, we will seize Paul and kill him."

But Paul's nephew heard about the plan. He hurried to the castle at once and told his uncle what the Jews were planning to do.

547

Quickly Paul called one of the captains and said, "Take this young man to the chief captain, for he has something important to tell him."

Because Paul was a Roman citizen, Lysias, the chief captain, took more interest in him. Lysias knew the Jews had no evidence against Paul. When he heard about their plan to kill Paul, he told the nephew, "Do not let anyone know you have told me this." With these words he sent the young man away.

At once there was much activity at the castle. The chief captain called two of his men and told them to get ready to take Paul to Caesarea that night. To make sure Paul would be safe, Lysias commanded two hundred soldiers, seventy horsemen and two hundred spearmen to accompany Paul. When everything was ready the captain wrote a letter to the Roman governor, Felix, at Caesarea and explained why he was sending Paul.

At nine o'clock that night the sound of horses' hoofs clattered on the pavement in front of the castle door. Paul was brought out and mounted on a horse. Then the small army moved rapidly down the dark street. None of the Jews knew what these soldiers were doing.

The next afternoon Paul was brought safely to the Roman governor, Felix. He opened the letter the chief captain Lysias had written. These are the words he read: "This man is a Roman who was taken by the Jews. They would have killed him if my soldiers had not rescued him. I brought him before the council of the Jews to find out why they accused him, but they had no charge worthy of death or even imprisonment. When I found out they were plotting to kill him, I sent him to you. I have commanded his accusers to come to you for his trial."

Until the trial Felix had Paul put in the palace that had been Herod's.

Paul Before Felix

Acts 24:1-26

Paul's enemies were angry when they found out that Lysias, the chief captain, had sent Paul out of Jerusalem safely. They arranged to go down to Caesarea and accuse Paul before Felix. The high priest, the Jewish leaders and a skillful lawyer named Tertullus hurried to Caesarea.

A boy saves Paul's life

Felix brought Paul before this council. Tertullus rose to speak. First, he flattered Felix in the hope that Felix would side with the Jews. Tertullus said, "Honorable Felix, by your leadership we enjoy peace. Your good work is known in this province and throughout the nation. We accept your leadership, most noble Felix, with all thankfulness. Now I do not want to bore you, but I pray that you will be kind enough to listen to a few words."

Felix knew well how the Jews hated Roman officials. He was not fooled by Tertullus' flattery.

Then Tertullus began to speak about Paul. No longer did he speak in a gracious tone. Instead he lashed out, "We have found this man Paul a terrible troublemaker. He has caused trouble among the Jews throughout the world. He is the ringleader of a group known as the Nazarenes.

"When he attempted to dishonor our temple, we tried him according to our law. But the chief captain Lysias came and took him away from us by force. Now we come to you, most noble Felix, so you will know what we have against Paul."

And the Jews agreed that Tertullus had spoken for all of them. Now Felix wanted to hear Paul's side of the story. He motioned to Paul to speak.

Paul said, "Honorable Felix, I speak for myself more cheerfully because you have known this nation for many years. You can easily find out that it was only twelve days ago that I went up to Jerusalem to worship God. The leaders did not find me stirring up the people. They seized me while I was alone in the temple. The men who now accuse me cannot prove their charges.

"They condemn the way I worship God. Yet I believe all that is written in the Law of Moses and in the books of the prophets. I have always tried to keep my heart free from wrong toward God and man."

As Felix listened he knew the Jews did not have any real charges or evidence against Paul. He said, "I will wait until Lysias comes so I can find out more about this matter." With that he dismissed the council.

Paul delivered to Felix

Felix commanded a captain to watch Paul but allow him to have some liberty. Friends could come and go whenever they liked.

Several days later Felix sent for Paul again. He and his wife wanted to hear about the gospel of Christ. As Paul talked earnestly with them, Felix was convicted of his sins. Trembling he told Paul, "Go away for now. When I have more time, I will send for you."

Two years passed and Paul was still a prisoner at Caesarea, though he had many privileges. Felix had called for Paul often, hoping to be bribed to set Paul free. Even though he knew Paul did not deserve to be kept a prisoner, he refused to let him go.

Paul Appeals to Caesar

Acts 24:27–25:12

After two years a new governor was appointed to Caesarea. To please the Jews, Felix left Paul in prison. Festus, the new governor, was not acquainted with the Jews' customs and religion. After three days at Caesarea, he went to Jerusalem to learn more about the people he was to govern.

As soon as Festus arrived in Jerusalem, the high priest and leaders of the Jews began to tell him about Paul. They tried to get Festus to send for Paul. If Paul were brought to Jerusalem, they planned to kill him.

But Festus said, "I'm going back to Caesarea. You come down there and accuse him."

Ten days later Paul was brought before the Jews and Festus at Caesarea. The Jews made many serious charges that they could not prove. Paul said, "I have never done anything against the Jews or against the temple or against Caesar."

To do the Jews a favor, Festus asked Paul, "Are you willing to go to Jerusalem and be judged before me there?"

Paul answered, "I stand before Caesar's judgment seat. To the Jews I have done no wrong, as you know very well. If I have done anything worthy of death, I am willing to die. I appeal to Caesar."

Festus knew that every Roman citizen had a right to appear before Caesar, the head of the great Roman Empire. To Paul's request, Festus could give only one answer. "You have appealed to Caesar and to Caesar you shall go."

King Agrippa Hears Paul's Story

Acts 25:13—26:32

Several days later King Agrippa and his sister Bernice came to visit Festus at Caesarea. Agrippa governed the land east of the Jordan River.

During their stay Festus told them, "Felix left a prisoner whom the chief priests and rulers of the Jews want to kill. When I heard their case, I found they had no real charges against the man. Because the Jews insisted, I asked if he would go to Jerusalem to be tried, but he appealed to Caesar."

At once Agrippa was interested. He said, "I would like to hear the man myself." And Festus promised to arrange it.

The next day Agrippa and Bernice were ushered into the judgment hall. Among the guests were many important people. Then Festus commanded that Paul be brought.

Festus stood to introduce the prisoner to the king. "Before you," he said, "stands the man who the Jews say is not fit to live any longer. When I heard the case, I found he had done nothing to deserve death. He has appealed to Caesar, and to Caesar he shall go.

"However, I have no charge to make against him. I have brought him before you, King Agrippa, so you may hear him and find out why he is being held."

Agrippa said to Paul, "Tell your own story."

Paul stood up, stretched out his hand on which hung a heavy chain, and said, "I am glad, O King, that I may speak for myself and tell why the Jews have accused me. You understand the customs and questions of the Jews, and you will understand my words.

"From my youth the Jews knew all about me, for I was brought up in their city. They know I lived among the strictest Pharisees and kept the Law of Moses just as carefully as any of them. Now I am accused because I believe God has raised Jesus Christ from the dead.

"There was a time when I persecuted those who believed in Jesus of Nazareth. In Jerusalem I put many of the saints in prison. The high priest even gave me authority to persecute the believers in other cities.

"On my way to Damascus to persecute the Christians there, I had a vision from God. It was noon, O King, when suddenly a light more dazzling than the sun shone on my friends and me. We fell to the ground in fear and a voice spoke to me in Hebrew, 'Saul! Saul! Why are you persecuting me?' I cried, 'Who are you, Lord?' The voice replied, 'I am Jesus whom you persecute.' That voice commanded me to tell of Jesus, not only to the Jews, but to the Gentiles as well.

"Because I have obeyed that heavenly command, O King, I am being persecuted by the Jews who will not believe in Jesus. Again and again they have tried to kill me, but God has saved me from them. He has given me strength to tell everyone that Jesus is the Christ of whom Moses and the prophets wrote."

As Festus noticed how earnestly Paul spoke, he cried out, "Paul, you are out of your mind. Too much learning has made you crazy!"

Calmly Paul answered, "I am not crazy, most noble Festus, but I speak the truth sincerely. Since King Agrippa knows these things well, I have spoken freely to him. King Agrippa, you believe the prophets."

Agrippa answered, "Paul, you almost persuade me to be a Christian."

"I wish I could persuade not only you but everyone here," Paul said. "I wish all of you could be as I am except for these chains."

The king, Bernice, Festus and the others left the judgment hall to discuss Paul's case. Agrippa told them, "This man has done nothing to deserve death or even imprisonment. He could be set free if he had not appealed to Caesar."

Paul stands before Agrippa

Paul Is Shipwrecked

Acts 27

On a ship leaving Caesarea was Paul, the prisoner. As the shore faded in the distance, Paul saw for the last time the land that is dear to the heart of every Jew. Never again would he return to the country of Judea.

Paul was not the only prisoner on board. At Caesarea he and several others had been given over to the Roman captain, Julius. Festus ordered Julius and his men to take the prisoners safely to Rome and deliver them to Caesar.

Probably the Christians at Caesarea gathered at the seashore to say good-bye to their beloved friend and no doubt many of them wept as they saw Paul in chains.

Paul was not the only Christian among the passengers. Two of his friends, Doctor Luke and Aristarchus, went along.

The next day the ship stopped at Sidon. By this time Paul had won the respect of the Roman officer and was given permission to go ashore to visit his friends. Paul, Luke, Aristarchus and a soldier guard had time for a short visit with the Christians at Sidon.

The ship docked at Myra, its last stop. The Roman captain found another ship ready to sail for Italy. He had the soldiers and their prisoners board this ship. It set sail and soon they were back in the great Mediterranean Sea.

Sailing was not good for the winds were strong and from the wrong direction. No wonder the passengers were glad when they stopped at the harbor Fair Havens on the island of Crete.

Winter was coming on and sailing was already dangerous. But the captain was eager to get back to Rome, and the owner of the ship was willing to sail on.

Paul told the owner and the captain, "Sirs, this will be a dangerous voyage. You will cause much injury and damage if we sail now."

Because Fair Havens was not a good place to spend the winter, the owner decided to go farther south before stopping for the winter. The ship glided out of the harbor and into the broad sea.

They had not gone far when a tempestuous wind swept down upon them. Now there was no turning back and they could not go

556

ahead. How the angry waves tossed the ship! They did not know how soon the ship might be torn to pieces. The captain and the owner of the ship remembered Paul's advice.

First they tried to lighten the ship by throwing things overboard. Then they waited anxiously for the storm to pass, but it raged on. They could not see the sun by day or the stars by night.

One morning Paul called everyone to him. Above the roar of the storm he told them, "Sirs, if you had listened to me, this would not have happened. But be of good cheer, even though we shall lose the ship, no one will lose his life. Last night an angel of the God I serve told me this."

Still the storm did not lessen. The people were afraid they would be drowned. Two weeks passed. Then one night the sailors discovered they were nearing land. No one knew where they were, since they had drifted on the waves for many days. They did not even know whether they were nearing a rocky coast or a sandy beach. For fear of being wrecked on the shore, they threw the anchors overboard and waited anxiously for morning to come.

The sailors knew they were in danger. They could not bring the ship safely to land, so they planned to escape and save their own lives. They began to lower a small boat, but they pretended to be casting more anchors into the sea.

Paul knew what the sailors were doing. He told the centurion, "We cannot be saved unless these sailors stay in the ship."

This time the Roman officer did not even stop to question Paul's words. He cut the ropes that held the small boat and let it drift away.

Toward morning Paul said, "This is the fourteenth day we have been without food. I ask all of you to eat now so you will be strengthened. No one will be lost."

Before all the people, Paul took bread and gave thanks to God. The people took courage and ate with Paul.

At daybreak they could see the land. The sailors did not recognize the place, but ahead was a sandy shore. Lifting the anchors they tried to steer the ship into a small stream. Soon the ship ran aground and stuck fast. The sea beat against the back of the ship so violently that the ship began to break up.

The soldiers wanted to kill their prisoners for fear some would escape. If one got away, a soldier would have to pay with his own life. The Roman captain did not want Paul killed, so he refused to let the soldiers harm any of the prisoners.

At the captain's orders those who could swim jumped into the water and swam to shore. Others found broken pieces of the ship and floated ashore. Not one of the two hundred and seventy-six people was drowned.

Safe on an Island

Acts 28:1-10

On the shore of the island a group of excited men anxiously watched those who were shipwrecked make their way to land. These natives felt sorry for the strangers who were wet and cold. They built a fire, and those who had been shipwrecked gathered around it eagerly. How glad they were to have a fire!

As they talked with the islanders, they discovered that they were on the island of Melita, south of Italy. The islanders noticed that among these strangers were several soldiers and prisoners.

The fire began to burn low, and Paul went to gather wood to keep it burning. As he laid his sticks on the fire, the heat from the flames aroused a poisonous snake that was hidden among the sticks. The snake bit Paul's hand.

The islanders knew that Paul was a prisoner. When they saw the snake hanging from his hand, they whispered to each other, "This man must be a murderer. Even though he has escaped from the sea, the gods will not allow him to live."

They watched expecting to see Paul's arm swell or to see him drop over dead. But nothing happened; he had not been harmed at all. In wonder the islanders looked at one another. They said, "This man must be a god, for even a deadly snake does not hurt him."

Nearby lived Publius, the ruler of the island. He invited Paul and his friends to his home and entertained them for three days. While there Paul discovered that Publius' father was very ill. The old man had a disease that often causes death. When Paul prayed for him, Publius' father was made well.

Paul reaches shore after the shipwreck

News of this healing spread quickly over the island. The people brought all their sick to Paul, and he healed them.

The islanders and those from the ship saw God's power at work. And Paul preached to them about Jesus. Those who received the good news were made happy. For three months Paul and the others stayed on this island.

Paul Arrives in Rome

Acts 28:11-31

When spring came Julius, the Roman captain, had his soldiers take their prisoners aboard a ship bound for Italy. The islanders came to see them off. They brought gifts for the Christian men who had taught them about the Lord. How thankful they were for Paul and his friends!

The boat docked at the Italian city Puteoli. Here all the passengers left the ship. Those going to Rome had to go the rest of the way by land. Before going on to Rome, the Roman captain let Paul and his friends spend a week with the Christians in Puteoli.

Then they started their trip on foot over the great highway to Rome. As Paul trudged along the road, his heart was heavy. Perhaps he was afraid he would not have many opportunities to preach the gospel in Rome since he was a prisoner. Perhaps he was afraid the people would not listen to a preacher who wore a heavy chain. Paul's discouragement was soon turned to joy. When Paul's company was forty miles from Rome, Christians came from the city to welcome him. At once he took courage and thanked God. Now he knew he would have true friends in this strange city. Ten miles farther on another group of Christians from Rome welcomed Paul.

In Rome Julius turned his prisoners over to the captain of the guard. Julius must have tried to get the captain to treat Paul as well as possible, for Paul was allowed to rent a house of his own and live by himself. Of course he was always chained to a soldier. Julius did not have the authority to do anything about that.

Paul had been in Rome only three days when he sent for the chief Jews. He told them how the Jews in Jerusalem had accused him and caused his imprisonment. He explained how this had happened.

The Jews at Rome were greatly surprised, for they had heard nothing about this trouble. Eagerly they asked Paul to preach to them about Jesus Christ. They had heard much about the Christians, but they did not know what the Christians believed.

With a glad heart Paul preached to them. He told how Jesus came to earth, suffered, died on the cross for the sins of men and rose from the dead.

The Jews listened carefully. Some believed and rejoiced that God had sent his Son to be their Savior. Others resented Paul's preaching and refused to believe.

When Paul saw that many did not believe that Jesus was the Savior, he said, "It is just as Isaiah said by the power of the Holy Spirit, 'The heart of this people has grown hard, and their ears will not hear my words.' But the Gentiles," said Paul, "will hear and believe the salvation that God has sent to all men."

For two years Paul lived in his own house in Rome. First one soldier and then another was chained to him. Not only did Paul preach to his guards but to all who came to see him. He taught many people about Jesus.

During this time he wrote letters to the Christians in the cities where he had preached. Some of these letters are in our Bibles. They are called epistles.

Onesimus, the Runaway Slave

Philemon

While in Rome Paul met Onesimus, a runaway slave. Strangely enough Paul knew Onesimus' master Philemon, a Christian who lived in Colosse.

Like many others Onesimus heard Paul tell about Jesus Christ, and he became a Christian. For a time he took care of Paul, and Paul taught him more about Jesus.

Paul would have liked to keep Onesimus, for he loved the young man. Also Onesimus made things easier and more comfortable for Paul. Yet according to the law the runaway slave still belonged to Philemon. In those days many people owned slaves just as people today own animals. Onesimus would never feel right until he had made things right with Philemon. So he decided to go back.

Paul hated to see Onesimus leave. To make sure that Philemon would treat his runaway slave kindly, Paul sent a letter with Onesimus for his master.

In the letter Paul wrote, "I appeal to you for Onesimus who has been like a son to me while I am in prison. I have sent him back for you to receive as your own. I would have liked to keep him, but I could not do that. Receive him not as a servant but as a brother. Treat him as you would treat me. If he has wronged you or owes you anything, charge it to me and I will repay it."

Then Paul added, "Get a room ready for me. I trust through your prayers that I shall be able to come to see you." After sending special greetings to the Christians who met at Philemon's house, Paul closed his letter with this prayer, "The grace of our Lord Jesus Christ be with your spirit. Amen."

Paul's letter to Philemon is in our Bibles. Probably when Onesimus took this letter to his master, he also carried a letter to the church at Colosse. This letter, called Colossians, is in our Bible.

Paul Finishes His Race

1 and 2 Timothy and Titus

We do not have an accurate record of the rest of Paul's life. From some of his letters, it is believed that he was pardoned after spending two years as a prisoner in Rome. For the next few years, he went from one place to another preaching the gospel.

Paul left Timothy in charge of the churches around Ephesus. It is thought that Paul may have gone from Ephesus to Macedonia and even Spain. When he visited the island of Crete, he left Titus to care for the Christians there.

How Paul loved the Christians! With all his heart he wanted them to be true to their faith in Jesus Christ. To help them be true, he wrote them letters of encouragement and advice.

After perhaps three or four years, Emperor Nero of Rome began a great persecution against the Christians. Paul was again arrested, and this time he was killed.

Onesimus brings Paul's letter to Philemon

While still in prison Paul wrote Timothy that he would soon meet his death. But he did not seem discouraged. "I have fought a good fight," he said. "I have finished the race the Lord gave me to run. I have kept the faith. Soon the Lord will give me the crown of righteousness that is awaiting me in heaven." So Paul, the mighty soldier of the cross, went to be with his Lord.

The New Testament Letters

Romans—Jude

Not all the letters, or epistles, in the New Testament were written by Paul. Some were written by other apostles. Peter wrote two, and John wrote three. James and Jude, probably the brothers of Jesus, each wrote one.

From these letters we learn about the teachings of the preachers in the early church. Many parts of the gospel that are not explained in the stories of Jesus are told in these letters.

We read in the epistles that all people are sinners. Although everyone deserves to be punished for his sins, God gave his Son, Jesus, for the sins of the world. Those who believe that Jesus died for their sins will be saved from sin and its punishment. God lives in the hearts of the believers by the Holy Spirit whom he gives them.

These New Testament letters also teach us how Christians should live. Christians are described as being honest, good to the poor, willing to suffer for Jesus' sake, kind to their enemies and ready to forgive them, having love for one another, and eager to win others to Jesus Christ. Christians are happy people, for God gives them joy.

The preachers of the early church wrote that Jesus is coming again. When he comes, he will take to be with him all who believe in him. The dead will rise. All who believe in Jesus will rise to meet him in the clouds. Those who do not believe will cry out for fear and look for a place to hide, but there will be nowhere for them to go. No one knows when Jesus will return, but Jesus taught that his followers should always be ready.

These letters were read many, many times when Christians met together. Copies were made and shared with churches in other places. These letters were very valuable. They helped the Christians know how to live. As a part of our Bible, they do the same today.

John on the Isle of Patmos

Revelation

On a lonely island far from his friends and homeland sat an old man. In his younger days he had been a fisherman on the Sea of Galilee. One morning he had left his fishing to follow a dear friend. Ever after, he had tried to please this dear friend, Jesus.

The old man was John, one of the twelve apostles. John was now a prisoner on this island because he believed in Jesus.

As John thought about God, he remembered that this was the day the Christians always met to worship. They called it the Lord's day. Then John heard a voice that sounded like the blast of a trumpet.

The voice said, "I am Alpha and Omega, the first and the last. Write what you see in a book and send it to the seven churches of Asia."

John turned to see who was speaking. He saw seven golden candlesticks. Among them was one who looked like Jesus. But never before had John seen his Master look like this.

Now Jesus wore a long robe. Around his chest was a girdle of gold. In his right hand were seven stars. His face shone like the noonday sun. When he spoke his voice sounded like the rushing of mighty waters.

John fell as if dead at Jesus' feet. Jesus bent over, touched John and said, "Do not be afraid. I am the one who was crucified, but now I am alive forevermore. Write the things you see and hear."

Jesus then told John that the seven stars represented the seven ministers who preached to the seven churches of Asia. The seven golden candlesticks were for the seven churches to whom John was to write letters. One of the letters was for the church at Ephesus where Paul had preached the gospel.

John wrote in the letters the words Jesus told him. The churches took good care of these messages, and today we have them in the Book of Revelation, the last book of the Bible.

Later John had a vision of God's throne in heaven. He saw the door of heaven open and heard a trumpet-like voice calling him to come up. Around God's great throne, John saw twenty-four old men dressed in white and wearing gold crowns. Other heavenly beings were there and all worshiped God.

John noticed a sealed book in God's hands. An angel cried out with a mighty voice, "Who is able to break the seals and open the book?"

A search was made in heaven, but there was no one worthy to break the seven seals and open the book. John wept that no one could open it. He longed to know what was written inside.

While he wept, one of the old men near the throne told him, "Do not weep, for One has been able to open it." And John realized that Jesus who was called the Lamb of God was able to open the book.

The heavenly beings around the throne rejoiced and fell down before the Lamb of God. They sang a new song, praising the one who had given his life to redeem them from sin so they could enter heaven.

When the Lamb of God opened the book, John saw the strange things that were in it. He wrote about those things so that others could know what he had seen.

Afterwards John saw a new heaven and a new earth, for the old earth seemed to pass away. In the clouds he saw the city of God coming down to the new earth.

And he heard a great voice from heaven say, "Behold, God's house is with men and he will dwell with them. They shall be his people and he will be their God. And God will wipe away all tears from their eyes. Never again shall they weep for sorrow. Never again shall they cry for pain. For sorrow, pain and death shall be no more."

And John saw the beautiful city of God—far more beautiful than anything he had ever seen on earth. The citizens of that city did not need the sun for light because God was their light.

John saw people from every nation of earth in that city, people whose sins had been forgiven because they believed in Jesus. He noticed that nothing wrong or unclean entered that city. Only those whose names were written in heaven's book were admitted.

John works on the Book of Revelation

John saw a river of crystal water flowing through the city. Along the banks grew the tree of life, bearing ripe fruit. And the leaves of that tree were for healing the nations.

When John saw all these things, he fell down to worship at the angel's feet. But the angel lifted him up and said, "Do not worship me, for I am just a servant. Worship God. And blessed are they who keep his commands, for they shall enter the gates of the beautiful city and eat of the fruit from the tree of life."

Jesus then said to John, "I have sent my angel to tell you these things. And whoever wishes may come and drink of the water of life freely, for the invitation is to all men. But only those who hear and obey God's words may share the blessings of heaven." Finally Jesus said, "Surely I come quickly."

And John, the aged prisoner, replied, "Even so, come, Lord Jesus."

List of Pictures

570

QUESTIONS AND ANSWERS
ON THE STORIES

QUESTIONS AND ANSWERS ON THE STORIES

These questions and answers are simple, yet clear and comprehensive. They are suited to children of junior age and above, and follow the outline of the stories as told in the Bible Story Book.

Sunday school teachers and leaders of youth will find them invaluable. Parents, after reading or telling the stories in the home, will find these questions helpful in developing the child's knowledge of Bible facts and emphasizing the thoughts presented in the stories.

Stories of the Old Testament—The Patriarchs

How the World Was Made—Page 11
1. Who made the world in which we live? (God)
2. How many days did it take God to create the world and everything in it? (Six days)
3. What did God say about everything he had made? ("It is good!")
4. What did God give to man that he did not give to other living creatures? (A soul that would never die)
5. How did God spend the seventh day of creation? (He rested)

The First Home—Page 12
1. Where did God place the first home on earth? (In the Garden of Eden)
2. Who lived in the beautiful home? (Adam and Eve)
3. What did the tempter who came to Eve look like? (A serpent)
4. Why were Adam and Eve afraid to meet God after they had eaten the forbidden fruit? (They knew they had disobeyed him)
5. What happened to them after they disobeyed God? (They had to leave the beautiful garden)

The First Children—Page 15
1. Who was the first child born into the world? (Cain)

2. What kind of work did he do when he grew up? (He worked in the fields)
3. Who was the second child born into the world? (Abel)
4. What kind of work did Abel do when he became a man? (He tended flocks of sheep)
5. What kind of offerings did these brothers bring to God? (Cain brought a fruit offering; Abel a lamb)
6. Whose offering pleased God the most? (Abel's offering)
7. Which of these men killed his brother? (Cain)

The Great Flood—Page 16
1. Who was the oldest man that ever lived? (Methuselah)
2. Why did God plan to destroy the people in the world? (They were evil and disobedient)
3. How did Noah and his three sons please God? (They tried to do right)
4. How did God save the lives of Noah's family? (He shut them in the ark when the Flood came)

The Tower of Babel—Page 18
1. On what mountain did the ark land when the floodwaters went down? (On a mountain in Ararat)

572

2. Why did the people plan to build a city and a great tower? (They did not want to become scattered over the earth)

3. What did God think about their work? (He was unhappy)

4. What did God do to the people? (He caused them to speak different languages)

5. Why did many of the people move away and leave the great tower unfinished? (They could not understand the different languages)

Abram Follows God—Page 20

1. Why did the people of Chaldea name their city Ur? (To honor the god they knew by that name)

2. How was Abram different from his neighbors and friends? (He believed in the true God and worshiped him only)

3. Who left Ur of Chaldea? (Terah and his family and servants)

4. Where did Abram's aged father die? (Haran)

5. What land did God promise to give to Abram and to his children? (The land of Canaan)

Abram and Lot Separate—Page 23

1. Who was Lot? (Abram's nephew)

2. Why were the servants of Abram and Lot quarrelling? (Over who would get the best pasture lands)

3. How did Abram show unselfishness? (He offered Lot the first choice of the pasture land)

4. To whom had God promised all the land of Canaan? (Abram)

Lot Is Captured—Page 24

1. Where did Lot move with his family? (Into Sodom)

2. What did God think about the people of Sodom? (They were wicked)

3. What happened to the people of the city? (They were captured)

4. How did Abram again show kindness to his nephew, Lot? (He rescued Lot and the other Sodomite captives)

5. Why didn't Abram accept a reward from the king of Sodom? (He had promised God he would not accept a reward)

Abram's Tent Home—Page 25

1. What reward did God promise to Abram—if he was faithful? (God promised to give him a son)

2. Why did the servant girl, Hagar, try to run away from her mistress, Sarai? (Sarai had punished her)

3. Who found her lying down to rest beside a fountain in the wilderness? (An angel of the Lord)

4. What did the angel of the Lord tell Hagar to do? (To return to her mistress and try to please her)

5. What name did Abram give to Hagar's infant son? (Ishmael)

6. Who changed the names of Abram and his wife? (God)

7. What did their new names mean? (Abraham means "The father of many;" Sarah means "princess")

Abraham's Strange Visitors—Page 28

1. How did Abraham show kindness to the strange visitors who came to his tent home? (He provided rest and food)

2. Who did Abraham's visitors turn out to be? (Heavenly beings)

3. Where were they going? (To Sodom and Gomorrah)

4. Why did Abraham plead with God to spare Sodom? (Because Lot lived in Sodom)

5. How many righteous people were living in Sodom? (Ten)

What Happened to Sodom—Page 29

1. Who entertained the angel visitors at Sodom? (Lot)

2. Whom did Lot take with him when he fled from the city? (His wife and two daughters)

3. What happened to Lot's wife? (Her body turned into a pillar of salt when she looked back)

4. Where did Lot and his daughters make their home after they left Sodom? (In a cave on the mountainside)

573

Hagar and Ishmael—Page 32

1. What did Abraham name the son God had given to him and Sarah? (Isaac)
2. Why did Sarah ask Abraham to send Ishmael and his mother away from their home? (Because Ishmael was unkind to little Isaac)
3. Who found Ishmael and his mother when they were lost in the great wilderness? (God)
4. Where did Ishmael and his mother live after they left Abraham? (In the wilderness)
5. What kind of man did Ishmael become? (A strong, wild hunter)

Abraham Offers Isaac—Page 33

1. Why did God ask Abraham to give Isaac back to him as an offering? (To test Abraham's love and obedience)
2. How did Abraham feel about God's strange request? (He felt he should obey God)
3. Who went with Abraham on his journey to the place God had appointed? (Two servants and Isaac)
4. Who carried the wood up the mountain to place on the altar? (Isaac)
5. What did Isaac ask his father as they climbed the mountain together? ("Where is the lamb for an offering?")
6. How did God provide an animal for the offering? (He caused a ram to become entangled in the bushes)

A Wife for Isaac—Page 36

1. Where did Abraham send his servant to find a wife for Isaac? (To Haran)
2. How did God answer his servant's prayer at the well? (Rebekah came to water the camels)
3. Why did Rebekah's father allow her to go with Abraham's servant to become Isaac's wife? (He believed God had guided Abraham's servant to them)

Esau Sells His Birthright—Page 39

1. What were the names of Isaac's two sons? (Esau and Jacob)
2. What did the older brother look like? (He was redheaded and hairy)

3. What was the birthright? (Twice as much inheritance as the other children would receive from their father)
4. Did Esau value his birthright? What did he do? (No. He sold it for something to eat)

Isaac and the Wells—Page 40

1. What did Isaac's jealous neighbors do to him? (They took his wells and filled them with dirt)
2. What did Isaac do about it? (He moved to another place and dug out old wells)
3. Who had dug these wells? (Abraham)
4. What did Isaac's enemies do finally? (They made peace with him)
5. Why do we remember Isaac? (He was a great peacemaker)

Isaac Blesses Jacob—Page 41

1. Why did Rebekah want Jacob to have Isaac's blessing? (Jacob was her favorite son)
2. Why couldn't Isaac tell Jacob from Esau? (Isaac was blind)
3. How did Esau feel when he learned Jacob had received the birthright? (Esau was brokenhearted and wanted to get revenge)

Jacob's Dream—Page 43

1. Why was Jacob afraid to stay at home after he received his father's blessing? (Esau was angry and threatened to kill him)
2. Who sent Jacob back to his mother's home country? (His father Isaac)
3. Why was this done? (So he would find a wife who worshiped the true God)
4. How did God encourage Jacob one night while he slept with a stone for a pillow? (God appeared to him in a dream and talked to him)
5. Jacob met someone at a well near the city of Haran. What was her name? (Rachel)

Laban Tricks Jacob—Page 45

1. How did Jacob's uncle show that he was glad to see him? (He welcomed him into his home)
2. What payment did Jacob ask for when he worked for his uncle? (He asked permission to marry Rachel)

3. How did Jacob's uncle cheat him?
(He first gave Jacob Leah for a wife instead of Rachel)

4. When Jacob started his journey home, what others went with him?
(His wives, children and servants)

5. Who warned Laban not to harm Jacob? (God)

Jacob and Esau Meet Again—Page 49

1. Why was Jacob afraid to return to Canaan?
(He thought Esau might still be angry)

2. Jacob wrestled all night with someone. Who was it? (An angel of the Lord)

3. What new name did the angel give Jacob? (Israel)

4. What did the name mean?
("A prince of God")

5. What happened when Jacob and Esau met again? (They met peaceably)

Joseph Becomes a Slave—Page 51

1. How many sons did Jacob have?
(Twelve)

2. Which of these sons was his favorite?
(Joseph)

3. Why did the older brothers hate Joseph?
(He told their father of their wrongdoing)

4. What did their hatred cause them to do?
(Sell Joseph into slavery)

Joseph, a Prisoner in Egypt—Page 54

1. Where did the Ishmaelites take Joseph?
(Egypt)

2. What did they do with him? (Sold him to an officer in the king's army)

3. Why did the Egyptian officer put Joseph into the king's prison? (The officer's wife lied about Joseph)

4. Who showed kindness to Joseph in the prison? (The keeper of the prison)

5. What did Joseph do for two of the prisoners? (He revealed the meaning of their strange dreams)

Joseph, a Ruler in Egypt—Page 56

1. Why did Pharaoh send for Joseph?
(He wanted Joseph to interpret his strange dreams)

2. What did Joseph tell Pharaoh?
(That God would make known the meaning of the dreams)

3. What did the king's dreams mean?
(Seven years of plenty, then seven years of famine in Egypt)

4. What honor did Pharaoh give Joseph? (He made him ruler over all the land of Egypt)

5. How did Joseph show his wisdom as a ruler? (He prepared for the coming famine)

6. When the years of famine came what did Joseph do with the grain he had stored away? (He sold it to the needy people)

Joseph's Dreams Come True—Page 59

1. Why did Joseph's ten brothers come to Egypt? (To buy food)

2. What did Joseph remember when his brothers bowed before him?
(His boyhood dreams)

3. Why didn't he tell them who he was right away? (He wanted to test them)

4. What did Joseph learn about his brothers' actions that pleased him?
(They had become honest men)

5. Which of the ten brothers did he keep in Egypt? (Simeon)

Joseph's Brothers Return to Egypt— Page 61

1. Why was Jacob unwilling to send Benjamin to Egypt? (He was afraid Benjamin would be hurt)

2. Why did Jacob finally let him go?
(Their food supply was nearly gone)

3. What did Joseph do when his brothers returned the second time?
(He entertained them at his own house)

4. How did Joseph feel when he saw Benjamin? (He cried)

Joseph Makes Himself Known—Page 64

1. Why did Joseph tell the steward to put his silver cup in Benjamin's sack?
(To find out how the older brothers would treat Benjamin)

2. How did the ten brothers show their love for Benjamin? (They all returned to plead for Benjamin)

3. Which of the brothers offered to become a lifetime slave in place of Benjamin? (Judah)

4. How did Joseph reveal who he was to his brothers? (He dismissed the servants, then told his brothers he was Joseph)

Joseph's Family Moves to Egypt—Page 66

1. How did Jacob react to the news that Joseph was still alive? (At first he could not believe the good news)

2. Who spoke to Jacob in a vision, telling him not to be afraid to go to Egypt? (God)

3. In what part of Egypt did Joseph place his brothers? (Goshen)

4. Where did Jacob die, and where was he buried? (He died in Goshen but was buried in Canaan)

5. What were the names of Joseph's two sons? (Manasseh and Ephraim)

Job, a Man Who Loved God—Page 69

1. What kind of man was Job? (A very rich man who feared God)

2. Who accused Job before God? (Satan)

3. How did God permit Satan to trouble Job? (Satan caused Job to lose all his possessions)

4. What kind of diseases did Satan then bring upon Job? (Very painful boils covered his body)

5. How did Job's three friends act when they visited him? (They accused him of wrongdoing)

6. How did God comfort Job at the end of his severe trial? (He blessed Job in many ways)

LAWGIVER AND LEADER

A Baby and a Basket—Page 73

1. What were the descendants of Abraham, Isaac and Jacob called? (Israelites)

2. How did the new Pharaoh treat them after they had become strong in Egypt? (He made slaves of them)

3. Why did Pharaoh command that all the baby boys should be thrown into the Nile River? (He wanted to decrease the Israelites)

4. What did Moses' mother do when she could no longer hide him? (She placed him in a basket on the Nile River)

5. What did the princess do when she found baby Moses? (She took him to be her own son)

6. Whom did she hire to be his nurse? (His mother)

Moses Becomes a Shepherd—Page 75

1. How do we know Moses did not forget his people while he lived in the king's palace? (He visited the Israelites)

2. What wrong did Moses do when he tried to help one of his people? (He killed a cruel taskmaster)

3. Why did Moses flee from Egypt? (He knew Pharaoh would try to kill him)

4. What work did Moses do in the land of Midian? (He was a shepherd)

5. How many years did Moses spend in that country? (Forty)

Moses and the Burning Bush—Page 77

1. Where was Moses when God spoke to him from a burning bush? (On the mountainside of Horeb)

2. What did God tell Moses to do? (To take off his shoes)

3. Where did God want to send Moses? (Back to Egypt)

4. Why was Moses at first unwilling to go? (He believed the task was too great)

5. What signs did God give Moses to prove that God was with him? (Moses' rod became a serpent; his hand became leprous)

6. God sent someone with Moses to speak for him. What was his name? (Aaron, Moses' brother)

Moses and Aaron Before Pharaoh— Page 80

1. Why wouldn't Pharaoh let the Israelites leave his country? (Their work helped to make Egypt rich)

2. Why did the Israelites accuse Moses and Aaron of bringing greater trouble upon them? (Pharaoh treated them worse than ever)

3. Who comforted Moses when he was unhappy because Pharaoh would not listen to his request? (God)

4. What miracle did Moses and Aaron perform when they met Pharaoh on the riverbank? (All the water in the rivers, lakes and ponds turned to blood)

"Let My People Go"—Page 82

1. How did the plague of frogs affect Pharaoh? (It worried him very much)

2. What did the Egyptian magicians tell Pharaoh when the plague of lice and fleas came? (That God's power was greater than theirs)

3. In what way was the plague of flies different from the other plagues that God had sent? (It did not affect the Israelites)

4. How did the terrible hailstorm frighten Pharaoh? (Heavy hailstones and fire fell, destroying lives and property)

5. Why did the Egyptians beg their stubborn ruler to let the Israelites go? (They feared their country would be ruined)

The Death Angel—Page 86

1. Tell about the first Passover Supper. (The Israelites ate roast lamb with cooked vegetables at midnight)

2. Why had the Egyptian people grown friendly toward the Israelites? (They believed God had sent Moses to help the Israelites)

3. What did the Israelites take with them when they left the land of Goshen? (Everything their Egyptian neighbors had given them)

4. What signs did God send to show the Israelites he was leading them on their journey? (They saw a cloud in the daytime and a pillar of fire at night)

5. Whose coffin did the Israelites carry when they left Egypt? (Joseph's)

Crossing the Red Sea—Page 88

1. Where did the Israelites make their first camp? (Along the shore of the Red Sea)

2. Why were the Israelites frightened when they realized Pharaoh's army was following them? (They saw no way to escape)

3. Whom did they blame for this trouble? (They blamed Moses)

4. How did God answer Moses' prayer? (He made a way through the Red Sea)

Water for Thirsty Travelers—Page 91

1. How was the wilderness of Shur unlike Goshen? (It was a desert)

2. Why were the Israelites disappointed when they camped at Marah? (The spring water tasted bitter)

3. How did God heal the bitter spring water at the camp? (He told Moses to cut down a tree and throw it into the water)

4. What did God promise the Israelites if they would obey him? (He would protect them)

5. Where did the Israelites pitch camp the second time in the wilderness of Shur? (At Elim)

Food for Hungry Travelers—Page 91

1. What sign did God give when he wanted the people to break camp and start on their journey? (The cloud lifted and began to move away slowly)

2. In what way did the Israelites behave like fussy children? (They found fault with Moses and Aaron)

3. How did God supply meat and bread in the wilderness of Sin? (He sent quails for meat and manna from heaven for bread)

4. How many days each week did the people gather the bread from heaven? (Six days)

5. What happened to those who disobeyed Moses by not gathering enough food for two days on the sixth morning? (When they went out on the seventh day to gather manna, they found none)

The Second Passover—Page 109

1. Where did the Israelites keep the second Passover? (In the camp near Mount Sinai)

2. Why did they keep it? (To remember the time the death angel passed over their homes in Goshen)

Quail for a Complaining People—Page 110

1. Why did God send a fire into the camp at Taberah? (Some of the people complained)

2. What did God do when the people cried for meat? (He sent lots of quail)

3. Why did Miriam get leprosy? (She complained about Moses)

4. How did Moses show his forgiveness? (He prayed for Miriam and God healed her)

The Twelve Spies—Page 113

1. Why did the Israelites want to spy in Canaan? (God told them to do it)

2. How many spies did God tell Moses to send? (Twelve)

3. What kind of report did ten of the spies bring back? (Unfavorable)

4. Who were the two faithful spies? (Caleb and Joshua)

Korah Rebels—Page 115

1. Who did Korah and his friends envy? (Moses and Aaron)

2. What happened to Korah and his friends? (They were killed by earthquake and fire)

3. What was done with the brass censers Korah and his friends had carried? (They were flattened to cover the altar as a reminder to the people that only Aaron and his sons were chosen to be priests)

Aaron's Rod—Page 117

1. How did God use a rod to prove to the Israelites his choice of a high priest? (He caused Aaron's rod to blossom)

2. Where was Aaron's rod placed? (In the tabernacle so the people would never forget that God had chosen Aaron to be the high priest)

Water at Meribah—Page 117

1. Where did Miriam die? (Kadesh)

2. What happened when the wells dried up at this same camp? (The people complained again)

3. How did Moses and Aaron displease God? (They hit the rock instead of speaking to it as God commanded)

4. How were they punished for disobeying God? (They were not allowed to lead the people into Canaan)

Troubles on the Way—Page 118

1. Why didn't Moses lead the Israelites through the land of Edom? (The Edomites would not give him permission)

2. On what mountain did Aaron die? (Mount Hor)

3. Who became the high priest in Aaron's place? (His son Eleazer)

The Brass Serpent—Page 120

1. Why did God permit fiery serpents to enter the camp of Israel? (To punish the people for complaining against him)

2. What happened to those who were bitten by the serpents? (They died)

3. Why did Moses make a serpent of brass and hang it on a pole? (God told him to do this so those who were bitten could look at it and be made well)

Victory for the Israelites—Page 121

1. What did the people do this time when they needed water? (They trusted God for it)

2. What kind of people were the Amorites? (Heathen)

3. What happened to Sihon, king of the Amorites, and to the Amorites' country? (The king was killed and the people driven out of their land)

4. Who told Moses not to be afraid of Og, the king of Bashan, or of his army? (God)

5. Near what river did the Israelites pitch their camp after taking possession of the countries of these kings? (Near the Jordan River)

579

Joshua and the Judges

2. How many days did the Israelites march around the city before the wall fell down? (Seven)

3. How many times did they march around the city on the last day? (Seven)

4. What did they do after they had marched around the city for the last time? (They stood still and shouted with a great noise)

5. Whom did the Israelites save alive? (Rahab and her family)

6. What did God command the people to do with the treasures they took from the ruined city? (He told them to carry the treasures to the tabernacle)

Because Achan Stole—Page 136

1. Why were the Israelites defeated in their first attack against Ai? (Because of Achan's sin)

2. How was Achan punished? (He was killed)

3. Tell about the Israelites' second attack against Ai. (They were victorious)

Joshua Builds the Altar of God's Law— Page 138

1. Why did Joshua lead all the Israelites to the bowl-shaped valley that lay between Mount Ebal and Mount Gerizim? (God told him to do this)

2. Who, many years before, had built an altar and worshiped God at that place? (Abraham)

3. Who read to all the people from the book in which Moses had written the laws of God? (The priests and the Levites)

4. What did the people mean when they said "Amen!" to the reading of the Law? ("Let it be so")

5. Where were these words afterwards written that everyone passing through the valley might read them? (On the stones of the altar)

Joshua Is Tricked by Strangers—Page 139

1. Why did the people of Gibeon wish to become friendly with the Israelites? (The Gibeonites were afraid of Israel)

2. Tell of their plan to deceive Joshua. (They pretended to be from a far country)

3. How did the men of Israel feel when they found out they had been fooled? (They felt angry)

4. In what way were the Gibeonites punished because they had lied to Joshua? (They became servants of the Israelites)

The Sun and the Moon Stand Still— Page 140

1. Why did the five kings of Canaan make war against the Gibeonites? (Because the Gibeonites had made peace with the Israelites)

2. Who helped the Gibeonites to gain a great victory? (Joshua and his army)

3. Why were Joshua and his soldiers not afraid to meet these kings in battle? (Because God had promised to give them the victory)

4. Why did Joshua command the sun and the moon to stand still? (His army needed more time to defeat the enemies)

5. What effect did the news of this great victory have upon the other inhabitants of Canaan? (They greatly feared the Israelites)

The Israelites Settle in Canaan— Page 141

1. Into how many parts was the land of Canaan divided? (Twelve)

2. What was each tribe to do with the Canaanites who lived in their part of the country? (They were to destroy them)

3. What request did faithful old Caleb make of Joshua? (He asked to be given the mountain and the cities where the giants lived)

4. Why was Caleb not afraid to fight against the giants of Canaan? (He knew that God would help him destroy the giants)

5. How many times each year did God want the people to meet at the tabernacle to worship him? (Three times each year)

Cities of Refuge—Page 143

1. What special work had God given to the Levites? (Teaching the law of God)

2. How many cities did God give them to live in? (Forty-eight)

3. Why were these cities scattered all through the twelve tribes? (To remind the other Israelites of the law of God)

581

4. For what purpose were the "cities of refuge"? (To protect persons who accidentally killed someone)

5. How many cities of refuge were there among the Israelites? (Six)

The Altar Beside the Jordan—Page 144

1. How many tribes had their homes on the east side of the Jordan? (Two and a half tribes)

2. Who did Joshua send with the men from these tribes when they returned to their homes after the conquest of Canaan? (He sent Levites)

3. Why did these men build an altar on the bank of the river? (To prove to coming generations that they were true Israelites)

4. Where had God commanded the Israelites to offer all sacrifices? (At Shiloh)

5. Why did the men on the west side of the river feel angry when they heard about the new altar? (They feared that these tribes were planning a separate worship)

6. Who did they send to learn why the new altar had been built? (Phinehas and ten princes of Israel)

Joshua's Farewell—Page 147

1. Why did Joshua send for all the tribes to meet him at Shechem? (He wanted to talk to them once more before he died)

2. How old was Joshua when he talked with the Israelites for the last time? (One hundred and ten years old)

3. What good promise did the people make when Joshua talked to them? (They promised to keep on obeying the words of God)

4. Why did Joshua set up a great stone under an oak tree at Shechem? (To remind the people of the promise they made to him)

5. Who became high priest after Eleazar died? (Phinehas, his son)

The Israelites Forget God—Page 149

1. What trouble came upon the Israelites because they failed to drive all the heathen nations out of Canaan? (They grew too friendly with their heathen neighbors)

2. Why did God's message bring sadness to the Israelites? (They knew that God would no longer help them drive out the heathen)

3. What great work did Othniel do for Israel? (He set them free from the rule of a cruel enemy)

4. Why did God permit the king of Mesopotamia to defeat the Israelites in battle and rule over them? (Because the Israelites had turned to idol worship)

Ehud Judges Israel—Page 150

1. Why were the Israelites unhappy when the king of Moab ruled over them? (Because the Moabites oppressed them)

2. Where did they go to sacrifice when they asked forgiveness? (To Shiloh)

3. Whom did God send to deliver them out of their troubles? (Ehud)

4. How many years did the Israelites enjoy rest from their enemies? (Eighty)

5. Who was the third judge of Israel? (Shamgar)

Deborah Leads Israel—Page 153

1. Why did the people of Israel show great respect to Deborah, the prophetess? (Because they knew God talked to her)

2. Who did Deborah call to lead the Israelites to battle against Sisera's army? (Barak)

3. Why did Barak refuse to go unless Deborah would accompany him? (Both he and his soldiers needed the encouragement she could give)

4. How did God destroy Sisera's army? (Many were drowned in a flood while the others were killed)

5. Who killed Sisera? (A woman named Jael)

Gideon Tears Down an Altar of Baal—Page 155

1. Who were the Midianites and how did they trouble Israel? (They were tent dwellers, and they robbed Israel of land and food)

2. Why did Gideon try to hide from the Midianites when he threshed out his grain? (He knew they would take his grain if they saw him at work)

3. How did God tell Gideon that he was chosen to deliver Israel? (He sent an angel)

4. How did Gideon destroy the heathen god his relatives and neighbors had worshiped? (He and ten servants tore the idol down at night)

Gideon and the Fleece—Page 158

1. What two signs proved to Gideon that God had chosen him to drive the Midianites out of the land? (First, Gideon asked for dew on the fleece only; then on the ground but not on the fleece)

2. What was Gideon's response to these two signs? (He believed God would help him)

Gideon Attacks the Midianites—Page 159

1. Why did God make Gideon's army so small? (So the Israelites would know God had given them the victory)

2. How many men left camp before the battle even began because they were so afraid? (More than two-thirds of the men)

3. How many men were left to go to battle with Gideon? (Three hundred)

4. Gideon divided his men into how many companies? (Three)

5. What did he tell them to carry in their hands? (A trumpet and a burning torch hidden inside an empty pitcher)

6. What happened during the midnight attack? (Gideon's soldiers surrounded the enemies' camp and frightened the Midianites so much they killed each other as they fled)

Abimelech Makes Himself King—Page 161

1. After Gideon died how did his son Abimelech prove himself unfit to rule Israel? (He used dishonest means to become king)

2. Why did Abimelech kill his brothers? (He feared they would not want him to rule over them)

3. Where was Abimelech crowned king? (Under an oak tree near Shechem)

4. Who spoke a parable about the trees wanting a king? (Jotham, Abimelech's youngest brother)

Jephthah Leads Israel to Victory—Page 163

1. Why did Jephthah go live in the land called Tob? (His brothers hated him and drove him away)

2. Who heard about his brave deeds and sent for him to help them? (The Israelites)

3. What foolish promise did Jephthah make to God? (That he would sacrifice the first thing that should meet him on his return home)

4. Who first met him when he returned home victorious? (His daughter)

5. For how many years did Jephthah judge Israel? (Six)

Samson's Birth Is Announced—Page 164

1. What kind of person was a Nazarite? (He was consecrated to God)

2. In what way did Samson differ from other men when he grew to manhood? (He drank no wine, nor did he ever shave or cut his hair)

Samson Chooses a Wife—Page 166

1. Where did Samson go to find a wife? (To Timnah, a Philistine town)

2. What happened at the wedding feast? (Samson's wife told her friends the answer to a riddle he had told)

3. What did Samson do then? (He became angry, left his wife and went back to his home)

Samson Angers the Philistines—Page 168

1. Why did Samson set fire to the Philistine's cornfields? (He was angry with them)

2. How did he do this? (He tied firebrands to the tails of foxes and let them run free)

3. How did Samson show his great strength to the men of Gaza? (He carried away the gates of the city on his shoulders)

Samson and Delilah—Page 169

1. The Philistines asked someone to help them discover the secret of Samson's great strength. Who was it? (Delilah)

2. Why did Samson finally tell Delilah the truth? (He became tired of her asking)

3. How was Samson captured
by his enemies?
(They cut off his long hair, then bound
him as if he were a common prisoner)

Samson Dies—Page 170

1. In what cruel way was Samson treated?
(The Philistines blinded him then made
him do heavy labor)

2. How did Samson die?
(He died with many Philistines when he
destroyed their temple)

Ruth Goes with Naomi—Page 171

1. How did Ruth the Moabitess learn
about the true God?
(From the family of Elimelech)

2. Why did Naomi and Ruth leave Moab?
(To return to Israel)

3. In what city of Israel did they make
their home? (Bethlehem)

Ruth Gleans in Boaz's Fields—Page 173

1. What rich man of Bethlehem showed
much kindness to Ruth? (Boaz)

2. How did Boaz help Ruth?
(He let her glean in his fields and made
sure she was well treated)

Boaz Marries Ruth—Page 174

1. How did God bless Ruth later?
(She and Boaz were married and
God gave them a little son)

2. What was the name of Ruth and
Boaz' son? (Obed)

Hannah Gives Samuel to the Lord—Page 176

1. What did Hannah ask God for while
she prayed at Shiloh? (A baby boy)

2. What did Hannah call her baby boy?
(Samuel)

3. Why did Hannah take little Samuel to the
Lord's house and leave him there?
(She had promised to give him
back to God)

4. What old man did Samuel live with in
Shiloh? (Eli)

God Speaks to Samuel—Page 177

1. How did God speak to Samuel one night?
(God called him by name)

2. Who told Samuel that it was God calling?
(Eli)

The Ark of God Is Captured—Page 180

1. Why did the men of Israel take the ark of
God to battle? (They believed God would
honor the presence of the ark)

2. Why did God not protect them when
the ark was in their midst? (Because the
Israelites had disobeyed him)

3. What happened to the ark of God?
(It was captured by the Philistines)

4. What happened to Eli when he heard
the ark of God had been captured?
(He fell dead)

The Ark of God Troubles the Philistines—Page 181

1. Where did the Philistines first set up
the ark? (In Dagon's temple)

2. What happened to the god Dagon
when the ark stood in his temple?
(The idol fell down before the ark)

3. What happened to the people of the
city after they had stolen the ark?
(They suffered from painful sores)

4. Why did the Philistines finally become
afraid of the ark? (They believed that the
ark had brought on their suffering)

5. How did they send the ark back to Israel?
(In a new cart drawn by two young cows)

Freedom from the Philistines—Page 184

1. What did Samuel tell Israel to do if they
wished to be delivered from the rule of the
Philistines? (Forsake idols and serve God)

2. What happened at Mizpeh when
the Israelites met with Samuel to
ask God's forgiveness?
(God frightened their enemies)

The Israelites Want a King—Page 185

1. Why did the people finally desire a king
to rule over them? (They wanted to be
like the nations around them)

2. Who gave permission for the people
to have a king? (God)

The Three Kings of United Israel

Samuel Anoints Saul—Page 187

1. The first king came from which of Israel's tribes? (Benjamin)

2. How did Samuel first meet Saul? (Saul and a servant were searching for his father's lost donkeys)

3. Why did Samuel treat Saul with such great respect at the feast? (He knew God had chosen Saul to become king of Israel)

4. Who anointed Saul to become Israel's first king? (Samuel)

Saul Is Proclaimed King—Page 189

1. Why did Samuel call the men of Israel to meet him at Mizpeh? (To present the man God had chosen to be their king)

2. Where was Saul when Samuel wanted to present him to the people? (Hiding in the baggage)

3. What did the people shout when they saw their king? ("God save the king")

Saul Rescues His People—Page 191

1. What did the Ammonites plan to do to the people of Jabesh? (Put out each person's right eye)

2. How did Saul show his kingly authority when he heard the news? (He called an army together and went to fight against the Ammonites)

Samuel Resigns as Judge of Israel— Page 192

1. At what place did Saul and his army sacrifice to the Lord after their victory over the Ammonites? (Gilgal)

2. What importance did the thunder and rainstorms at Shiloh have? (Samuel asked God to send this storm to show Israel their sin)

King Saul Offers a Sacrifice—Page 193

1. How did Jonathan, Saul's son, prove himself to be a brave leader? (He and his soldiers drove the enemy away from Gibeah)

2. With which people were the Israelites at war? (The Philistines)

3. What had the Philistines done to frighten the Israelites and to weaken their army? (They had taken away all the weapons from the Israelites)

4. Who sent for Saul to meet him at Gilgal? (Samuel)

5. How did Saul act unwisely at this time? (He offered the sacrifice that Samuel should have offered to God)

Jonathan Attacks the Philistines— Page 195

1. Who did Jonathan trust when he went with his armor-bearer to the Philistines' camp? (He trusted the Lord)

2. How did God show that he was pleased with Jonathan? (He sent an earthquake to frighten the Philistines)

3. What foolish command did Saul give that day? (That none of the soldiers should eat until evening)

4. Who disobeyed the command? (Jonathan)

5. Why did Jonathan disobey? (He did not know of the order, and he was hungry)

6. How was Jonathan's life spared? (The people would not allow Saul to kill Jonathan)

Saul Disobeys God—Page 197

1. Who did King Saul appoint as captain of his army? (Abner, his cousin)

2. Why did God send King Saul to destroy the Amalekites? (Because they had fought against the Israelites)

3. What part of God's command did the king disobey? (He spared King Agag's life, along with many cattle and sheep)

4. Who told Samuel that Saul had disobeyed God? (God)

5. Who did King Saul try to blame? (The people)

Samuel Anoints David—Page 198

1. Why was Samuel at first afraid to go to Bethlehem at God's command? (He feared that Saul might kill him)

2. What man and his sons did Samuel ask to the feast at Bethlehem? (Jesse)

3. Which of Jesse's eight sons did he not bring with him? (David)

4. What work was David doing when the messenger found him in the fields near Bethlehem? (Tending sheep)

5. What did God tell Samuel to do when David came into his presence? (Arise and anoint him to become the king of Israel)

David Plays for King Saul—Page 201

1. Why did David not become king at once after Samuel had anointed him? (Saul still claimed the throne and ruled as king)

2. What terrible thing happened to King Saul after he refused to obey God's words? (A bad spirit came to trouble him)

3. Why did King Saul send for David to come to his palace home? (He wanted a musician to entertain him)

4. In what way did David help the troubled king? (He played soft, sweet melodies that calmed troubled thoughts)

David Kills Goliath—Page 203

1. To what nation did the giant Goliath belong? (The Philistine nation)

2. What did Goliath ask the army of Israel? (To send one of their soldiers to fight him)

3. On what two occasions had God given wonderful strength to David, the shepherd boy? (When he killed a lion and a bear)

4. Why did David leave the sheep and visit the camp of Israel? (His father sent him to check on his brothers)

5. How did David show his courage and his faith in God when he heard the giant defy the army of Israel? (He asked permission to accept the giant's challenge)

6. How did David kill the giant? (With the help of Israel's God, David killed Goliath with a pebble)

Saul Becomes David's Enemy—Page 206

1. After he had slain the giant Goliath, David formed a lifetime friendship with what brave young prince? (Jonathan)

2. Why wouldn't King Saul permit David to return to his father's home? (He needed brave young men in his army)

3. What made King Saul jealous of David? (He heard others praise David more highly than himself)

4. How did Saul try on two occasions to kill David? (Saul threw a spear at David while he played on his harp)

Jonathan and Michal Save David's Life—Page 209

1. How did Prince Jonathan prove himself to be David's friend? (He pleaded for David's life)

2. How did David's wife help him to escape from the king's guard? (She let him out of a window and he escaped in the darkness)

3. Where did David go when he ran away from Saul? (To Samuel)

4. What happened to the messengers and to King Saul when they came to Samuel's home seeking David? (Instead of harming David, they bowed and worshiped God)

Jonathan Warns David—Page 210

1. What did Prince Jonathan take into the fields one day? (A little boy)

2. What did the prince ask the boy to do? (To pick up the arrows he shot)

3. Who was hiding behind a great rock in the field? (David)

4. What sad news did Prince Jonathan bring to David? (King Saul was determined to kill David)

5. What promise did David make to the prince before they parted? (That he would always be kind to Jonathan and to his children)

David Flees for His Life—Page 213

1. Why did David visit the tabernacle and talk with the high priest? (He was hungry and without weapons)

2. Who saw David talking with the high priest? (Doeg)

3. Why did David afterwards go to the land of the Philistines? (He feared that Doeg would tell Saul what happened at the tabernacle)

4. In what cave did David hide? (Adullam)

5. How did three of David's soldiers risk their lives to please him? (They drew water from Bethlehem's well to bring him a drink)

Saul Orders the Priests' Death—Page 214

1. Why did King Saul send for Ahimelech, the high priest?
   (Doeg had told Saul that Ahimelech had given food and a sword to David)

2. How did Ahimelech's reply to the king's question cost him his life?
   (Ahimelech spoke well of David)

3. Why wouldn't King Saul's soldiers obey his command to kill all the priests? (They feared God more than they did Saul)

4. Who finally consented to do the wicked deed? (Doeg)

5. Who was with David when he heard the sad news? (One of Ahimelech's sons who escaped)

Saul Hunts David—Page 216

1. How did David show his kingly spirit at Keilah? (He drove away the Philistines who had been troubling the people)

2. Who warned David to leave the city lest King Saul kill him there? (God)

3. Where did David and Prince Jonathan have their farewell visit? (In the woods)

David Spares Saul's Life—Page 217

1. Why wouldn't David permit his soldiers to kill King Saul when Saul lay asleep in the cave? (Because Saul was God's anointed king over Israel)

2. How did Saul act when he discovered that David had spared his life? (Saul was sorry he had ever tried to kill David)

David Finds Saul Asleep—Page 218

1. What happened during David's visit to King Saul's camp one night?
   (Everyone was asleep and David took Saul's spear and water bottle)

2. Who was the captain of Saul's army? (Abner)

Saul Dies—Page 220

1. Why did King Saul decide to visit the witch at Endor? (He wanted advice)

2. What message did King Saul receive? (He and his sons would be killed the next day)

3. What noble prince was killed the following day? (Prince Jonathan)

4. How did King Saul die?
   (He fell on his own sword)

David Mourns for Saul and Jonathan—Page 222

1. What happened to the city where David and his soldiers lived?
   (It was burned)

2. What did David do when he heard of Jonathan's death?
   (He mourned bitterly for his friend)

3. How did David act when he heard that his enemy, King Saul, was dead?
   (He showed genuine sorrow)

4. Where did David make his home when he returned to the land of Israel?
   (Hebron)

David Becomes King—Page 224

1. Why did the chief men of all the tribes finally ask David to be their king?
   (They saw that God was with David)

2. In what city did David set up his capital?
   (Jerusalem)

3. How did the ark finally get to the new tabernacle in Jerusalem?
   (Priests carried it on their shoulders)

The Lame Prince—Page 225

1. Whose son was the little lame prince?
   (Jonathan's son)

2. How did he become crippled?
   (He was dropped by his nurse)

3. Why did King David send for him after he had grown to manhood?
   (David remembered his promise to Jonathan)

4. What kindness did King David show to Mephibosheth for Jonathan's sake?
   (He restored to him his grandfather's land and servants)

David's Sin—Page 227

1. God sent someone to speak to King David about his great sin—who was it?
   (Nathan, the prophet)

2. What punishment did God say would fall upon the king because of his wrongdoing?
   (He would have much trouble in his home life)

3. How did King David show that he was sorry for his sin against God?
   (He wept and prayed for God's forgiveness)

Absalom Tries to Become King— Page 228

1. What kind of prince was young Absalom? (Proud, selfish and deceitful)

2. How did he succeed in stealing the hearts of the people away from his father David? (He performed kind services for them)

3. What excuse did he make when he asked the king permission to go to Hebron? (He said he wanted to worship God there)

4. Why did King David and his faithful servants leave Jerusalem when they heard what had taken place at Hebron? (They feared they would all be killed)

Absalom Loses His Life—Page 230

1. Why did Absalom go to battle with his soldiers? (He believed his soldiers would be more eager to fight if he led them)

2. How many companies did David divide his servants into before sending them out to battle? (Three)

3. In what woods did the battle take place? (Ephraim)

4. How did Absalom meet his death? (He was caught by his hair in the limbs of a tree and Joab killed him)

5. What did King David do when he heard how the battle had ended? (He mourned bitterly for Absalom)

David Counts His Soldiers—Page 232

1. Why was God displeased when King David counted the number of soldiers in Israel? (He did not want Israel to trust in its own strength)

2. What did David do when he saw the angel over Jerusalem? (He cried to God and confessed his sin, pleading for mercy)

3. Why did the king build an altar on the top of Mount Moriah? (He wanted to present his offerings to God at that place)

Solomon Becomes King—Page 234

1. Who tried to take the throne when King David became too old to rule over Israel? (Adonijah, his son)

2. Why was the prophet Nathan displeased with Adonijah's plans? (He knew God had chosen Solomon to be the next king)

3. How did King David show the people the one he had chosen to take his throne? (He had Solomon ride on the king's mule and had servants proclaim him king)

4. How did Solomon show kindness to his older brother? (By allowing him to live in safety)

God Gives Solomon a Gift—Page 237

1. What kind of man was Solomon? (He trusted God and tried to do right)

2. How did God speak to him at Gibeon? (In a dream)

3. What did Solomon ask God for? (Wisdom to rule the people well)

4. How can we know today that Solomon was indeed a wise man? (By his writings and deeds)

Solomon Builds the Temple—Page 238

1. Why was God unwilling for King David to build the temple? (Because King David had been a man of war)

2. Where did Solomon get wood for the temple building? (In the mountains of Lebanon)

3. How many years did it take to finish the great temple? (Seven)

4. Who attended the first religious service at the temple? (All the men of Israel)

5. What sign did God send so the people would know he was pleased with the temple? (God filled the temple with a cloud of glory)

The Queen of Sheba Visits Solomon— Page 241

1. Why did the Queen of Sheba come to see Solomon? (To see if he was as wise and as rich as people said)

2. What did she discover? (Solomon was twice as great and wise as had been reported)

Solomon's Last Days—Page 242

1. Who led King Solomon into idolatry? (His heathen wives)

2. Why did the people of Israel become dissatisfied with Solomon's rule? (They had to pay heavy taxes to carry on his building projects)

3. Who was Jeroboam?
(The overseer of Solomon's workmen)

4. What happened at a meeting of Ahijah the prophet and Jeroboam in a field outside Jerusalem? (A strange sign showed Ahijah that Jeroboam would rule over ten tribes of Israel)

The Divided Kingdom

Revolt Against Rehoboam—Page 245
1. Who was chosen to sit on David's throne after King Solomon died?
(Rehoboam, Solomon's son)
2. Who did the people of Israel call back from Egypt before they were ready to crown their new king? (Jeroboam)
3. To whose advice did Prince Rehoboam listen? (The young men's)
4. What was the result?
(Nearly all the people refused to acknowledge Rehoboam)
5. Which one of the twelve tribes crowned Rehoboam king? (Judah)

Idol Worship Under Jeroboam—Page 246
1. The ten tribes chose what person as their ruler? (Jeroboam)
2. Where was the new kingdom set up?
(At Shechem)
3. Why did King Jeroboam plan to change the religious worship of his people?
(He feared a united worship might lead to a reuniting of all the tribes)
4. Where did he set up new altars?
(At Bethel and Dan)
5. What form of idolatry did he introduce?
(The worship of golden calves)

Jeroboam's Wife Visits Ahijah—Page 249
1. Why were the king and queen of Israel worried about their little son Abijah?
(He was very ill)
2. Who did King Jeroboam want to speak with about this child? (A prophet of God)
3. Why did the queen disguise herself as a poor woman when she went to visit the prophet? (She did not want him to know her)
4. What did Ahijah tell Jeroboam's wife?
(The kingdom would be taken away from Jeroboam)

Rehoboam Turns to Idols—Page 250
1. Who taught Prince Rehoboam to worship idols? (His mother, a heathen princess)
2. What did the people do when their king bowed down to idols?
(They worshiped idols too)

Asa Follows God—Page 251
1. In what way was King Asa different from his father and his grandfather?
(He ruled wisely and tried to restore the worship of God)
2. Why did King Asa refuse to permit his grandmother to be queen of Judah?
(She was an idol worshiper)
3. How did God help King Asa when a strong army came to fight his people?
(His smaller army defeated the enemy with God's help)

Trouble Between Israel and Judah—Page 252
1. What mistake did King Asa make when he tried to hinder the plans of King Baasha?
(He asked a heathen king to help him instead of trusting in God for help and victory)
2. Who warned Asa that he had done wrong?
(The prophet)

Elijah Is Fed by Ravens—Page 253
1. What kind of person was Ahab's wife, Queen Jezebel? (A heathen)
2. Why did God send the prophet Elijah to speak to King Ahab?
(To warn Ahab of the drought)
3. Why did Elijah seek a hiding place by the brook Cherith?
(God told him to hide there from the angry king)
4. Tell how God cared for his prophet while he lived by the brook.
(He caused birds to carry food to Elijah every morning and evening)

A Widow Feeds Elijah—Page 254

1. Where did God send Elijah when the waters of the brook dried up? (To a poor widow who lived in a heathen city)

2. How did Elijah reward the widow for her kindness to him? (When her son died Elijah prayed and God restored him to life)

Elijah Comes Out of Hiding—Page 256

1. How long did the famine and drought last in the land of Israel and countries nearby? (Three years)

2. Why did King Ahab search everywhere for the missing prophet? (He believed it would not rain until Elijah announced it)

3. Why wasn't Elijah afraid to meet the angry king? (He knew God had sent him back to speak to Ahab)

Elijah and the Prophet of Baal—Page 257

1. Why did Elijah want to meet the prophets of Baal? (To prove to them who was the true God)

2. How did Elijah prove to all the people that the Lord is God? (He called down fire from heaven to consume his sacrifice)

Elijah, the Little Cloud and the Great Rain—Page 260

1. What happened to the priests of Baal after God sent fire to burn up Elijah's sacrifice? (They were all killed)

2. What was Elijah doing while King Ahab and the people feasted on top of the mountain? (He was praying)

3. How many times did Elijah ask God to send rain? (Seven times)

4. What message did Elijah send to King Ahab when he heard that a little cloud was rising in the sky? (He told him to hurry back to the city before the rain came)

Elijah Under the Juniper Tree—Page 262

1. Where did the angel find Elijah? (In the wilderness south of Judah)

2. Why was the prophet feeling so unhappy? (He feared Queen Jezebel)

3. For how many days did Elijah live on the strength he received from eating the angel's food? (Forty days)

Elijah and the Still Small Voice—Page 264

1. Who talked with Elijah when he hid in the cave? (God)

2. How did God comfort the unhappy prophet? (He told Elijah that many others were true worshipers)

3. What person did Elijah anoint to be the next great prophet? (Elisha)

Ahab and the King of Syria—Page 265

1. Who helped King Ahab's soldiers drive the Syrian army out of the land of Israel? (God)

2. Why did the Syrians plan to fight in the valley? (They believed Israel's God was a god of the hills)

3. What happened to the city where many of the Syrian soldiers had run to hide? (Its wall fell down and killed thousands of soldiers)

4. Why did Ahab spare the life of the Syrian king? (He felt sorry for him)

5. How did God's prophet accuse King Ahab? (He said, "You must pay for his life with your own")

Naboth's Vineyard—Page 267

1. Why didn't Naboth want to sell his vineyard to King Ahab? (Because it was his inheritance)

2. How did the king act when he found he could not have Naboth's vineyard? (He pouted like a spoiled child)

3. How did Jezebel help Ahab get the vineyard? (She ordered the rulers to try Naboth for treason and have him killed)

4. Who met Ahab when he went to take Naboth's vineyard? (Elijah)

5. What message did Elijah have for Ahab? (That he and Jezebel and all their sons would soon be killed)

Ahab's Son Becomes King—Page 268

1. Who became king when Ahab died? (His son Ahaziah)

2. When Ahaziah was ill who did he call for help? (An idol in Philistia)

3. What message did God send to him through Elijah? (God said that he would never be cured)

4. How did King Ahaziah feel toward Elijah for sending him such a message? (He was angered)

Elijah and the Chariot of Fire—Page 269

1. Who accompanied Elijah on his last journey to visit the young prophets' schools? (Elisha)

2. Why wouldn't Elisha leave Elijah? (He wanted to be with Elijah when God sent for him)

3. In what miraculous way did God provide a crossing at the river Jordan for his two prophets? (God made a dry path through the river)

4. What last request did Elisha make of his master? (He asked for a double portion of Elijah's spirit)

5. How was Elijah taken to heaven? (With a chariot of fire in a whirlwind)

Elisha Saves Two Boys from Slavery—Page 271

1. A poor widow told her troubles to what prophet? (Elisha)

2. What did the prophet advise her to do? (Borrow many empty vessels)

3. Who helped her obey the prophet's words? (Her two sons)

4. Why didn't the widow's pot of oil run out? (Because God miraculously kept it filled)

5. How did she pay off the debt her husband had owed the rich man? (She sold the oil in the borrowed vessels)

A Room for Elisha—Page 273

1. Who entertained Elisha and his servant whenever they passed through Shunem? (A rich woman and her husband)

2. How did God reward the Shunammite woman and her husband for their kindness to his prophet? (He gave them a child)

Elisha and the Shunammite's Son—Page 274

1. What great sorrow came to the Shunammite family? (The son became sick and died)

2. Why did the Shunammite woman at once search for Elisha? (She believed that Elisha could restore the child's life)

3. How did God answer Elisha's prayer? (God brought the child to life again)

The School of the Prophets—Page 276

1. How did Elisha remove the poison from the food the prophets were eating? (He threw some meal into the dish of poisoned food)

2. What was the miracle of the twenty barley loaves and some ears of new grain? (God multiplied the food until there was enough to feed one hundred men)

3. When did God cause iron to float? (When an ax head fell into the Jordan)

A Little Slave Girl Helps Naaman—Page 277

1. How did the little Israelite girl come to live in Syria? (She had been stolen and sold as a slave)

2. Where did she live as a slave? (In the home of Naaman who was captain of the Syrian army)

3. What terrible disease afflicted Naaman? (Leprosy)

4. Who told Naaman that Israel's prophet could cure him? (The slave girl)

5. What happened when Naaman followed Elisha's instructions? (He was entirely cured of the leprosy)

Elisha's Foolish Servant—Page 281

1. What did Elisha's servant do that was foolish? (He accepted the gifts Naaman offered Elisha)

2. How did Elisha feel about this? (He was disappointed in his servant for going behind his back and lying about it)

Joash, the Boy King—Page 282

1. How old was Prince Joash when he was crowned king? (Seven years old)

2. He had been hidden from what member of his family? (His grandmother)

3. Why had this been done? (She had killed his brothers and sisters)

4. What happened to wicked Queen Athaliah after Joash was crowned king? (She was killed)

Joash Repairs the Temple—Page 285

1. Who ruled the people until Joash became old enough?
(His uncle Jehoiada the high priest)

2. How did Joash collect money to repair the temple? (He had a box placed at the door of the temple, and the people put offerings in the box)

God Protects Elisha—Page 286

1. How did Jehoram learn about the plans of the Syrian king?
(Elisha the prophet told him)

2. Why was Elisha's servant alarmed when he saw the Syrian army?
(He feared that he and Elisha would be captured and killed)

3. What wonderful sight did the servant behold after Elisha asked God to open his eyes? (He saw the angels God had sent)

4. What kindness did the prophet command King Jehoram to show to his captives?
(To feed them and send them away)

Food for a Starving City—Page 287

1. Why were the people of Samaria starving?
(Because the Syrian army camped around the city and would not allow food to be brought in)

2. Who did King Jehoram say was to blame for the famine in the city?
(Elisha the prophet)

3. What strange words did Elisha tell the king when the king came to kill the prophet? (That food would be plentiful in the city the next day)

4. What frightened the Syrian army away from the city? (God caused them to hear a strange noise that sounded like an army approaching)

5. Who first discovered that the enemy had gone? (Four lepers)

Jonah Disobeys God—Page 290

1. Why did God wish to send a prophet to Nineveh? (No one had ever warned the Ninevites of God's punishment)

2. Who did God choose to go on this errand?
(Jonah)

3. Why did Jonah try to run away from God?
(He did not want to preach to the Ninevites)

4. How was Jonah's life spared?
(God heard his cry for mercy and gave him a second chance)

Jonah Preaches at Nineveh—Page 292

1. What did the people of Nineveh do when they heard Jonah's words?
(They repented of their great sins)

2. How did Jonah feel when the people repented? (Disappointed)

Isaiah and Hosea, Two Great Prophets—Page 293

1. Where was Isaiah when the Lord called him to be a prophet?
(In the temple at Jerusalem)

2. How many kings of Judah reigned during Isaiah's life? (Four)

3. Which king paid most attention to God's messages? (Hezekiah)

4. Hosea preached to what people?
(To the kings and people of Israel)

Israel Is Enslaved—Page 294

1. Why did God permit the kingdom of Israel to be destroyed?
(The people refused to return to true worship)

2. Who came to live in the land of Israel after the Israelites were carried away into captivity? (Heathen people from countries lying to the east)

3. Who did the King of Assyria send to teach the new people about the true God?
(A priest of the Israelites)

4. What kind of religion did the people of that land then have?
(A mixture of the false and true religions)

Good King Hezekiah—Page 295

1. How did King Hezekiah restore the worship of the true God in Judah?
(He commanded the people to keep the Passover Feast)

2. Why was King Hezekiah frightened when he heard the message the Assyrian king had sent?
(He knew the Assyrians could easily destroy his kingdom)

3. Why didn't the Assyrians attack?
(The soldiers became very sick and many died)

God Spares Hezekiah's Life—Page 297

1. Why did God add fifteen years to King Hezekiah's life? (To answer Hezekiah's prayer)

2. By what sign was Hezekiah assured he would be made well? (The shadows on the sun dial moved backward instead of forward)

Josiah and the Forgotten Book—Page 298

1. Why had the book of Moses been forgotten? (Because the true worship of God had been neglected so long)

2. Who found the book under rubbish in the temple? (The high priest)

3. What did King Josiah do when he heard the words read from the book of Moses? (He tore his clothes and wept bitterly)

4. How do we know that Josiah was a good king? (He tried to serve God)

Five Other Prophets—Page 301

1. What kind of work did Amos do? (He was a shepherd)

2. What prophet was a descendant of Hezekiah? (Zephaniah)

3. What prophet was one of the temple singers? (Habakkuk)

4. What messages did Micah and Nahum bring? (Micah spoke for the poor and Nahum warned Nineveh)

Jeremiah Answers God's Call—Page 302

1. Who was Jeremiah's father? (Hilkiah, a priest)

2. Why did Jeremiah become a prophet? (God called him)

Jeremiah Warns the People—Page 303

1. What did Jeremiah warn the people about? (Punishment for sin)

2. Why was Jeremiah put out of the temple? (Because the people did not like to listen to his warnings)

Jeremiah Writes God's Words in a Book—Page 304

1. Why were the princes of Judah alarmed when they heard the words of God that Jeremiah's friend had written? (They believed God's punishment would surely fall upon them)

2. How did the words of God affect the wicked king? (He burned the scroll Jeremiah's friend had written)

Jeremiah in the Dungeon—Page 305

1. Why was Jeremiah thrown into a dungeon beneath the prison? (Because he spoke the words God gave him)

2. How was Jeremiah later taken out of the dungeon? (He was pulled out with ropes that had been lowered to him)

3. Why is Jeremiah called the weeping prophet? (Because he wept for the sufferings of his people)

Stories About the Jews

Captives in a Strange Land—Page 309

1. What were the Israelites called after they were taken captive to Babylon? (Jews)

2. How did their new ruler treat them? (He gave them fields and houses)

3. What faithful prophets brought God's messages to them? (Jeremiah wrote letters to them and Ezekiel lived among them)

4. Why wouldn't the Jews worship the idols of their heathen neighbors? (They knew that idol worship had brought them into captivity)

Daniel in the King's Court—Page 311

1. Why were Daniel and his three friends unwilling to eat food from the king's table? (They wanted to keep the laws of God)

2. What request did Daniel make of the king's officer? (He asked to be fed only vegetables, water and bread)

3. What favorable change did the officer observe in Daniel and his friends at the end of the ten days' trial? (They looked healthier than their companions)

4. What did the king's examination of these young princes reveal? (They were the wisest men in all of the kingdom)

Daniel and the King's Dream—Page 312

1. What strange request did King Nebuchadnezzar make of his wise men? (He asked them to tell what his dream was and what it meant)

2. Why did he threaten to kill every one of them? (Because they said that no one could tell what his dream was or what it meant)

3. Who asked the king to spare the lives of the wise men? (Daniel)

4. How did the king honor Daniel after he had told the dream and its interpretation? (He made Daniel ruler of all the province of Babylon)

The Fiery Furnace—Page 316

1. Why did King Nebuchadnezzar command all the princes, rulers and officers in his kingdom to come to the plain of Dura? (He wanted them to worship the god he had made)

2. Why had the king prepared a fiery furnace? (He threatened to cast those who would not bow to this image into the furnace)

3. Why did Shadrach, Meshach and Abednego refuse a second opportunity to bow down before the image? (They loved God and would not dishonor him)

4. What strange sight did King Nebuchadnezzar see in the fiery furnace? (He saw a fourth person walking in the furnace with the three men)

5. What did King Nebuchadnezzar now think about the God of those three men? (He believed the God of the Jews should be respected by everyone)

Nebuchadnezzar Loses His Mind—Page 319

1. Why was Daniel at first afraid to tell King Nebuchadnezzar the meaning of his second strange dream? (He knew the dream pronounced judgment upon the proud king)

2. How did God cause the dream to come true? (The king lost his mind and became like a wild beast)

3. How did Nebuchadnezzar show his change of heart after God permitted his mind to be restored? (He thanked God for his mercies)

The Handwriting on the Wall—Page 320

1. How did Belshazzar dishonor the vessels of gold which his grandfather King Nebuchadnezzar had taken from the temple in Jerusalem? (He and his companions drank wine from them)

2. Why did happiness suddenly die out of King Belshazzar's heart during the feast? (He saw the fingers of a man's hand writing strange words on the wall)

3. What did Daniel tell the king that the strange writing meant? (He said that God would take the kingdom from him)

4. What happened to the kingdom of Babylon that same night? (An enemy entered the city, killed Belshazzar and overthrew the kingdom)

Daniel in the Lions' Den—Page 323

1. What honorable position did King Darius give to Daniel? (He made Daniel the first president in his kingdom)

2. Why did the princes and presidents hate Daniel? (They envied him)

3. How did these wicked men plan to get rid of Daniel? (They flattered the king into making an unfair law)

4. How did the king feel when he heard that Daniel had broken the decree? (He regretted having made the law)

5. Tell how God cared for Daniel in the lions' den. (He shut the mouths of the hungry beasts and made them harmless)

Daniel Prophesies—Page 326

1. What did Daniel pray for very earnestly when he became an old man? (He wanted God to forgive the sins of his people)

2. Who did God send to comfort Daniel? (An angel)

3. Who visited Daniel at the riverside? (God sent an angel to tell Daniel many things which he later wrote in a book)

4. How did Daniel rank among the prophets? (He was one of the greatest)

The Homecoming of the Jews—Page 327

1. What king permitted the Jews to return to Judah and rebuild the temple? (King Cyrus)

2. Who became leader of the company of returning Jews? (Zerubbabel)

3. Why didn't all the Jews return to Jerusalem? (Many did not want to)

4. What did the priests and the Levites do as soon as they had located the ruins of the temple?
(They rebuilt the altar and offered sacrifices to God)

Trouble in Rebuilding the Temple—Page 329

1. How did the people celebrate when the foundation of the new temple was laid?
(They praised God with shouting and singing and with musical instruments)

2. Why weren't Zerubbabel and Jeshua, the high priest, willing to let the Samaritans assist in building the new temple?
(Because the Samaritans did not worship God the right way)

Beautiful Esther Becomes Queen—Page 330

1. Who did Esther live with as she grew up?
(With her cousin, Mordecai)

2. Who sent Esther to the king's palace?
(Mordecai)

3. What did the king do when Esther was brought before him?
(He chose her to become the new queen)

4. How did Mordecai save the king's life?
(He warned the king of a secret plot to kill him)

Haman Plans to Kill the Jews—Page 331

1. Why was Haman angry with Mordecai?
(Because Mordecai would not bow to honor Haman when he passed)

2. How did Haman finally plan to get revenge on Mordecai? (He planned to have all Jewish people destroyed)

3. Why did the king consent to Haman's wicked plan? (He thought the Jews were an unprofitable people)

4. Why didn't Mordecai go to the palace to send a message to Queen Esther?
(No one dressed in mourning dared enter the palace gate)

Queen Esther Is Troubled—Page 334

1. Who told Queen Esther about Haman's wicked plot?
(A messenger she had sent to talk with Mordecai)

2. What did Mordecai tell Esther to do?
(To go to the king and plead for her life and the lives of her people)

Esther Goes to the King—Page 335

1. Why did Haman feel honored when Queen Esther invited him to attend her banquet? (Because he was the only invited guest to eat with the king and queen)

2. Who urged Haman to erect a gallows for Mordecai's hanging? (His wife and friends)

The King Honors Mordecai—Page 336

1. Why did the king plan to honor Mordecai?
(Mordecai had saved the king's life)

2. Who did Haman think the king planned to honor? (Haman)

3. Who led Mordecai through the streets shouting, "This is done to the man the king delights to honor"? (Haman)

Esther Pleads for Her People—Page 337

1. Who was hanged on the gallows Haman had built for Mordecai? (Haman)

2. What feast do Jews observe in honor of the time Esther saved her people? (Purim)

The Temple Is Finished—Page 338

1. Who encouraged the people to rebuild the temple? (Haggai)

2. Who tried to stop the work?
(The Samaritans)

3. Who had commanded the Jews to rebuild the temple? (Cyrus)

Ezra Teaches God's Law—Page 340

1. Why was Ezra the priest called a scribe?
(Because he wrote the words of God in books)

2. For what purpose did the king of Persia send Ezra to Judah? (To teach the Jews the law of God)

3. Why was Ezra ashamed to ask the king for soldiers to protect his company from bands of robbers along the way to Judah? (He had told the king that God would care for those who served him)

4. Who did they ask to take care of them?
(They asked God to protect them)

5. How did Ezra show his interest in the true service of God when he reached Jerusalem?
(He taught the people God's law)

Nehemiah, the King's Cupbearer—Page 341

1. Who brought messages to Nehemiah from the land of Judah? (His brother and other men from Judah)

2. Why did Nehemiah weep when he heard the news from Jerusalem? (He was upset by the sad news)

3. What kindness did the king show to Nehemiah? (He sent Nehemiah to rebuild the walls of Jerusalem)

4. How did Nehemiah's midnight ride around Jerusalem strengthen his resolve? (He rode quietly around the ruined walls to see how much work needed to be done, then decided to begin the work at once)

The Walls of Jerusalem Are Rebuilt—Page 344

1. Who tried to hinder the rebuilding of Jerusalem's wall? (Sanbalat and Tobiah, two enemies who lived near Jerusalem)

2. Why did Nehemiah and his workmen carry swords and spears while they worked on the wall? (Their enemies threatened to engage them in battle)

3. How long did it take to finish the wall? (Fifty-two days)

The People Worship God—Page 345

1. What feast did the Jews keep after they heard the words of the Law? (Feast of the Booths)

2. Who was the last prophet that God sent to speak to the Jews during Old Testament times? (Malachi)

Stories of the New Testament—Stories about Jesus

An Angel Visits the Temple—Page 355

1. Why had Zacharias left his home in the hill country of Judah and gone to Jerusalem? (His turn had come to work in the temple)

2. What was Zacharias doing when an angel visited in the temple? (He was burning incense on the golden altar in the holy place)

3. What were the people who stood in the court outside doing? (Praying)

4. What wonderful news did the angel bring to Zacharias? (That he and his wife Elizabeth would have a son)

5. Why was Zacharias stricken dumb? (At first he did not believe the angel's message)

The Angel Visits Mary—Page 356

1. Gabriel visited what young woman in Nazareth? (Mary)

2. What did he tell her? (Jesus would be born)

3. What other promised child did the angel mention to Mary? (The child soon to be born to Zacharias and Elizabeth)

4. Why was Elizabeth glad when Mary came to visit her? (God let her know that Mary would become the mother of Jesus)

5. Who told Joseph about the secret of Jesus' birth? (God's angel)

A Baby Named John—Page 357

1. What did Zacharias and Elizabeth prepare to do when their child was eight days old? (To announce his name)

2. What did the relatives and friends want to name the child? (Zacharias, after his father)

3. Why did both his parents wish to call him John? (Because the angel had told Zacharias to call the child by that name)

4. What happened to Zacharias after the baby had been given a name? (His speech was restored to him)

A Wonderful Baby's Birth—Page 358

1. Why did Joseph and Mary journey to Bethlehem? (As descendants of David, they were required to register for taxation in that city)

2. Where did they find lodging when they came to Bethlehem? (In the stable of the inn)

3. Why did the angels watch over Bethlehem one night while Mary and Joseph were there? (Because Jesus the Savior was born on that night)

4. Who heard the glorious message of the angels? (Shepherds in a field)

5. Where did the shepherds go after they had heard the angel? (Bethlehem)

The Wise Men Follow a Star—Page 362

1. What wonderful meaning did the new star have to the Wise Men in the East? (They believed it announced the birth of the Messiah)

2. Why did the Wise Men decide to journey to Judah? (They wanted to worship the newborn king of the Jews)

3. When the Wise Men stopped in Jerusalem who did they ask about the newborn King? (They asked Herod, king at that time)

4. What request did King Herod make of the Wise Men when he sent them away to Bethlehem? ("Bring me word at once when you have found the child")

5. How did God help the Wise Men to find the baby Jesus? (The star led them to the place where Joseph and Mary were living)

When Jesus Was a Boy—Page 364

1. How old was Jesus when Joseph and Mary took him to the feast at Jerusalem? (He was twelve years old)

2. How did Jesus disappoint Joseph and Mary? (He remained behind when their group started homeward)

3. How many days did they search before they found Jesus? (Three)

4. What was Jesus doing when they found him? (He was asking questions of the wise teachers in the temple)

John Preaches in the Wilderness— Page 368

1. Why was the wilderness preacher called John the Baptist? (Because he baptized many who came to him in the Jordan River)

2. John reminded people of what great prophet? (Elijah)

John Baptizes Jesus—Page 371

1. Why did Jesus ask John to baptize him? (He knew God wanted him to receive John's baptism)

2. How did John know that Jesus was God's promised Savior? (The Spirit of God in the form of a dove landed on Jesus' head)

Jesus Is Tempted—Page 371

1. Who found Jesus alone in the wilderness? (Satan)

2. How long had Jesus been without food? (Forty days)

3. Why wouldn't Jesus turn stones into bread? (Jesus would not use his great power to please himself)

4. Why did Satan want Jesus to throw himself down from the pinnacle of the temple? (To prove that he was the Son of God)

5. What did Satan promise to give to Jesus if he would fall down and worship him? (All the kingdoms of the world)

Jesus Makes Five New Friends—Page 373

1. What did John say when he saw Jesus walking by? ("Behold the Lamb of God, who bears the sin of the world")

2. Why did two of John's disciples follow Jesus that day? (They wanted to learn more about him)

3. Who brought Simon to Jesus? (His brother Andrew)

4. What new name did Jesus give to Simon? (Peter)

5. Why did Philip become a follower of Jesus? (He believed Jesus was the Messiah—the one God had promised)

6. Who did Philip then bring to Jesus? (His friend, Nathanael)

The Wedding at Cana—Page 376

1. Where did Jesus perform his first miracle? (In Cana, a town in Galilee)

2. Why were the servants careful to do just as Jesus told them? (Because Mary, his mother, told them to do so)

3. What did the governor of the feast say about the wine that Jesus had made from water? (That it was the best they had served at the feast)

Jesus Keeps the Passover—Page 377

1. What did Jesus do when he saw the disorder in the temple court? (He drove out the oxen and the sheep and the men who sold them)

2. What did Jesus say that his Father's house should be used for? (A place of prayer)

Nicodemus Comes to Jesus—Page 378

1. What Pharisee wanted to meet with Jesus? (Nicodemus)

2. What did Nicodemus think of Jesus after he had visited with him? (He believed more strongly than ever that Jesus had come from God)

The Woman at the Well—Page 380

1. Why did Jesus stop by the well in Samaria? (He was tired)

2. Who came to draw water from the well while Jesus sat there? (A woman from Sychar, a city nearby)

3. Why was the woman of Samaria surprised when Jesus asked her for a drink? (Because the Jews did not associate with the Samaritans)

4. Why did the woman believe that Jesus was a prophet? (Because he seemed to know about everything she had done)

5. Who did Jesus tell the woman that he was? (The Messiah for whom the people were looking)

Jesus Heals a Nobleman's Son—Page 382

1. Why did the nobleman from Capernaum wish to see Jesus? (Because his son lay sick with a burning fever)

2. Where did he go to find Jesus? (He went to Cana)

3. Why didn't Jesus go with the nobleman? (To test the man's faith)

4. What happened to the sick child while the father was talking with Jesus? (The fever left him)

Jesus Speaks at Nazareth—Page 384

1. Why did the people of Nazareth become displeased with Jesus' teaching? (They did not want to believe God cared for people who were not Jews)

2. What did they attempt to do with Jesus? (To kill him)

3. In what city did Jesus make his home? (Capernaum)

Many Fish—Page 385

1. From whose boat was Jesus teaching the people? (Peter's)

2. How did Jesus help his friends who had fished all night and caught nothing? (He told them where to find lots of fish)

Fishermen Leave Their Nets—Page 387

1. Why did the four fishermen leave their boats and follow Jesus? (Because he called them to follow him)

2. Who were these four men? (Andrew, Simon, James and John)

3. How did Jesus help the demon-possessed man in the synagogue of Capernaum? (He commanded the evil spirit to come out of the man)

4. What did Jesus do for Simon's mother-in-law who lay sick with fever? (He touched her hand, and the fever left her)

Jesus Calls Matthew—Page 388

1. Why were the publicans called "sinners"? (They were Jews who worked for the Roman government)

2. What work was Matthew doing when Jesus called him to be a disciple? (He was collecting tax money from the people)

3. Why did Matthew prepare a great feast at his house? (He wanted his friends to meet Jesus)

4. Who came to this feast to find fault with Jesus? (Some scribes and Pharisees)

5. What book of the Bible is called by Matthew's name? (The first book in the New Testament)

The Cripple at the Pool of Bethesda—Page 390

1. Why did many afflicted people gather at the pool called Bethesda? (They came hoping to be healed)

2. How long had the crippled man Jesus talked to been there? (Thirty-eight years)

3. What did Jesus tell this man to do? (To rise, take up his bed and walk)

4. Why did the Jews find fault with the man when he obeyed Jesus? (Because he was carrying his bed on the Sabbath day)

5. What did Jesus tell the man when he found him in the temple? (He told him to sin no more)

Jesus Heals a Withered Hand—Page 392

1. Why did the rulers of the Jews dislike the way Jesus kept the Sabbath? (Jesus thought people were more important than rules)

2. Why were the Pharisees angry at Jesus for healing the man with the withered hand? (Because he healed the man on the Sabbath)

The Twelve—Page 393

1. Why did Jesus choose twelve men to be his disciples? (He wanted to train them to help in his great work)

2. How did Jesus have the wisdom to choose his twelve helpers? (He spent the night on a mountain in prayer to God)

3. What did Jesus give these twelve men before he sent them out to work for him? (He gave them power to cure diseases and to cast out devils)

The Sermon on the Mount—Page 394

1. Where did Jesus take his twelve apostles to teach them? (He took them to a quiet place on a mountainside)

2. Who did Jesus say were blessed? (The poor, the sorrowing, the meek, the merciful, the pure in heart, the peacemakers and others)

3. Jesus said those who hear his words and obey them are like what? (They are like the man who builds his house on a foundation of rock)

Jesus Heals a Leper—Page 396

1. Why were leprous persons not permitted to come near other people? (Leprosy is contagious)

2. As this leper knelt in the dust of the roadside, what did he tell Jesus? ("If you are willing, I know you can make me well")

3. Why was Jesus not afraid to touch the leper? (Because he had power over all kinds of diseases)

4. What did Jesus tell the man to do after he was healed? (To go to the priests in Jerusalem and make an offering to God)

A Roman Captain Shows Great Faith—Page 397

1. What kindness had the Roman captain shown toward the Jews? (He had built them a synagogue)

2. Why was he glad when he heard that Jesus had returned to Capernaum? (He hoped that Jesus would heal his sick servant)

3. Who did he send to speak to Jesus about coming to heal his servant? (Some Jewish elders or teachers in the synagogue)

4. What message did the friends of the Roman captain take to Jesus before he came to the house where the servant lay ill? (Jesus should just speak the word and the servant would be healed)

Four Men Tear Up a Roof—Page 398

1. What strange thing happened while Jesus was teaching in a house in Capernaum one day? (A crippled man was lowered into the presence of Jesus through a hole in the roof)

2. Why had the four men brought their crippled friend to Jesus in this strange way? (They could not pass through the crowd with him)

3. How did Jesus encourage the poor man's faith? (He said, "Son, be of good cheer, for your sins are forgiven")

4. After he had read the thoughts of the faultfinders, what did Jesus say to the cripple lying on the mat? ("Arise, take up your bed and return to your own house")

A Widow's Son Is Raised to Life—Page 401

1. Who stopped a funeral procession outside Nain? (Jesus)

2. How did Jesus show his great power there? (He spoke to the dead man and life returned to his body)

John the Baptist in Prison—Page 403

1. Why did John the Baptist send two friends to speak to Jesus? (He was in prison and could not visit Jesus)

2. What was the sad end of John the Baptist? (He was beheaded at the command of Herod)

A Woman Anoints Jesus' Feet—Page 403

1. Why did Simon the Pharisee ask Jesus to dine at his home? (He wanted to watch Jesus closely and find some fault in him)

2. Who washed Jesus' feet with tears that day? (A sinful woman)

3. What did the proud Pharisee think of Jesus when he let the woman touch his feet? (He thought that if Jesus were a prophet he would not allow her to touch him)

4. How did Jesus rebuke Simon for his wrong thoughts? (By telling him a story and then asking him questions)

5. How did he show his pity for the sinful woman? (By forgiving her sins and sending her home in peace)

The Story of the Sower—Page 405

1. What is a parable? (A short story that teaches a lesson)

2. Who asked Jesus why he spoke in parables? (The disciples)

3. To whom did Jesus explain his parables? (The disciples)

4. What is the parable of the sower? (The good seed he sowed fell on different kinds of soil and yielded accordingly)

Stories About the Kingdom of Heaven—Page 406

1. What three things did Jesus say were like the kingdom of heaven? (A man who sowed good seed, a mustard seed and leaven)

2. What did he say the good seed represented? (The people of God)

Jesus Calms the Storm—Page 407

1. Why did the disciples of Jesus become frightened one night on the Sea of Galilee? (Their boat was beginning to sink because of the fury of the storm)

2. How did Jesus show his great power that night? (With a word of command he calmed the storm, and the sea grew quiet)

Jesus Heals a Wild Man—Page 409

1. Who met Jesus and the disciples when the ship came to land at the other side of the sea? (A wild man in whom evil spirits lived)

2. What did Jesus tell the man to do after he had made him well? (To return home and tell his friends what great things God had done for him)

Jesus Answers Calls for Help—Page 410

1. Why did Jairus ask Jesus to come to his house? (He wanted Jesus to heal his little daughter who was dying)

2. Who pressed through the crowd that followed Jesus to touch the hem of his garment? (A woman who had been ill for twelve years)

3. What happened to the daughter of Jairus before Jesus reached her bedside? (She died)

4. How did Jesus change sorrow into joy in Jairus' home? (He restored the girl to life)

A Boy's Lunch Basket—Page 413

1. Why did the people follow Jesus to a desert place? (Some came to hear his teaching; others, to be healed)

2. The throng of eager people reminded Jesus of what? (Sheep without a shepherd)

3. Who in that crowd had brought a lunch with him? (A boy who had followed along with the crowd)

4. Which of the disciples brought the boy to Jesus? (Andrew)

5. What happened to the little boy's lunch? (With Jesus' blessing it was multiplied until it fed over 5,000 people and there were leftovers!)

Jesus Walks on the Water—Page 415

1. Where was Jesus when the disciples were rowing against the windblown waves? (He was praying on the mountainside)

2. How did Jesus come to them across the water? (Walking on the waves)

3. Why were the disciples frightened when they saw Jesus? (They thought he was a spirit)

4. Why did Simon Peter begin to sink into the sea? (He looked at the waves instead of looking straight at Jesus)

5. What happened after Jesus brought Simon safely into the ship? (The wind ceased blowing at once)

A Gentile Mother Comes to Jesus— Page 418

1. Why did Jesus take his disciples into the land of Phoenicia?
(He wanted time alone to teach them)

2. Who came to ask Jesus for help?
(A Gentile mother)

3. How did Jesus treat her at first?
(He paid no attention to her)

4. What did the disciples urge him to do with her? (Send her away)

5. How did Jesus answer the mother's prayer? (He told her she would find her daughter well)

Jesus Heals and Feeds the Crowd— Page 419

1. How did the people of Gadara receive Jesus when he came the second time to visit their country?
(They received him gladly)

2. How long did they stay without food in the desert with him? (Three days)

3. Why did Jesus tell his disciples to feed the people before sending them away?
(He knew they might faint from weakness)

4. How much food did Jesus have to feed this crowd?
(Seven loaves and a few little fishes)

5. How many people were fed?
(More than four thousand)

The Blind Man of Bethsaida—Page 421

1. Why did Jesus lead the blind man out of town before he healed him? (He did not want to attract multitudes to himself)

2. How many times did Jesus touch the man's eyes before he saw clearly?
(Twice)

Peter's Great Confession—Page 421

1. What important question did Jesus ask his disciples one day?
("Who do you men believe I am?")

2. How did Simon Peter answer that question?
(He said, "You are Christ the Son of the living God")

3. Why did Jesus need to rebuke Simon Peter?
(Peter spoke tempting words to Jesus)

The Mount of Transfiguration— Page 422

1. Which of the twelve disciples did Jesus take with him up on the mountain?
(Simon Peter, James and John)

2. What did these disciples do while Jesus prayed? (They slept)

3. Who came to visit with Jesus?
(Moses and Elijah came from heaven)

4. What wonderful sight met the disciples' gaze when they awakened?
(Jesus appeared transfigured in glory before them)

5. What did Simon Peter want to do when he saw the heavenly visitors with Jesus?
(He wanted to build tabernacles for Jesus and his visitors)

6. What did the voice from the cloud say to the disciples? (The voice said, "This is my beloved Son; hear him")

Jesus Heals an Epileptic Boy—Page 424

1. How had the nine disciples failed when Jesus was not with them?
(They could not heal an epileptic boy who was brought to them)

2. Who came running to meet Jesus when he came down from the mountain with the three disciples?
(The father of the epileptic boy)

3. Why had the nine failed to heal the boy?
(They did not have faith)

4. How did Jesus make him well?
(He commanded the evil spirit to come out of the boy and it obeyed)

Who Is the Greatest—Page 425

1. Where did Jesus send Peter to find money to pay their tax?
(He sent him on a fishing trip)

2. What lesson did Jesus try to teach his disciples with a little child?
(A lesson in humility)

3. Who did Jesus say would be greatest in the kingdom of heaven?
(Those who humble themselves and become like little children)

4. What did Jesus teach his disciples about the Father's will for little children?
(The heavenly Father wants children to keep their faith in Jesus)

601

Peter Learns About Forgiveness—Page 426

1. What question did Peter ask Jesus about forgiveness? (He asked whether seven times was enough to forgive his brother)

2. How many times did Jesus say Peter should forgive his brother? (Seventy times seven)

3. How is God similar to the king in the story that Jesus told Peter? (When God forgives us, he expects us to forgive others)

4. Why is it necessary to forgive those who wrong us and ask forgiveness? (God will not forgive anyone who is unwilling to forgive others)

On the Way Through Samaria—Page 428

1. Why did two of Jesus' disciples want to call fire from heaven to destroy a Samaritan village? (The Samaritans refused Jesus and his disciples lodging for the night)

2. How did Jesus reply when the disciples asked him to destroy the village? (He said, "The Son of man is not come to destroy men's lives, but to save them")

The Ten Lepers—Page 429

1. What did the ten lepers ask of Jesus? (They asked him to heal them)

2. What happened as they hurried to obey Jesus? (They were healed)

3. How many returned to thank Jesus for what he had done? (Only one)

4. What nationality was the thankful man? (He was a Samaritan)

Would-Be Followers—Page 429

1. What was wrong with the three men who wanted to be Jesus' followers? (They would not put Jesus and his work first in their lives)

2. Why wouldn't the men follow Jesus at once? (One wanted to wait until his old father died; another wanted to spend time with his relatives)

Jesus Attends the Feast in Jerusalem—Page 430

1. What great feast was held each autumn in Jerusalem? (The Feast of Tabernacles)

2. What did Jesus do at the feast? (He taught the people in the temple)

3. Why did the officers his enemies sent refuse to arrest Jesus? (They said of him, "Never did a man speak like this man")

4. How was Nicodemus unlike the other Pharisees? (He believed in Jesus)

A Sinful Woman Is Brought to Jesus—Page 432

1. Jesus' enemies brought someone to him one day. Who was it? (A woman who was a great sinner)

2. Why did Jesus stoop down and write in the dust with his finger? (He knew they were setting a trap for him)

3. What did Jesus finally tell them to do? (He said, "Let the man among you who is without sin cast the first stone at her")

4. Why were the men afraid to throw stones at the woman? (They knew in their hearts that they were sinners)

5. What did Jesus tell the woman when all the men had gone away? (He said that he did not condemn her but that she should sin no more)

Questioned by His Enemies—Page 434

1. Who did the Pharisees think was Jesus' father? (Joseph)

2. Why were the Pharisees angry when Jesus spoke of knowing Abraham? (Because Abraham had lived hundreds of years before)

Jesus Heals a Blind Man—Page 435

1. How long had the blind beggar been without his sight? (All his life)

2. Why did Jesus send him to the pool of Siloam? (To strengthen his faith)

3. Who brought the man to the Pharisees? (The neighbors)

4. Why did the Pharisees call the parents of the man who had been blind? (They thought the man might be only pretending that he was born blind)

5. What did they do with the man when he spoke in defense of Jesus? (They cast him out of the synagogue)

Little Children Are Brought to Jesus— Page 437

1. Why were the disciples displeased with some women one day? (Because they brought their little children to Jesus)

2. How do we know that Jesus loves children? (He took them in his arms and blessed them)

The Rich Young Ruler—Page 438

1. What important question did a rich young man ask Jesus? ("What good thing must I do that I may receive eternal life?")

2. How many of Moses' commands had the young man kept? (All of them)

3. What did Jesus tell him to do if he wished to please God? (To sell all his goods, give his money to the poor and follow Jesus)

4. Why did the young man turn away from Jesus with a sad heart? (Because he loved his money more than he loved God)

Seventy Other Disciples Sent Out— Page 438

1. Why did Jesus send out seventy more disciples? (Because he needed more helpers doing his great work)

2. How did the seventy minister to the people? (They preached the kingdom of heaven and healed the sick)

The Good Samaritan— Page 440

1. How did a lawyer try to trick Jesus? (By questioning him)

2. Why did Jesus tell him the story about the Good Samaritan? (To answer the lawyer's question, "Who is my neighbor?")

3. Whose example did Jesus tell the lawyer to follow in his treatment of his fellow men? (The example of the Good Samaritan)

Lazarus Is Raised from the Dead— Page 442

1. What message did Mary and Martha send to Jesus? (Their brother, Lazarus, was ill)

2. Why did Jesus not go at once to help his dear friends? (He said, "This sickness is for the glory of God")

3. How many days had Lazarus laid in the grave before Jesus came to Bethany? (Four days)

4. Why had many Jews from Jerusalem come to the grave with Martha and Mary? (They were trying to comfort the grieving sisters)

A Sick Man Is Healed—Page 445

1. Who did Jesus heal one Sabbath when he dined at a Pharisee's house? (A man afflicted with dropsy)

2. What did the Pharisees think of this healing? (They were angry because Jesus healed the man on the Sabbath)

The Parable of the Supper—Page 446

1. How did Jesus teach the guests a lesson in humility? (He told them to seek the lowest place when invited to a wedding)

2. What did Jesus teach the guests in his parable about the kingdom of God? (The Jews were first invited into the kingdom, but they refused to come. God welcomes everybody)

A Crippled Woman Is Healed— Page 448

1. Why was the ruler of the synagogue unhappy when Jesus healed the crippled woman? (Because he had healed her on the Sabbath Day)

2. Why was Jesus angry with the Pharisees? (Because they only pretended to be righteous)

Jesus Answers the Pharisees—Page 449

1. How did some Jews try to frighten Jesus about King Herod? (They told him that Herod was seeking to kill him)

2. What beautiful story did Jesus teach to show God's love for the sinner who repents? (The story of the lost coin)

The Prodigal Son—Page 449

1. What did a younger son ask of his father? (His share of the inheritance)

2. What did the young man do with it? (He left home and spent his money foolishly)

3. How did the father act when his wandering son returned?
(The father was so glad to have his son home again that he gave him special gifts and had a party for him)

The Rich Man and Lazarus—Page 452

1. Why did the rich man who failed to help the beggar Lazarus later wish that Lazarus would help him?
(Because he was tormented and Lazarus was comforted)

2. What did he want Lazarus to do?
(Go back to earth and warn his brothers to repent of their sins)

The Unjust Judge—Page 453

1. Why did the wicked judge help the poor widow?
(He grew tired of having her come so often to ask his help)

2. Why did Jesus tell this story?
(To encourage people to keep on praying until they get an answer)

The Pharisee and the Publican—Page 455

1. Was God pleased with the Pharisee or the publican?
(God was pleased with the publican)

2. Why was God pleased with the publican?
(Because he was sincere)

James and John Want to Be Honored—Page 455

1. What did the mother of James and John request of Jesus?
(She asked Jesus to give her sons the best places in his kingdom)

2. How did the other disciples feel when they heard about this request?
(They were jealous)

Blind Bartimeus—Page 456

1. When Jesus came to Jericho, who wanted to see him but couldn't because he was blind? (Bartimeus)

2. What did the blind beggar do when some who heard him calling after Jesus told him to keep quiet?
(He called louder)

3. How did Bartimeus please Jesus?
(By believing that Jesus could heal him)

Zacchaeus Climbs a Tree—Page 457

1. Why did Zacchaeus climb into a tree when he heard that Jesus was passing?
(He was not very tall and he wanted to see Jesus)

2. Who called him to come down from the tree? (Jesus)

3. How did Jesus' visit change Zacchaeus?
(He received Jesus gladly and promised to make his wrongs right)

4. What great blessing did Jesus bring to that home? (Salvation)

The Parable of the Pounds—Page 459

1. What did the servants do with the money their master entrusted to them?
(All except one servant used it to make more money)

2. What did the Master do to the unfaithful steward?
(He took away the one pound he had and gave it to the servant who had ten)

Mary Anoints Jesus—Page 460

1. When Jesus came to Bethany who made a supper for him?
(Simon, who had been a leper)

2. What interesting man from Bethany sat among the invited guests at this supper?
(Lazarus, who had been raised from the grave)

3. How did Mary show her great love for Jesus at this supper? (She anointed Jesus' head and feet with expensive perfume)

4. Who found fault with Mary?
(The disciples, especially Judas Iscariot)

5. Where did Judas Iscariot go when supper had ended? (He went to the enemies of Jesus to betray Jesus for money)

Jesus Rides into Jerusalem as King—Page 461

1. Why did Jesus have to borrow a colt to ride into Jerusalem?
(Neither he nor his disciples owned one)

2. Who did he send to borrow the colt?
(Two of the disciples)

3. How did the disciples and friends of Jesus show their pleasure as he rode towards the city?
(They spread their cloaks on the ground for him to ride over)

4. Who found fault when the people praised God? (The Pharisees)

Jesus Teaches in the Temple—Page 463

1. How did the children in the temple displease the chief priests and scribes? (They sang, calling Jesus the Son of David)

2. Why wouldn't Jesus' enemies tell him what they thought about John's baptism? (They were afraid to offend the listening people who believed that John was a prophet)

The Parable of the Two Sons—Page 465

1. When the father asked his sons to work in his vineyard, how did they answer? (One refused and one promised to help)

2. Who did go to work in the vineyard? (The son who had refused)

The Parable of the Wicked Farmers—Page 465

1. In the story Jesus told, why did the owner send his son to bring fruit from his vineyard? (Because the keepers of the vineyard had killed the servants he sent)

2. Why were the chief priests and scribes angry when they heard this parable? (They knew it was spoken against them)

The Parable of the Wedding Feast—Page 466

1. How did the guests who had been invited to the wedding act? (They refused to come)

2. Who did the king invite next? (Everyone who would come)

Jesus' Enemies Come with Questions—Page 467

1. Why did Jesus ask his enemies to show him the tax money? (They had asked him whether the Jews ought to pay taxes to Caesar)

2. What did Jesus tell them? (Give to Caesar the things that are Caesar's and to God the things that are God's)

Jesus' Last Hours in the Temple—Page 468

1. What country did the Gentile strangers who asked to see Jesus come from? (Greece)

2. Why was Jesus troubled at this time? (He knew the time was near when he would suffer and die on the cross)

3. What did Jesus say about the poor widow's offering that she threw into the temple treasury? (He said that her small offering was more in God's sight than the large offerings of the rich)

The Parable of the Ten Virgins—Page 470

1. Why were five of the virgins called foolish? (Because they did not prepare for the wedding feast by filling their lamps with oil)

2. What did Jesus want to teach his disciples from this parable? (The importance of being ready to meet the Lord)

Jesus Tells About the End of the World—Page 471

1. Jesus said Christians and sinners were like what two animals? (He likened Christians to sheep and sinners to goats)

2. What did Jesus teach by this story? (His followers should treat people in need as they would treat Jesus)

The Last Supper with the Twelve—Page 472

1. What errand did Jesus send Peter and John to do in Jerusalem? (To prepare their Passover Feast)

2. What sign would lead the disciples to the guest room where they would eat the Passover? (They were to follow a man who would be carrying a water pitcher)

3. What strange example of humility did Jesus set before his disciples in that guest room? (He washed their feet and dried them with a towel)

4. What did Jesus tell John he would give to the one who would betray him? (A piece of bread)

5. What did Jesus do with the bread and wine after the supper was over? (He blessed the bread and wine and gave it to his disciples)

Two Disciples Fail Their Lord—Page 475

1. For how many pieces of money did Judas Iscariot sell his Lord? (Thirty)

2. Where did Jesus and the eleven disciples go when they left the guest room? (To the Garden of Gethsemane)

3. Which of the eleven did Jesus take with him to the place of prayer? (Peter, James and John)

4. What sign did Judas use to betray Jesus? (A kiss)

5. How did Peter try to defend Jesus? (He drew a sword and cut off an enemy's ear)

6. Who denied his Lord? (Peter)

The Darkest Day in All the World—Page 477

1. Before what Roman ruler was Jesus led? (Pilate)

2. Who urged Pilate to set Jesus free? (Pilate's wife)

3. The Jews asked to have someone else released instead of Jesus. Who was it? (Barabbas)

4. What kind of crown did the Roman soldiers put on Jesus' head? (Crown of thorns)

5. Where was Jesus crucified? (On a hill called Calvary)

6. What writing did Pilate have nailed on the cross above Jesus' head? ("This is Jesus, the King of the Jews")

7. What did the Roman captain who saw Jesus die say of him? ("Truly this man was the Son of God!")

The Watchers at the Tomb—Page 480

1. Who asked permission of Pilate to take the body of Jesus from the cross? (A rich man named Joseph)

2. Where was the body of Jesus buried? (In Joseph's new tomb in a garden)

3. Why did Pilate place his Roman seal on the stone at the tomb? (The enemies of Jesus asked him to do so)

4. Why did Pilate station Roman soldiers in front of the tomb? (To guard the place so the disciples could not steal the body of Jesus)

5. Who came to visit the tomb at early dawn the first day of the week? (A group of sad women)

Jesus Rises from the Dead—Page 482

1. Who ran to tell Peter and John that the body of Jesus had been stolen? (Mary Magdalene)

2. What message did the other women hurry to bring to the disciples? (The glad news that Jesus had risen from the dead)

3. Why did Mary Magdalene return the second time to weep at Jesus' grave? (She did not know that Jesus had risen)

4. To whom did Jesus first appear after he had risen from the dead? (Mary Magdalene)

The Stranger on the Road to Emmaus—Page 484

1. What were Jesus' two friends talking about as they walked toward Emmaus? (They discussed the trial and crucifixion of Jesus, and the report of his resurrection)

2. How did these two men finally recognize Jesus? (When they ate supper, Jesus took bread, blessed it and gave it to them)

Doubting Thomas—Page 486

1. Why did the two friends hurry back to Jerusalem? (They now believed that Jesus was alive and wanted to tell the others)

2. To which disciple had Jesus appeared that same day? (Simon Peter)

3. Why were these disciples frightened when Jesus suddenly stood in their midst? (They supposed he was a spirit)

Jesus' Last Meeting with His Disciples—Page 488

1. Jesus told the disciples he was sending someone to them after he went away. Who was it? (The Holy Spirit)

2. Where did Jesus have his farewell talk with his disciples? (On the Mount of Olives)

3. Why were the disciples filled with joy when they returned to Jerusalem from the Mount of Olives? (They knew that Jesus truly was the Christ)

Stories about the Apostles

The Coming of the Holy Spirit—
Page 490

1. Why did the one hundred and twenty men and women meet daily in the upper room? (They met to pray)

2. What happened on the morning of the tenth day? (The Holy Spirit came and filled them with joy and courage)

3. Why were there many strangers in Jerusalem that day? (It was the Day of Pentecost)

4. What happened when Peter spoke boldly for Jesus? (Three thousand persons believed and were baptized)

The Lame Man at the Gate Beautiful—
Page 492

1. Why was the crippled man carried to the temple gate every day? (So he might ask money of those who entered the temple to pray)

2. How long had he been crippled? (From birth)

3. From which of the disciples did he beg money? (Peter and John)

4. In whose name did Peter command the cripple to walk? (In Jesus' name)

5. What effect did this miracle have on the people who had met to worship at the temple? (All who saw the man walking and leaping were amazed and listened to Peter's words about Jesus)

Peter and John in Prison—Page 494

1. Why were Peter and John put in prison? (Because they preached about Jesus)

2. What did the Jewish rulers want Peter and John to promise? (That they would not speak to anyone in the name of Jesus)

3. What did Peter and John say to that? (That they could not keep from telling what they had seen and heard)

Sharing in the Early Church—Page 495

1. How did the people in the first group of believers show their unselfishness? (Those who had plenty shared with the needy ones)

2. Why did Ananias and Sapphira sell their property? (They wished to appear as generous as the others)

3. What did Peter say when Ananias brought his bag of gold to the apostles? (He asked Ananias why he was lying to the Holy Spirit)

An Angel Opens Prison Doors—
Page 497

1. How did the Jewish rulers try again to crush out the teaching of Jesus? (They imprisoned the apostles)

2. Who set the apostles free? (An angel of the Lord)

3. Why did the apostles return to the temple to teach about Jesus? (The angel told them to do so)

4. How did the rulers mistreat the apostles? (They beat them severely)

Seven Are Chosen—Page 501

1. Why were there bad feelings between the Grecian Jews and the Hebrews? (The Grecians thought their poor people were not getting proper care)

2. How did the apostles solve this problem? (They had the believers choose seven men to care for the needs of all)

Stephen Is Stoned—Page 503

1. Where did Stephen go to preach the gospel? (Into a synagogue where foreign Jews met to study the Scriptures)

2. Who became angered with him there? (The leaders of this synagogue)

3. In what cruel manner was he put to death? (He was stoned)

4. How did Stephen show his courage and love when wicked men were killing him? (He prayed God would forgive them)

Simon Tries to Buy the Holy Spirit—
Page 506

1. To what city did Philip go to preach the gospel? (Samaria)

2. What effect did Philip's preaching have on the people of Samaria? (Many of them accepted Jesus as their Savior and Lord)

607

3. How did Simon regard the teachings and miracles of Philip? (He wondered at them since he saw that they were genuine)

4. Why did Peter and John visit the Samaritan believers? (They came to pray for them to receive the Holy Spirit)

Philip and the Ethiopian—Page 507
1. Who sent Philip on an errand from Samaria? (An angel of the Lord)

2. Where did Philip go? (South toward Gaza)

3. Who did he see traveling on the road? (An officer of the queen of Ethiopia)

4. What did Philip ask the Ethiopian when he heard him reading from the Scriptures? (He asked the Ethiopian if he understood what he was reading)

5. How did Philip help the Ethiopian? (He taught him about Christ)

Saul on the Road to Damascus—Page 509
1. Why was Saul, the young Pharisee, angry with the believers in Jesus? (He believed the teachings of Jesus were wrong)

2. How did he mistreat the believers in Jerusalem? (He cast many into prison and stopped their public services)

3. What did he plan to do in Damascus? (Persecute the believers)

4. Who spoke to Saul in a vision by the roadside? (Jesus)

Saul Becomes a Follower—Page 512
1. Why did Ananias go lay hands on Saul so he might receive his sight? (God told him that Saul had become a believer)

2. What was Saul's first request? (He wanted to be baptized as a believer in Jesus Christ)

Saul Escapes in a Basket—Page 513
1. How did Saul's enemies in Damascus plan to capture him? (They set watchers at the city gates to seize him)

2. How did Saul's friends help him to escape? (They lowered him in a basket from a high wall to the ground outside the city)

3. Where did Saul go when he escaped from Damascus? (Jerusalem)

4. Why were the believers in Jerusalem afraid of him? (They remembered how cruelly he had persecuted other believers)

5. Who befriended Saul? (A believer named Barnabas)

A Man Is Healed of Palsy—Page 516
1. What miracle did Peter perform while he was visiting the saints at Lydda? (He healed a man who had been sick with palsy for eight years)

2. What did the people of Lydda think of Peter? (Many came to hear him preach and believed on Jesus Christ)

Dorcas Is Raised from the Dead—Page 516
1. Why did the saints at Joppa send for Peter to come at once? (Because Dorcas had died)

2. Who spoke to Peter about the good work that Dorcas had done? (Widowed mothers helped by Dorcas)

3. How did Peter bring gladness again to the weeping friends of Dorcas? (He prayed and God restored Dorcas to life)

Peter and Cornelius—Page 517
1. Why was Cornelius unlike other Gentile officers? (He feared the true God and worshiped him)

2. Who appeared suddenly to him one afternoon while he was praying? (An angel of the Lord)

3. What did the angel tell him? (To send for Peter who would tell him what to do)

4. What remarkable vision did God give Peter? (He saw a sheet let down from heaven containing all kinds of animals)

5. Why was Peter willing to go to Caesarea with the messengers Cornelius had sent? (The Spirit of God told him to go)

An Angel Lets Peter Out of Prison—Page 521
1. Why had King Herod begun to persecute the believers at Jerusalem? (He was trying to please the rulers who were enemies of Jesus)

2. What had Herod done with Peter? (He had shut him up in prison)

608

3. Who woke up Peter the night before King Herod intended to kill him? (An angel from God)

4. Where did Peter go after the angel left him? (To the home of Mary, the mother of Mark)

5. What were the saints doing at Mary's home when Peter arrived? (Praying)

6. Why wouldn't they let him enter right away? (They did not believe that it was Peter)

Barnabas and Saul at Antioch— Page 522

1. Where were the believers in Jesus first called "Christians?" (At Antioch, in Syria)

2. The church at Jerusalem sent what man to visit the Gentile church at Antioch? (Barnabas)

3. Why did Barnabas look for Saul? (He needed another helper)

4. Why were Barnabas and Saul going to Jerusalem? (To take the money the church at Antioch was sending to the poor saints in Jerusalem)

5. What young man did they bring back with them when they returned to Antioch? (John Mark)

Barnabas and Saul, First Missionaries— Page 523

1. Who were the first missionaries sent out in the early church? (Barnabas and Saul—now called Paul)

2. Why did Paul cause a certain man in the island of Cyprus to become blind? (Because this man was a wicked deceiver)

3. What effect did this example of God's power have on the governor of the island? (He was astonished and believed in the power of God)

Paul and Barnabas at Antioch and Iconium—Page 524

1. How were the missionaries treated in Antioch and Iconium? (They were persecuted)

2. Who persecuted them? (The Jewish leaders)

Paul and Barnabas Mistaken for Gods—Page 526

1. Why did Paul command the cripple at Lystra to stand on his feet? (He saw that the man had faith to be healed)

2. Who did the people of Lystra believe Paul and Barnabas were after they had seen this miracle? (Their gods, Jupiter and Mercury)

3. How did they decide to honor these miracle workers? (By offering sacrifices to them)

4. What did Paul and Barnabas do when they saw the intentions of the people? (They begged with them not to do it)

5. How did these people treat Paul after that? (They stoned him and left him for dead)

A Serious Problem—Page 528

1. Why did the visitors from Jerusalem look unkindly on the Gentile Christians at Antioch? (They believed that Gentile Christians should keep Moses' law)

2. Who did the church at Antioch send to Jerusalem to answer this question? (Paul and Barnabas)

3. Why did Peter, Paul and Barnabas believe that Gentiles could be saved without obeying the Law of Moses? (They had seen many Gentiles become true believers in Jesus)

4. Who returned with Paul and Barnabas from Jerusalem to Antioch? (Judas and Silas, who also were preachers)

5. Which of the two visitors decided to remain at Antioch? (Silas)

Paul Begins a Second Journey—Page 531

1. Who did Paul take with him on his second missionary journey? (Silas)

2. What young man decided to travel with Paul and Silas? (Timothy)

3. Why did Paul and his companions plan to visit Macedonia? (Because in a vision Paul had seen a man from that country calling to him)

4. Who joined Paul's company at Troas? (A doctor named Luke)

5. Where did the missionaries first
preach the gospel in Philippi?
(In an open-air prayer meeting
by the riverside)

6. Who was the first Christian convert
in Macedonia?
(Lydia)

The Philippian Jailer—Page 532

1. Why were Paul and Silas cast
into the Philippian jail?
(Because they commanded an evil
spirit to come out of a slave girl)

2. Tell how Paul and Silas glorified God
in the prison.
(They sang praises to God)

3. Who prevented the jailer from taking
his own life? (Paul)

4. What important question did the jailer
ask Paul and Silas?
("Sirs, what must I do to be saved?")

5. After his conversion how did the jailer
treat these two men?
(He washed and bound up their wounds,
took them into his home and set food
before them)

In Other Cities of Macedonia—Page 535

1. When Paul and Silas preached about
Jesus in Thessalonica, who were they
preaching to? (Jews and Greeks)

2. Who became jealous of the missionaries
at this place?
(Some Jews who refused to believe
in Jesus)

3. Why did friends of Paul and Silas send
them away at night to another city?
(To escape persecution from
unfriendly Jews)

4. How did the Jews of Berea receive
the words of the missionaries?
(Many of them believed the
gospel message)

Paul Preaches on Mars' Hill—Page 536

1. What strange altar did Paul find
on the streets of Athens?
(An altar erected to the Unknown God)

2. Why did the wise men of Athens
bring Paul to Mars' Hill?
(They wanted him to tell them
about the doctrine of Christ)

Many Believe at Corinth—Page 538

1. What kind of work did Paul do while he
waited at Corinth for Silas and Timothy?
(Tent making)

2. How did God encourage Paul
in a dream one night?
(He told Paul to speak boldly, for many
people in that city would believe)

3. Paul took what two people with him
when he sailed away from Greece?
(He took Aquila and Priscilla)

The Gospel Is Preached in Ephesus—Page 540

1. Aquila and Priscilla taught a Jew about
Jesus Christ. What was his name?
(Apollos)

2. How long did Paul teach in a school
in Ephesus? (Two years)

3. What happened to the seven brothers
who tried to cast out an evil spirit
in the name of Jesus?
(The man who was possessed by the
evil spirit beat them)

4. What did the Ephesian Christians do
with the books of magic?
(They burned the books)

Riot at Ephesus—Page 542

1. What heathen goddess did the Ephesians
worship? (Diana)

2. Why did Demetrius, the silversmith,
feel uneasy about the teachings of Paul?
(He feared people would no longer
buy the images he made)

3. How did he cause a great uproar
in the city?
(He told his friends that the worship
of Diana was about to be overthrown)

4. For how long did the excitement last?
(Two hours)

5. Who quieted the people? (The town clerk)

On the Way to Jerusalem—Page 543

1. What happened during Paul's farewell
visit with the saints at Troas?
(A young man fell asleep and fell to the
ground from an upstairs window)

2. Where did Paul have a farewell meeting
with the elders from Ephesus?
(They met with Paul at the seacoast)

3. What part did the children have in Paul's farewell meeting with the saints at Tyre? (They were in the group of believers who bade Paul farewell)

4. How did Agabus, the old prophet from Jerusalem, upset the minds of Paul's friends? (He said Paul would be seized and imprisoned at Jerusalem)

Paul Is Taken Prisoner—Page 545

1. Why did Paul visit the temple and perform the ceremony of cleansing, according to Moses' law? (To please the leaders in the church at Jerusalem)

2. Who seized Paul in the temple? (Some old enemies of Jesus)

3. How did they treat him? (They began beating him)

4. Who rescued Paul from these angry men? (The Roman captain and his soldiers)

5. Why did Paul's speech on the castle stairs excite the Jewish listeners? (He told them that God had sent him to preach to the Gentiles)

A Young Man Saves Paul's Life— Page 547

1. What did the Lord tell Paul as he lay sleeping in the castle prison? (That Paul would witness for the Lord in Rome)

2. What foolish thing did a group of forty Jews decide? (To eat nothing until Paul was killed)

3. Who warned Paul about the plan of these men? (His nephew)

4. How did the Roman captain save Paul from these men? (He sent Paul away to Caesarea that night)

Paul Before Felix—Page 549

1. What did Felix think of the charges the Jewish leaders made against Paul? (He felt they were unimportant)

2. Why did Felix, the Roman governor, tremble when he heard Paul preach the gospel of Christ? (Felix knew he was a great sinner)

Paul Appeals to Caesar—Page 552

1. Why did Paul ask the new governor Festus to send him to Rome instead of to Jerusalem? (Paul knew he would be killed if he were taken to Jerusalem)

2. How did Festus answer Paul's request? ("You have appealed to Caesar and to Caesar you shall go")

King Agrippa Hears Paul's Story— Page 553

1. Who came from east of the river Jordan to visit Festus? (King Agrippa and Bernice, his sister)

2. Why did Festus bring Paul before King Agrippa? (Because Agrippa wished to hear Paul's defense)

3. How did Agrippa receive Paul's words? (He said, "You almost persuade me to be a Christian")

4. Why did the king think Paul deserved to be set free? (Because he had done nothing worthy of punishment)

Paul Is Shipwrecked—Page 556

1. Who accompanied Paul on his last journey away from Palestine? (Luke and Aristarchus)

2. Why did Paul wish to remain at Fair Havens for the winter? (He knew the time of year was dangerous for sailing)

3. What was the result of the centurion's unwillingness to heed Paul's warning? (They were caught in a terrible storm)

4. Why did the sailors plan to escape from the ship? (They knew they could not bring it safely to shore)

Safe on an Island—Page 559

1. How did the islanders receive the shipwrecked passengers? (Kindly)

2. What caused them to think that Paul must be a god? (He was not harmed when bitten by a poisonous snake)

3. What kindness did the ruler of the island show to Paul and his friends? (He invited Paul and his friends into his home)

4. How did Paul repay him for his kindness? (He prayed for this man's sick father and the man was healed)

5. Tell how Paul brought joy to the islanders. (His prayers healed many of their sick)

HELPFUL BIBLE INFORMATION
How We Got Our Bible

Our Bible is printed in English. But the Bible was not originally written in English, but in Hebrew (the Old Testament) and in Greek (the New Testament). In both Old and New Testament times men wrote on writing paper made from a plant called papyrus or on parchment made from the skins of animals. The sheets of papyrus or parchment were joined together to make rolls long enough for a book. Jesus used one of these rolls in preaching at Nazareth. We do not have the rolls on which the Bible books were first written, for papyrus breaks up easily when it becomes old and many parchment rolls were destroyed for one reason or another.

In the time of Ezra the Scribe he and a large company of men, called the Great Synagogue, collected the writings of Moses, Samuel, David, the prophets and others. A few more books were added later, and this made the Old Testament as we have it. About 280 B.C. these books were translated into Greek. We call this version the Septuagint, or LXX, because about seventy men did the work.

Jesus did not leave any writings but many of the earliest Christians did. The four Gospel writers who recorded Jesus' life and works, and the other New Testament authors, wrote in the Greek language of their time. We have over four thousand Greek copies of the various portions of the originals. Some of these manuscripts are very old. One, called the Vaticanus, now in the library at Rome, was copied on antelope skin in the fourth century. Another, the Sinaiticus, now in the British Museum, was found about 1862 on Mount Sinai by the great scholar Tischendorf, when it was just about to be burned up as rubbish. It also dates from the fourth century.

John Wycliffe was the first man to translate the whole Bible into English. He completed it about the year 1388, translating from the Latin Vulgate. William Tyndale translated the New Testament and parts of the Old from the Hebrew and Greek manuscripts they had in the years 1525-1535. His pupil, Miles Coverdale, finished the Old Testament translation from Latin and German Bibles. A committee appointed by King James for that work translated our King James, or Authorized Version, in 1611. They did a magnificent piece of work, but they did not have many of the ancient parchment and papyrus manuscripts that we have now. Ancient manuscripts are continually coming to light. For instance, in 1948 a copy in Hebrew of the Book of Isaiah, dating from about 100 B.C., was found in a cave near the Dead Sea.

In 1885 another committee of English scholars presented to the world the Revised Version of the Scriptures, which was followed in 1901 by the American Standard Version, and in 1946 and 1952 by the Revised Standard Version.

The Books of the Bible

Thirty-nine books in the Old Testament and twenty-seven in the New total sixty-six books in the Bible. The Old Testament books fall into five divisions—law, history, poetry, Major and Minor Prophets. The sections of history and Minor Prophets have twelve books each. The other divisions have five books each.

The New Testament also contains five divisions—biography, history, Pauline Epistles, General Epistles and prophecy. The four books of biography, called Gospels, are Matthew, Mark, Luke and John; one book of history, the Acts; thirteen Pauline Epistles; eight other epistles, including Hebrews; and one book of prophecy—the Revelation.

Old Testament Books

Books of the Law

The books of the Law are Genesis, Exodus, Leviticus, Numbers and Deuteronomy. Many of the stories and records that make up these books were written down many hundreds of years before Christ.

GENESIS. This first book of Moses describes how the world began. It tells the story of the creation of the world and of man, tells how man fell away from God and gives God's original promise of a Savior who would redeem man. We also read of the great Flood and the beginning of the history of the Jews. Genesis ends at the death of Joseph.

EXODUS is named from the "exodus," or going out, of the Hebrews from Egypt. This book tells about the bondage of Israel in Egypt, the ten plagues, the wandering of the children of Israel in the wilderness and the giving of the Law on Mount Sinai. Exodus also lists the Ten Commandments.

LEVITICUS contains the religious laws for Israel. The tribe of Levi, after which the book is named, was responsible for seeing that these laws were carried out.

NUMBERS is so named because it tells of the numbering of the children of Israel. It gives the history of the thirty-eight years' wandering after Israel left Sinai. It also contains some of the laws to govern Israel and directions for dividing the land of Canaan.

DEUTERONOMY. The name of this book means "The Second Law." Moses repeated much of the Law and pleaded with the Israelites to keep it. The last chapter reports Moses' death on Mount Nebo.

Historical Books of the Old Testament

The historical books of the Old Testament are Joshua, Judges, Ruth, First and Second Samuel, First and Second Kings, First and Second Chronicles, Ezra, Nehemiah and Esther.

JOSHUA tells how Joshua became Israel's leader in place of Moses and about the entrance of the Israelites into the Promised Land. It also relates the conquest and division of Canaan among the twelve tribes. In the latter part we find the farewell, death and burial of Joshua.

JUDGES covers a period of over three hundred years, during which time Israel was conquered by other nations. God raised up "judges" to deliver them. Some of these judges were Jephthah, Deborah, Gideon, Samson and Samuel.

RUTH is the story of a Moabitess who came to Israel with Naomi, her mother-in-law, during the time of the Judges. Ruth married Boaz, and they became ancestors of Jesus. Ruth contains only four short chapters and we do not know who its author was.

THE BOOKS OF SAMUEL were named after Samuel, the great prophet-judge of Israel. First Samuel is a history of the judgeship of Samuel and the reign of Saul; Second Samuel is about the reign of David.

FIRST AND SECOND KINGS tell of the reign of Solomon and of the division of the kingdom under Rehoboam. They trace the story of Israel to its overthrow by Assyria and the story of Judah to the captivity in Babylon. The works of the prophets Elijah and Elisha are also given here. The writer is unknown.

FIRST AND SECOND CHRONICLES contain the history of Judah from the death of Saul to the Captivity. They contain many important family records of Judah. Probably Ezra compiled them.

EZRA takes up the history of the Jews, beginning with the return from captivity and continuing for a period of nearly eighty years. The rebuilding of the temple in Jerusalem and the religious reformation that took place after the return are of special interest.

NEHEMIAH was originally called the Second Book of Ezra. Nehemiah, who was a great Jewish historian and statesman, wrote most of it. He directed the rebuilding of the walls of Jerusalem after the return from captivity.

ESTHER shows the providential care of God for the Jews while they were scattered in lands under Persian rule.

Poetical Books of the Old Testament

The poetical books of the Old Testament are Job, Psalms, Proverbs, Ecclesiastes and Song of Solomon.

JOB describes the sufferings of Job and his faithfulness through those sufferings. The author and date of writing are not known. This book teaches that to know God is better than to understand the mystery of evil.

Psalms is made up of five songbooks. This collection was the Hebrew hymnal. Some of the songs are Messianic, i.e., they predict the life, character and sufferings of the Savior. David is regarded as the author of many of the Psalms; however, unknown writers wrote others.

Proverbs is a collection of wise sayings written or compiled mainly by Solomon.

Ecclesiastes is believed to have been written by Solomon. Its name means "the preacher." The chief lesson of this book is, "Fear God, and keep his commandments: for this is the whole duty of man."

Song of Solomon. Many have treated this book as an allegory setting forth the love between Christ and the church. It is a wedding song and exalts family love.

Major Prophets

The books of the Major Prophets are Isaiah, Jeremiah, Lamentations, Ezekiel and Daniel.

Isaiah takes its name from its author, whose work covers the years from about 739-701 B.C. Chapters 1—39 are concerned with Judah and her neighbors during the reigns of Jotham, Ahaz and Hezekiah. Chapters 40—55 concern the events of the Exile and return. They contain the peak of Messianic insight. Especially is this true of chapters 52—53. Some have called this part of the book "Isaiah's Gospel" because it is so full of evangelical truth.

Jeremiah is named after the great prophet who wrote it. He prophesied before and during the siege of Jerusalem by Nebuchadnezzar and during the early captivity of Judah. During Zedekiah's reign, Jeremiah was arrested because of his prophecy and cast into prison where he remained until Jerusalem was captured. Some of the prophecy in this book was given to Jeremiah in Egypt, where he went after the captivity.

Lamentations is a sort of funeral dirge. The prophet bewails the doom of his people. The book was written after the destruction of Jerusalem and is remarkable for its poetic beauty and novel construction.

Ezekiel wrote during the Captivity. The prophet helped to keep the exiles true to the Law and inspired many of them to keep alive the hope of return. Ezekiel's visions helped the captives to believe, especially the vision of a restored temple.

Daniel is named for its chief character, a young prince who was captured from Jerusalem and taken to Babylon. In it is the story of Daniel in the lions' den and of the three Hebrews in the fiery furnace. Some of the book is written in the style of the Revelation in the New Testament.

Minor Prophets

The Minor Prophets are Hosea, Joel, Amos, Obadiah, Jonah, Micah, Nahum, Habakkuk, Zephaniah, Haggai, Zechariah and Malachi. Each of these books was written by the prophet for which it was named.

HOSEA prophesied in the Northern Kingdom of Israel during the reign of Jeroboam II, who died 744 B.C. He rebuked Israel for their gross wickedness and pleaded with them to return to God. Hosea was the first prophet to understand that God loves sinners and wants to forgive them.

JOEL lived before the fall of Samaria. He uses a plague of locusts and a severe drought as symbols of conquering foes sent to punish Judah.

AMOS was a citizen of Judah but he preached in Israel. He probably wrote his book about 750 B.C.

OBADIAH is the shortest of the prophetical books. It contains only one chapter and is directed against Edom, which had helped to destroy Judah.

JONAH was a prophet of the Northern Kingdom. The book describes his experiences when God sent him to prophesy against Nineveh. The book also shows the spread of the knowledge of God among nations other than Jews.

MICAH, although a prophet to Judah, also prophesied to the Northern Kingdom. He lived to see the fall of Samaria in 722 B.C. Micah 5:2 foretells the birth of the Messiah in Bethlehem.

NAHUM is directed against Nineveh, the capital of Assyria and enemy of Israel. Little is known about Nahum, its author.

HABAKKUK lived during the reign of Jehoiakim and prophesied in the kingdom of Judah about 608-597 B.C. The prayer in the last chapter of this book is noted as one of the most sublime poems in literature.

ZEPHANIAH prophesied during the reign of King Josiah of Judah before the reformation by that king. He foretells judgment not only on Jerusalem and Judah, but also on the surrounding nations. His description of the day of wrath is graphic.

HAGGAI, along with Zechariah, urged the returned captives to rebuild the ruined temple.

ZECHARIAH, second of the prophets of the restoration, describes the destruction of the foes of Jerusalem and the revealing of the Messiah. He ranks the moral law above the ceremonial.

MALACHI closes the Old Testament. He prophesied in the days of Nehemiah, foretelling the coming of both John the Baptist and Christ.

New Testament

Biography

The books of biography, or Gospels, are Matthew, Mark, Luke and John.

MATTHEW was written particularly for the Jews; hence the book abounds in statements of fulfilled Old Testament prophecies. Jesus is presented as the Messiah and King predicted by those prophets. This book is especially important because it contains so many of Jesus' discourses.

MARK was written particularly to the Romans. This book is noted for its powerful, yet concise style. It reveals the mighty character of the Son of God. Mark wrote down what he had heard Peter tell about Jesus.

LUKE was written particularly for the Greeks. Luke was a physician of Gentile birth who accompanied Paul on part of one of his missionary journeys. It is the most beautiful of the Gospels.

JOHN is often called the Gospel of the divine Son of God. It was written later than the other Gospels, probably about A.D. 95. John dwells especially on the divinity of Christ. The first part of Jesus' public ministry is given only in this Gospel.

History

The only historical book in the New Testament is the Acts of the Apostles.

ACTS provides a partial history of the church during the generation after Christ's ascension. It describes the coming of the Holy Spirit and his workings in the church through Peter and Paul and other apostles. Also the conversion and missionary journeys of the Apostle Paul are related. Luke is its author.

Pauline Epistles

The Pauline Epistles are Romans, First Corinthians, Second Corinthians, Galatians, Ephesians, Philippians, Colossians, First Thessalonians, Second Thessalonians, First Timothy, Second Timothy, Titus and Philemon.

ROMANS. The keynote of this book is "justification by faith." It was written to the Roman brethren about A.D. 57. The book's main argument is that God's law condemns all men as sinners, but his love manifested through Christ offers to all justification through faith in Christ's name.

FIRST AND SECOND CORINTHIANS. These books were written to the church in Corinth, principally to correct certain abuses that had entered into the congregation there. Many great doctrines and truths of the church are established in these epistles.

GALATIANS was written to the Christians of Galatia, in Asia Minor. Here Paul points out that they should not be in bondage to the Law but should take

618

advantage of their freedom through the gospel. Certain Jewish teachers were trying to turn these churches away from the faith.

EPHESIANS. Ephesus was a city in the province of Asia, famous for its great temple of Diana. In his epistle to this church, written from Rome about A.D. 62, Paul describes the ideal church and the work of its members.

PHILIPPIANS was also written at Rome during Paul's imprisonment, about A.D. 62. It describes the self-denial of Christ in taking upon himself the form of a servant, and calls upon the Christians at Philippi likewise to deny themselves for Christ's sake. Paul thanks the Philippians for their expressions of regard for him.

COLOSSIANS was written about the same time as Philippians and was sent to the Christians at Colosse, in Asia Minor. They had made inquiry as to Paul's health and welfare. He warns this church against heresy and tells them how to be complete in Christ.

FIRST AND SECOND THESSALONIANS. First Thessalonians was the earliest of Paul's epistles and the first New Testament book to be written. Both letters speak of the second coming of Christ. Paul commends the Thessalonians for turning to God from idols and for their faith and love.

FIRST AND SECOND TIMOTHY were written to Timothy, Paul's son in the faith and a young minister. They exhort him to pastoral wisdom. Second Timothy was evidently written not long before Paul's martyrdom.

TITUS is also a pastoral epistle, laying special stress upon the life that God approves as worthy of those in his service.

PHILEMON was written to a person of that name whose servant, Onesimus, had run away. The purpose of the letter was to reconcile the master with the slave. It is a beautiful example of Christian courtesy and brotherly kindness.

HEBREWS. The author of this book is not known though the King James translators attached Paul's name to its title. It was particularly addressed to Jewish Christians who were suffering persecution. Christ is lifted up as the great High Priest of his people. The writer particularly points out the danger of falling back to Judaism. This book is not really a letter. It is more like a sermon or essay.

General Epistles

The General Epistles are James, First Peter, Second Peter, First John, Second John, Third John, Jude and Revelation.

JAMES records much practical wisdom. He explains the "works" side of the gospel. The keynote is, "Faith without works is dead." Holy living is enjoined.

FIRST AND SECOND PETER represent the Christian as a pilgrim to another country and point out that he must conduct himself as a citizen of that country to which he is going. The style is peculiarly vigorous. The books are full of exhortations to purity of life.

First, Second and Third John are the works of "the beloved disciple" who wrote the Fourth Gospel. He continually says, "We know." He argues strongly against sin and points out that the Christian should conduct himself before the world as a son of the Father.

Jude is a warning against apostasy. The writer warns believers to keep themselves from stumbling.

Prophecy

The one prophetic book of the New Testament is the Revelation of John.

Revelation is also called the Apocalypse. John wrote it on the Isle of Patmos about the year A.D. 95. The book's purpose was to encourage the early church to consider their heavenly reward amidst the troubles and persecutions of the times. Most of it is symbolic in character.

Interesting Facts about the Bible
(King James version)

The Bible Contains:

66 books	(39 in the Old Testament; 27 in the New Testament)
1,189 chapters	(929 in the Old Testament; 260 in the New Testament)
31,175 verses	(23,216 in the Old Testament; 7,959 in the New Testament)
773,692 words	(592,439 in the Old Testament; 181,253 in the New Testament)
3,567,180 letters	(2,728,800 in the Old Testament; 838,380 in the New Testament)

The middle verse is Psalm 118:8.

The longest verse is Esther 8:9.

The shortest verse is John 11:35.

The longest chapter is Psalm 119.

The shortest and middle chapter is Psalm 117.

The longest name is in Isaiah 8:1—Mahershalalhashbaz.

The word "and" occurs 46,227 times; 35,543 times in the Old Testament and 10,684 times in the New Testament.

The word "Lord" occurs 8,000 times.

Isaiah 37 and 2 Kings 19 are alike.

Ezra 7:21 contains all the letters of the alphabet except "j."

The name of God is not mentioned in the Book of Esther.

Old Testament

The middle book is Proverbs.

The middle chapter is Job 29.

The middle verses are 2 Chronicles 20:17-18.

The shortest verse is 1 Chronicles 1:25.

New Testament

The middle book is 2 Thessalonians.

The middle chapters are Romans 13 and 14.

The middle verse is Acts 17:17.

The shortest verse is John 11:35.

Great Prayers of the Bible
Old Testament Prayers

Offered by	Subject	Where Recorded
Abraham	For God to spare Sodom	Genesis 18
Eliezer	For success in seeking a wife for Isaac	Genesis 24
Jacob	For success	Genesis 28
Jacob	For deliverance from Esau	Genesis 32
Moses	For forgiveness of Israel's idolatry	Exodus 32 Deuteronomy 9
Moses	For God's presence	Exodus 33
Moses	For help to lead Israel	Numbers 11
Moses	For cure of Miriam's leprosy	Numbers 12
Moses	For forgiveness of Israel's murmuring	Numbers 14
Moses	For a successor	Numbers 27
Moses	For entrance to Canaan	Deuteronomy 3
Joshua	Reason of defeat at Ai	Joshua 7
Manoah	For guidance in training his child	Judges 13
Samson	For vengeance on Philistines	Judges 16
Hannah	For a son	1 Samuel 1
David	For blessing on his house	2 Samuel 7
David	For God's mercy on Israel	2 Samuel 24
Solomon	For wisdom to govern Israel	1 Kings 3
Solomon	Dedication of the Temple	1 Kings 8
Elijah	For restoration of widow's son	1 Kings 17
Elijah	For divine proof of truth of his mission	1 Kings 18
Elijah	For death	1 Kings 19
Elisha	For his servant's eyes to be opened	2 Kings 6
Elisha	For blindness upon the enemy	2 Kings 6
Hezekiah	For protection against Sennacherib	2 Kings 19
Hezekiah	For recovery from illness	2 Kings 20
Jabez	For God's protection from evil	1 Chronicles 4
David	For blessing on Solomon	1 Chronicles 29
Asa	For victory over Ethiopians	2 Chronicles 14

622

Offered by	Subject	Where Recorded
Jehoshaphat	For protection against invading armies	2 Chronicles 20
Hezekiah	For the unprepared at Passover	2 Chronicles 30
Ezra	For blessing on the people	Ezra 9
Nehemiah	For the Jews of the day	Nehemiah 1
Nehemiah	For protection against Sanballat	Nehemiah 4
Levites	For pardon of nation's sins	Nehemiah 9
David	For pardon of his heinous sin	Psalm 51
Agur	For moderate earthly blessing	Proverbs 30
Jeremiah	For removal of famine	Jeremiah 14
Jeremiah	For comfort in his trials	Jeremiah 15
Ezekiel	For mercy upon the people	Ezekiel 9
Daniel	For pardon and restoration	Daniel 9
Jonah	For deliverance from the fish	Jonah 2
Jonah	For death	Jonah 4
Habakkuk	For revival of God's work	Habakkuk 3

New Testament Prayers

Offered by	Subject	Where Recorded
Christ	The Lord's Prayer	Matthew 6
Christ	Praise for revelation of God's truth	Matthew 11
Christ	In Gethsemane	Matthew 26
Christ	On the Cross	Matthew 27
Pharisee	Self-righteous boasting	Luke 18
Publican	For mercy	Luke 18
Christ	For his murderers	Luke 23
Dying Thief	For remembrance in glory	Luke 23
Christ	Thanksgiving that his Father heard him	John 11
Christ	For his Father's aid	John 12
Christ	For his disciples through all ages	John 17
Apostles	On choosing Judas' successor	Acts 1
Christians	For help in persecution	Acts 4
Stephen	For pardon of his murderers	Acts 7

Our Lord's Parables

Parable	Matthew	Mark	Luke	Principal Point
Recorded in One Gospel only				
The Tares	13:24			Good and bad grow together.
The Hidden Treasure	13:44			True value of God's kingdom.
The Goodly Pearl	13:45			Looking for and finding salvation.
The Draw Net	13:47			Not all who say they are Christians are true Christians.
The Householder	13:52			Truth is old but ever new.
The Unmerciful Servant	18:23			We must forgive.
The Laborers in the Vineyard	20:1			The Lord rewards all his workers as he sees fit.
The Two Sons	21:28			God expects deeds rather than mere words.
The Marriage of the King's Son	22:2			We should have on the robe of righteousness.
The Ten Virgins	25:1			Be ready for the Lord's coming.
The Talents	25:14			Use well the powers the Lord has given you.
The Sheep and the Goats	25:31			We serve Christ by serving the needy.
The Seed Growing Secretly		4:26		The gradual growth of God's kingdom.
The Two Debtors			7:41	He who feels his sin deeply will love deeply when forgiven.
The Good Samaritan			10:30	All who need help are our neighbors and we should help them.
The Importunate Friend			11:5	Do not stop praying.

Parable	Matthew	Mark	Luke	Principal Point
The Rich Fool			12:16	Do not love earthly things so much we do not love God.
Servants Watching			12:35	Expect the Lord to come.
The Wise Steward			12:42	Serve the Lord faithfully at all times.
The Barren Fig Tree			13:6	The Lord gives us time to repent.
The Great Supper			14:16	God calls everybody to come into his kingdom.
Tower; King Going to War			14:28	It pays to count the cost of entering the kingdom of God.
The Lost Piece of Money			15:8	Joy over those who are saved.
The Prodigal Son			15:11	The Father's love to a returning sinner.
The Unjust Steward			16:1	Be faithful in taking care of what the Lord has left with you.
The Rich Man and Lazarus			16:19	We need only God's Word to point us to salvation.
Unprofitable Servants			17:7	We must not think our own good works are sufficient.
The Unjust Judge			18:2	Pray until you get the answer.
The Pharisee and Publican			18:10	Be humble and trust in God rather than in your own good works.
The Pounds			19:12	Workers will be rewarded, the lazy punished.
Recorded in Two Gospels				
House on Rock and House on Sand	7:24		6:47	Not only hear the Lord's words, but obey them.
The Leaven	13:33		13:20	Christianity will spread throughout the world.
The Lost Sheep	18:12		15:4	The Lord does not want to see one person lost.

Parable	Matthew	Mark	Luke	Principal Point
Recorded in Three Gospels				
Light Under the Bushel	5:15	4:21	11:33 8:16	People will see your good works if they are there.
New Cloth on Old Garment	9:16	2:21	5:36	The new life in Christ will find new ways to manifest itself.
New Wine in Old Bottles	9:17	2:22	5:37	The new life in Christ will find new ways to manifest itself.
The Sower	13:3	4:3	8:5	Men must prepare their hearts to obey God's word.
The Mustard Seed	13:31	4:30	13:18	God's kingdom will make great growth.
The Wicked Husbandmen	21:33	12:1	20:9	Rejection of Christ by the Jews.
The Fig Tree and All Trees	24:32	13:28	21:29	Signs of the Lord's second coming.

Maps

Maps are drawings that show us details of the earth, such as countries, states and cities—even mountains, lakes, highways and streets.

The maps on the following pages show us what the Holy Lands were like before, during and after Jesus lived. They can help you understand and even picture in your mind where Moses and the Israelites, Jesus and the disciples, and Paul, the missionary, traveled on their many journeys.

Here is a key that will help you understand the different symbols and sizes of fonts used on the maps.

- A round, red dot is used to show a town or city.

▲ A small triangle represents a mountain.

Dead Sea Italic fonts are used for places such as oceans, seas, lakes, rivers, mountains, deserts and so forth.

Caesarea This size font is used for all cities and towns.

JUDEA Large capitals are used for nations, countries and continents.

The Holy Land during Old Testament Times

After Jacob's name was changed to Israel, his children were called Israelites. For more than 400 years, they lived in Goshen and became a strong nation. But then a new Pharoah came to the Egyptian throne. Because he feared the Israelites were becoming too powerful, he began to oppress them. The Israelites cried out to God, and he answered their prayer. Soon a man named Moses would lead them to the Promised Land.

To learn more about what happened on the Israelites' journey with God read the section, Moses, Lawgiver and Leader (pp. 73-128) in this book or read Exodus, Leviticus, Numbers and Deuteronomy in your Bible.

- - - - The Exodus from Egypt to the Promised Land

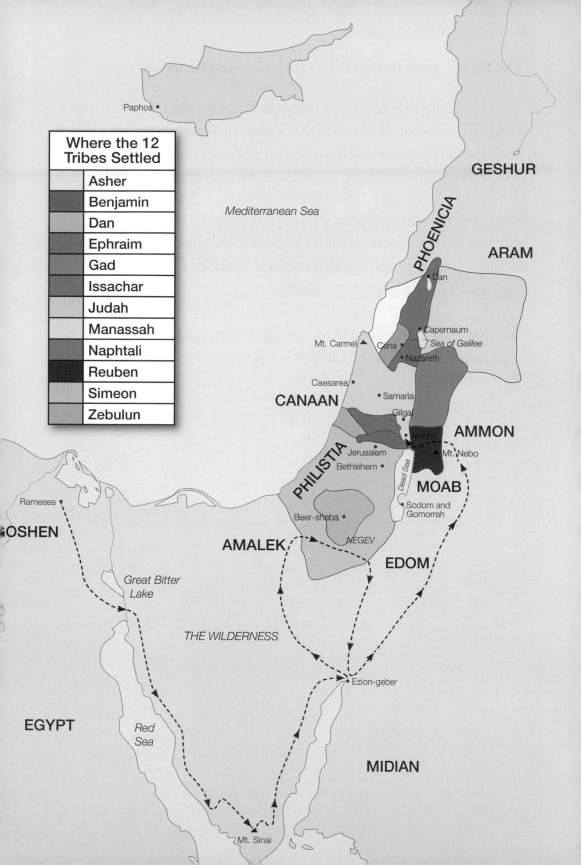

Where the 12 Tribes Settled

	Asher
	Benjamin
	Dan
	Ephraim
	Gad
	Issachar
	Judah
	Manassah
	Naphtali
	Reuben
	Simeon
	Zebulun

GESHUR

ARAM

PHOENICIA

Mediterranean Sea

Dan

AMMON

Capernaum

Sea of Galilee

Mt. Carmel ▲   Cana ▲

Nazareth

Caesarea

CANAAN

Samaria

Gilgal

Jericho

Mt. Nebo ▲

PHILISTIA

Jerusalem

Bethlehem

Dead Sea

MOAB

Sodom and
Gomorrah

Beer-sheba

NEGEV

Rameses

GOSHEN

AMALEK

EDOM

*Great Bitter
Lake*

THE WILDERNESS

Ezion-geber

EGYPT

*Red
Sea*

MIDIAN

Mt. Sinai

The Holy Lands in 900 B.C. – The Divided Kingdom

After the death of Solomon the kingdom was divided. The Northern Kingdom was called Israel and the Southern Kingdom Judah. Because the kings and their subjects disobeyed God, he sent prophets to warn them.

Elijah was the main prophet who appeared to the king of Israel. He was followed by Elisha, and later by Jonah, sent by God to preach in Nineveh. The prophet Amos scolded Israel for worshiping a golden calf instead of the true God.

You may read about The Divided Kingdom on pages 245-308 or read 1 and 2 Kings; 1 and 2 Chronicles; Jonah and Jeremiah in your Bible.

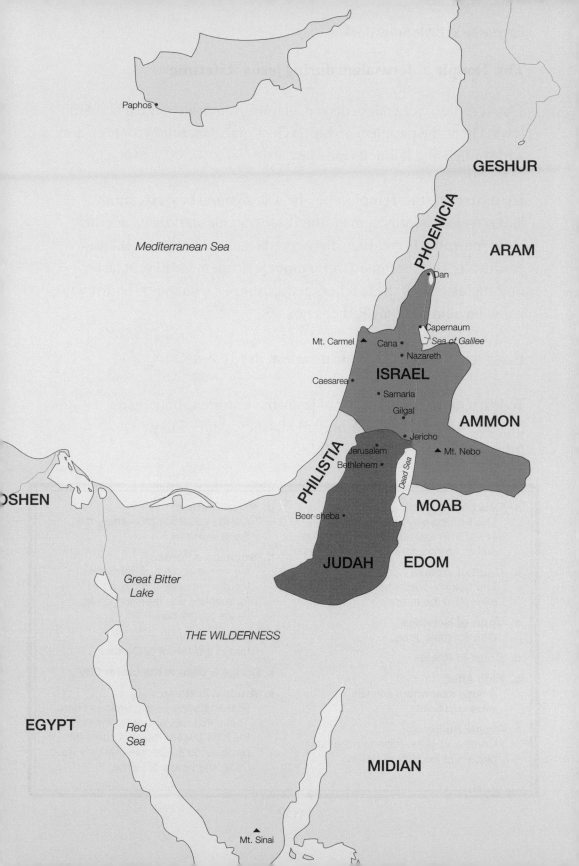

Paphos •

GESHUR

Mediterranean Sea

PHOENICIA

ARAM

• Dan

• Capernaum

Mt. Carmel ▲   • Cana   *Sea of Galilee*

Caesarea •   • Nazareth

ISRAEL

• Samaria

Gilgal

AMMON

• Jericho

PHILISTIA   • Jerusalem   ▲ Mt. Nebo

• Bethlehem   • *Dead Sea*

OSHEN

MOAB

Beer-sheba •

JUDAH   EDOM

Great Bitter Lake

THE WILDERNESS

EGYPT   *Red Sea*

MIDIAN

▲ Mt. Sinai

The Temple at Jerusalem during Jesus' Lifetime

The Temple at Jerusalem played an important role in the lives of the Jews. There the people worshiped God, made sacrifices for their sins and studied and learned God's law.

Jesus first saw the Temple when he was a young boy. His family had traveled to Jerusalem for the Passover celebration. When they were returning home, they discovered Jesus was not with them. Frantically, they searched throughout Jerusalem for him, at last finding Jesus with the teachers at the Temple. Jesus said, "Didn't you know I would be at my Father's house?"

Later, Jesus would teach the people at the Temple.

To learn more about the life of Jesus read Stories about Jesus (pp. 355-489) in this book or read Matthew, Mark, Luke, John and Acts 1:1-14 in your Bible.

---

a. **Court of the Gentiles**
   This was the only area open to non-Jews. This was also where the traders and money changers did their business.

b. **Court of Women**
   The farthest point where women were allowed in the temple.

c. **Court of Israelites**
   Only for male Jews.

d. **Court of Priests**

e. **High Altar**
   A huge altar where animals were sacrificed.

f. **Temple Building**
   Consisting of the entrance, the holy place and the Holy of Holies.

g. **Royal Portico**
   A large covered porch where the Sanhedrin met.

h. **Solomon's Portico**
   A covered porch that surrounded the temple area. It provided a place for meeting and teaching, and Jesus taught here.

i. **Shushan Gate**
   Led to the Mount of Olives.

j. **Bridge & Gate to the Lower City**

k. **Antonia Fortress**
   Roman troops were garrisoned here. This place was also used for storing the high priests' robes, a constant reminder to the people that they were under the power of Rome.

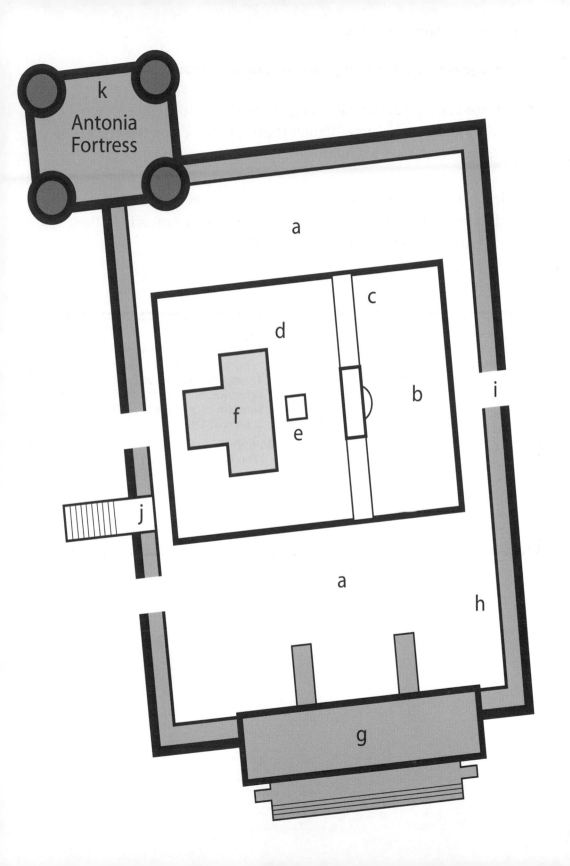

k
Antonia
Fortress

a

c

d

f

e

b

i

j

a

h

g

Jerusalem at the Time of Jesus' Death and Resurrection

Jesus rode into Jerusalem as a king to shouts of "Hosanna." All too soon those shouts became, "Crucify him." Jesus died on the cross for the sins of the world, but three days later he rose again.

To learn more about what happened during Jesus' last days on earth read Stories about Jesus (pp. 461-489) in this book or read Matthew, Mark, Luke, John and Acts 1:1-14 in your Bible.

Upper Room
Where Jesus and his disciples ate the Passover meal and the Last Supper, which we now observe as communion.

Mt. of Olives
Jesus and his disciples went here after the Passover meal.

Garden of Gethsemane
Jesus prayed here and was then arrested.

House of Caiaphas
Home of the high priest. Jesus was taken here for questioning.

Herod's Palace
Pilate, the Roman governor, sent Jesus to Herod. Herod had wanted to meet Jesus, but when Jesus made no reply to his questions, he mocked Jesus and sent him back to Pilate and ultimately to be crucified.

Golgotha
"The Place of the Skull." Jesus was crucified here between two robbers.

Garden Tomb
Jesus' dead body was placed in a new tomb here until he rose to life again.

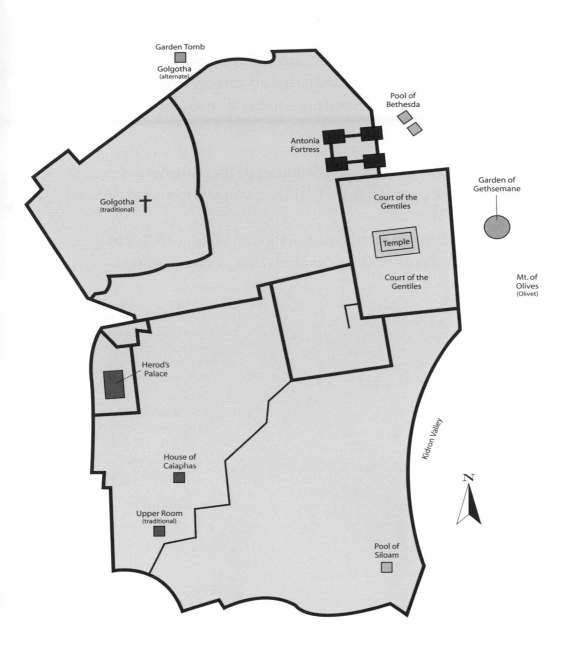

Garden Tomb

Golgotha
(alternate)

Pool of
Bethesda

Antonia
Fortress

Court of the
Gentiles

Temple

Garden of
Gethsemane

Golgotha
(traditional) †

Court of the
Gentiles

Mt. of
Olives
(Olivet)

Herod's
Palace

Kidron Valley

House of
Caiaphas

N

Upper Room
(traditional)

Pool of
Siloam

The Holy Land in New Testament Times

This is the land where Jesus was born; where he played as a child; where he grew to be a man and started his early ministry. It is where he performed many miracles: healed the sick, raised the dead, and cast out evil spirits.

This is also where Jesus was accused, hung on the cross, died for our sins, and was resurrected so we could live with him forever in heaven.

Read about Jesus' life in the pages of this book (355—489) or in your Bible read the books of Matthew, Mark, Luke, John and Acts 1.

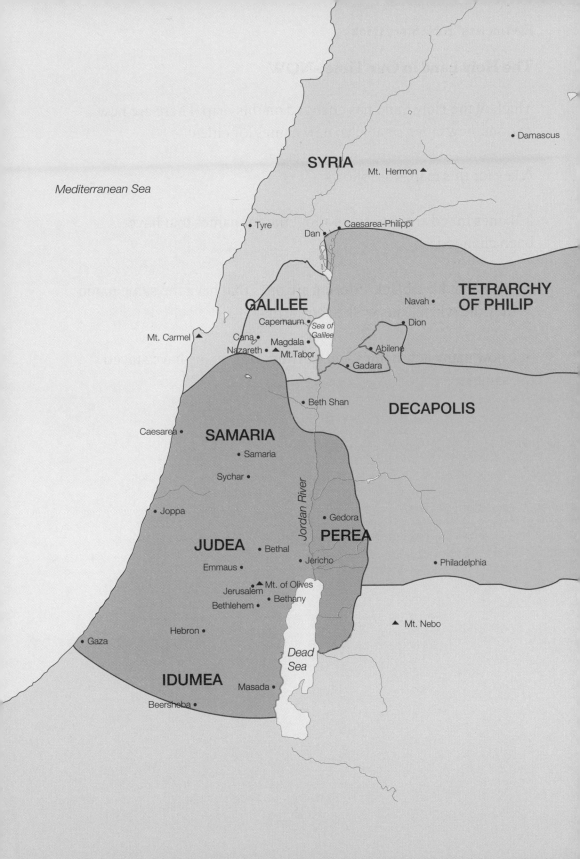

The Holy Land in Our Time—NOW

Much of the Holy Land has changed on this map. There are new regions, new cities, or at least new names for cities.

A key for this map is as follows:

1. Names in red are new cities altogether or names that have been changed.

2. Cities that have black lettering are ones that have the same name as they did when Jesus walked on earth.

See how many new names you can find. How many have stayed the same?

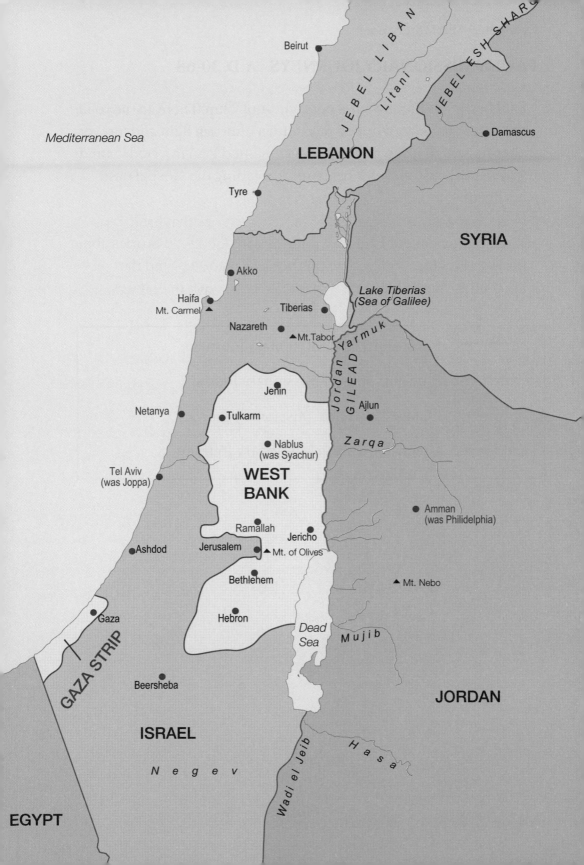

PAUL'S MISSIONARY JOURNEYS - A.D. 30-68

Paul began his life as Saul, a persecutor of Christians. On the road to Damascus, Jesus stopped Saul with a blinding light and forever after he served Jesus. Saul who was renamed Paul traveled far and wide, speaking boldly for Jesus and spreading the Gospel until his death.

To learn more about Paul's adventures with God read Stories about the Apostles (pp. 490-568) in this book or read Acts and the Epistles in your Bible.

Purple line: First Missionary Journey

Blue line: Second Missionary Journey

Orange line: Third Missionary Journey

Green line: Fourth Missionary Journey

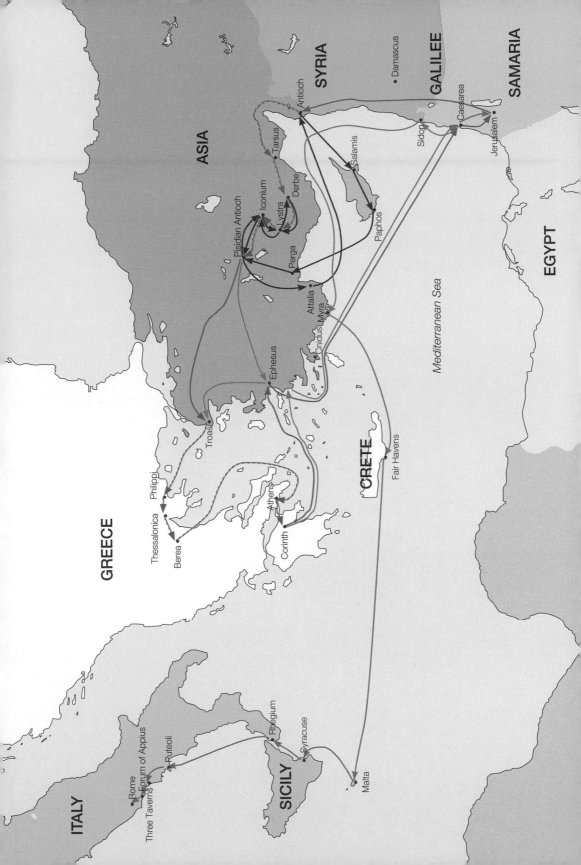

ITALY

Rome
Forum of Appius
Three Taverns
Puteoli

SICILY

Rhegium
Syracuse

Malta

GREECE

Thessalonica
Philippi
Berea

Athens

Corinth

Troas

CRETE

Fair Havens

Mediterranean Sea

Ephesus

Pisidian Antioch
Iconium
Lystra
Derbe
Perga
Attalia
Cnidus Myra

Tarsus

ASIA

Antioch

SYRIA

Damascus

Salamis

Paphos

Sidon

Caesarea

GALILEE

Jerusalem

SAMARIA

EGYPT